FOLLOW IN THEIR FOOTSTEPS

True pioneer's blaze trails, they lay down the paths that we all follow whether we realise it or not. Hanwag have been pioneering alpine footwear for over 90 years, and they're still blazing new trails, redefining what we expect from our footwear, so we can explore the mountains like never before. Get hands on with the latest Hanwag footwear in your local store, or find more colours and more choice online at cotswoldoutdoor.com/hanwag

THE
ALPINE JOURNAL
2017

A study in ambition: the young Edward Whymper, a major figure
in Gilles Modica's beautifully illustrated new history *1865*,
last year of the Golden Age, reviewed on page 361.

THE
ALPINE JOURNAL
2017

The Journal of the Alpine Club

A record of mountain adventure
and scientific observation

Editor: Ed Douglas

Production: Jane Beagley

Volume 121

Number 365

Supported by the
MOUNT EVEREST FOUNDATION

Published by
THE ALPINE CLUB

© 2017 by the Alpine Club

THE ALPINE JOURNAL 2017
Volume 121 No 365

www.alpine-club.org.uk

Address all editorial communication to the Hon Editor:
Alpine Club, 55 Charlotte Rd, London, EC2A 3QF
email: journal.editor@alpine-club.org.uk

Address all sales and distribution communications to:
Cordee, 11 Jacknell Rd, Dodwells Bridge Ind Est, Hinckley, LE10 3BS

Back numbers:
Apply to the Alpine Club, 55 Charlotte Rd, London, EC2A 3QF or, for
1969 to date, apply to Cordee, as above.

First published in 2017 by The Alpine Club
Typeset by Jane Beagley, Vertebrate Publishing
Printed and bound by Novoprint SA, Barcelona

A CIP catalogue record for this book is available from The British Library

ISBN 978-0-9569309-6-5

Front cover: A great prize, long admired. Skip Novak during the first ascent,
via the north face, of Mt Baume in South Georgia. (*Stephen Venables*)

Endpapers
Front: Climbing steep ice on *Lost in China* on Kyzyl Asker. (*Luka Lindič*)
Back: The wild grandeur of the Spenceley glacier, South Georgia.
(*Stephen Venables*)

Foreword

Long before his face appeared on Mount Rushmore, and 20 years before he was elected to the White House, a fresh-faced New York State assemblyman called Theodore Roosevelt wrote to his sister Anna from Zermatt: 'Darling Bysie, day before yesterday, at nine in the morning, I started off, accompanied by two guides, to make the ascent of the Matterhorn. I was anxious to go up it because it is reputed very difficult and a man who has been up it can fairly claim to have taken his degree as, at any rate, a subordinate kind of mountaineer.'

As president, in May 1903, Roosevelt visited Yosemite in the company of that great champion of nature John Muir, camping on a snow pack that was still five feet deep near Sentinel Dome, talking into the night round a campfire and enduring a snowfall that dumped another few inches. Roosevelt said he could not imagine a better way of exploring Yosemite than in the company of the man who knew it best and had written about it so beautifully. For Muir, by then more than 10 years the president of the Sierra Club, it was the ideal moment to press the case for federal protection of this jewel in American's natural crown. 'There can be nothing in the world more beautiful than the Yosemite,' Roosevelt said after his visit. '… our people should see to it that [such places] are preserved for their children and their children's children forever, with their majestic beauty all unmarred.'

The links between mountaineering and conservation are very strong in the United States. Practising climbing skills went hand in glove with campaigning for more and better protection of wild country. John Muir was not just the founding president of the Sierra Club – an organisation with few equivalents in Europe and none, regretfully in my opinion, in Britain – he was also a founding member and second president of the American Alpine Club. The origins of this Club are older than the conservation movement that rose to prominence with the establishment of organisations like the Open Spaces Society and the National Trust. A cynic might argue that in Britain the wild was already lost by then. John Muir was appalled at what the increase in sheep grazing was doing to Yosemite: he called sheep 'hooved locusts' and they were evicted. Britain's uplands had been sheep farms for centuries, with the deep human culture and heritage that implies.

Mountaineers and their institutions on this side of the pond may not always be such instinctive environmentalists as their American equivalents, but that makes no difference to the mountains. Editing this year's *Alpine Journal*, I was only too aware, among all the extraordinary stories of first ascents, from Tibet to Greenland, from the Rwenzori to South Georgia, from India to Indonesia, how quickly the mountain environment is changing as the climate changes and glaciers retreat, sometimes with devastating consequences for populations relying on their water or threatened by floods.

Of course, nature is entropic and mountains are no exception. Disasters happen in mountain ranges around the world without any interference from us. In the *AJ* 2013, the Oxford geologist Mike Searle reported on the immense rock fall from the summit ridge of Annapurna IV that caused the Seti river to flood, killing more than 70 people. The well-known mountain geographer Alton Byers was writing in the *Nepali Times* much more recently about another flood, on the Arun river in April 2017. This disaster was triggered with a glacial lake outburst flood (GLOF), a familiar danger in the Himalaya but one that has worsened with climate change. Byers was careful to establish the context: 'Although Nepal has most likely entered an era of increased GLOF risk, these are natural events and a normal part of Himalayan geomorphology ... GLOFs are not only the result of climate change processes but also that of the dramatic geologic setting of the Himalaya. Every glacial lake and glacial lake outburst flood in Nepal is different, complex, and defies oversimplification.'

This is the problem. What drives climate and weather is a complex subject not easily reduced to headlines. In the last edition of the *Alpine Journal* we published an explanation for natural variation in the earth's climate. This year, on page 143, we publish the powerful, and to me unanswerable, argument that human activity is driving current climate change. Quite what John Muir would have made of Donald Trump and his decision to withdraw the US from the Paris climate agreement can only be guessed at. It's hard to imagine Trump bedding down for the night beside a campfire. How we as mountaineers respond is a personal choice but as humans who interact with nature in a unique and profound way, I feel we have something unique to offer.

This year's contributors to the *Alpine Journal* deserve our gratitude, filling its pages as always with a diverse range of experiences and views. I would like to thank in particular the AJ's assistant editors, Susan Jensen, who has done such a great job with the Area Notes, and Catherine Moorehead, for her assiduous and careful work editing the Obituaries section. Sadly, she steps down from that role with this volume and I offer her my thanks.

Ed Douglas

Correction

In the last edition of the *Alpine Journal*, in the article 'Walter Bonatti and *The Ghosts of K2*', we stated that Mick Conefrey, author of *The Ghosts of K2*, had not approached Erich Abram to check the details of oxygen equipment used during the first ascent in 1954. This was incorrect; Erich Abram for reasons of health was no longer giving interviews. We apologise to Mick for any suggestion he had been dilatory in his research.

Contents

ART & PHOTOGRAPHY

HISTORY

AREA NOTES & MEF

This year's section lead pages celebrate the philanthropy of Paul Mellon (1907-99), and in particular his enthusiastic collection of British art, with mountain drawings from that collection. Fifty years ago his endowment was in place to build the Yale Center for British Art as a home for his enormous collection of prints, drawings and books, and 40 years ago the Yale Center was completed and opened to the public. In 1970 he founded the Paul Mellon Centre for Studies in British Art in Bloomsbury. An introduction to the works featured appears in AC Notes, written by Robin Campbell, who curated these pages.

India

Sasso di Pelmo as seen from St Luzia, Tyrol
Elijah Walton (1832-80)
1866. Watercolour, gouache and graphite on very thick,
slightly textured, cream wove paper. 13⅞ × 9⅞ inches.
Yale Center for British Art, Paul Mellon Collection.

1

MICK FOWLER

The Sersank Redemption

Mick Fowler on pitch three of day five during the first ascent of the north face of Sersank, in the Kishtwar region of the Indian Himalaya. *(Victor Saunders)*

'Blurgh.'

It was the middle of the night and Victor awoke with a start. He knew immediately what was wrong.

'I'm so sorry ...' he began. But it was too late.

The liquid in our water bottle was most definitely not the refreshing water I had expected. Up until this point I had been snoozing contentedly in our little tent at 5,200m sucking in as much thin air as possible ahead of our attempt on the unclimbed north face of Sersank (c6050m) in the Pangi valley area of the Indian Himalaya.

As I fumbled around to melt water to wash my mouth out and ignored the unappetising taste of Victor's urine, I noticed the stars were out. This at least was a positive. It had been snowing non-stop for several hours but now an improvement in the weather looked to be on the cards and that would greatly ease access to our planned climb.

It was the British mountaineer Martin Moran who prompted our interest in Sersank. He led a trek across the Sersank La in 2011 and wrote that

3

Putting the band back together. Saunders and Fowler in the Karakoram in 1987 for their historic ascent of the Golden Pillar of Spantik, and 29 years on in Kishtwar, still going strong. *(Mick Fowler)*

the north side presented a 'tremendous north face of linked white spiders. Victor and I knew Martin well enough to read between the lines. We contacted him, confirmed our suspicions and found our 2016 objective.

Vic and I had not climbed together since we did the Golden Pillar of Spantik in Pakistan in 1987. Over the intervening 29 years we had a boxing match in a seedy East London pub [See 'Seconds Out', *Alpine Journal* 2016] and intermittently kept in touch but essentially we went our separate ways. Victor became a mountain guide based in Chamonix and I stayed with my tax office job in England. Then, in 2015, a joint selection of our memoirs was published in France, a literary award was won and talk of a fresh trip together was born. And so it ended up that Vic and I, at 66 and 60, were back together in the mountains: 29 years after our Spantik experience.

Himalayan trips have changed a lot in 29 years. Back in the 1980s we freighted gas cartridges, spent hours in customs sheds, negotiated with porters and generally did everything ourselves. Now gas cartridges can be bought in India, bigger baggage allowances to Delhi mean there is no need to freight kit and a plethora of in-country agents means that mountaineers can lay back and let others take the strain. We embraced the new world. Simplicity is all.

With logistics all arranged through Kaushal Desai, our ever-reliable agent in Manali, our first job was a quick drop-in to the Indian Mountaineering Foundation (IMF) in Delhi. Here we met Sanju, our liaison officer, and were subject to the mandatory briefing exercise. Mainly this involved officials staring intently at Victor and asking if we had a satellite phone. (Victor having been arrested and fined for using one a couple of years ago.) Denials complete, an air-conditioned 16-hour Volvo bus ride to the honeymoon town of Manali followed. Here we met Kaushal and Devraj our cook before boarding a mean vehicle called a Force Traveller to cross the Rohtang pass into the heart of the Himalaya.

The Rohtang is just under 4,000m and enjoying a 'snow experience' on the pass has become outrageously popular for Indian tourists. Even out of season the traffic queues were memorable. In spring Sanju told us that there is now a restriction of 800 taxis per day ferrying people to the snowline but

The north face of Sersank (6050m) with route and bivouacs marked.
(Mick Fowler)

before this limit was introduced the numbers reached 5,000 to 6,000 per day. Judging by the congestion with a lot less than 800 we could hardly imagine what that would look like.

Road signs on Indian Himalayan roads never cease to amuse me. As we zigzagged up the pass we saw signs urging us to 'Keep Nerves on Sharp Curves' and pointing out that 'Safety on Road (leads to) Safe Tea at Home.' On the far side of the Rohtang the atmosphere changes abruptly. A sign saying 'last fuel for 365km' sums up the new remote mood. Downstream from here, in the Chenab gorge, the tarmac runs out and the road deteriorates fast. It took 12 hours or so from Manali before we turned away from the Chenab into the Sural valley where, in line with so many of the valleys hereabouts, the road-head has now been extended to the last village, Sural Batori.

From here mules were hired and never turned up, porters were engaged and after a halting two days of slow walking and negotiation, base camp was established in sight of the Sersank La at an altitude of about 4,400m. And then, after a day of rest and sorting, two days of getting us and our heavy sacks up the energy-sapping screes to the col and a further day of descending the far side and traversing to a high vantage point, Victor and I were able to lie in the tent staring at the face we had come to climb and enjoy a robust discussion about differentiating between our pee bottle and our water bottle.

Our initial plan of accessing the face via a very steep chute was soon dismissed as too exposed to anything falling down the face. But like minds

Above: Fowler leading on day five.
(Victor Saunders)

Left: Leaving the bivouac site at the start of day four: the crest below was the end of day three. *(Mick Fowler)*

spied a single safe line accessing the face via a buttress to the left. It would add a few hundred metres to the climbing and no doubt increase the time we would spend on the route but the fact we both homed in on it was refreshing. Like-minded thinking in the mountains is important and we had both wondered whether we would still feel the same way after 29 years apart. Our personalities have always been very different but by the time we were settled into our acclimatisation routine the banter was flowing as freely as it did in the 1980s, albeit with old-man subject matter. Our mountain judgement looked as if it was in tune too. Already we were agreeing that it was great to be back in the mountains together.

Photographs gleaned from the internet suggested the face can be very dry and dangerous in the summer and it was a relief to see that it appeared quiet and well frozen for us. It did though look distressingly steep. With some trepidation, we couldn't wait to get going.

First though we had to re-cross the Sersank La, drop down to base camp, sort ourselves out, fill our stomachs and then cross the Sersank La again to the foot of the face. I could see that I was going to be quite weary of the steep screes of the pass by the time we had finished.

Four days later we had crossed the pass for the third time and were at the base of the buttress. Already I was being reminded of Victor's wiry strength and enviable ability to plod through deep snow and carry huge loads at great speed. I had hoped that my fell-racing efforts might have levelled us out in this respect but that appeared not to be the case.

Victor Saunders enjoying a brew at the fifth bivouac. Note the duct tape holding his fingers together. *(Mick Fowler)*

The buttress was steep with powdery snow stuck to all but the very steepest rock. What looked to be straightforward from a distance was terribly precarious and painfully slow involving clearing perhaps 15cm of snow, hooking crampon points over rugosities in the rock and teetering upwards. It was not until early on our second day that the ground changed as we reached the knife-edge crest of the buttress. The pitch that Victor led to get us to this point was a heroic performance that left me in no doubt that years of commercial expeditions have not dented the Saunders ability.

The way forward now was to traverse the sharp crest which sported intermittent overhanging walls on either side. It wasn't the kind of ground that lent itself to abseiling and if we should fail higher on the face it was clear that our descent would involve reversing these pitches followed by climbing back over the Sersank La. I very much hoped we were good enough to get up.

'My stomach is not feeling too good,' Victor announced.

It was at the end of our second day on the face that this problem first became apparent. By the end of day three, as we were being buffeted by spindrift in our precariously positioned tent, it was clear it had worsened.

'Got to get out,' came the urgent call from the far end.

Being of slight build and with minimal blubber Victor likes to wear a lot of clothes both in his sleeping bag and whilst climbing. We were testing various items of Berghaus clothing and Victor was wearing them all together. This meant that he was dressed in five layers and a harness. Sadly there was not enough time

'Agh! Agh! Agh! Oh no! Oh no!' I heard above me as Victor scrabbled for the door. A full assessment revealed that Vic's favourite Calvin Kleins had taken the brunt of the force.

Fowler leading on the sixth day of the climb. *(Victor Saunders)*

'What shall I do?' he asked no one in particular.

What with all the other layers, his harness and the need to be tied on at all times, simply taking them off wasn't easily achieved.

'Cut them off,' I announced unhelpfully being keen to both stem the flow of spindrift into the tent and generally see a quick resolution to the odorous problem that was playing out above my head.

'Great idea,' said Vic producing an Opinel knife of the kind that I thought were only used for peeling vegetables. For the rest of the night we lay with our own thoughts. The accumulation of spindrift was pushing the tent off the ledge but Vic's predicament was a more serious problem for us both. Four days out from base camp and three days up the face it was not the best position to have this kind of difficulty.

Come the morning there was no improvement but Victor was irrepressibly positive.

'Looks brilliant ahead,' he enthused, 'but can you lead the first pitch while I get myself sorted out?'

One of the great things about Himalayan north faces is that the temperature is always below freezing. The accident of the previous night was well frozen but our ropes in particular had suffered and I did not envy Vic as he fought to feed them through his belay plate.

He was right that the climbing was becoming brilliant. The conditions on this upper part of the face were much better than lower down. It felt as if every pitch looked uncertain to begin with but turned out to be just

The route of descent on the south-west flank of the peak proved far more complex than anticipated. *(Mick Fowler)*

about within our limits. The ice was a bit soft which meant our ice screws were less secure than we would have liked but progress was slow and steady. On this difficult ground it was interesting that I readily recognised Victor's distinctive way of moving from 29 years before. He too commented that he instantly recalled my habit of resting my head against the slope when tired.

A fantastic day ended with us at a little snow crest where we were able to cut two small ledges, one above the other. Victor was still not feeling well.

'I think perhaps it is the dehydrated food,' he announced, leaving most of his portion.

This was unfortunate as, aside from boiled sweets, we didn't have anything else. It also struck me that Victor had told me that his usual weight is 59kg (compared to my 70kg) and our pre-climb blubber comparison had suggested I had more reserves. As I boosted my calorific intake by polishing off his food I couldn't help but comment that even Victor wouldn't be able to run on empty forever. The man himself though appeared not to be concerned.

'Not a problem. Perhaps it's just the evening meals and the porridge for breakfast will stay down.' Whatever the situation it was becoming increasingly clear that finishing the climb and descending the far side would be considerably easier than retreating down the face and re-crossing the Sersank La.

Descending the chaotic glacier at the back of Sersank on day eight. *(Mick Fowler)*

The porridge only partially stayed down and day five on the face proved both challenging and memorably fine. By the time we had solved the difficulties of the headwall and had the cornice in sight the Saunders body was surging forward. Where he found the energy from I do not know. Not once did he complain about a situation that would have ended the climb for lesser beings. At the age of 66 he is a truly remarkable man.

The cornice provided an acrobatic finale before, at 6.30pm, we flopped out to a new panorama and the relatively amenable slopes of the south-west side of the mountain. Hopes of being able to pitch the tent were quashed by hard ice just 20cm down but a clear and cold night on nose to tail ledges saw us through to a perfect dawn and a lazy start. Unknown to us, Sanju and Devraj had their binoculars trained on us; they wondered why we were starting so late. In fact, there was no need to rush; ahead was just the 150m summit pyramid and what we hoped would be a leisurely descent.

The summit pyramid itself had never been climbed. In 2008 a team of Japanese climbers and high-altitude porters had reached its foot via the glacier systems to the south-west but they did not proceed further as local people had apparently asked them to leave the summit untouched. Knowing this beforehand we had quizzed locals at Sural Batori who assured us that they had no objection to us climbing to the highest point.

From the side we approached the pyramid it was not particularly difficult

Running on empty. A thinner Saunders enjoys tea and nibbles brought up from base camp. *(Mick Fowler)*

and by 12.30pm on our seventh day out from base camp we stood on the top and built a little cairn to mark our passing. The panorama of the Kishtwar, Pangi valley and Lahaul peaks was inspirational. Every time I stand on a summit in this area I seem to see exciting new objectives. It was a first for Victor in this area and he was like a playful puppy faced with an array of new chews.

It was left just to descend the glacier systems of the south-west side. Martin Moran had suggested the descent might prove easy. Let's just say on that front he was wrong. After a day and a half of complex glacier travel, including several forced abseils through icefalls, we eventually escaped onto rocky ground and descended to a welcome tea encounter with Sanju and Devraj. Three days later our porters had ferried our kit down to Sural Batori and we were ensconced in a local house watching satellite television. It seemed somehow fitting that Bear Grylls appeared on the screen eating a variety of insects and drinking his own urine.

'Appears to be more refreshing than mine,' concluded Victor as Bear licked his lips enthusiastically. All we have to do now is agree a follow up re-union climb. There's a lot to be said for them.

- This article is adapted from the English edition of *Himalaya: the Tribulations of Mick & Vic* by Mick Fowler and Victor Saunders, published by Eric Vola, available as a paperback on demand from *Lulu.com* and amazon.

JIM LOWTHER

Gupta

Spot the vehicle: driving the notorious Chandra Bhaga
road to access the Kishtwar range. *(Jim Lowther)*

The idea of climbing in Kishtwar first cropped up in the early 1990s. Graham Little was my climbing partner at the time and he told me about a 5,618m unclimbed mountain called Gupta that he'd seen from the top of nearby Rohini Shikhar, which he climbed in 1989. It's a shapely rock peak dominating the Dharlang Nala and knowing how good the granite was likely to be, we both thought Gupta would be a plum objective.

Unfortunately our application to climb the mountain was rejected three days before we were due to leave the UK in September 1996. We were told there had been some insurgent activity in Gulab Garh and the government of India had decided to close Kishtwar to climbers. It remained closed for the next 17 years. This didn't matter to us though; Graham pulled a rabbit out of a hat with a superb alternative suggestion for a new route, the north face of Kullu Eiger in Himachal Pradesh's Parvati valley. The timely intervention of Dr M S Gill secured us Indian Mountaineering Foundation (IMF) permission in three days and the expedition went ahead successfully.

Then in 2013 Mick Fowler sprung open the doors to Kishtwar by getting consent to climb Kishtwar Kailash. Although he may not have been the first

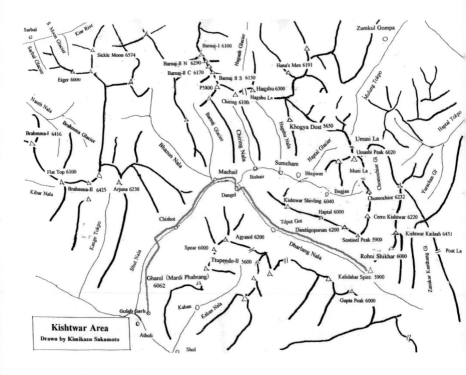

The approach to Gupta.

to re-enter the area, this widely reported climb brought Kishtwar to every-one's attention and prompted what felt like a headlong gold rush of climbers, drawn to a paradise of amazing unclimbed granite walls and peaks. I thought we needed to get in there and climb Gupta before anyone else did.

I sent Mick's picture of Gupta's majestic north face to my good American friends Mark Richey and Mark Wilford; they were instantly on for another trip together to follow our last epic to Saser Kangri II in 2009. The thing I like about these guys is they put every last ounce of effort into everything they do, so I knew we'd have an adventure to remember.

The road along the Chandra Bhaga gorge, particularly the section between Udaipur and Gulab Garh, has to be one of the most extreme road-building endeavours in the world and travelling along it is not for the faint-heart-ed. Meeting two American teams on our journey certainly added to the impression of a gold rush, even if collectively we were the only visitors to the area in 2017.

Kaushal Desai organised our trip for us and we met him at his HQ in Manali after an overnight 'super deluxe' sleeper bus journey from Delhi on 9 September that was so uncomfortable we decided to hire a private jeep for our return journey. Kaushal was Mick's recommendation and he did a great job for us throughout the trip, with prompt and helpful replies to emails during the planning period all the way through to providing us with a great crew and good base camp kit and food, not to mention hard-core jeep drivers and proficient horsemen.

Military sensitivities required us to approach Kishtwar from the Rohtang pass, which is why we were starting from Manali and contemplating the scary two day jeep journey down the Chandra Bhaga gorge with an overnight stop at Udaipur. The latter part of the road route is cut out of vertical granite and a 500m sheer drop into the river gorge yawns on one side; we only saw three other vehicles on the road that day. After a very dusty, teeth-rattling journey we finally arrived at Gulab Garh late in the evening of 11 September and stayed in the comfortable Satyam Shiram guest house.

After completing formalities with the police the following morning we started our trek up the Dharlang Nala with 15 horses carrying our gear. The pony drivers didn't hang around: progress was so swift the villages we passed through on the way went by in a blur. But what were memorable was the lushness of the valley, the heady scent of the cedar forest and the ever-present roar of the river in post-monsoon spate. The village houses are painted bright primary colours of red, blue and even yellow that contrast with the dun browns of the farmland in full harvest: stubble fields, stacked stoops of cut barley and hay and standing crops of nearly mature maize.

The two Marks are more familiar with the scrub approaches of arid parts of the Karakoram, so green and verdant Kishtwar was a welcome break for them as well as providing a feast of birdwatching opportunities. In my case the virgin forest was a dendrologist's paradise with no evidence of logging and a wide variety of tree species to admire such as southern beech, chestnut, walnut, different types of cedar, sugar pine, maple, sycamore and the most enormous elm trees I've ever seen.

We stopped at the village of Chishot where our super-organised liaison officer Rajender Sharma (aka Rinku) arranged for us to sleep in the grounds of the temple. First thing the following morning, Chishot was alive and busy with major outbound traffic of sheep and goats driven by their Muslim shepherds heading down to the Kashmir valley now that winter was approaching. Walking against the flow of animals along winding, dusty paths, we eventually broke through the top of the tree line to be greeted by wide open fields around Machel, also spelled Machail, the temple site of the Hindu goddess Chandi Mata and the focal point for many thousands of pilgrims, who unfortunately leave a lot of litter behind them. Here we completed the last formalities with police and continued to Dengel, the last bridge in the valley, where we met two young American climbers, Crystal and Whitney Clark from Colorado. They were stranded in Dengel because their horses had bolted the night before; they were awaiting the arrival of new ones, so we said goodbye and good luck and never saw them again close up. Each team progressed up the valley on opposite sides of the river, aiming for different objectives, so we could only wave at them on the couple of occasions that we saw them afterwards.

The route took us first through more cedar pine forest, then birch and the river became smaller and quieter. After two or three climbs, the valley

Top left: Mark Richey crossing the Tyrolean on his way to climb Gupta. *(Mark Richey)*

Above left: The two Marks, Wilford and Richey, at camp three. *(Jim Lowther)*

Right: Mark Richey traversing the north-east face on day three. *(Mark Wilford)*

levelled off at 3,500m and became a series of wide open pastures, the river a braided gravel bed that looked deceptively crossable (which it wasn't). This continued all day and by 4pm we found a decent enough base camp opposite Gupta – but on the wrong side of the river. We were underneath lots of granite towers, amidst huge climbable boulders and we could see Mick Fowler's superb route up Kishtwar Kailash.

Our camp staff, Pritam Yangthangi and Amit Bodh, made a delicious dinner of chicken from one of the six that made it to base camp alive inside a metal box on the back of one of our horses. We were told that we had 90 unbroken eggs left from the 150 we set off with, which meant plenty of omelettes every morning we were in base camp. Getting drinkable water was a challenge: we were camped beside a river draining the Chomochoi glacier that was thick with rock flour and required filtering. However, we'd brought a horse load of beer to compensate.

The ponies left us on the morning of 15 September after we arranged for them to come back on 1 October for the return journey. That gave us a fortnight to scope the mountain and climb it. First we had to work out how to cross the river, which looked possible lower down but wasn't an appealing prospect at base camp. I've lost two friends to river crossing accidents and treat Himalayan rivers with the greatest of respect. Richey came up with the bright idea that one of us should swim across the river. It was decided that person would be me, with a rope for a safety that would then be tensioned across a shorter span of river between the framing of a collapsed shepherd's bridge. Amazingly this worked, so feeling rather chuffed with ourselves we pushed on up Gupta following a series of grassy ledges and the tracks of bharal goats, or blue sheep, and left a cache of hardware at 4,300m.

Although the Tyrolean rope bridge worked quite well at first, however hard we tightened the 7mm Kevlar, the 25m span was too wide and we got

Gupta with route and camps marked. *(Mick Fowler)*

wet each time we pulled ourselves across. Wilford solved the problem with
the introduction of an 8.5mm dynamic rope to augment the cord, which we
fixed the following day and Richey tested this a couple of times, floating
across a good six feet above the water. Pleased with this, we went back to
base camp and assembled three days of food and clothing for a carry up
to a new high camp we established at 4,600m on 18 September on scree
beside a small snowfield in the middle of the north-east face. This required
rock shifting and dirt scraping to make a level platform for a bivy tent and
one sleeping position for a person outside, but was worth it: this was our
launch pad for the technical climbing above. We ferried a second load up
from the cache next day and spent another night there before descending
to base camp on 20 September.

Up until this point the weather had been consistently good and stable
and since we were ahead of schedule we decided to have two days' rest.
This suited me because I came down with a fever and was bed ridden. The
two Marks went bouldering but Richey had a fall and cracked his heel
bone on landing, although didn't know this until he got back to the States.
In the meantime he bore the pain and hobbled around base camp and
suffered during the climb. I then succumbed to a tick bite that brought me
out in a livid itchy rash from head to toe, so we extended the rest period by
another two days to allow both Richey and me to recover. It then rained in
base camp on 24 September for the whole day, which made us feel less guilty

about having a rest. This was our only day's bad weather and when the clouds parted the dark granite of the north face had a thin covering of powder snow and the temperature adjusted downwards for the rest of the trip.

We adjusted our tactics and took a three-man tent to swap with the two-man bivy tent at the launch pad on 25 September in case we had to sit out bad weather waiting for the summit push. In the event the weather was fantastic and we had clear views of the whole of the Kishtwar range and beyond for the duration. The route to the launch pad – camp one – was pretty convoluted but very safe, linking together grassy terraces, animal trods, scree rakes and the like. When we arrived at the camp the two Marks had enough energy to walk to the top of a tower above the camp to spy out the route across the north-east face towards the east ridge. They spied a promising line and left a fixed rope for the first pitch in the morning.

On 26 September we jumared this to the top of a pinnacle ridge that connected to the main face. Richey lead about six pitches up snow-covered rocks over the next six hours to a decent bivy tucked well into the north-east face. We did some heavy engineering to make flat ledges out of dirt and settled down for the night after a frugal meal of salami, cheese, crackers, Ramen noodles and tea. Wilford slept outside on an enormous yellow blow up mattress and Richey and I had the two man bivy tent to ourselves.

The sun hit camp two at 6.20am but we decided to wait for our gear to dry. There was no hurry; it was warm and blue skies promised glorious mixed climbing across the north-east face to the east ridge. Richey lead off across a snow ramp and scratched his way up a strenuous pitch through an overhanging chimney and a snow-filled rake towards another snow patch. Another pitch followed and then the best pitch of the whole climb, an upward-slanting traverse left across snow-covered slabs with frozen turf placements for tools and tiny incuts for mono points, all of it about grade M5. Wilford and I followed, reaching the sunlit east ridge, to be greeted by an ebullient Richey. We were now looking across the breadth of the east ridge, which consisted of climbable granite slabs and ledges; this narrowed to a finer ridge above and we thought easier ground would be found by traversing across towards the south face, the side of the mountain we couldn't see from base camp.

I led a couple of pitches, then Wilford a couple and then Richey took us up to a snow patch that cut through the east ridge onto the broad south face. We scrambled up this for about 100m and found a superb bivy perched hard on the east ridge with the summit beckoning above us. The mountain was not throwing any nasty surprises at us and spirits were high as we brewed up for summit day; the Americans slept in the tent and I had a spacious ledge outside with awesome views of peaks to the south and stars above.

The sun woke us at 6.30am on 28 September but we weren't on our way until 9am: we wanted the rock to be warm. Wilford wore rock shoes again and climbed three straightforward pitches up the ridge. Richey followed this with two harder pitches of about 5.9 in big boots on truly immaculate granite with lots of gear placements and chicken heads for holds. I seconded

Mark Wilford leading on the east ridge on day four. *(Mark Richey)*

all of this and then pitched through up snow to the summit ridge, which was a snow cornice overhanging a vertical drop down the featureless north face.

The others came up to join me and we pushed on to the summit proper, an arrangement of tottering blocks. Unrestricted views into Zanskar, Pangi and towards Kashmir greeted us at the top. The sun shone and there wasn't a breath of wind. We did some self-timed photos and whilst looking around noticed a tiny red dot 1,000m below us on the glacier to the north of Gupta. It must have been the two American girls in their tent so we shouted down at them and got some faint shouts and waves back. Camaraderie in the mountains and an unclimbed summit all to ourselves with expansive views under a windless blue sky: our trip climaxed at that moment.

To the south-east we could see the imposing profile of Shib Shankar, also known as Sersank, the north buttress of which was at that very moment being climbed by Mick Fowler and Victor Saunders. I remembered failing miserably on this mountain in 2007: Graham Little and I turned back halfway up the north-west ridge when we encountered friable shale so it was nice to know that it was being climbed in good style by some Brits.

Feeling well pleased with our efforts and thoroughly enjoying ourselves, we slowly started a descent back to camp three, which went in about four raps. All of us were exhausted. I have to hand it to my two partners for their intuitive route finding, gutsy but safe climbing and perpetual good humour, which is why I like climbing with them so much.

Wilford and Lowther close to the summit on day four. *(Mark Richey)*

Hoar frost coated my sleeping bag as a weak sun tried to penetrate swirling clouds at 6.30am next morning. I got up and made some brews but the others weren't going to budge, so I melted snow for the day's water canisters. We had that sinking feeling of knowing the descent was going to be difficult so we weren't in a hurry. The descent was first a scramble to the snow patch on the east ridge, then three raps to a ledge system that we could walk along to the edge of the east ridge. Wilford persuaded us to take a direct line straight down the north-east face, down a snow gully filled with rock spikes, about 10 raps in all, until we were back at the camp one tent. It was a miracle we didn't get our ropes stuck. We left there at 2.30pm and were down at the Tyrolean by dusk, concluding an excellent five-day alpine-style climb. Rinku met us with a big smile and walked us back to base camp whereupon we were greeted by Pritam and Amit with cups of tea, chicken and whisky.

The sun stayed with us for two more days at base camp and the two-day walk out with the horses. We waved at the American girls across the river when we passed their camp. They shouted their congratulations and news of their adventures but I don't think they climbed anything. If you haven't got a fixed objective to go for it's easy to get blown away by all the possibilities. As we left the Dharlang Nala we carried with us memories of a happy and successful trip in beautiful unspoilt surroundings. The journey to Kishtwar is a long one but there is plenty of scope for future exploration of unclimbed peaks that make it worthwhile.

MALCOLM BASS

Gangstang

Looking up towards the north-west ridge of Gangstang (6163m).
(All images Malcolm Bass and Guy Buckingham)

The primary aim of the expedition in June 2016 was the first ascent of the north-west ridge of Gangstang (6163m) in Himachal Pradesh. Gangstang lies near the Chandra-Bhaga river and is usually approached from Keylong (3350m) for the south-west ridge, the voie normale, from the Gangstang glacier. This expedition approached from the road head of Naingarth further to the west. The expedition, comprising Malcolm Bass and Guy Buckingham with support staff, enjoyed excellent weather and achieved its objective in short order.

Gangstang, reportedly first climbed by Italians in 1945 and again in 1973 by a team from Calcutta, is most commonly climbed via the south-west ridge. Successful parties have approached from the Gangstang glacier to the east. In 2001 a Japanese party broke new ground, approaching the peak via the glacier below the north face and from here made the first approach of the east ridge. In 2007, Martin Moran brought a commercial expedition to the Thirot valley. His team successfully climbed what they called Thirot Shivling (5324m), a prominent rocky bastion at the far end of the north of Gangstang (PD-) and established a partial new route up a curving snow couloir on the west face of Gangstang before joining the standard south-west ridge (D-). (A local professor from a nearby college, Mr Suresh Kumar, told

22

A closer view of the north-west ridge. The peak was first climbed from the south-west in 1945.

us the traditional name for Thirot Shivling is Neelkantha, which we use in this report.)

The expedition had originally planned to go back to Rimo III (7233m) in the east Karakoram. Rimo III lies near the head of the North Terong glacier, a tributary of the Siachen. This area is militarily sensitive and unfortunately permission was turned down at the last moment, leaving us looking for a suitable project on an 'open' peak to avoid further problems. After long discussions covering numerous ranges and countries, with the help and support of Martin Moran we settled on Gangstang. The north-west ridge had yet to be climbed and pictures from the previous expedition promised an excellent line on a peak reminiscent of the Matterhorn or Shivling.

The nearest open peak is Phabrang (6172m) for which we applied through the Indian Mountaineering Foundation (IMF) and permission was duly granted. As a requirement of the permission, the IMF appointed a liaison officer and we were lucky in being allocated Mr Parmender Sharma, a young, ambitious climber who was both friendly and amenable to our objectives. Our other Indian members were employees of our agent. The application for this open peak took less than a month. Insurance for mountaineering above 6,000m remains expensive; the most cost effective method we found was an extended policy from the Austrian Alpine Club plus basic cover for lost luggage and so forth. Satellite phones are still an issue in India. Although there is the intention by the government to change the law banning them, they are still not allowed. The use of a satellite texting device, such as the Alpine Club's InReach, was deemed acceptable.

We arrived in Dehli on 27 May and met our liaison officer and Rimo Expeditions representatives at the Indian Mountaineering Foundation (IMF). Having completed the world's fastest IMF briefing, thanks to the vice-president being double booked, we had a long and fruitful shopping trip and departed for Chandigarh, Le Corbusier's regimented contribution to Indian urban planning cheerfully supplemented with the Indian compulsion towards colour and chaos. Then it was the long drive to Manali, fighting through holiday traffic, where we met our cook Santabir Sherpa, and his assistant Dawa Bhutiya. Santabir was shy but an excellent cook; Dawa was more outgoing and provided excellent service with a real care for his charges.

From Manali, we continued over the Rohtang pass (4000m) down into the Chandra Bhaga valley. The Rothang is exceptionally popular with local tourists; there's a flourishing trade hiring snowsuits to allow those from the plains their first experience of snow. The road is under constant threat of rock fall and repair gangs are ever present, but it's still busy and we queued at times. It never ceases to amaze me how, despite the instinct for anarchy that bewitches Indian drivers, the traffic still flows.

Once over the pass, the roads were quieter. There is a huge engineering project to drive a tunnel from Manali through to the Chandra Bhaga valley which will ease the journey, but it won't be completed for five years. After travelling through numerous small villages we turned off towards the road head at Naingarth. Once we arrived, our Rimo guide, Bhim Bahadar Lama, introduced us to one of the elders of the village who was most gracious in allowing us to camp close to the village that night. Bhim remained with us for a few days to ensure we were properly settled, our mother hen, clucking around to make sure we didn't get into trouble – and very welcome it was.

Naingarth was idyllic: last stop on the popular pilgrim route to the sacred lake of Neelkantha. There seemed to be a real sense of community with everyone sharing in the work with humour and diligence. It was the time for planting of crops and the animals were being moved further up the valley as the snows melted.

The walk-in to base camp took two days, the intermediate camp being in a pleasant meadow, lush with flowers and with some large boulders to play on. Both days were short, and after a relaxed start we were in camp by 11am. Some of the porters visited the sacred lake prior to leaving. The camp was in a pleasant spot next to the main river with an excellent view of the main objective. This was our home for the next three weeks, visited only by a few passing pilgrims.

Our liaison officer, Palmi, was keen to join us on our acclimatisation programme and had some excellent previous experience. He has a plan to climb Everest in the next couple of years. Our first objective was simply to gain height; we headed up some moraine and continued past a huge rock buttress we named 'The Lump', continuing up snow ramps until we reached

Malcolm Bass leading the first rock tower on the north-west ridge.

around 4,900m. It was a beautiful day and we were able to hang around to admire the view and let our bodies adjust. We were still back by midday, fortunately since it got unbearably hot in the afternoon.

Next day was due to be a rest, but seeing how everyone was feeling well, we pushed our next acclimatisation phase forward by 24 hours, packing up for a night out. Guy, Palmi and I headed back up the moraine before heading east across the front of the north-west ridge of Gangstang towards the base of Neelkantha (5324m). This peak stands as the bastion at the end of the ridge with a very distinctive rock feature on top looking like a figure in a lotus position watching over the sacred lake. As we went past the lake, Palmi took the opportunity to offer a prayer while we paid our respects. On the side of the lake is a small monument surrounded in gifts, especially small iron tridents or *trisul*; there is also a small box with donations to help establish a proper temple on the site.

Once past the lake, we established our camp on a moraine band (4500m) and after an uncomfortable night getting used to the tiny tent rose early to head around to the west face as soon as possible and head up the slopes to the summit. It was a long way round before we found a snow gully that wound its way through a series of rock buttresses. The slope was pockmarked with some serious debris from snow and rock fall, concentrating our minds on getting back down before the sun hit the face. The slope remained at an almost constant 30° until we reached the north-west summit after about

Guy Buckingham on the difficult grey tower higher on the ridge.

four and a half hours. There was time for the quickest of photographs and then we were moving with alacrity back down the slope towards our tents and then base camp for a rest.

Feeling we had just about enough acclimatisation, it was time for the main objective. We spent a day sorting food and equipment. Not knowing what was in store, we planned for five days, thinking that would allow us enough contingency for unforeseen eventualities without adding too much to the packs. Early on 6 June, we headed back up the moraine towards the base of the glacier that sits under the north face of Gangstang. It was unfortunate, but we could see no way around getting on the glacier early, climbing a frozen stream before the sun hit it and then waiting all day in the heat for an early start next morning. Once on the glacier we were in luck; there was a large boulder under which we could get shade and during the day produced a small puddle of melt-water for drinking. We used the time to head up towards the start of the climb, giving us a marker in the dark to follow and allowing a good look at the proposed route onto the ridge.

A large debris cone accessed an easy-angled snow-slope which led to the ridge; the bergschrund above was covered over and it looked steady. We went to bed with the usual sense of anticipation, both engrossed in our own thoughts for the days ahead. At 1am, we headed back to the snow cone and made our way up towards the couloir. For the first half of the climb to the ridge everything was smooth. The climbing was grade II and we were able to move together smoothly and efficiently. It was not until we traversed left under the rocky outcrops that the angle steepened and the extreme effect of the sun on the snow came into play. As we approached the ramp, we had a

Continuing up the ridge in worsening conditions.

choice between unconsolidated snow and brittle grey ice. I spotted a small couloir to the side, a grade IV mixture of dinner-plating ice and loose rock. It did allow us to approach the upper reaches. Then it was unconsolidated snow to the cornice, which was exceptionally insecure.

We reached the ridge at 7.30am and after a short break continued towards the first tower and the start of the ridge. We stuck mostly to the ridgeline, climbing in crampons on ground that was mostly V Diff to Hard Severe with one or two moves of 5a. The rock was mostly okay as long as you took care where to stand and what to pull on. We made good progress up towards our next key crux, dubbed the 'Citadel', but as evening approached, we started looking for a campsite. Settling on a small snow ledge half over-hanging the north face, we anchored everything, including ourselves, to the rock around it. We didn't get much sleep but at least we were able to rest.

Next day we took on the Citadel, an imposing and large buttress blocking our path. It was obvious we were not going to tackle it head on and the route on the north side meant a precarious day working between unconsolidated snow bands with little protection. This left the dank west face, which lived up to its promise of uncompromising and loose terrain. After a 5a traverse onto the face, we spent the day on loose mixed at around a technical grade of IV/V. Views were limited and we had to guess when we were far enough around the Citadel before heading up again to the ridge, relieved to find we had got it right. Luck remained on our side as we soon came across a bivy site, which, after a solid hour chipping away, became a flat campsite where we didn't need to tie on. Consequently, we had a better night's sleep and were looking forward to the challenges of the next day and hopefully the summit.

Next morning, 9 June, things started well: having crossed some snow slopes we approached a grey rock tower, different in appearance and feel to rock we'd experienced so far. Although still loose, looking similar to a large pile of Jenga, it allowed good progress if taken with care. It was here that the technical crux of the climb came, with a slabby pull onto a large block. It was only when fully committed to the block, that you could see it was completely overhanging the west face and felt some distance apart from the main ridge.

Once above the tower, the climbing became a monotonous round of small rock buttresses interspersed with sections of grey ice that was both hard and brittle. By this time the altitude and previous work was taking it toll, with a sequence of very slow pitches with both of us making a beeline to any rock showing from the ice to rest our calves. By now the weather had deteriorated with a barrage of icy wind and snow being blown across the west face. It was getting towards evening and we'd both donned duvet jackets to battle the cold when the top finally came in sight. We were fairly subdued when we finally topped out, with a quick 'selfie' before finding somewhere to camp. The route down was none too obvious and visibility was in and out, so we only went about 100m to some soft dry snow which made for an easy final bivy site.

Next morning the weather started badly, but it soon cleared and we were able to see the way down. It was easy enough, with only a small section of grey ice before an easy stroll down snow ridges towards the west face, making our way along the route taken by Martin Moran. Unfortunately this included a short climb up a small tooth on the ridgeline, wading through knee and thigh-deep snow. It felt like the mountain reminding us who was boss. Then we were at the couloir leading to the basin at the bottom of the west face and with four abseils, a lot of down-climbing and bum-sliding, we were at the corrie floor and in relative safety: man-hugs all round. Then it was a matter of six hours of moraine bashing with heavy packs until we reached base camp and gorged on Tang and pakora. With the weather on our side we had achieved our objective much quicker than anticipated, ten days after reaching base camp, and were able to leave earlier than planned.

Support for the expedition

Expeditions are inevitably expensive and would be untenable if it weren't for the excellent grants available to support British alpinists attempting new routes and first ascents. The British Mountaineering Council, Mount Everest Foundation, Austrian Alpine Club and the Montane Alpine Club Fund supported us with grants. We are extremely grateful to all four bodies. Montane also supported with equipment. High5 Sports Nutrition kindly provided us with bars, gels, sports drinks and recovery drinks, very convenient for quick recovery in bivouacs. Lyon Equipment helped Malcolm with footwear and hardware. Rab supported Guy with clothing and the summit tent.

COSMIN ANDRON

Zanskar's Supercouloir

Climbing solid rock high on the first ascent of *Supercouloir* (ED, 75° max,
WI 4+, M5/6, 6b) on T16 (6431m) in Zanskar. *(Cristina Pogacean)*

*Southern Zanskar has many unclimbed and little known peaks. In June 2016, the
Romanians Cosmin Andron and Cristina Pogacean climbed a stunning line on
a peak known as T16 (6431m) in the Gompe Tokpo area south-west of Padum.
Dubbed Supercouloir, they graded their line 1200m, ED, 75° max, WI 4+, M5/6,
6b, climbed in three days from an ABC at 5,200m.*

In the sweltering early summer of 2016 my wife Cristina and I met a
couple of Indian friends in Delhi. Prerna Dangi and Karn Kowshik
were participants in the 2013 'Climbathon' organised by the Indian Mountaineering Foundation (IMF). I had been an instructor. Our plan was simple
yet complicated: Cristina and I were short, really short, of cash but still
keen to have an expedition. We peered at maps and reports and one area
seemed interesting to us: Zanskar. We tried to translate the map of Japanese

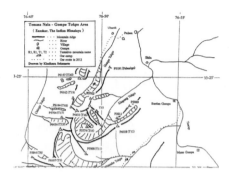

Above: Kimikazu Sakamoto's sketch-map of the mountains south-west of Padum showing the location of T16.

Right: The Supercouloir of T16.
(Cosmin Andron)

mountain traveller Kimikazu Sakamoto onto Google Earth and identified a peak we liked, without having any photos of it. Trawling the internet for more information – mainly photos – we discovered that Sakamoto's report of the area was still the best resource.

The expedition would be as cheap as possible, the upside being we had no commitments to sponsors or the media. The plan was simple: make our way to Padum using public transport, source some local help to reach a suitable base camp and from there try to climb the chosen peak, initially by any easy enticing route in teams of two: Prerna and Cristina, Karn and myself. Then we would try its north face. The peak chosen was 'baptised' as P6436 in the IMF registry and as peak T13 on the Sakamoto map.

Our merry band was joined by two more: Nishit, a rock climber from Pune, and Karn's dog, Argos, and on 2 June we left Delhi in two batches:

Karn, Nishit and Argos the dog with part of our luggage in Karn's Duster
and Cristina, Prerna and I by public transport with the rest of the luggage.
Public bus from Delhi to Jammu took 10 hours, then we switched to a
shared taxi and 12 hours later were in Srinagar, after a bit of a detour around
a village to avoid a gunfight between Indian troops and Islamists. From
Srinagar, where we spent the night, we took another van for the 10-hour
drive to Kargil for another 10-hour journey. After a depressing night in a
squalid hotel we left early next morning after an extended shopping session
for veggies, rice, flour, eggs, fruit, Coke and whatever else the girls decided
would be our diet for the next few weeks.

Twelve hours later, on the night of 5 June, we were in Padum (3600m),
slightly less shattered than we expected after the travel. We promptly and
totally by chance met Karn, Nishit and Argos in the first restaurant we

Above: Cristina Pogacean after the tiring first bivouac. *(Cristina Pogacean)*

Right: Cristina Pogacean near the top of the ice in the couloir. *(Cosmin Andron)*

visited to rest our weary bodies. Also by chance, a local boy, Tenzing Thapa, a taxi driver by trade, was officially appointed sirdar, cook and base camp manager. Next day was spent on a recce trip up the valley towards our objective looking for a way across the river, which the Japanese party had trouble crossing, hence skipping entirely our intended destination.

On 8 June we set up base camp on a moraine at around 4,900m. A quick recce up the moraine and glacier showed our initial objective, T13, was quite unlike it appeared on Google Earth. On 11 June at 3am four of us left base camp leaving Nishit, Tenzing and Argos behind. We moved efficiently over moderate ground with only a couple of belays up to close to 5,900m. Unfortunately, the ridge was not continuous as it appeared on Google Earth but more a convergence of ridges running from south to north to converge with the west ridge of T13. From where we stopped, a couloir of snow on the north side of the west side seemed the way to go, but the route beyond looked progressively more difficult culminating with several abseils and walls before the summit. Despite having bivy gear, we deemed the undertaking a tad too much for our merry band in its current configuration and decided to bail.

Cristina and I were pondering on our next target. We could try a line on the north face of T13 but it would be a confection, a linking together of snow islands and I didn't much like the odds of being in the firing line for three days or so. Each night at ABC we heard the rumble of avalanches.

The alternative was the south side of what we identified on Sakamoto's map as T16, right opposite the north face of T13. From the ridge I had seen a beautiful, natural line: a couloir running from bottom to top. The problem was that the upper third of the couloir seemed pure rock, possibly overhanging. Would we be able to find a way through that? The choice was between forcing a line through dangerous terrain on T13 and following a natural, safer line with a major question mark right at the top on T16. In the end we decided to set up an ABC in the middle of the glacier, right between the two faces, giving us the option to decide after examining both faces in more detail.

Karn and Prerna were having their own powwow. They reached the conclusion that all the lines on T13 and T16 were beyond what they were ready, as a team, to tackle. Karn decided to take Nishit and Argos down to Padum and arrange porters for 18 June, when we hoped we should be off whatever route we chose to try, while Prerna would remain with Tenzing in base camp to keep us company on the mountain.

We feasted on pasta, lard, sausages and *matar paneer* mainly thanks to the kitchen labour of the girls: Tenzing's progress from steering wheel to ladle was tortuous but ended with dal and boiled veggies. As a matter of pre-caution, we brought from Romania a solid stash of blue and green cheese and other goodies just to be safe. After three days at base camp, all our companions, whether Tibetan Buddhist, Indian Buddhist, non-practising Hindu and vegetarian Hindu were converted to Romanian ways and soon the fat Romanian omelette with cheese, lard and sausages was the staple of each breakfast.

On 14 June, after two days of rest and gluttony, Karn, Nishit and Argos left for Padum while Cristina and I left to set up ABC at around 5,200m and make up our minds. Prerna and Tenzing stayed at base camp to ponder how lard had changed their lives and finish season two of *Arrow*, the American TV series we had got them addicted to on our iPad. That night at ABC our decision was made for us. The north face of T13 was rumbling with avalanches and rock fall. It wasn't wise to be up there any time of day and there was a much better alternative just opposite. We set our alarms for 3am.

The couloir was pretty straightforward, as we expected it to be, with a couple of shortlived 75° sections. We simul-climbed pretty much all of it with a quick brew and breakfast stop on a ledge halfway up. We were hoping to get off the snow and into a sheltered spot before the sun hit the couloir as we were anticipating slush and rock fall. The snow section of the couloir ended with a constriction and a foretelling of what was to come higher up. The five metres or so of mixed ground looked anything but pleasant and Cristina drew the short straw: rotten ice and polished rock required some inventive shimmying up the pitch.

By the time we were done the sun was moving in and we scurried to find shelter. Rocks were whizzing around and we played dodgems until we found a ledge, if you can call it that, under a small overhang. Then we sat down to wait. By 5pm the sun went over the ridge and by 7pm the rocks

Cosmin Andron leading thin ice at the top of the couloir. *(Cristina Pogacean)*

had stopped falling. We did another pitch on easy snow up to an icefall but that was more of a waterfall. Since it wouldn't be easy frozen, let alone melting, we decided to return to our little ledge, sort out a bivy and have an early start in the morning. We felt queasy and sun-struck. Conversation was merely functional and with a hint of irritation. We were, literally, cooked. As we settled down to sleep, I said: 'At least it's not snowing!' It wasn't half an hour before the first snowflakes were dancing down onto our bivy bag. My wife told me, quite justifiably, to shut up.

It was a beautiful morning though, and, grunting and aching, we extracted ourselves from our bags, unclipped ourselves from the anchor and started up. It was my day to lead and I was expecting it to be glorious. The icefall was indeed frozen but the surprises soon came thick and fast. Sorting the gear, I took the opportunity to congratulate myself for only bringing two ice screws. One was promptly sunk in the base of the icefall and I assumed that the other would be enough for the next 30m, the limit of what I could see. Out of sight, however, the icefall continued, cork-screwing up a full rope-length. Halfway up, with sinking heart, I was forced to call down to Cristina asking for the lower screw to be sent up on one of the ropes, quite a matter of dexterity as I was hanging off one tool with feet in ice and a crack. The ice was old: brown and thin. The exit was burly and mixed: I managed to clean the upper bit straight onto Cristina's belay below. It wasn't the prettiest start, but heaving and grunting gets you a long way if you're persistent. My sack followed, then Cristina.

Pogacean following the move left and up through a band of overhangs to avoid an area of loose rock. *(Cosmin Andron)*

A pitch higher, the couloir was blocked by vertical, frozen mud with rock stuck in it: some sort of dubious-looking, 'improvised' conglomerate. An attempt up it produced little progress, moderate amounts of fear and loads of doubt. We opted for the 'sporty' option, negotiating overhangs and thin mixed ground. I felt well in control of my tools but not necessarily of my emotions since protection was scarce, the run-outs long and the ice thin. Luckily I was so tired I couldn't strike it too hard, thus preserving some for Cristina when it was her turn.

Cristina Pogacean leading on the last day, going light for the summit.
(Cosmin Andron)

Not knowing what lay ahead and having wasted time on the 'fake' conglomerate, we started looking for a bivy spot. The sun was moving in although we were blessed with a cloudy day and the firing range opened up a tad later. We finally found a spot and excavated it: it was perfect, as long as you were tiny – and alone. The morning was bright but that couldn't make up for a sleepless night, sitting on one butt-cheek. Grumpy was my middle name, on the morning of 17 June.

After a few wet and snowy pitches on decent rock but with fingery moves we ended up on a beautiful face. The sun was out, the rock was dry, protection about right and I was happy seconding. We left all the bivy gear at the bivy spot and took only what we deemed necessary, climbing in rock shoes. We soon passed a fake summit, the white triangle visible from base camp, on the face to its right and kept going. The higher we got the better the climb became. Towards the exit to the final ridge we both experienced some of the best rock climbing we have done in the higher mountains.

At the base of the final arête we left behind the backpack, the camera, taking only my phone, and our big boots. The afternoon was approaching and we were keen to start down. As on T13, the final ridge was the meeting point of several ridges, including the two sides sheltering our couloir. We had exited the couloir by its left, west side onto the face and the ground ahead was fairly moderate. One could see the flat table-top north summit ahead and the south summit above. It was now after 4pm and with the end in sight we moved with a high sense of urgency.

The north summit was at least a kilometre away and the ridge was up and down with quite a few pinnacles in between, all pretty much at the same height. We weren't keen on visiting each and every one of them and weren't planning to tag the north summit either. Quite a bit past 5pm we started descending, down-climbing what we could, abseiling where we couldn't or where it was faster.

Having recovered the backpack, then the stuff left at the bivy, as darkness set in we were abseiling in a void, past the overhangs, past the icefall, past the first bivy and into the snow couloir. We started down-climbing until tiredness caught up and we reached the steeper bits. Then we alternated between abseils and down-climbing until the slope gave in and we started walking face out towards the glacier below. There was a little light down on the glacier, near our ABC: Prerna has sent someone up to help us dismantle it and head down to base camp since the porters were due that evening. By 3am we were in base camp with a mug of hot chocolate in hand. Sleep was never sweeter nor the sleeping bag softer.

From Padum we decided to close the circle and travelled, again by public transport, all the way to Leh and from there to Manali and back to Delhi. Karn, Nishit and Argos went back via Srinagar in their Duster. Given the geographical data, we were not comfortable claiming the first ascent of T16. The north summit may be higher and the two are, at least as it stands, bundled together. In February 2017, a photograph arrived from the Slovenian alpinist Matic Jost taken from Rangtik Tokpo to the north-west that makes me wonder how far south we were on the ridge – and whether what is marked on the Sakamoto map as T16 is actually the same peak they photographed from Gompe Tokpo. Whatever the truth, we decided to leave such problems to the geographers. We are content to have climbed our 'Supercouloir'.

Modern Times

Chamonix, Mer de Glace
Charles Gore (1729-1807)
Between 1778 and 1779. Watercolour with pen and black ink
over graphite on moderately thick, slightly textured, cream laid paper,
pasted on thick, rough, blue wove paper. 10 × 16¾ inches.
Yale Center for British Art, Paul Mellon Collection.

TOM LIVINGSTONE

The Year of Living Dangerously

Tom Livingstone climbing *The Vicar* (VII,7) on Coire an Lochain, Cairngorms, during the British Mountaineering Council's winter meet in early 2016. *(Raphael Slawinski)*

At 26, Tom Livingstone is one of the best young alpinists in the UK, as well as a high-performance rock and winter climber. In 2016 he had an exceptional year, which included high-level ascents in Scotland, a winter ascent of the Walker Spur, his first rock climb of E9, an ascent of Divine Providence and the American Direct in the same week, the third ascent of the House-Anderson route on the north face of Mt Alberta in Canada and finally, in early 2017, an ascent of the Supercanaleta route on Fitzroy in Patagonia.

January

My year began with a yell, and the steady drip, drip of blood. Working on a rope-access job, two of my fingers were squashed in a drill. I ripped off my glove in horror, expecting to have lost digits. When I saw crimson splashing into the mud, I thought I'd be doing a 'Tommy' [Caldwell: see Reviews] and having to amputate. Luckily, one finger was only broken and another scarred, and they soon began to heal.

Four days later, I drove up to Scotland for the start of my annual winter climbing trip. I'd called my partner, Uisdean Hawthorn, and explained there 'might be a minor complication ... nothing serious.' My sausage-shaped fingers throbbed in their bandages but conditions and the weather were looking great. Uisdean and I spent many fine days in the mountains; highlights included the second ascent of *The Vaporiser* (VIII,8) on Creag an Dubh Loch and an early repeat of *Shoot the Breeze* (IX,8) on Beinn Eighe. We also visited many Scottish hospitals and GPs as I needed near-daily dressings for my fingers. The GP in Glenelg gave me quite a scolding when I told my story.

March

I rented an apartment in Chamonix with Pete Graham and Uisdean for March and April. Our box-like room was filled with huge piles of climbing equipment. We lived off coffee, porridge and French 'cake-bars'. When I arrived, the valley had just received a huge snowfall, and my trusty Peugeot skidded and crashed into barriers as we careered down the roads.

Happily the weather quickly improved and I met up with a grizzled Australian named Kim. Although we'd never climbed together before, we got on well and lifted our eyes to the Dru. Conditions were dry this spring, with little ice in the mountains, so we opted for a winter ascent of Pierre Allain's route on the north face.

For two days we inched higher, forming a strong partnership. Kim's straight talking kept me laughing: 'It's not this way, what a bugger!' he'd say if we took a wrong turn. When he reached a belay he'd shout: 'Hell mate, that's a good pitch!' At the bivy at the end of the first day, I dropped fistfuls of snow into the stove and watched them saturate. A crimson sun dipped into a cloud inversion. Shortly afterwards, the orange lights of Chamonix glowed ghostly from beneath the white blanket. I took it all in. This was where I needed to be.

Late in the evening on the second day, as night drew in, we sprinted for the summit, the metal statue of the Virgin Mary flashing in my headtorch's beam as the Chamonix streetlights came on again. My breaths came in heavy, slow gasps as I belayed Kim up the final step. I had dreamed of climbing the Dru for many years; to finally be there after a winter ascent let me contented. I almost enjoyed the 14 rappels back to our tent.

After some serious 'inactive recovery' and more cake-bar, Pete and I made a winter ascent of the *Walker Spur* on the Grandes Jorasses, with three bivouacs and numerous interesting moments. I particularly remember

Livingstone leading the final pitch of the *Walker Spur* on the Grandes Jorasses in winter. *(Pete Graham)*

being caught in a small storm just a pitch below the summit on the third evening; we huddled in our yellow bivy bag, perched on a small ledge, and slowly froze in our icy sleeping bags. Social media and alpinism is a modern combination. Thankfully, Pete is good at these things, coming up with the hashtag: *#freezing-our-asses-on-the-Grandes-Jorasses*. When I topped out next morning, moving from shade to sunlight for the first time in three days, I felt I could actually taste the warmth. It prickled my cheeks and a sense of joy bubbled up from within.

My girlfriend, Victoria, came to Chamonix for a long weekend afterwards and we did some skiing and went to a techno party, redressing the life balance. I'm lucky she gives me a lot of independence. The weather was poor for April, unfortunately. I made a few attempts in the mountains, but they always resulted in the same scenario: standing in swirling snow, looking up at a mountain wreathed in cloud. I put the poor weather to use and climbed my hardest sport grade with *La Ligne Noire* (8a+). Who says alpine climbing gives you heavy legs? I felt ready for home and trad climbing.

May

I joined a few DMM climbers for a trip to the Isle of Arran. James McHaffie led us straight to *The Great Escape* (E8 6c) and we spent the rest of the trip debating which of us he'd sandbagged most. Ryan Pasquill didn't seem to notice the crux moves as he flashed the main pitch, but I had plenty of time to appreciate the exposure when I fell on my attempt.

June

I really enjoy climbing in Pembroke and it's a great place to push your grade. I spent some time here with James Taylor. I hadn't done much headpointing before, but learnt plenty when I climbed *Boat to Naxos* (E7 6c) in Huntsman's Leap. I'd originally tried this line on sight, but took the 'monster lob' in the middle of the run-out. I went back and, due to time pressures, tried it on top rope. I went for the lead shortly after, with a giant swell crashing and booming in the zawn.

Tony Stone and I cancelled a trip to the Alps due to poor weather, and instead drove north for *The Long Hope Route* on Hoy. The island has a few eccentric characters, many thousands of angry fulmars, and one giant overhanging wall of semi-choss: St John's Head. It's undoubtedly one of the most impressive cliffs in the UK, and *The Long Hope* weaves a 450m line through some incredible terrain. Overhanging walls are interspersed with ledges and slots, which stretch deep into the rock. We gently crimped on the sandstone faces, clambered onto ledges and shuffled, sometimes on stomachs, along slotted breaks. The remote and committing feel, with fulmars wheeling and screaming in the wind, eyeing us as we tiptoed past, make it feel like Jurassic Park.

We repeated the E7 version of the route, originally put up by Ed Drummond and Oliver Hill, but I'd like to return for Dave MacLeod's direct pitch. There were a few memorable moments, such as trying not to weight the

Livingstone on the 'heel hook' traverse, high on the *Long Hope Route*, St John's Head, Hoy. This comes just before the crux E7 pitch. *(Tony Stone)*

belay at the end of the 'grass pitch', and making a mental note to get a health check after thrutching up the 'vile crack'. We trundled giant blocks and snapped holds. The belays usually required five pieces of gear. A stuck wire near the top forced us to escape out left, and we returned the following day to remove it, then clean the crux pitch. Tony dispatched this in fine style and we soon topped out to glorious sunshine.

July
It was my childhood dream to climb E9. I knew, one day, it had to be done, and I found myself drawn to the soaring arête of *Rare Lichen*, on the Gribin Facet in the Ogwen valley. The route follows such a striking feature, it's like being slapped in the face. You can see the line from Bethesda, a perfect right-angle cut from the mountain. I couldn't take my eyes from it as I swerved up the road.

I approached this route from above, on the safety of a top rope, with Oli Grounsell, but all I felt was fear. I saw it as an opportunity to learn, to develop, to fall off without dying. I certainly did fall off on my first visit; I punted off virtually every move. Oli is light and strong and described locking each hold, moving between them as if they were jugs. In bitter winds, high on the arête I couldn't feel my hands, but that wasn't why I couldn't do the moves: I was weak from winter, fingers soft after months of gloves and ice axe jugs. The ratty crimps were horrible, skin-shredding, tip-trashing little edges.

Returning as summer 2016 started in North Wales again, I was jealous of those who'd felt strong on the initial moves, flowing through the no-fall zone. 'I get butterflies every time I think of just being up there!' I confessed to my friend. 'I won't fall ... but if I do, the gear might rip; and if that happens, I'll crater from 20m.' I found a 'tall-man's' way to climb the middle section which felt a bit like cheating, but now I could climb the route cleanly on a top-rope and the proposition of leading became a reality. The devil on my shoulder chanted: 'you're off!' The angel said: 'crimp harder!'

Next day I stood beneath the route with only two half ropes tied to my harness; the top rope lay in a crumpled heap by my feet. I hoped the few brass wires might stop me from the same fate as the top rope if I fell. The Ogwen valley was in bright sunshine, a contrast to our shady cliff. I wanted to be swimming in the lake below. Instead, I waited for the internal chatter to quiet and then I stepped off the grass. The route hadn't changed: only my perception of its danger. Where I'd previously slumped onto the top rope, now I'd risk clattering into the ground. I tried to kid myself as I wedged in tiny wires: 'they'll definitely hold me.' Then I moved from left to right on the arête, on autopilot.

The top arête, a fat bottomless wedge jutting into space, was the only thing between the finishing jug and me. I closed my eyes. I tried to imagine myself on a top rope again: nine quick movements of my hands and four subtle foot moves were all it would take, but I couldn't commit. Why am I here? Do I really want to take this risk? The breeze grew stronger and my mind spoke louder, and when I opened my eyes I knew what to do. I just had to switch off my brain and execute. Committing, I bumped my left foot higher, squeezing

John McCune, Tom Livingstone and Uisdean Hawthorn on the summit of Mont Blanc after *Divine Providence* (900m, ED4, 7b, A3). *(Tom Livingstone)*

Left: John McCune, just before the crux corner on *Divine Providence* on the Grand Pilier d'Angle, Mont Blanc range. *(Uisdean Hawthorn)*

the arête with everything I had. Slapping my hands up, my brain came back to life: I had this, I have this, and I have the finishing jug in my hands.

I should have felt elated. The sunshine should have been warm. Instead my mind was raw and could barely comprehend. I felt the effects of a heady cocktail kick in slowly, a mix of satisfaction, boldness – pleasure. My voice bubbled up, so I let out a long whoop of joy, rippling round the valley. I sat for a long time at the top of the crag, finally at peace with myself.

August

At the start of July I received a call from the European brand Tendon. I'd entered a writing competition many months earlier, but heard nothing since. Now they announced I'd won and was being treated to a week's sport climbing on the Norwegian crags of Flatanger, to spend a few days with Adam Ondra. It was an incredible experience in a truly world-class sport climbing destination and Adam was great company. He gave me beta so I could project his warm-ups, and I tried not to mess up as he worked his 'Project Hard' and 'Project Big.' The cave of Flatanger is so vast, so impressive and so good, it's impossible to fully describe. I left having redpointed a few 8as and flashing 7c+, and with a deeper awe and respect for Adam and his friends. Their projects are on another level of difficulty and length.

Then a quick hit to the Alps that coincided with good weather and conditions. On the Friday night Uisdean and I bounced into the bar in Chamonix, celebrating our good friend John McCune's success: he had just completed the British Mountain Guides scheme. Beer flowed, and John, already two *pichets* ahead, was in full swing.

Uisdean Hawthorn climbing above the 90m corner on the *American Direct*, Les Drus. *(Tom Livingstone)*

'You're going to Divine!' he shouted in his Irish accent. 'And I'm coming with you.'

It's always a pleasure to climb with John and we'd talked about *Divine Providence*, the hard rock climb on the Grand Pilier d'Angle, before. Now he was free and psyched.

'Fine,' I replied. 'We leave on Sunday.' I wondered if John would be sober by then.

From the Fourche bivy hut we studied the Grand Pilier d'Angle. Snow covered the lower and upper faces, but the 300m headwall appeared dry. I hoped snowfall the previous day wasn't going to cause any wet sections on the route, but we had our doubts. I told the story of Twid Turner and Dai Lampard nicking a hut blanket when they climbed *Divine* in the 1980s. Uisdean and I had our insulated trousers so we'd be fine. John only had a pair of leggings. His eyes began flicking between our trousers and the lovely hut blankets.

As is so often the case in Alpine climbing, the experience of *Divine Providence* was richer and more fulfilling than I imagined. The physical difficulties of the route were harder and longer. But it was also easier and shorter than the stories made it out to be. Mentally, just getting on the route was a major crux and I felt great relief when I started the first pitch. Of course, this was soon replaced with the usual uncertainty and fear of the unknown. We made good progress with the leader climbing free, and the seconds carrying bigger packs. Strong winds caused melting ice to rain down on us, making it feel very Patagonian. Our dreams of freeing the route also came crashing down when we reached the crux pitches: they were dripping wet despite the outrageous steepness. We resorted to aid.

As we climbed higher and the sun moved off the wall it became very cold and windy. The temperature dropped but we reached easier ground near the top of the wall, while still being buffeted by the wind. To continue along the ridges and snow arêtes to the summit of Mont Blanc would have been dangerous, despite reaching the top of *Divine Providence* if not the top of the Grand Pilier at about 6.30pm after 13 hours. We found a small bivy ledge and spooned through the long night. At dawn we thawed ourselves out, finally huffing and puffing our way to the summit of Mont Blanc at noon.

On Thursday morning, barely 36 hours later, I puzzled at the reflection staring back at me in the window. I was awake, but my reflection was asleep and badly sunburnt. I rubbed my eyes and drank more coffee. The forecast gave us two more days of sunshine, but we were both satisfied; we'd climbed the big one and were left wondering what to do. I thought most people would be content to sip beers in the sun, rather than suffering all over again. Then we bumped into Jon Griffith. He was a bundle of energy: 'what's next, boys?' Within an hour a message arrived from him, listing all the options of routes to do. We knew we had to make the most of the opportunity, but our bodies felt slow and sluggish. We couldn't go big, but we had to do something.

When we stepped off the Montenvers train that evening and walked towards the Dru, it didn't feel right. We'd set our sights on the *American Direct*, but the walk-in took ages; we reached the bivy at 10pm, ready for only five hours sleep.

We were already awake when the alarm sounded at 3am. The night before we'd talked about our doubts; they still hung in the air in our bivy cave. But when we crawled out, neither Uisdean nor I were willing to break first. We strolled over to the base, just to take a look, and started climbing. The initial ground was easy and we followed the circle of light cast by our headtorches. Uisdean climbed his pitches quickly and the ground dropped away. An imposing black wall stretched above us but we had no sense of scale until dawn hit the summit far above. Then we realised how far we'd come, and pushed on. My brain-fog began to clear; positive thoughts returned.

By the time we reached the Jammed Block at about one-third height, I felt I was ready to 'punch up'. I was fixated on the summit rather than the ground. Uisdean's encouragement spurred me on. But I was still an amateur in crack climbing, and the 90m corner looked menacing. At the first technical pitch a few hours ago, I'd had to ask Uisdean how to tape my hands for the rough granite. The 90m corner didn't disappoint; it made Dinas Cromlech look like a kindergarten. The two open-book walls soared and soared, and I climbed and climbed until there was nothing left in my arms. At the top of the corner an aid traverse out left brought us to the north face. I wobbled out over the 90m corner hanging from thin rusting nails, eyeing the finishing ledge. The air below me made it feel like flying.

I'd climbed this way during the winter ascent earlier in the year. Where previously we'd used axe torques we could now jam our hands and pad up slabs. Skirting round the summit of the Petit Dru and reaching the top of the Grand Dru at dusk was very special, because it marked a place I thought was unattainable only yesterday.

We had a long night ahead: I'm always wary of the descent from any mountain but these rappels sounded especially tricky. In the fading grey light we hurried down, turning our headtorches left and right, searching for the tell-tale flash of metal. Of course we lost the bolted belays, spinning down the 800m cliff in the dark, resorting to hollow flakes for anchors. Our minds slowed and the brain-fog returned. Uisdean's phone alarm went off again at 3am; I would have laughed if I wasn't so tired. We started falling asleep at belays, waiting for the other person to find the next anchor or make something out of a piece-of-shit spike. I didn't care what we abseiled off any more. I just wanted to be down.

At last – at last! – we both stood on the glacier, dizzy and hungry, with the mountains shadowed above. We wanted to be in the Charpoua refuge, just a short walk beneath us, but the mountains played one final trick; the glacier was a jumbled mess of crevasses and we had no idea how to get through. So we found a rognon of rock and slumped onto the least lumpy area. The shivering was life enhancing. The hunger and thirst was a reminder to consume more next time. The fatigue was absolute, our heads nodding forward and then snapping back. Cramp screamed through my muscles like fire.

But dawn finally came. The morning sun glowed orange on the summit of Mont Blanc and crept down towards the valley. We shook ourselves upright and walked towards the refuge.

September

Uisdean Hawthorn and I had attempted the *House-Anderson* route on the north face of Alberta (3619m) last year, having been inspired by Nick Bullock and Will Sim's second ascent, but we had to bail due to poor

Tom Livingstone leading one of the crux ice pitches on the *House-Anderson* route (1,000m, WI5+, M8) on the north face of Alberta in the Rockies. *(Uisdean Hawthorn)*

conditions. This year, however, we found the mountain in much better shape: the ice was well formed and the rock was well frozen and mostly bare.

On our first day we left the nearby hut – in reality, more of a shed – at 1am and rappelled down to the glacier beneath the face. It felt incredibly committing as we walked beneath the mountain, with no real chance of a rescue if something went wrong. Having just come from the Alps, with a phone signal, cable cars and helicopters everywhere, it felt pretty 'out there' beneath the towering, 1,000m face, wholly self-reliant.

We climbed the bergschrund and moved quickly together up the ice field as dawn broke, reaching the base of the headwall at 8am. Uisdean quickly climbed past the wire we had bailed off on the first M7 pitch during our attempt in September 2015. We climbed a few more mixed pitches around the same grade, and a short section of aid where there should have been ice, to reach a gully clogged with solid clear ice and snow mushrooms. In a moment of sheer amateurism, I fell off the start of the steep WI5+ pitch when I stepped too high on my axe. I didn't fall far but the bruise on my hip reminded me to be more careful.

I crossed a section of severely undercut ice on aid; this was no place to take a big fall. Then it leant back to vertical, leading to the cave bivy, which we reached at 6pm. The cave is in reality a tunnel that twists and turns into the heart of the mountain, one of the craziest features I've ever seen on a mountain. We spent the night here, feeling very lucky to be relatively warm and lying down.

On the second day we climbed the final three pitches to reach the top of the headwall, and then Uisdean climbed the last 150m to the summit in one big pitch. It was 1pm and we were surprised at how early we'd arrived. Unfortunately cloud had covered the upper part of the headwall since daybreak. We were worried about being caught in a storm but occasional patches of blue sky helped our descent down the long ridge of the *Japanese Route*. By the time we reached the start of the rappels, we were below the cloud and relaxed. It began to snow and rain during our descent and we still had to negotiate numerous cliff bands, so kept our focus throughout. It felt so sweet to reach the hut just as it got dark, late on the second day. It had been an epic route, which kept us involved and tested us, mentally and physically.

I know a lot of the draw of climbing in the Canadian Rockies is about adventure, and 'the unknown'. I realise we weren't very original in our route choice: essentially copying Will and Nick. If I were to nitpick our ascent, it's only for this. I realise with each ascent, an almost mythical route like the *House-Anderson* becomes slightly more 'known'; slightly less mythical. Yet despite our lack of originality, I'm very content.

October

I spent most of October working and then climbing George Smith's *Rock of Ages*, an impressive E7 which, to my knowledge, hadn't been repeated. It climbs up an overhanging ship's prow in a giant cave, a true Gogarth pumpfest, but thankfully has good gear. I tried it once with James Taylor, leaving some cams near my highpoint, aiming to return a few days later. Two weeks went by and I still hadn't returned due to tides, weather, swell and partners. Finally I made it back with Tony Stone, finishing a great day by the light of my headtorch.

December

After some rope-access work fell through, I sold Christmas trees for a few weeks in December. My life seems permanently strapped to a roller-coaster, with frequent money worries from my hand-to-mouth existence and monthly peaks and troughs. I can't complain: it's all self-inflicted because I devote so much to the mountains. I do wonder how sustainable this lifestyle can be.

Calum Muskett, Tony Stone and I flew to Patagonia in December, drawn south by recent seasons of good weather. We spent a few weeks in Torres del Paine, sitting in base camp waiting for stable conditions. Unfortunately, settled weather never arrived, and we moved to El Chaltén and the Fitzroy massif. In January, Calum flew home but Tony stayed, sitting out poor weather. We walked into the mountains five times for various objectives, each time turning around. On the sixth and final time, right at the end of our seven-week trip, we climbed the 1,600m *Supercanaleta* on Fitzroy. We had plenty of excitement battling giant fins of rime ice on the final gendarmes. It felt special to reach the summit on a calm, sunny day, just with our return flight beckoning. It was time for home and the end to a fantastic year.

SIMON RICHARDSON

The Diamond Ridge

The Tronchey Wall on the Grandes Jorasses. The 1,600m-long Diamond Ridge
follows the sunlit crest just right of centre. *(Simon Richardson)*

Major unclimbed lines on the biggest mountains of the Mont Blanc range are almost by definition rare, but a few plums remain. This is the account of the first ascent of the Diamond Ridge (1600m, 5c, A0) on the south-south-east face of the Grandes Jorasses by Simon Richardson and Micha Rinn between 28 and 30 July 2016.

Ten years ago the Italian mountaineering historian Luca Signorelli contacted me about a book he is writing on the Grandes Jorasses. I was delighted that the ascent of the *Gervasutti* route on the east face that Nick Kekus and I made in 1982 would merit a tiny mention in the book, but it started me thinking that it would be wonderful to have a route on the Grandes Jorasses that I could call my own. I'd been fortunate enough to climb new routes on the other two great mountains in the range, Mont Blanc and the Aiguille Verte, so the Jorasses would complete the set.

I was well aware that this was an ambition bordering on fantasy. The Grandes Jorasses is one of the most celebrated mountains in the Alps and home to dozens of long and testing routes. The stupendous north face is crisscrossed with lines and was unlikely to yield anything novel, so it was

Above: Simon Richardson climbing perfect granite on the crest of the Diamond Ridge at the start of day two. This is the section above the crux tower. *(Michael Rinn)*

Left: Michael Rinn approaching the crux tower at the start of day two of the Diamond Ridge. *(Simon Richardson)*

natural to turn to the Italian side where the summit ridge towers an awe inspiring 3,200m above the beautiful Val Ferret. The east face is the most beautiful aspect on this side of the mountain, but it has attracted significant attention in recent years and the remaining lines look extremely difficult. Similarly, I quickly dismissed the south-south-east face, or Tronchey Wall as it is often called, due to its reputation for stone fall and a difficult glacier approach. I spent many winter evenings studying photos of the south face, but the unclimbed ground lacked logical lines and carried significant objective danger from hanging seracs and falling rocks.

Then almost by chance, I came across a photo on the internet where sunshine and shade highlighted a snaking ridgeline winding up the right side of the Tronchey Wall. The Diamond Ridge, as it later became called, was so prominent it had almost become invisible. In my search for more tenuous and subtle routes I had completely missed it. But, best of all, the Diamond Ridge appeared to be unclimbed: I could scarcely believe my luck.

Over 1,400m high, the Tronchey Wall is the highest in the Mont Blanc range. It is framed by two huge structural features: the Pra Sec and

Michael Rinn climbing steep ground on day two. *(Simon Richardson)*

Tronchey ridges that meet at the summit of Pointe Walker enclosing the huge scooped-out rock wall with the tiny Pra Sec glacier nestling at its foot. The first team to climb the face was Alessandro Gogna and Guido Machetto in August 1972. They approached via the previously untravelled Pra Sec glacier and spent two days braving the significant stone-fall threat whilst climbing difficult ice-worn slabs and discontinuous grooves before gaining the safety of a pronounced pillar in the upper third of the face. Although their route description is remarkably understated, and they only graded the route TD, this three-day tour de force has never been repeated and ED2 is thought to be a more realistic rating.

It was another 13 years before the Tronchey Wall was climbed again. The visionary Italian ice climber, Giancarlo Grassi was attracted to the huge gully slicing through the centre of the wall. Grassi chose June for his attempt, looking for rarely formed ephemeral ice on the lower slabs to take him, Renzo Luzi and Mauro Rossi into the gully. The first part of the plan worked: thin ice led through the lower section. But unfortunately the gully itself was bare. Instead of retreating, Grassi and his team made an irreversible leftwards traverse across the 1972 route and finished up steep gullies in the upper part of the face. Unsurprisingly, *The Phantom Direct* (ED3) remains unrepeated.

There was no further activity on the wall for another 25 years until May 2010 when a French-Italian team attempted to complete Grassi's vision and climb the gully in its entirety. This time modern equipment and dry tooling techniques took them within a couple of pitches of the exit onto the *Tronchey Ridge* but they were shut down by blank rock on the vertical sidewalls of the cleft. I was excited when their bold attempt was reported widely in the mountaineering press. At first I was intrigued that someone had identified a major new line on the Jorasses. Perhaps this was the route that I should have been chasing? But when I studied the associated topos, they confirmed the Diamond Ridge itself was still unclimbed, and I became even more excited!

By early last year I could wait no longer. The Diamond Ridge was too good an objective to ignore so I made it the primary objective for a visit to Chamonix in July 2016. My partner was Michael (Micha) Rinn from Germany. We had climbed together in January during the BMC International Meet in Scotland and instantly clicked. Micha shares my love of adventure and the unknown, and despite the atrocious weather during the meet, we sealed our partnership with a new route on Lochnagar.

But of course, there was a glitch. The Diamond Ridge starts at the head of the heavily crevassed Pra Sec glacier and is severely undercut at its base. The obvious way to bypass these obstacles was to start 200m lower down the mountain, climb the small peak of Punta Grassi on the right, one of the last summits in the range to be climbed in 2006, and then traverse left to gain the ridge just above the initial overhangs. Unfortunately our photos showed the traverse threatened by a hanging icefall originating from the left branch of the Tronchey glacier, and it looked potentially dangerous. As always, the only way to resolve this was to go and have a look.

Simon Richardson climbing towards the Tronchey towers on day two.
(Michael Rinn)

On 16 July I flew to Frankfurt. Micha drove us to Chamonix and we walked up to the Envers des Aiguilles hut that evening. Over the next two days we climbed the modern classics *Children of the Moon* and *Subtitles Dulferiennes* on the Aiguille du Roc, and then carried our bivouac kit (there was no room in the hut), up the more traditional *Mer de Glace Face* of the Grépon. So a good start, but then the weather became poor and Micha picked up a nasty stomach bug. Once he recovered we went up to the Torino hut and climbed the elegant pinnacle of the Roi de Siam in the Vallée Blanche and then joined the crowds on the Dent du Géant. It was all very laid back and relaxed but, crucially, our time up high was allowing us to acclimatise.

After another night in the hut we spent the day in Val Ferret scoping out the route. It became clear that the best way of accessing the Diamond Ridge was to climb the left flank of Punta Grassi to gain a crossing point in the couloir below the icefall. Viewed from the valley through binoculars the hanging glacier didn't look too bad. Glacial recession had worked in our favour, and the overhanging ice in our photos had relented to more of a rounded snout. It was still a worry, but it didn't look excessively dangerous. Beyond the couloir was an easy-angled snowfield that would quickly take us out of danger onto the crest of the ridge itself.

We bivouacked in Val Ferret and started the approach just before dawn on 28 July, with food and fuel for two nights. The weather forecast promised two dry and cloudy days before bad weather swept in on the third. So not perfect, but good enough. We reached the foot of Punta Grassi

Michael Rinn on an awkward mixed section late on the second day.
(Simon Richardson)

at 2,600m and started climbing at 9am. The line up the left flank slotted together well: there was a blank slabby section past a cave and then easier ground led to the couloir below the hanging glacier snout.

It was tricky climbing down into the couloir, but we were across it in seconds and soon moving across the snowfield to the safety of the Diamond Ridge itself. We started this about midday and climbed ten pitches to a notch in the ridge. The rock was marvellous. It reminded me of the east side of Mont Greuvetta: perfect fine-grained granite with loads of excellent features. Whenever you reached up there was a perfect hold just where you needed it.

There was not a bivouac site big enough for two but we found separate ones about 15m apart. The cloud had been swirling around all day, but it cleared and we spent a comfortable night. Next morning, a steep step above the notch proved to be the crux of the route and we used three points of aid before continuing up the crest of the ridge for another 16 pitches. We thought we'd be drawn rightwards towards the Tronchey Ridge, but the natural line took us straight up to the base of the Second Tower.

Here things began to get a little awkward. The cold spring meant that ledges were still banked up with winter snow, so there was lots of changing out of boots into rock shoes and taking crampons on and off mid-pitch. We crossed an icy couloir and climbed a steep wall left to gain the prominent right traverse below the imposing Third Tower. We expected easy ledges here, but instead we found smooth unprotected slabs that were soaking wet with dripping snow.

Simon Richardson on mixed ground high up on day two. *(Michael Rinn)*

The belay was poor and Micha led a full 50m rope length before coming back saying he couldn't complete the final moves because the final slabs were covered in ice. There was no foothold big enough to stop and put on crampons, so Micha had to repeat the entire traverse in crampons so he could climb the ice at the end. It was now getting dark, so it was a pretty tense time for both of us, and an outstanding lead by Micha. We bivouacked immediately afterwards by digging into a snow bank on top of the Second Tower.

The next day we continued up the original route of the *Tronchey Ridge*, by traversing above the top of the steep section of the east face to join the upper crest. We were on the summit of the Grandes Jorasses (4208m) at midday just as the forecasted bad weather was sweeping in from Mont Blanc. The descent went smoothly and we reached the Boccalatte hut at 5pm to a great welcome from guardians Franco Perlotto and Roberta Cutri. The hut was empty because of the poor weather, and at first, they couldn't understand where we'd come from or what we'd climbed. Once we explained they both became very excited, and Franco immediately contacted the Italian Alpine Club and also Luca Signorelli who was staying in Courmayeur.

It snowed hard that night, almost to the level of the hut, and after a leisurely breakfast we walked down in the rain and were met by Luca halfway up the trail. This in itself was rather special; we had been corresponding for ten years so it was great to finally meet. Luca was charming and enthused about our ascent.

'You have made history,' he said. 'This is only the third time the Tronchey Wall has ever been climbed, and each time by a separate route!" Until that point I hadn't really considered our climb to have anything but personal significance, but a 1,600m-high new line on one the most important peaks of the Alps was not going to pass unnoticed. As we sped back up the motorway to Germany later that afternoon, the internet hummed as news of our ascent on the CAI website spread fast. In a climbing world where technical difficulty is often king, it was rather refreshing that a route that could have been climbed eighty years ago could still capture the wider imagination.

Tibet

The Pays de Valais
John Robert Cozens (1752-97)
Between 1780 and 1785. Watercolour, graphite and red-brown gouache
on medium, slightly textured, cream laid paper. 14¼ x 20½ inches.
Yale Center for British Art, Paul Mellon Collection.

PAUL RAMSDEN

Nyenchenthanglha South-East

Climbing towards the crux steep headwall low on the north buttress
of Nyenchenthanglha South-East (7026m).
(All images Paul Ramsden and Nick Bullock)

*Paul Ramsden and Nick Bullock overcame bureaucratic hurdles and steep technical
ground to make the first ascent of Nyenchenthanglha South-East's (7026m) huge
and impressive north face (1600m, ED+) between 1 and 7 October 2016. The ascent
was recognised with a Piolet d'Or, Ramsden's fourth overall.*

As well as referring to the highest peaks in the area, the name Nyenchenthanglha (Tibetan pinyin: Nyainqêntanglha) is also applied to the
whole mountain chain running west to east, north of Lhasa, in parallel
with the Himalaya. I had actually driven past the Nyenchenthanglha peaks,
which top 7,000m, nine years earlier, on my way to the Nyenchenthanglha
East range with Mick Fowler to make the first ascent of Manamcho. From
the road the potential of these peaks looked minimal, not helped by heavy
cloud, a characteristic of the area.

The magical thing about climbing new routes in China and Tibet is
that after being lucky enough to complete a few successful expeditions
you suddenly start receiving *Japanese Alpine News*. One day it just pops
through the letterbox and then just keeps on coming. It's a great source of

Above: Nick Bullock and Paul Ramsden, who won his fourth Piolet d'Or for their climb.

Right: Nick Bullock on his way to the bottom of the north face in new snow.

information about Tibet, acting as a record of the activities of the Tibet explorer and chronicler Tamotsu Nakamura, or Tom to his friends. A few years ago, perusing his latest article, I was struck by his set of pictures of the four 7,000m Nyenchenthanglha peaks. Taken from the north-east, they showed a large north wall falling away from the four summits, with a particularly striking arête at the north-west end. A plan started to formulate.

Wanting to go to Tibet is very different from actually getting there. First of all the China Tibet Mountaineering Association (CTMA) is not easy to contact. Email addresses exist but getting a response is a different matter. Once in contact, the granting of permits is based on the local political situation. If the locals have been kicking off against the authorities then you will never get a permit. If you do get a permit the situation may change on a week-by-week basis leading to last minute cancellations. With Mick we had been applying for a peak in the Nyenchenthanglha for eight years to no avail. When the CTMA eventually agreed, I was amazed. Nine months later we arrived in Lhasa, although it wasn't that easy: the CTMA announced the week before they couldn't email me the Tibet entry pass so we would have to go and collect it in China before proceeding to Tibet. Expensive flight changes quickly ensued: Tibet is never cheap.

I have been climbing with Mick Fowler off and on for the last 15 years and consistently for the last four expeditions but at over 7,000m, Nyen-chenthanglha was a bit high for the now sexagenarian Mick, so I had to shop around for a new climbing partner. This was not an easy decision:

A photo-diagram of the north buttress of Nyenchenthanglha South-East
(7026m) showing the line and camps.

a climbing partner for such routes needs to be the right person and the pool of people interested in technical climbing on Himalayan peaks is actually not that big, although I can't imagine why.

I first met Nick Bullock in Namche Bazaar many years ago. At the time he seemed a wild, intense, scary character but when I popped over to visit him in North Wales last year, he was writing his second book, while doing a spot of cat sitting: an altogether calmer person. The last 12 years living out of the back of his van had clearly been good for him. Amazingly, the first pitch of the climb in Tibet was the first time we had ever tied on together. Over the course of the expedition we got on really well, never a cross word between us, just a steady stream of mild mutual verbal abuse: just the way I like a team to behave.

Tibet had changed a lot since my last visit nine years earlier. Lhasa was about five times bigger with high-rise buildings everywhere. The Tibetans are now swamped with new settlers. The road network is totally overloaded with vehicles, though I was pleased to see that many of them are now electric which improves the air quality a lot.

Beyond Lhasa, all the small towns have grown considerably with extensive Chinese developments everywhere. It's only when you get into the remote villages and farms that things look pretty much as they always have, except for the satellite dishes and mobile phone masts. It's quite a surprise when a yak herder whips out his iPhone 6 and demonstrates that he has a 3G signal just an hour's walk from base camp.

Acclimatisation requirements made the short journey to base camp take a long time. Lhasa is at 3,700m so we had two nights there after flying in. We then drove for half a day to Damshung at 4,200m and spent two nights there. Then we drove for an hour and spent a night at the road head at 4,700m in the headman's house, then walked for just four hours to base camp with packhorses. It took six days to base camp and at the end of the expedition six hours back to Lhasa.

As we arrived in bad weather, there was much confusion over which valley we should walk into. Maps of the area are quite poor and location names confused. It worked out, but the locals warned us we were approaching the mountain from the wrong side, saying it was too steep to climb, which sounded brilliant. They also warned us the area was infested with bears that would 'bite you in the face'. Following Nick's infamous Canadian grizzly incident, which made national news in 2015, his face was a real picture.

We had no staff at base camp, since they're so expensive in Tibet, so it was just the two of us for a month, pretty intense with someone you don't know that well. But it was a pretty location and once settled in with our psychedelic cooking shelter we felt right at home and ready to explore. On the first day Nick decided to take it easy, bed being his natural habitat, while I wandered up the valley to see if we were in the right one after all. Expectations were low due to heavy cloud but a few hours up the valley it cleared and there was our mountain, big and steep.

Our original plan had been to climb the north buttress of Nyenchen-

Tackling the steep band barring access to the upper mountain,
the crux of the route.

thanglha's main summit, which looked just brilliant in Tom's pictures. However as we walked below the face we realised there was a hidden monster. The lowest 7,000m peak and first on the ridge, Nyenchenthanglha South-East, had a recessed north face not really visible from anywhere other than directly below it. As we edged into position the clouds cleared to reveal a huge north buttress that was just incredible. It was the sort of route you always dreamed about finding and here it was. We were speechless.

The buttress itself was very steep in the lower half before giving a bit and forming an impressive arête in the upper section. The headwall of the lower face in particular looked problematic. Steep rock with what appeared to be a thin veneer of ice looked like it might go – but only just. If that veneer of ice turned out to be just a bit of powder snow from the last storm then we would have big problems. Hardly able to contain our excitement we headed back down to base camp for a rest and to get ourselves prepared.

Our first attempt on the route is best forgotten about. We camped under the face, it dumped snow, the tent nearly blew away and we retreated. Let's just call it a gear carry to ABC. We needed to let the mountain slough some of that snow for a few days so we headed to base camp and read, made bread, ate enormous meals, debated whether to take a toothbrush or not, all the usual base-camp stuff. Eventually conditions were deemed suitable, or as good as it was going to get, so we set off for our second attempt. Luckily the only two really nice days of the trip coincided with our walk back up and our first day on the face. It wouldn't last.

Weather in the Nyenchenthanglha is notoriously mixed.

Camped once again under the face things were looking good: perfect weather and a lot less snow on the face. We decided the direct start looked a bit thin in the first rock-band; there is nothing more dispiriting than failing on the first pitch. A gully to the left offered more ice and would allow us to traverse into the centre of the face a bit higher up, avoiding the regular spindrift sloughs coming down the centre of the face.

I always enjoy the walk to the foot of a face. As the perspective changes the face rears up alarmingly but as the upper face disappears, the lower pitches become visible in more detail. Suddenly the whole thing looks more manageable. I suppose it's burying your head in the sand but I always think its best to think about such a big route just one pitch at a time. Deal with what's in front of you and worry about the rest later. If you think about the route as a whole it's just too easy to get intimidated.

Once on the face we soon discovered that we weren't going to get any névé on this trip. The snow was deep, really deep, and the only ice existed when things steepened up. That first day working our way up the lower slopes was really hard work, never-ending post-holing as we worked our way towards the planned first bivy ledge below the ever-steepening rock bands above.

I was convinced that the snow arête we were aiming for would give us an excellent camp spot but it turned out to be knife sharp with rocks just below the surface and only offered two semi-reclining spots to sit on. Grim. With us on separate ledges there was no way to put up the tent so I wrapped myself in the fabric, pulled on my duvet jacket and settled down to try and melt some water with the wind frequently blowing the stove out. Open bivouacs in mediocre weather are best avoided; a bad night on your first night is a recipe for retreat. As the sun came up we could see the good weather had gone and we were back to the usual Nyenchenthanglha cloud and precipitation. But the night had not been that bad; we were ready to get stuck in. Above our bivy ledge, things steepened up alarmingly. From below we thought this would be the crux of the route. A steep rock band crossed the full width of the face; in most places it was too steep for ice but in the centre there was a thin veneer of white covering the rock. Whether this was powder snow or ice remained to be seen. At least we would find out if the line would go or not.

We traversed diagonally up and rightwards aiming for some steep runnels and the elusive ice. Much of what had looked like ice from below turned out to be powder snow stuck to the underside of overhangs and a thin delaminated snow crust on the vertical rock itself. Luckily a series of shallow runnels did hold some goodish ice. Often it wasn't thick enough to take a full ice screw but if you dug around on the adjacent rock, bits of rock gear were available.

Slowly we worked our way up some absorbing pitches, occasionally hauling sacks. The climbing was excellent; Nick thought it reminded him of the upper part of the *Colton-MacIntyre* on the Grandes Jorasses. Eventually the groove ended and Nick was forced to climb a steep rock wall; fortunately beneath the snow veneer was a series of flakes that allowed for good if scary hooking: a fine lead.

Then we were through the rock band and looking for somewhere to camp. Determined to have a better night's sleep I announced it was time to test out my latest version of the 'snow hammock'. Originally a Russian invention, it employs the fabric base of a portaledge to trap snow and build an artificial ledge. I have experimented and produced lightweight versions. The first version was used last year on Gave Ding with Mick and proved effective but not robust enough. When it froze to the face and we pulled it off, it would rip. The second version is a totally different beast. High-tech rip-stop fabric and Kevlar webbing make it both strong and lightweight. It's essentially a large rectangle of fabric you attach to the face with ice screws and fill with snow before pitching your tent on top. Now it worked brilliantly: we finished with a nearly flat camp spot in a truly ridiculous position.

It had been a tough day and we woke pretty exhausted. From this point we had two options, either follow the crest of the buttress or the more mixed ground on the right. Concerns about avalanche potential on some of the snowfields and the feasibility of some of the rock bands meant the crest of the buttress was clearly the best option. Traversing leftwards we hit the crest and climbed an arête in a pretty wild position. The previous two days had tired us more than we realised so we decided to make day three a short one and stopped as soon as we could find another good spot for the snow hammock. The ledge was even better this time and the tent fitted

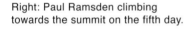

Above: Ramsden's honed technique of packing a fabric sheet, hung from ice screws, with snow to create a tent ledge.

Right: Paul Ramsden climbing towards the summit on the fifth day.

comfortably. In the evening we had great views of the adjacent Nam Tso lake. We could literally see moisture being sucked off the surface ready to dump on us. The lake was so big the route felt like a sea cliff.

Now we were following the crest of the buttress, the setting was dramatic but as the route became less technical the snow got deeper. Combined with the altitude, this made for some lung-busting pitches. Our fourth camp was good but that night it started to dump snow and at 6,700m you start to realise what a serious position you are in. Retreat down the line would be difficult, due too a lack of ice, making abalakovs time-consuming. We didn't have enough rack to abseil on rock anchors all the way. Upwards to the summit and hopefully down an easier ridge was the best option but this snow could make that option hazardous.

Dawn brought more snow and cloud. Post-holing upwards we made the summit about midday. It was the second ascent of the peak and my first time over 7,000m: we were both knackered. There wasn't any view so after a quick 'selfie' I was keen to get off down. I was pretty sure our best option was to descend the east ridge until it terminated in a huge cliff at which point we would abseil down the north side on abalakovs before regaining the ridge again at a col. From here it looked like an easy walk down to the valley and base camp. In the end dense fog turned the relatively easy but

complex east ridge into a navigational challenge. I loved it. However, after falling into three bergschrunds I decided to call it quits for the day. The tent fitted quite nicely into the last hole I made.

By now there was little food left, it dumped snow all night and we didn't actually know where we were due to the dense cloud, so it wasn't the best night. Dawn brought poor visibility so we stayed put for a few hours until it improved, which it did and we pushed on. At this stage avalanches were our main concern but there wasn't actually anything we could do about it. There was no Plan B.

Fortunately the cloud cleared and we identified our location exactly, allowing us to descend to the col without incident. From here we had planned to descend to the north, towards our base camp. However, from the col it was clear that the southern slope was easier and safer, even if it did descend into an unknown valley. We had no map but it got us safely down to the moraine without incident. The following day was a purgatory of loose boulders and soft muddy moraine. Not a day I'd care to repeat. Amazingly the valley then opened out onto grassy slopes just above the small hamlet where out liaison officer was living with the village headman. They seemed amazed to see us, even more amazed to hear we had summited. After all we had gone up the 'wrong valley'.

TAMOTSU NAKAMURA

The Holy Mountain

A Climbing Paradise in Yunnan?

The east face of Balagezong (5545m). None of the peaks in this
region have yet been climbed. *(All images Tamotsu Nakamura)*

In January 2004 a letter arrived from William M Bueler living in Colorado. It contained a brief note about his reconnaissance of Balagezong in October 2003 with maps and pictures and his book *Roof of the Rockies: A History of Colorado Mountaineering*. Our contact had begun through the *American Alpine Journal* and *Japanese Alpine News*. I knew of this soaring peak having seen it in the far distance in 1993. But to the best of my knowledge, he was the first to reconnoitre Balagezong for climbing.

The following month, however, he told me a tumour had been found and it was difficult for him to write, being paralyzed on one side. In April 2004 a letter arrived from his wife Lois with news of his death, thanking me for the pictures and information I had recently sent him. 'Thank you for your correspondence with Bill,' she wrote. 'His travels to the Sino-Tibetan borderlands were the great adventures of his last ten years and he enjoyed those adventures to the full. He felt that you were a kindred spirit.'

A wide-angle view of the south face of Shangbala Stupa (c5000m) and to the right, or east, another rock peak of a similar height.

After that, Balagezong stayed in my mind as somewhere to explore one day, although before I knew it a decade had passed. In the meantime, Damien Gildea, the well-known Antarctic expert, visited, and also Dr Liu Yong, from Sichuan University. In May 2016, I had my chance.

Mountain scenic places are a hive of industry in Yunnan and Sichuan. Tourism development is progressing at a tremendous speed. New roads with bridges and tunnels are under construction through mountains and valleys wherever you go in the frontier regions. Driving distances are becoming shorter and roads faster. Traditional industry such as agriculture is being replaced with tourism. Tourists are rushing here from every corner of China. The Dagu Glacier Scenic Park has a ropeway to a 4,800m lookout point. It is only one day drive north from Chengdu and is busiest for the 'autumn leaves' season.

You can now get to Deqen, an early field of exploration, famous for Meili mountains, in three and a half hours from Zhongdian, itself rebranded as Shangri-La in 2001 to boost tourism. It previously took a full day. My lack of urgency in getting to Balagezong means that it has changed dramatically since Bueler visited. There are four and five-star hotels at Shuishuang (2320m), the base for sightseeing. When Bueler visited 13 years ago it took eight days for Bueler to trek on foot to Balagezong for

The view from the tourist village of Bala.

reconnaissance. Now it takes less than two hours to drive from Shangri-La airport. Balagezong is an important project for Shangri-La County, which has already invested $118m.

Among the region's main attraction is the holy mountain of Balagezong (5545m), called Gezongsongben in Tibetan, the physical embodiment of three beautiful princesses from legend. These peaks, a 'natural stupa', Shang-bala Stupa (c5000m) and other prominent rock peaks (4700m-5000m), alluring alpine meadows and mysterious high mountain lakes are impressive and attractive. All peaks remain unclimbed.

Located at the meeting point of Sichuan, Yunnan and Tibet, Balagezong is famous for its Shangri-La Grand Canyon with a 2.5km hanging path to bring walkers through it. They have the option of rafting back down. Bala (3200m) is a 'typical' Tibetan hamlet, recently enlarged. Some 300 years ago a Khampa family looking for paradise, an ideal homeland with no warfare and misery, finally settled here after overcoming hardships. Tibetan-style wooden houses have been built in layers up the mountainside.

The paradox of this opening up of the region is that controls and regulations are being tightened. As tourism development progresses, controls over Tibetans have become tighter and tighter. When you travel through eastern Tibet, Qinghai, Sichuan and Yunnan, you often come across a board reading 'New Village' on the roadside. Tibetans and other minorities formerly living in remote areas are being forced to move to these houses newly built near a main road, so that the local government may more easily control them. Old villages and trails are abandoned; remote regions are thus less populated.

Unnamed rock peaks between 4700m and 5000m in the Balagezong region.

My Tibetan guide, Gerong, who lives in Deqen, complained he could no longer visit foreign countries. Even though he became a member of the Communist Party, the county government doesn't allow him to renew his passport since he visited Dharamsala last year. Awang, a Tibetan guide from Lhasa, is also not allowed to have a new passport after he returned from Nepal and India two years ago. The Xi Jinpin administration is strengthening the control and observation of Tibetans. In Sichuan, for example, Tibetans in Danba County, one day's drive north-west from Chengdu, are required to have a permit from the local government to go to Lhasa, while Han Chinese may travel freely.

Restrictions on foreigners entering eastern Tibet are being strengthened and more tightly enforced. Two or three years ago, foreigners could enter eastern Tibet by road from Yunnan and Sichuan. Now it's impossible. Foreigners cannot travel from Deqen in Yunnan to Yanjing in the Tibetan Autonomous Region (TAR) crossing the provincial border by road. They cannot cross the upper Yangtze, the provincial border on the Tibet-Sichuan Highway from Batang in Sichuan to the old salt and tea-trading town of Markam. Foreigners aren't allowed in Chamdo Prefecture. Tsawarong, along the upper Salween north-west of Meili mountains, is the same. Damyon is inaccessible. A friend who is secretary of the TAR's sports administration centre says that the procedure for foreigners to enter restricted areas is becoming more complicated and time-wasting.

Our journey was in May. The team, as usual, was myself, aged 81, and 83-year-old Tsuyoshi Nagai. We flew from Chengdu to Shangri-La airport in Yunnan. We planned two stages to our trip: Balagezong and the Sichuan-Dagu Glacier Scenic Park, to look at a little-known 5,500m massif in the area. Bad weather hampered us in the second part.

We started early on 16 May, the rainy season having already started, but trusting to the luck of Tom 'Blue Skies' Nakamura. My agent and old friend Lu Weidong, from Kunming, and our Tibetan guide Gerong from Deqen welcomed us. A new highway took us to the junction of the Jinsha Jiang,

Above: Chinese investment has rapidly transformed what was once a wild region into a tourist honeypot. The so-called Shangri-La Canyon.

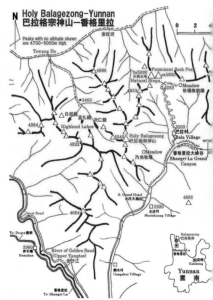

or upper Yangtse, and its tributary, Gang Qu, through tunnels and across bridges that cut hours off the old road. We arrived at the Suishuang Grand Hotel at 11am, having left Chengdu at 7.30am. The next few days, the weather was poor: we visited Bala, the 'Tibetan-style' village, drove to Deqen over the Baimang Shan pass (4280m) and on 18 May went to the Shangri-La Grand Canyon. Happily, on 19 May, we had some clear weather and were able to photograph the peaks. We chartered a shuttle bus and rushed to the pass below Shangbala Stupa via Bala village where the east face of Balagezong towered above the valley. Climbing a path from Bala village to the pass, beautiful rock peaks of 4,700-5,000m appeared in succession. Though these peaks were only a part of Balagezong massif, they were magnificent and fascinating. We were deeply touched.

• See also Area Notes in this edition of the *Alpine Journal* for Tom Nakamura's images of unclimbed peaks along the Yarlung Tsangpo.

Far-flung Places

Mountain Landscape, Macugnaga
John Ruskin (1819-1900)
1845. Pen and brown ink, brown wash, graphite and scraping out
on thick, smooth, cream wove paper, 11¾ x 15¾ inches.
Yale Center for British Art, Paul Mellon Collection.

STEPHEN VENABLES

Return to South Georgia

Approaching South Georgia, a British territory since 1775 when Captain Cook
made the first recorded landing, naming the island for King George III.
King Edward Point was set up to administer the whaling industry, after Anton
Larsen established the first shore whaling station at the adjoining cove of
Grytviken in 1904. Hugely profitable at first, by the mid 20th century the
industry was no longer viable; the last base closed in 1964. Seasonal
government staff help administer the South Georgia fishery, with the Falklands
fishery the biggest protected marine zone in the world outside Antarctica.

*Stephen Venables recently organised his seventh expedition to the sub-Antarctic
island of South Georgia. The team made several first ascents including
Mt Baume and Starbuck Peak, which Venables had wanted to climb for 27 years.
Starbuck was possibly the hardest technical climb yet achieved on the island.*

South Georgia is a very long way away and it's very hard to get to. If it
hadn't been for Julian Freeman-Attwood's suggestion in 1989 that we
organise an expedition to this very remote island, 750 miles from the nearest airstrip, I probably would never have contemplated the idea. Lacking
a private yacht, we needed the blessing of the military, in charge since
Argentinean 'scrap-metal merchants' landed illegally seven years earlier
as a prelude to the Falklands War. So, cheered on by Julian, I pulled strings

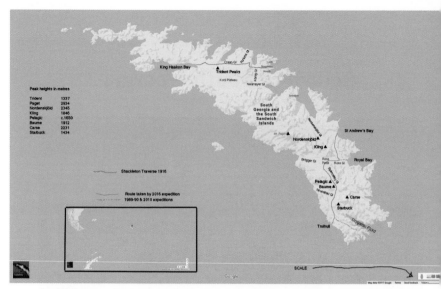

Peak heights in metres

Trident	1337
Paget	2934
Nordenskjöld	2345
Kling	1846
Pelagic	c.1650
Baume	1912
Carse	2231
Starbuck	1434

South Georgia and
the South
Sandwich
Islands

Shackleton Traverse 1916

Route taken by 2016 expedition
1989-90 & 2010 expeditions

SCALE

South Georgia is about 100 miles long and is entirely mountainous with over 60 named glaciers. The highest summit is Mt Paget (2934m), first climbed by a British joint-services expedition in 1965. Like the Antarctic Peninsula, South Georgia provides graphic evidence of recent climate change. Since Venables first went in 1989 many glaciers have shrunk dramatically. The Ross glacier, which was an easy walk 30 years ago, has now become so shrivelled and broken its lower reaches are now almost impassable. Glacier tongues have also retreated in the last few years, with a new bay of open water at the site of the former tongue of the Twitcher glacier.

at the Ministry of Defence, grateful for the generosity of influential top brass prepared to vouch for us, and in October 1989 we delivered 36 barrels of food, gas and equipment, plus a bundle of skis, to HMS Endurance just before she sailed from Portsmouth on her annual southern patrol. A month later we flew down with the RAF and joined Endurance in the Falklands for the final 800 miles to South Georgia.

Captain, officers and crew were incredibly hospitable to the eccentric collection of civilians code-named SOMEX – the Southern Ocean Mountaineering Expedition – billeted on their already crowded ship. Lindsay Griffin, the legendary walking database of mountaineering history, resplendent in pink and turquoise fleece, had dreamed for years of coming south. Julian, an earthy tweed-clad throwback to the 19th century, just loves going to whacky new places. Kees t'Hooft, a charmingly vague Dutch cameraman from Clapham, had agreed to film us for an ITV documentary to pay the bills. Research chemist Brian Davison had already done time on the mainland with the British Antarctic Survey (BAS) but had never called at South Georgia. I, having had past job applications rejected repeatedly by BAS, enjoyed a smug glow of triumph as the sea air cooled perceptibly and, after years of dreaming, I finally crossed the Antarctic Convergence.

King penguins with Mt Kling in the background. The only way to get to South Georgia is by boat and the nearest port of departure is Stanley, in the Falklands, about 750 miles from Grytviken. All expeditions have to apply for a permit to the government of South Georgia and the Sandwich Islands, paying £1,000 for the vetting process, plus £100 landing fee per expedition member. Conservation is a major concern; rats have been eradicated from the island and expeditions have to follow clear environmental guidelines to avoid inadvertent introduction of alien species.

Once on the island, I was enthralled by the novelty of it all, in particular the constant interplay of decay and renewal. Grey whalebones speckled with orange lichen, littered on the beach beside a rusting hulk where blue-eyed shags nested in the tussock grass colonising her bows. Giant petrels, the yellow-eyed vultures of the south, squabbling over the placenta of a new-born elephant seal pup; the passive-aggressive whimper of the fur seals; the keening wail of the light-mantled sooty albatrosses nesting in the tussock; the massed trumpeting of the three hundred thousand or so king penguins we passed as we tramped round St Andrew's Bay on our way to Royal Bay. Here the 'Endurance Airways' helicopter pilot had kindly dropped eighteen barrels of food and fuel to see us well into 1990.

Then there was the weather. We chose initially to explore the Salvesen range at the southern, windier, end of the island. Load carries round the beach were abandoned due to intolerable sand blasting. Tents imploded as the katabatic 'williwaws' came screaming at us from every direction. Naïvely, perhaps, we chose to put our mountain base on the Ross pass: a logical access point to the glacial hinterland 600m above sea level, but also the most prominent wind funnel on the entire island. To limit the blast we dug into a scoop at the side of the glacier, excavating a large ice palace,

Left: The dramatic tower of Starbuck, with the corkscrew route of the first ascent marked.

which became home for 23 days. It was secure and comfortable and we read lots of good books. But, hunkered down in our dugout, we developed an unhealthy trench mentality, reluctant to put our heads above the parapet, exaggerating the menace outside.

Despite that timidity, we climbed some nice little peaks during short breaks, and then, just as the food was about to run out, we got a full two days weather window. Lindsay and Julian made the first ascent of a fine peak called Mt Kling, with Julian leading the headwall of rotten rock over-laid by sugar: the only bit of real technical climbing achieved in nearly three months on the island. Meanwhile, Brian and I skied 13 miles south, stopped to pitch the tent for afternoon tea, before continuing on foot to the prev-iously untouched summit of Mt Carse. It seemed a waste to be with one of Britain's finest mountaineers on a snow plod. But what a plod! Just to be there, at the end of a long, long day, crampons crunching up mushrooms of Patagonia-style rime, with the sun setting over the furthest edge of the Southern Ocean, a thousand miles from the nearest city in South America, felt very precious.

Sailing home on RFA Diligence in February 1990 I thought how lucky we had been and assumed that was that. South Georgia was a unique, never to be repeated, experience. But ten years later, out of the blue, I was invited to go back. It was Shackleton that did it. Or, to be more precise, the grow-ing resurgence of interest in his 1914-16 Imperial Antarctic Expedition, an ill-judged failure which transmuted into one of the greatest survival stories of all time, beginning, and culminating triumphantly, on South Georgia.

Sunrise on Mts Fraser and Paget, seen from Starbuck.

The epic tale was ripe for the giant screen and I was to join Conrad Anker and Reinhold Messner repeating the Edwardian hero's legendary 1916 trek across the mountains for the IMAX film *Shackleton's Antarctic Adventure*.

It was a jolly, convivial outing, with some seriously experienced people like Brian Hall, Paul Ramsden and Nick Lewis running the show, while we three – 'The Climbers' – tramped in the hallowed footsteps of Shackleton, Crean and Worsley, tracing their masterpiece of intuitive route-finding over thirty miles of what had in 1916 been totally unknown, unmapped glacial wilderness. We took about the same time, 36 hours, but in our case spread over three days, with the luxury of being able to stop and pitch a tent at night. Like Shackleton, Crean and Worsley, we travelled in the austral autumn – May in their case, April in ours – but unlike them we found the Crean glacier a hideous maze of open crevasses. Nowadays the isotherm is much higher than it was in 1916, and by late summer the former comforting snow blanket has gone. Leaping one humungous crevasse, Reinhold landed badly, fracturing a metatarsal. As he continued uncomplaining for the next two days, limping stoically on his broken foot, shuffling *à cheval* between chasms when required, we began to understand something of the iron will behind the legend.

Since 2000 the Shackleton Traverse has become quite a popular jaunt for seriously adventurous Antarctic travellers. In my case it has provided hugely enjoyable work on three further visits to the island, going in spring when the crevasses are still nicely bridged, leading parties with and for Skip Novak. He is a big cheese international yachtsman who also loves to go

Simon Richardson on the summit of Starbuck.

The camp on the Spenceley glacier below Mt Baume. Starbuck is on the extreme left of the photo.

climbing and has built two yachts – *Pelagic* and her reassuringly chunky sister *Pelagic Australis* – for that express purpose. The four or five days passage can be irksome, particularly the return to the Falklands when you tend to be hammering into the wind, but on a good day, with a fair wind on the beam, dolphins dancing in the bow spume and albatrosses circling overhead, it is a wonderful way to travel to your mountains, always in the safe hands of outstanding skippers and crews.

The Shackleton Traverse across the north-western end of the island takes in some fine country, but after my second crossing in 2008 I yearned to get back to the wilder end of the island. So in 2010 I found a team willing to finance a *Pelagic Australis* trip and ski from our old 1989 starting point in Royal Bay, continuing past Mt Carse, all the way down to the southern tip of the island. Alan Scowcroft and Ian Searle were seriously good skiers; Ian Calder, a distinguished retired anaesthetist, was more of a survival skier and mountaineering novice, but he rose splendidly to the occasion, towing his pulk by day, and in the tent at night regaling us with large tracts of H W Tilman's incomparable prose committed to memory. The company was great, the landscape was sublime and, unlike the static trench warfare of my first trip, on this occasion we were mobile, skiing with shelter and supplies in our pulks and, despite some mixed weather, able to travel every day.

It was one of the best ski tours I have ever done and the final steep descent into Drygalski Fjord made a fantastic grand climax, but earlier, on the fourth day, I couldn't help glancing up at the fine summit of Mt Baume, named after the Genevan watchmaker, bibliophile and mountaineer who had been here with the great map-maker Duncan Carse in the 1960s. Baume's fine eponymous summit was still untouched, as was Starbuck Peak, named after a famous American whaling dynasty (and the fictional first mate in *Moby Dick*), which I had first seen silhouetted against the setting sun from the summit of Mt Carse. Twenty years on Starbuck looked even more dramatic and pointy. And as we skied below the west face, I kept glancing up at a beguiling snow ramp rising diagonally across a wall of blank rock. I would clearly have to return again to the Salvesen range.

So I put together a suitably alluring prospectus and in August 2014 six of us plus our support team arrived off the coast, with Skip eying rue-fully the carapace of ice shrouding his floating life's investment, looking like the doomed vessel in the *Rime of the Ancient Mariner*. I had persuaded him that late winter would be a good idea. Good snow cover on the glaciers, right down to the beach. Nice safe freezing. And wasn't there a rumour that winter gave more settled weather? Alas, persistent south-westerlies stopped us landing at my chosen beach on the south coast and our attempts from the less convenient Drygalski Fjord fizzled out in the face of bitter, blasting spindrift. So, by way of alternative, we offered our 'clients' the unclimbed Trident peaks, which we had often skied past on the more accessible Shackleton Traverse. They proved a magnificent consolation prize, climbed on three successive days, with the central summit, now named Poseidon, giving some beautiful mixed climbing for Skip, myself, Nick Putnam,

The line of the first ascent of Mt Baume. *(David Lund)*

David McMeeking, Mark Dravers and the famous Chilean climber Rodrigo Jordan, the first person to climb Everest from east, south and north.

That was all fine and dandy, but those Salvesen summits were still unclimbed. So we drummed up another team for 2016 and last September, after a blissfully easy four days' passage from Stanley, anchored in perfect conditions at my favoured bay, Trolhull, with just one easy glacier pass between us and Starbuck. That afternoon, helped by our wonderful support team, we got all the gear and 16 days' supplies landed on the beach, stowed safely where no four-ton bull elephant seal might accidentally crush it. At dawn the next day we waved goodbye to *Pelagic Australis* and set off, towing hideously heavy pulks. Soon we were navigating by compass in a whiteout and by mid afternoon pitching camp in falling snow.

Excellent, I thought, as the wind blew from the north-west for the next four days, burying the tents in snow the consistency of concrete: the boys are getting the authentic South Georgia experience. In fact one of 'the boys' Crag Jones, knew the island better than me and Skip and had probably done more first ascents here than anyone. The other three, who *were* new to South Georgia, took the incarceration with admirable good humour. David Lund remained as phlegmatic as he had been when I had last climbed with him, on Monte Rosa in 1978. Henry Chaplin, expert skier and thoroughly sound all-round climber, endeared himself to me by saying I cooked the

Sunset from Mt Baume.

best risotto he had ever eaten in a tent. Sharing the other tent with Jones and Novak was the hardcore Scottish winter climber and ace alpinist Simon Richardson: our secret weapon.

Each night Novak telephoned our skipper for a weather forecast and by the fourth night we were promised a spell of settled high pressure over the island. Sure enough, we woke to blue skies and a stunning view of Starbuck plastered white. After the long chore of digging out the tents and packing, a quick descent and a three hour climb got us to a new camp right beneath the north ridge. While the old men pitched the new camp, the youngsters – Simon and Henry – skied up to nab a subsidiary little summit and recce the approaches to my ramp. Shortly after dawn the next morning five of us assembled on the east side of Starbuck and watched the sixth – the secret weapon – disappear over a little notch on the north ridge.

It was a brilliant opening move, getting us straight on to the west face ramp and, after six years wondering, I was thrilled to find solid climbable snow and ice sticking to it. The problem was how to climb the vertical headwall above. In the absence of any discernible weakness, Simon just kept working round the mountain, with the rest of us following obediently, admiring the eclectic selection of pegs, Bulldogs, ice screws, slings and hexes assembled at each improbable belay. One dramatic 'Traverse of the Gods' was protected with a back-rope. A pitch later we crossed a notch

onto the south ridge and then continued to spiral round onto the east face.

It was now mid afternoon. Simon was out of sight above and Skip was muttering gloomily about it nearly being his bedtime. But at last there was a shout and Skip and Crag set off up the only weakness in the entire headwall. Henry followed and I came last, marvelling at Simon's lead of a classic, udging shuffle up fathomless sugar stuck loosely to some of the most unhelpful rock any of us had ever seen, ending with a body belay standing in a hole just beneath a fantastically pointy precarious summit, on which we each took turns to stand. A snow bollard got us safely back down to the final belay, from where we reversed our upward spiral, abseiling and down-climbing into the darkness, back to our skis and eventually our beds at around midnight.

Standing on the summit of Starbuck, looking across at the snowy dome of Carse, where I had stood almost 27 years earlier and first wondered about this improbable pinnacle, was one of the great moments of my life. Even better was the realisation that, being blessed with an extraordinary sustained spell of high pressure, our show could go on. By way of relaxation, the next afternoon Simon, Henry and I skied round to two nice little unclimbed snow domes. Then we all spent a day in harness, moving camp to one of the highest cols on the island. From there Henry and David made the first ski ascent and descent of Mt Pelagic. Skip and Crag had made the first ascent 11 years earlier as consolation for a failed attempt on Mt Baume, which four of us now set off to try again.

We knew it would be a long day, so we set off at 11pm. In the dark Crag led us up several pitches of excellent mixed climbing, failing to recognise

Above: Skip Novak climbing the knife-edge summit ridge of Mt Baume.

Left: The wildness of South Georgia. Traversing the snow domes before the ascent of Mt Baume.
(Simon Richardson)

any of it from his previous attempt, until, at daybreak, he found a single forlorn bleached abseil sling at the 2005 highpoint. It was a beautiful, clever route, weaving sneakily up a safe buttress just to the side of some very dangerous seracs, to get onto a big upper snow and ice face. Here we toiled laboriously in the hot sun, with Simon leading the way, emerging finally beneath a typically vertiginous South Georgian summit nipple, climbed via a spectacular ice tube. Again, it was a one-at-a-time summit, with the most awesome 2,500m drop straight down to the ocean. Then the race was on to get back to the rock buttress before nightfall. This we just achieved, but the final six abseils were all done in pitch darkness and we had been on the go continuously for 27 hours when we finally joined Henry and David back at camp.

The weather forecast was now finally looking less promising, so it was time to quit while we were ahead. For me it was another trip down memory lane, trundling enjoyably north, over the Ross pass and down onto a Ross glacier transformed almost out of recognition since I had first seen it in 1989, and now looked virtually impassable in its lower reaches. But Novak, like Baldrick, had 'a cunning plan' to continue north, up the subsidiary Webb and Cook glaciers to St Andrew's Bay. The plan worked, but one route-finding mistake cost us a day's delay, tent-bound in ferocious winds, eking out the last scraps of food. In my tent, breakfast on day 16 was a biscuit. In Novak's tent they had conserved rations more judiciously and feasted royally on porridge and pesto. Then, in glorious sunshine, we packed the pulks for the final time and skied down to beach, where the penguins watched indifferently while the support team welcomed us with hugs and champagne.

SEBASTIAN WOLFRUM

Forgotten Giants
of the Rwenzori

Alexandra (left) and Margherita (right) as seen from the summit of Mount Baker.
(All photos by Sebastian Wolfrum)

Having read about the Rwenzori as a child in a popular German geographical journal, the range had been in the back of my mind for as long as I dreamt about exploring the wilder places of this planet. My chance of going there arrived in the summer of 2016. This being some of the wettest mountain-country on earth ascending the summits is generally an activity confined to the dry season, with the middle of June to the middle of August offering the best opportunities.

The border of Uganda and the Democratic Republic of Congo (DRC) runs through the massif and Margherita, its highest summit, can be climbed from both sides. However, the majority of the lower peaks are situated solely in Uganda. The Congolese section of the range is part of Virunga national park; since 1991 the Ugandan part forms the Rwenzori national park, declared a World Heritage Site in 1994. Access to the mountains is restricted to those enlisting the support of one of two Ugandan companies holding concessions to supply porters and guides. Rwenzori Mountaineering

Lake Kitandara from the north.

Tree heather covered in balls of moss.

On the receding glacial edge of the Stanley plateau.

Services (RMS), operates on the long established central circuit, the historic access route through the Mubuku and Bujuku valleys. Another, newer venture, Rwenzori Trekking Services (RTS), based in the mining town of Kilembe, opens up the mountains from the south.

As I had little interest in trotting behind guides to quickly climb to the highest point, a more elaborate idea was developed: the ascent of the respective highest summits of five of the six highest mountains of the range, with a sixth high mountain lying unreachable (or so I thought) across the border in the DRC. For this a 16 to 18-day expedition was planned.

It was impossible even to get a reply to my request for such an undertaking from RMS; RTS only agreed to a trip including remote Mount Gessi after lengthy correspondence. The vast majority of visitors to the mountains nowadays are trekkers who never stray far from the few established paths, with very little exploratory mountaineering being done. With it being mandatory to hire two guides, I could have found myself entangled in the stranglehold of tourism, but a first meeting with RTS in Kilembe eliminated any such fears. RTS is owned by an Australian long-term resident of Uganda and has invested effectively in guide training. Although they are by no means mountain guides in the European sense of the word, they are probably the best trained anywhere in central Africa and were certainly flexible.

On 17 July the expedition got under way and I left Kilembe with a posse of two guides, a trainee guide I had agreed to take along, as well as 17 porters. This large number was partly due to the fact that, despite huts along the way belonging to RTS, all domestic equipment such as pots and pans is carried up and down the mountains with each visitor, in order, or so I have been told, to avoid theft. Furthermore no cutting of firewood is allowed in the park so charcoal has to be carried up as well. While a smaller number might have been preferable, one has to note that the successful protection of environments like the Rwenzori can fully function only as long as the locals living in proximity to it have some economic incentive to engage in this process.

Winding our way through plantations of cassava and coffee, the latter being the main cash crop of this area, the park boundary at 1,727m was soon reached and after some last formalities we entered the dense montane rainforest characterising this lower part of the range. Following the course of the Mulyambuli river, walking speed soon slowed considerably to observe the flora and fauna, including blue monkeys, chameleons and the remarkable birdlife. Tall *Symphonia globulifera* trees, with their waxy red flowers, dominate the forest. Sine at 2,602m was our place for the night: one of several newly built huts with comfortable bunk beds.

I had been told there had been no rain for the two weeks preceding my visit, but this spell of unusually dry weather came to an end and during the night it started to rain, continuing into the morning. On the second day we soon reached the bamboo zone, although the floral strata are substantially overlapping. Further on giant tree heathers, covered in *Usnea* lichen and balls of moss as large as human heads form a fairy-tale forest of ethereal beauty. The forest floor below 3,000m is blanketed in *Scadoxus cyrtanthiflorus*, an herbaceous plant with attractive red tubular flowers, endemic to the Rwenzori.

Mutinda at 3,660m was our next station. The rain once again broke loose soon after nightfall, continuing heavily till noon the next day. Conditions underfoot were such that mountain boots had to be exchanged for wellies and still it was next to impossible not to get wet feet in the seemingly bottomless mud for which these mountains are famous. On the third day the Afro-alpine zone was reached. Giant *Lobelia*, up to eight metres and giant groundsel (*Senecio*) up to 10m dominated the scene; *Hypercium* (St John's Wort) occurs as bushy form up to 12m high in three species with yellow, orange and red flowers. Whole mountainsides are covered in *Helichrysum*, a silvery bush of everlasting flowers, rapidly opening as soon as the sun does shine.

All high east African mountains have their respective species of Afro-alpine plants but nowhere else is this type of vegetation as dense and luxuriant as in the Rwenzori. Yet at first a zone of regrowth had to be crossed. In 2013 a bushfire destroyed a large area of this precious environment, burning for weeks until a spell of rain lasting three days extinguished it. In the same year a flash flood coming off the mountains swept away

Jubilant mood on the summit of Mount Speke.

countless houses as well as the road surface in Kilembe, killing nine people and displacing nearly 10,000.

The third night was spent at Bugata camp (4059m), overlooking a small lake of the same name. My original plan had been to use the next day to climb Mount Luigi from the south and to descend via its north-western flank, but continuing heavy rainfall in the morning of the fourth day led to the decision to use this bad weather to penetrate further into the mountains by way of high passes. Butawu camp, close to the Kitandara lakes was reached via Bamwanjara pass (4450m). Beyond it the area of fire damage was exchanged for the most enchanting thickets of lobelias and groundsels; the all-enshrouding mists lifted for the first time in four days, the sun was shining and soon countless sunbirds fluttered from flower to flower and while it closed in again later, the evening at Butawu was spent admiring impressive views of Mount Baker to the north-east, Mount Stanley to the north-west, Mount Speke to the north and the steep cliffs of Mount Luigi to the south.

Any optimism regarding the weather was shattered next morning. Having started at 4.30am for the ascent of Mount Baker, it began to cloud over at 5am and to rain at 5.30am. Gaining height, this soon turned to snow. Although the chosen route up this mountain was never difficult, with long stretches of easy scrambling and only short pitches of grade III, the practical difficulties increased at once due to the extreme slipperiness of the rock when wet. This challenge would repeatedly arise throughout the expedition. As crustose lichen grow right up to the highest peaks, the danger of slipping had to be heeded.

Clambering on, we reached Edward, the highest summit of Mount Baker, at around 11.40am, which gave us a welcome excuse to prolong our stay

Typical forest of giant groundsel. Many kilometres had to be covered over such ground.

on the summit by lunching on it. Sitting in the thick clouds was of limited comfort, especially for the trainee-guide accompanying us, dressed as he was only in a hooded cotton jumper and no jacket of any description, but perseverance was rewarded with a short spell of sunshine and ten minutes of breath-taking views towards Mount Stanley, the only mountain in the range with any significant glaciers left.

The following day was spent continuing northward, past the upper and lower Kitandara lakes, a place of serene beauty and tranquillity, over Scott Elliot pass and on to the newly built Margherita camp (4487m). The weather was again clear and the imposing peaks of the southern Stanley group loomed impressively above the hut. No climbing has been done here for decades and the afternoon was spent musing about future objectives in this area.

The next day we climbed Margherita, at 5,109m the third-highest mountain in Africa. In 1906, when the Duke of Abruzzi first climbed this peak, its snows reached nearly down to the location of the present day hut. Nowadays over an hour of climbing over wet and loose rock is necessary to gain the gently sloping Stanley plateau, still the largest glacier in the range. This has to be crossed towards the south-east ridge of Alexandra, the second-highest summit, which in turn is crossed on rock, leading to the steep Margherita glacier. Whilst both these glaciers were formerly connected and their surface was one of firm snow, it is now one of hard ice, due to changes in precipitation-patterns with less snowfall and more rain.

This we followed upwards to a point close to the saddle between the two main peaks. We finally reached the summit of Margherita, scrambling for 30 minutes over verglas-covered rocks.

The whole climb was done in whiteout conditions and only on the way down was it possible to discern some of our surroundings, notably the front of glacial melting, a process so fast that the guides were able to point out where only a year ago there had still been ice. Having come down the mountain we continued to Bujuku. The hut there belongs to RMS and was in a semi-derelict condition, so the party camped under a rock shelter, which appeared insubstantial at first but kept everybody dry throughout the long rainy night and the following day.

It was on this eighth day of the expedition that the real adventures began. Directly to the north-east, Mount Speke, my next target, hid itself in the clouds. First we had to organise logistics for the days to come. The base of Mount Gessi, lying beyond Speke, could be reached in three ways. The most obvious would have been to descend to Bigo Bog and follow the Mugusu valley upstream. This was ruled out by RTS not being allowed to use the path from Bujuku to Bigo. The other options were to cross right over Speke or to find a way around its western and northern flanks, the latter necessitating a crossing of the border into the DRC.

Although the number of porters had been reduced at this point, even with our lower number it seemed inadvisable to try to climb the mountain in inclement weather and the slippery conditions, followed by a descent on the far side through difficult terrain. For this reason a group of three of the most experienced men, all of them former poachers with an intricate knowledge of the area, were sent ahead to reconnoitre a route around the mountain.

This group was supposed to meet us again on the evening of the seventh day at Bujuku, but was nowhere to be seen. With the weather progressively deteriorating to continuous heavy downpours, visibility reduced to less than ten metres and with the porters still missing at 10am of day eight, I called it as a rest day. In the later afternoon the rain finally abated and a search party was sent out. With these men coming back empty-handed the situation became more serious. After some consideration I called the guides and porters together. Having formed a strong bond with them by sharing their local food and spending most of the time not used for climbing in their midst, it was not overly difficult to convince them that a small number, carrying only the most necessary items should traverse with me over Mount Speke the next day, whilst others could search for their missing colleagues. Soon after coming to this agreement and sorting through gear I retired only to be woken at 11pm by wild exultations: the missing porters had finally returned.

Thus we reverted to the original plan, for porters to go around the mountain and to meet me and the guides on the other side, I found myself approached in the morning by three porters requesting to come over the mountain anyway. Reluctantly I agreed, and so we climbed Mount Speke in cloudy but dry weather as a group of seven people, some of them carrying

Giant lobelias on the shore of Lac du Speke.

heavy loads. The agility of the local Bakonjo being generally very high and this mountain being one of the easier ones, there were no significant problems, other than occasional delays. Once on the summit, a jubilant mood took hold and there were lots of pictures taken of them posing with helmets, ice axes and so forth. This joyful scene ranked as one of the expedition's most memorable experiences.

The descent on the other side was very intricate. Receding glaciers had left behind a wasteland of smooth slabs and loose rock; further down moss-covered rocks ensured we did not walk but slid off the mountain. Worse, however, was the fearsome tangle of *Senecio*, growing in a valley strewn with huge boulders hidden underneath a layer of moss concealing many a hole into which the unwary traveller would fall from time to time. Crossing several kilometres in this kind of forest, by far the most impregnable terrain I have ever encountered anywhere, was a thorough test of nerves and stamina. A camp was set up at a rock shelter called Skull Cave after a human skull had been found there, most likely originating from a porter who died from altitude sickness during an expedition in 1932. Although only at 4,000m the place seemed cursed. Our trainee-guide developed a strong headache and had to be sent down to lower altitudes.

The following day was blessed with the best weather of the expedition. For the first time the morning's blue sky lasted until the afternoon. In these sunny and dry conditions we set about climbing Mount Gessi, a mountain

Mount Luigi as seen from below Weisman. An unnamed peak (c4570m) in the foreground and Sella behind. Other unnamed peaks to the right.

that had last seen humans on its summit in 2006. First another hour of struggle through vegetation led to the Raccoti pass from where an ascent was made via mossy slaps up the western flank of Gessi. Higher up a scree gully with a chockstone, which we had to crawl under, led to the col of the main summit ridge. Following this easily we reached Bottego, the lower of the two main summits, retracing our steps to the col and continuing south along the ridge, we bagged the higher Iolanda, rewarded with outstanding views of the surrounding mountains, especially Emin across the valley to the west.

With a thunderstorm raging for the better part of the night, depositing 30cm of fresh snow, the next day could only be written off. Day 12 brought a return to sunny conditions and an attempt to climb Mount Emin seemed possible. Retuning to the Raccoti pass two snares designed to trap rock hyrax were found, most likely placed there by poachers operating from villages in the DRC. Breaking these I was warned by the guides of the powerful charms the Congolese trappers would now surely call upon me.

Emin, of all the main mountains one of the most technically imposing, has knife-edged ridges, serrated like shark's teeth, radiating from its summit. A steep scree gully running parallel to the east ridge of Umberto, the highest summit, was chosen as our point of attack. This ridge was gained above a prominent vertical section and followed over extremely loose rock further up. Some 50m below the top the rock became ever more rotten and ascending to the crest of the main ridge ended in a sheer precipice, most likely the abseil-pitch reported by Pasteur (see *AJ* 1964). Having unofficially crossed the border into the DRC, a wide margin of safety had to be observed, so owing to the loose rock the climb was abandoned at this point.

The extended stay at Skull Cave due to the thunderstorm resulted in a shortage of food; this prevented any further attempt on Emin via a different route. The journey back to Bujuku around Mount Speke turned out to be the most strenuous day altogether, the ground crossed being both overgrown with dense forests and very muddy. Other sections were, in want of better alternatives, tackled by descending steep brooks. Great was the joy when some of the porters who had remained at Bujuku came to meet us at Lac du Speke, bringing with them a liberal amount of cassava and peanut sauce.

Walking back to Butawu in the rain next morning, Mount Luigi still waited to be climbed. Weismann summit was easily reached and traversed to Bugata. A second unnamed peak was climbed but no attempt was made on Sella, the highest summit but with a height difference of just seven metres, due to poor visibility. With only our descent to civilisation to come, our last two days flashed by, but already in these last hours I was longing to come back to the otherworldly realm of the Rwenzori.

ROBERT POWELL

Renland, Eastern Greenland

Run-out slab climbing on Arctic Monkeys, Renland. *(Paul Seabrook)*

During July and August of 2016, Paul Seabrook, David Barlow, Geoff Hornby and Robert Powell travelled to an un-named glacier in Renland, eastern Greenland, with the aim of climbing new peaks and routes in this remote and largely unclimbed area. The glacier is located opposite the Bear Islands at N71°8.52', W25°38.56'.

The line of *Arctic Monkeys* (E2), on a wall five kilometres up the glacier from the team's landing point. *(Paul Seabrook)*

Alpine rock climbing on the summit crest of Cerro Castillito. *(Rob Powell)*

Our journey started with a three-hour charter flight from Akureyri in Iceland to Constable Point in Greenland. From there, we travelled in small rubber inflatable boats (RIBs) for 12 hours along the coast of the Scorbysund. The RIB journey proved to be equally spectacular and unpleasant, the beauty of the mountain views and icebergs quickly numbed away by unrelenting bouncing and frigid temperatures on the RIBs.

We landed on a beach at the snout of a glacier; the temperatures were pleasant and the location breathtaking. Base camp was on the hillside about a hundred metres above the beach with a convenient water source close by. Here we discovered that Greenland has no shortage of mosquitos.

Our first task was to establish an advanced base camp (ABC) about five kilometres up the glacier. It took us three hours to get there and we found a brilliant site on an alluvial silt plain located by the main bend of the glacier. We headed back to base camp and roughly a hundred metres before it, Geoff plunged through a snow patch and inverted his knee. This was terrible luck for Geoff and the end of his expedition.

Having established ABC, we decided to make an attempt on a 'warm-up' route. Next morning, we threaded our way up the glacier and scouted numerous big walls, eventually deciding to climb a crack that split one of 400m. The initial pitches were excellent with some loose rock, but mostly good climbing following an obvious and aesthetic line. Higher up, the route turned rather more committing with long run-outs and sections that required delicate climbing on dubious rock.

The line of ascent on Cerro Castillito, Renland. *(David Barlow)*

After threading our way through some large rotten overhangs, we finally popped out on a ridge where we had the choice of continuing up to an unremarkable summit, or abseil off. We chose the latter and arrived back at ABC 22 hours after setting off. We named the route *Arctic Monkeys* (400m, E2 5b). A rest day was needed after such an involved warm-up so we headed back down to base camp and celebrated our first route with a fine single malt.

For our next route, we opted for a big alpine objective. The first climbing expedition to this glacier had attempted our chosen peak and although they had not managed to summit it, they named it Cerro Castillito. We followed the same route the first team had attempted, up a glacier and over a massive bergschrund that led to a long and arduous snow gully. At the top of the gully we followed a complex ridge, sometimes with excellent rock and other times scary loose blocks. Route finding proved complex, involving venturing into deep chimneys and squirming into and out of slots as well as some abseiling from towers on the ridge. Finally, we all made it onto the very pointy summit blocks.

The weather had been coming in for some time and after hastily taking some pictures and GPS data, we set off down-climbing and abseiling to reach the snow gully. It started snowing during the descent but we finally reached the tent after a continuous 26-hour push. This was the first ascent of Cerro Castillito via the *South-East Ridge* (1,300m, AD+/D, V). As was now our routine, we headed to base camp to recharge our batteries, consume whisky and feed the mosquitos.

On the first ascent of *Polar Daze*, Mount Hannes. *(Rob Powell)*

Mount Hannes, showing the line of *Polar Daze* (1400m, TD, E2 5b, 50°).
The quality of rock varied from superb granite to 'granola'. *(Rob Powell)*

A shot from higher on the first ascent of *Polar Daze. (David Barlow)*

From ABC we had identified a snow and ice couloir sandwiched between two large peaks and decided to climb it as a reconnaissance mission prior to attempting the large peak to the left of it. Should the couloir fall easily, we were open to continuing up the left peak to the summit that we estimated was about 250m further up. To reach the base of the couloir, we had to negotiate a fairly complex glacier with many crevasses. Fortunately, the initial approach on the glacier was 'dry' so it did not prove difficult. Once at the base of the couloir, the glacier is 'wet' but the snow was firm and we encountered no difficulties with crevasses or the bergschrund.

We hugged the rock wall on the left of the couloir trying to stay out of the central part where we expected rock-fall might be a problem. However, as the couloir narrowed about halfway up we had little choice but to run this gauntlet with only a couple of small stones flying past. David and I hadn't expected to climb any ice routes in Greenland so we had brought only one ice tool each. Paul had come more prepared and had a pair of them, although comment was made as to which museum Paul had purchased them from. The leader got a pair of tools and each seconder had to make do with one. We had eight ice screws, two for each belay, leaving four for placing runners. The ice was bullet hard, inflicting considerable pump to our rapidly ballooning calf muscles. The route became steeper the higher we progressed but never exceeded 75°.

It soon became apparent that we had underestimated the length of the route. After what felt like an eternity, we reached the upper part of the couloir where the quality of the ice became somewhat concerning. Comprising of a series of large crystals, the ice cracked apart when an ice tool or ice screw was placed into it. Fortunately, this section was short-lived and a couple of pitches later we reached the col. At this point, the call of our sleeping bags was too strong and we abandoned our idea of continuing to the left summit. We descended directly down the route using abalakovs and a few pieces of rock gear on the left side of the couloir. We recorded 18 abseils and 150m of down-climbing on snow. Five minutes short of 24 hours after setting off, we crawled back into our sleeping bags. We named the route the *Double OO Couloir* (800m, AD, 55°-75°).

After a couple of rest days at basecamp, we returned to have an attempt at our main objective for the trip. Our previous scouting mission had identified a leftward trending ramp line from the lower section of the *Double OO Couloir* heading towards the arête between the north and east faces. Our plan was to ascend this ramp and then follow the arête to a series of steep corner systems where we expected to encounter the crux of the route.

We left ABC at 8.30am and retraced our steps through the maze of crevasses and up the initial section of the *Double OO Couloir*, making our first stance at the start of the leftward trending ramp. We alternated leads through varying degrees of loose horribleness, arriving at the end of the ramp where the rock steepened considerably. Where the rock was steep, it was generally good although the lower section of the north face had areas of thick black lichen covering the rock making protection hard to find. We encountered chimneys, cracks, flakes, laybacks and even an off-width on our way to the base of the steep corner systems.

Once at the base of the steeper corner systems, we were please to find perfect splitter cracks. What followed was steep, well protected and thoroughly enjoyable climbing for three long pitches. Feeling a little smug after completing the corner systems and on easier ground we were due for a little humbling. The rock quality deteriorated into possibly the worst rock I have ever climbed on. The rock crumbled into 'granola' in your hands and I think it's safe to say protection was purely of a psychological benefit.

Fortunately, this dire rock lasted for only a pitch-and-a-half and after a long and tiring day, we found the first possible bivy site since setting off. We built a rock wall to provide some shelter from the wind and climbed into our bivy bags. To save weight, we had decided not to bring sleeping bags so the night was a cold one.

The following morning, we flanked a loose steep crack and continued up steep ground on the north face, more than a little concerned that instead of easing off, the ground looked to be getting steeper. Nonetheless we continued weaving our way up the easiest line possible, passing another potential bivy site and crossing the arête onto the east face. Here we encountered more 'granola' and steep technical climbing. Finally, after two pitches on the east side of the arête, we hit the easy ground of the summit ridge;

Rob Powell, Paul Seabrook and Dave Barlow on the summit, with their dedication to Hannes Esterhuyse, the South African alpinist who died in Switzerland in 2008. *(David Barlow)*

350m later we were standing on the summit of our main objective.

Prior to setting off on this route, I had asked Paul and David if they wouldn't mind naming the peak after my old climbing partner, Hannes Esterhuyse, who had tragically passed away climbing the climbing in the Alps. Both were supportive of the idea. I had previously prepared a note to the Esterhuyse family and we took a summit photo with the note. This was the first ascent of the peak that we named Mount Hannes via the route *Polar Daze*, (1400m, TD, E2 5b, 50°).

From the summit, we descend the very loose ridge leading to the col at the top of the *Double OO Couloir*. We made five long abseils on steep rock that brought us to just below the col where our previous ice route finished. Reaching the first abalakov station we had set up previously, we were dismayed to find the abalakovs had melted out and we would have to re-set all of the abseils.

One incident worth forgetting on the descent occurred when a microwave-sized rock came bouncing down the couloir directly towards us and at the last second bounced right over our heads. We had a further five days until our boat pick-up, but after two new peaks and four new routes, we decided enough was enough and demobilised our ABC and headed to the relative warmth of beach. We strongly recommend any future parties use hard-bottomed boats. A local Inuit fisherman picked us up in a hard-

The view from the summit of Mount Hannes. The obvious steep tower offers future parties a major new big wall route. *(David Barlow)*

bottomed boat and the journey out was considerably faster and infinitely more comfortable.

There is fantastic potential for new routing in the area. There is a big wall with two summits on the right of the main glacier as one looks up the valley from ABC. This has two obvious and spectacular lines on the right (highest) summit. We estimate the wall to be between 800m and 1,000m high. Access to the wall is straightforward from ABC. The left line is a dihedral system that narrows to become a continuous crack system higher up. After c500m it becomes an easier-angled corner system where the crack intersects slabs coming in from the left. This rock looks clean and the climbing steep. The right line is an even larger dihedral system with a continuous crack that appears to turn thin and then very wide higher up. The finish to this line was not visible and would probably be steep. We expect these routes would be climbed in big wall style and require a portaledge.

From base camp, looking up the valley there is a smaller steep glacier intersecting the main glacier from the left. There is a short entry chute to a higher mini-glacier plateau. From there, the glacier heads rightwards before curving left to access the high glacier plateau and various unclimbed snow summits. While the route looks moderate, there are many crevasses visible and the initial entry chute and mini-glacial plateau are exposed to serac fall.

Central Asia

The Former Winter Capital of Bhutan at Punakha Dzong
Samuel Davis (1757-1819)
1783. Watercolour, pen and black ink, brown ink, gouache, graphite,
with scratching out and sponging on moderately thick, slightly textured,
cream, wove paper, mounted on thick, moderately textured, beige, wove paper,
17½ × 27½ inches. Yale Center for British Art, Paul Mellon Collection.

INES PAPERT & LUKA LINDIČ

Lost in China

Ines Papert warming up for Kyzyl Asker on the 2004 route Border Control
on the so-called Great Walls of China nearby. *(All images Luka Lindič)*

*The leading German alpinist Ines Papert and the Slovenian Luka Lindič made a
much-fancied first ascent on the south-east face of Kyzyl Asker (5842m) over two
days at the end of September 2016, via their new route Lost in China (1200m, ED,
WI 5+, M6). It was Papert's third attempt on the face, which has seen plenty of
attention from other climbers too. These details are drawn from Papert's account
and other sources.*

Kyzyl Asker, meaning 'red soldier', is a dramatic and hard to access
mountain in the western Kokshaal-too which straddles the border
between Kyrgyzstan and Xinjiang: part of the Tien Shan. After it was first
photographed in 1998, the south-east face became a magnet for some of
the world's leading alpinists. Among the feature's most appealing lines was
an elegant ice couloir. First to try were the British climbers Es Tresidder
and Guy Robertson in 2002 and 2004. They found out that in bad weather
the couloir is plagued with spindrift avalanches and in good weather the
ice quickly melts out. Having found conditions too warm on their second
expedition, when the couloir's ice simply disappeared, the two speculated
the line might only be possible in winter. They had plenty of consolation:

Left: Papert preparing for the ephemeral couloir on Kyzyl Asker's south-east face. The route takes the line above her head and slightly to the left. The pillar to the right was the route of first ascent in 2007.

their expedition, which included Matt Halls, Pete Benson and Robin Thomas, climbed five new routes, including Kyzyl Asker's north face, the mountain's second ascent, as well as a line on the granite walls to the south dubbed the Great Wall of China, a steep ice chimney called *Border Control* (650m, ED2, WI5, A1).

In 2007, a Russian team from St Petersburg, comprising the late Alexander Ruchkin, Mikhail Mikhailov and Alexander Odintsov, climbed the striking pillar to the right, coming in from the right to avoid the steep lower third; the Franco-Belgian team of Nicolas Favresse, Sean Villaneuva, Stéphane Hanssens and Evrard Wendenbaum climbed the entire pillar in 2011 via a hard new route, which shared some pitches with the Russian line, with climbing up to 5.12c and M6+, called *China Jam*. In the years since other lines have been added to the right of the pillar, most recently, in July 2016, *The Spear* (1300m, A3, M8) from the Russians Oleg Khvostenko, Vasya Terekhin and Alexander Parfyonov.

Papert had made two previous attempts on the couloir Tresidder and Robertson had tried, the first in 2010 when she retreated 300m shy of the summit due to heavy snowfall and avalanches. A second attempt a year later also failed after health problems in Papert's team. Five years later the haunting appeal of Kyzyl Asker persuaded Papert to try for a third time.

Both Papert and Lindič described the ice climbing as the best they'd experienced at altitude.

She brought with her the Slovenian climber Luka Lindič, as enthusiastic about the project as she was.

Papert and Lindič warmed up with a repeat of the Tresidder and Robertson route *Border Control*. Then they focussed on the ephemeral couloir. With only a narrow window of good weather, the pair set off at 5am on the morning of 30 September, simul-climbing the first few hundred metres in the dark. Papert and Lindič knew that they had to make progress quickly to reach the summit ridge that same day, before the weather worsened and they would have to retreat in the face of a snow storm and the inevitable spindrift.

The pair gained ground quickly, soon arriving at the steep ice that constitutes the route's main technical challenged. Papert recalled hearing Lindič, who was out of sight above her, screaming for joy when the upper section of the couloir came into view and he realised it continued up to the summit ridge. Papert said that neither she nor Lindič had climbed such a perfect ice and mixed route at that sort of altitude before. A thunderstorm set in as night was falling and the pair continued as darkness fell until they were two pitches below the summit ridge and then set up an uncomfortable and extremely exposed bivy exposed to heavy spindrift.

After a tough and severely cold night the two climbers began their ascent to the summit next morning, reaching the summit ridge at around 10am;

Facing south, the couloir is prone to melting out in good weather.

Towards the end of the first afternoon, worsening weather prompted the route's other great hazard: spindrift.

Papert photographed at dusk. The two climbers continued until it was dark to ensure success.

Despite a tough bivouac, Papert and Lindič were able to continue to the summit ridge.

Papert on the summit ridge. The pair descended the route on the same day, escaping just before another storm hit the peak.

they left ropes and gear behind and raced to the summit, Lindič making way for Papert, telling her that she should be first after all her experiences and hardships on the mountain. Papert and Lindič reached the top at 12.10pm local time.

The pair knew the weather was set to worsen so they rappeled down their route as quickly as possible, solely using abalakovs. They reached their ABC at 7pm and almost immediately a massive thunderstorm swept over the mountain, sending spindrift avalanches down the face. 'Failure is part of climbing,' Papert said afterwards. 'So is patience. After the second failed attempt I needed to let the idea rest, I didn't want it to become my purpose in life … but it's one route that begs to be climbed.'

ROBERT ESTIVILL

On Skis in the Ak-shirak

Séverine Stemmer skiing in Kyrgyzstan's Ak-shirak range. *(Arnaud Pasquer)*

From 15 March to 4 April 2016 a team of four ski mountaineers Rob Estivill, Séverine Stemmer, Arnaud Pasquer and Nicolas Valdenaire visited the Ak-shirak range in the central Tien Shan. The objective of the expedition was to explore these little-known glaciers and ski previously unclimbed summits. To their knowledge, ski-mountaineering activity in the region has been confined to Eagle Ski Club trips led by Dave Wynne-Jones in 2006, 2007 and 2008. Most alpinism has focused on the rocky, central-west part of the massif. A short video of the expedition is available on YouTube.

The best method of accessing the Ak-shirak is via the Petrov glacier, which gives access to the lake of the same name on the Ara Bell plateau. However, this option was barred by the mining concession that operates there and we were forced to approach from the south-west, up the Kara-say valley. This required a long detour, and a border permit due to the proximity with the Chinese frontier and the crossing of the Suek pass (4028m), which can be blocked due to snow accumulation.

On the morning of departure, we woke in Karakol to five centimetres of fresh snow covering the streets. Luckily conditions were good enough, and we were able to cross in our vehicle, before continuing through a military checkpoint. Having had our permits checked, the soldiers warned

The expedition's ski exploration of the Ak-shirak in the central Tien Shan. Their efforts build on those of the Eagle Ski Club. *(Rob Estivill)*

us about the cold and we continued over the wooden bridge across the Kara-say river, repaired in recent years, before continuing up the valley as far as we could. Unloading our gear in a raging snowstorm, we quickly set up camp hoping the weather would improve. Happily it did, and what's more the small amount of fallen snow would prove invaluable over the next days for pulling our heavy sledges over the grassy terrain.

The ambition to do some mountaineering in Kyrgyzstan had grown after a first visit in 2014. Hiking in the early autumn, I had a great time experiencing this incredible country and its people. After looking up at various unnamed snow-capped peaks, I vowed to return and ski them. Now, after all the preparation and logistics, it was time to start pulling the sledge. For the next few days we trekked north-east up the valley. Arriving at a fork we turned left, following the North Kara-say glacier. We set up a first base camp just before the foot of the glacier. Comparing our experience with previous reports, the ice front had clearly retreated.

From here we skied up the first valley to our west. Snow conditions were unstable, with a mass of fresh powder on a deep layer of depth hoar, which periodically gave way as we progressed. We climbed a peak, but found a cairn on top, but then Nico and Arnaud reached the top of a snow dome at the end of the glacier that was named Mt Elia (4750m, N41°46.41' E78°10.12). We rejoiced at our first success, reassured that by taking the necessary precautions with the snow cover it was indeed possible to climb these peaks. A second successful day followed, in which we skied up the valley immediately adjacent to the north. All four members reached the top of the twin tipped summit at the end, which we named Lion's Head (4750m, N41°46.41' E78°10.12'). On the way down we discovered the hard ice wasn't far beneath the layer of powder snow.

It was now time to move higher, so we started scouting the chaotic glacier, trying to find the best route for the sledges. The ice is not too deeply crevassed, but rather flows and rolls like a frozen sea or sand dunes. Leaving some gear and food buried next to our campsite, we made the tortuous crossing to gain the eastern side and set up our tent facing the huge

Lion's Head, south-west face

Lion's Head
4640 m

Line of ascent on the Lion's Head. *(Rob Estivill)*

SNK Kyrgyzia peak. From this camp we spent the next few days exploring in different directions. We took the right-hand branch of the glacier to verify if it was possible to cross the pass at the end and enter the valley above the Petrov lake.

Climbing the small hill above the col we saw that although skiable, it was much too steep for sledges, and presented several large overhanging cornices. Skiing down I broke through a large crevasse hidden just beneath the col. Luckily, I was roped up and being on skis, managed to reach the other side before it all caved in. In the meantime Nico had explored the west flanks of the steep peaks that separated the two branches of the glacier, but found the snow much too unstable. Instead, he made a repeat climb of Snow Cannon, climbed by the British in 2006.

Back at camp, Nico was still interested in climbing the steep peak. Having seen a large couloir on the east side, we all set off the next day to try it. The colouir had already cleared of fresh snow, so were much more confident about conditions. The slope is about 300m and 40-45° but overhung by an ominous looking serac. Arnaud led up to the cornice and cut a way through. Soon joined by Nico, the pair of them climbed the peak to the north but realising the highest point was in fact to the south, they came back and the four of us made it to the icy summit, which we named Dratpouet (4830m, N41°49.44' E78°15.52). It was an epic moment but with the weather closing in fast we beat a hasty retreat back to camp.

After a day spent waiting for a storm that never came, we set off for SNK Kyrgyzia, hoping to try and climb a new route up the east side. We found a

Fresh snow as the team arrived helped mobility but the trend for snowfall in the region is downwards. *(Rob Estivill)*

steep ice slope that led up to the east-west ridge but we turned back before the summit due to more ice. In better conditions this would be an aesthetic route to the top. That same day Arnaud climbed a spur behind our camp and paraglided off, possibly making the first flight in the Ak-shirak.

With our supplies of cheese, horse sausage and buckwheat dwindling, we had a day left so we decided to repeat another of the peaks climbed in 2006, Peak Karga: 'crow's peak'. After crossing the glacier again – by this time we knew every cliff and bump – we headed north-west. Arriving on the final ridge, we saw several large black birds flying around, confirming the peak is aptly named. But unfortunately a large crevasse barred our way a few hundred metres before the summit. After poking through the soft snow with our poles and looking down into its depth we decided to turn back. As this peak is right on the edge of the Ak-shirak range we could see across the beautiful Ara Bell plateau. We could also make out the sharp lines of the gold mine cutting into the mountains, chopping off pieces of glacier. The views as we skied back were more than enough to make up for the disappointment.

Next day we descended to our cache of provisions to find it had been ravaged. Although we had seen some wolf prints down in the valley, this was most probably the work of foxes. We had seen several circling our camp under the cover of darkness. They had managed to completely shred some clothes and a spare tent and make a mess of everything. Because it had snowed during the day, lots of our stuff had been reburied, making retrieval all the harder. Thankfully most of our food was untouched, but we had to stay put for the evening to sort everything out.

Line of ascent and ski descent of Dratpouet. *(Rob Estivill)*

Nico made good use of the next morning to make a fast ascent of the peak immediately to the west of our camp. Climbing mostly on foot he got to the top as the weather closed in. Hearing the buzzing of electricity on the summit he was forced to throw his ice axe and run for cover before lightning hit not far off. Of course, we named this Lightning Peak (4560m, N41°46.36' E78°14.5'). Moving camp again we went further down before heading to the base of the South Kara-Say glacier, which is much thicker and crevassed. The sides highlight the incredible pressures to which the ice is submitted. There are swirls and marbled veins that show how the different layers have folded in on themselves.

After admiring this spectacle we found it was easier to hike up the moraine on the west side with skis on our packs before crossing onto the snow. A long haul took us all the way to the end of one of the valleys and up a peak of beautiful red granite. In view of recent events we called this Thieving Fox (4800m N41°47.18' E78°17.16'). From the top we admired the central part of the Ak-shirak massif, rockier and steeper than the western side. As I stood on the snowy ridge, looking down into a new valley, I saw we were in fact on the watershed, not only of these particular mountains but of the Tien Shan as a whole. Upon getting back and carefully studying the map, I realised that a snowflake falling on this summit could take either one of the two different directions, representative of the identity of these mountains. On one side it would flow down the Kara-say valley and into the river of that name. From tributary to tributary, all the way past Naryn,

The team's fourth camp, at the foot of the North Kara Say glacier, from where they climbed their first peaks. *(Rob Estivill)*

across the border into Uzbekistan, it would finally end up in the Aral Sea. If it travelled down the other side, it would head straight off towards China, before being taken via irrigation channels to one of the oasis towns on the edge of the Taklamakan desert. Thanks to Central Asia's geography, it was destined never to reach the open ocean.

We spent the next couple of days packing up and hauling our sledges down the valley. The snow had melted from our first campsite, and we pitched the tent on grass. Driving back across the passes we encountered the first brave herders going the other way. They were taking their livestock over the mountains to find the best spots for grazing on the high plateau. Coming down from Ak-shirak felt like an extreme transition from winter to spring. As the black and white landscape of the high mountains gave way to green forests and the blue of the lake, we were greeted by the flowering apricot trees along the shore of Issyk-kul. The last few days were spent enjoying Kyrgyz hospitality and food in both Karakol and Bishkek.

These mountains offer serious possibilities for both ski mountaineering and alpinism, although as remarked by the previous teams, the lack of snow is ever more pronounced. In our case, many of the peaks were barely covered with ice not far below. This makes crossing the Suek pass much easier, which together with the repaired bridge means that access via the Karak-say valley is a good means of entering the massif. The sloping terrain and the nature of the glaciers lend themselves to pulks. There is a lot of potential for beautiful lines and new ascents.

Mount Everest Foundation

Loch Scavaig, Isle of Skye
William Daniell (1769-1837)
c1819. Watercolour with gouache and scraping over graphite
on medium, slightly textured, cream wove paper, pasted on very thick,
slightly textured, cream card. 8¼ x 12¼ inches.
Yale Center for British Art, Paul Mellon Collection.

BILL RUTHVEN

Recollections of
an MEF Secretary

Bill Ruthven meeting Her Majesty the Queen during the
60th anniversary celebrations of the first ascent of Everest in 2013.

I am sometimes asked how I became involved with the Mount Everest
Foundation. The basic reason can be traced back to the early 1950s, when
as a student at Loughborough College I was a keen member of the college
mountaineering club. One fellow member was a guy called Bob Pettigrew,
and in 1954 I took part in an expedition to Lyngen in Arctic Norway led
by Bob: at the time he was the club chairman, and I was the secretary. Our
paths crossed again in 1977, when he was president of the BMC and I was
honorary secretary of the Lake District Area Committee.

By 1985, Bob was chairman of the MEF Screening Committee, and
when the then secretary found the work too much, Bob asked if I would
be interested in taking it on. At the time I was going through a bad patch
at work and this seemed an ideal opportunity to get involved in something
entirely different. So once again it was 'Chairman Bob' and 'Secretary Bill'.

Meetings of the Screening Committee were always interesting. At one of the earliest, we were interviewing a couple of 'young hards' who thought that they were going to the ends of the earth, when an elderly bespectacled gentleman sitting at the end of the table asked where they planned to establish their base camp. They mumbled the name of a well-known village, to which he suggested that if they progressed slightly further up the valley they would find a level grass area on which to pitch their tents, with good water in a nearby stream. The elderly gentleman was Sir Edward Peck, who had explored mountains all over the world while serving his country in a variety of diplomatic postings.

For some years the MEF Committee of Management had a separate secretary, Bill Risoe, but in 1988 he decided to retire, and the chairman at the time, George Band, asked if I would be interested in taking over. His idea was that I would take on the C of M, and a new secretary would be appointed for the 'Screeners'. However, as the Screeners' secretary I did not attend meetings of the C of M so while I was the only person in direct contact with expedition leaders, I always had to wait some time to hear the outcome of the meetings from Bill before I could let the expedition leaders know the results of their grant applications. It therefore seemed sensible to revert to a single secretary (i.e. me) serving both committees, and this was agreed.

Between then and my 'retirement' in December 2013, the MEF kept me pretty busy dealing with several hundred leaders and expeditions, and attending over 130 meetings of one committee or another, tendering apologies for absence from just three due to spells in hospital. As now, the only real commitment of an expedition awarded a grant was to submit a report on the trip. But I soon discovered there were a number of past expeditions, which did not seem to have met this simple requirement. I felt it my duty to chase them until they did so. For this Ted Peck bestowed me the nickname 'Ruthless Ruthven'. But it had its results, revealing that one leader, having received an MEF grant, cancelled his trip and joined another one, which had also received an MEF grant, on the other side of the world. The 'diverted' grant was recovered, and future applications from the errant leader monitored carefully.

Although the majority of expeditions were made up of university students or graduates, I was shocked by the spelling and sometimes grammar displayed in the resultant reports. One example that sticks in my mind included the phrase: 'After much discussion, we all agreed to take alpine guitars.' Thoughts of an unusually musical expedition were dashed when I realised the team had selected 'alpine gaiters' as the best equipment to deal with the deep snow that was anticipated.

One day in 1987 I received a telephone call from a lady in New York called Wendy Davis, who told me that she was employed by an expedition being planned to celebrate the thirty-fifth anniversary of the first ascent of Everest by attempting a new route: the first alpine-style ascent of the east face without the use of bottled oxygen. It was hoped the team would include the sons of both Ed Hillary and Tenzing Norgay, and she asked if I could give her the telephone number of John Hunt, who was to be invited to be 'honorary co-leader'. While I would not normally pass on a number, this seemed to be a very special case, and I did as she asked. Later I discovered that John had suggested including a British climber in the team to make it truly international. His proposal was Stephen Venables. Over the next months I received several more calls from Wendy, culminating in one in which she excitedly told me that of all the team, only Stephen had reached the summit of Everest, and he was now back in UK, about to appear on the 'Wongan Show'. A few hours later I watched on TV as Terry 'Wongan' interviewed not only Stephen, but also Dr Charlie Clarke, who had by chance met up with him in Kathmandu, and treated his frostbitten nose and toes.

In May 1993, the MEF celebrated the fortieth anniversary of the first ascent of Everest with a lecture and reception at the Royal Geographical Society. Our patron, Prince Philip, was already committed to attend another event, but we were delighted Her Majesty the Queen and Princess Anne accepted instead. As we chatted informally with the Royals I looked round hopefully for the official photographers, but in vain. Later I learned that the Queen had requested no photos during this part of the evening. Bob later consoled me: 'But I'm sure she'll tell her friends that she met you.'

In those days, the Screening Committee tended to be a group of specialists, who remained as long as they desired, with no specified time limit. Most expeditions applying for support were interviewed, which led to some very long meetings, the longest being in March 1989 which started at 9am and finished at 9pm, during which time no less than 36 trips were interviewed. But in 1994 the C of M decided that like themselves, the Screeners should be subject to a six-year period in office: this took effect in 1995 and Stephen Venables was transferred from the C of M to chair the Screeners. About the same time, it was decided more applications should be considered 'on paper'.

In May 1995 I received an enquiry from a Mr White, deputy head of mission in the British Embassy in Tel Aviv. He asked me to comment on the achievements of 'K D', a British subject currently living in Israel, who claimed to have climbed many of the world's highest peaks, including Everest twice, and was seeking a reference for an expedition he was planning to New Zealand. He intended to include an Israeli and an Arab in his team, and make the first ascent of an unnamed peak, which he intended to dedicate to peace. At the time I kept a database of successful Everesters, on which his name was conspicuously absent. He claimed that his second ascent, in 1990, was on an expedition led by Stephen Venables, but Stephen confirmed he had not been back to Everest since his dramatic ascent in 1988. And, like me, Stephen had never heard of KD. Other claims included being a top competition climber – fourth in Britain – and acting as a stunt double in several well-known films. A long and fanciful article about him, in the *Jerusalem Post*, carried the sub-heading: 'K D has not lived down his reputation as the country's top sport climber.' Why should he?

This was my first experience of the Walter Mitty type; not so for Mr White, who as a diplomat in Israel was familiar with the well-documented Jerusalem syndrome: 'I suspect that Mr D is the possessor of a rather fanciful imagination … It is likely that he will be numbered amongst the many we meet who claim close kinship or actually to be the Messiah, but who unfortunately have lost their passports, have no money etc.'

With more and more ascents of Mount Everest being recorded, some people seem to forget that it is the highest mountain on earth, and is still not 'an easy day for a lady'. In addition to relevant enquiries, I have received some from individuals with remarkably little mountaineering knowledge or experience. Possibly the ultimate was a telephone call from a young man I received in November 1993. After general introductions, the call went something like this:

Caller: I've decided that I would like to climb Mount Everest

MEF: Oh! Are you very rich?

Caller: Not particularly. Why?

MEF: Well, it is a rather expensive exercise these days, but let's come back to that later. When were you thinking of going to Everest?

Caller: Next summer, when I have finished college. I would prefer to climb it in the summer, as I don't like climbing in the cold. [!]

MEF: Have you climbed in the Himalaya before?

Caller: No.

MEF: Okay, then tell me about your Alpine experience.

Caller: Well, I've never actually been to the Alps.

MEF: What have you climbed then?

Caller: I climbed a mountain in South Africa once.

MEF: How high was that?

Caller: About five thousand.

MEF: (With tongue in cheek) Feet or metres?

Caller: Feet, I think.

MEF: I think that you ought to have a few seasons of Alpine climbing and then maybe one or two trips to the Greater Ranges before you consider Everest.

Caller: But that is going to cost a lot of money! Do I have to pay some sort of fee to climb Everest?

MEF: Yes. Assuming you plan to climb from the Nepali side, the local authorities charge a peak fee, which is currently $50,000 for a party of up to five.

Caller: But that's ridiculous. Is there a reduction for students?

MEF: Highly unlikely. The mountain is in their country, so whatever we think or do, they can charge what they like. There are many other costs to consider, apart from just getting to and from Nepal. I think that you'd be most unlikely to stage an expedition to Everest these days for less than, say, £100,000.

Caller: But I can't afford that!

MEF: I suggest you might talk to one of the British companies, which are offering commercial trips: one has just succeeded in getting several clients to the summit. But I think they would expect a reasonable level of experience before they would be prepared to accept you as a paying team member.

At this stage the caller, by now thoroughly demoralised, thanked me for my assistance and said goodbye. I wonder what happened to him? These days, he might well find someone to take him.

After 50-odd years carrying heavy rucksacks up hills in many countries, I was suffering severe back pain. All attempts to relieve this proved to be short-lived at best and mostly ineffective, so in 1997 I was referred to a 'top' spinal surgeon. His proposed solution was an operation to 'decompress' my spine, and construct internal 'scaffolding' to hold it in position. Although the surgery was successful, during or immediately after the operation I developed an epidural haematoma, or blood clot, which was not addressed for a whole week, by which time I was paraplegic due to cauda equina syndrome. Thus what was expected to be about two weeks in hospital was extended to six months. Having walked into hospital, when I eventually left it was in a wheelchair. But unlike most of the patients on my ward, I wasn't idle. Apart from reading many books, particularly during physiotherapy sessions, I endeavoured to keep up to date with MEF work, using a borrowed laptop to write letters onto floppy discs, which were then given to my daughter to print and post. During this time I received letters of support from many people, including John Hunt and Chris Bonington, encouraging me not to give up my MEF work. This was excellent advice, and gave me a reason to get up each morning.

The Duke of Edinburgh has been patron of the MEF from day one, and I have had the honour of meeting him on several occasions. The first was in 2003 when he and the Queen joined us in celebrating the fiftieth anniversary of the first ascent of Everest. We were arranged in groups around a sumptuous room in Spencer House. Unfortunately, the edge of the carpet became caught up in my wheels, and I was busy trying to untangle things when I suddenly became aware of a tall figure looking down on me.

'You don't need to back away from me,' he said.

Forgetting the detailed instructions we had received on how to address royalty, I replied: 'Oh, hello there!'

In fact, Philip could usually be relied on to have a (not always tactful) cheery quip. In December 2011 a reception for 'explorers' to celebrate the centenary of Captain Scott's trip to the South Pole was held at Buckingham Palace. All attendees were provided with cards bearing their names and professions, which were read out by a palace official as they reached the head of the queue to meet the Queen and Duke. On learning that Malcolm Bass was a clinical psychologist, Prince Philip commented: 'You've come to the right place.' And at the 60th anniversary of Everest's first ascent, he met a number of people who had been closely associated with Everest expeditions, including Jan Morris who – as James Morris – had been *The Times* correspondent on the 1953 expedition. Moving on, he met Ronald Faux, who held a similar position on the army expedition of 1975. Prince Philip asked Ronnie: 'Has anything interesting happened to you since Everest?'

In 1987, I received a letter from a New Zealand publishing company enclosing a complimentary copy of a newly published book entitled

The Story of Everest National Park. At that time, the book was only available within New Zealand, but the letter offered further copies to the MEF at a very favourable rate, with profits to go to the Foundation if I would act as their UK agent. After discussion with the C of M, it was agreed I should investigate further and, if a viable proposition, I should import one hundred copies to sell for a figure that would ensure a reasonable profit for the MEF.

Although possibly outside my terms of reference, this was the first of a number of minor fund-raising schemes in which I was involved, with the three-fold aim of raising the profile of the MEF, celebrating outstanding expeditions and educating those who might want to go on future trips. In the early 1990s it was agreed that the MEF should initiate a series of annual lecture evenings. Although the first of these was originally intended to take place at the RGS, due to confusion over costs it was held in the Alpine Club in January 1992, and titled 'Mountain Expeditions of 1991', with the leaders of four very different trips talking about their achievements.

To avoid becoming too much of a drain on resources, for future events – held at various universities, Newcastle (1993), Sheffield (1994), Glasgow (1995), Bath (1996) and Manchester (2007) – I managed to raise some sponsorship. I had started work on a similar evening to be held at Oxford Brookes in January 1998, but had to hand over to other committee members when I went into hospital for my spinal operation in May 1997 and was still recovering in January, so could not even attend as a guest. In 2000, these events were to some extent replaced by a regular slot at the Kendal Mountain Film Festival.

In 1994, its 50th anniversary, each place setting at the annual dinner of the British Mountaineering Council included a specially engraved (but fully functional) souvenir karabiner. With the 50th anniversary of the first ascent of Everest looming, it occurred to me that if suitable terms could be agreed a similar karabiner could be sold to raise funds for the MEF: once more the C of M agreed. The inscription was '1953 – EVEREST – 2003' and until all one hundred were sold, I could be seen wearing a 'necklace' of karabiners whenever I attended mountain events like the Kendal festival.

After several years of negotiations, in November 2008 a settlement was finally reached regarding the photographs taken on Everest expeditions between 1921 and 1953. As part of the compensation for allowing the RGS to retain ownership of the photographs in perpetuity, it was agreed that the MEF would receive free use of the Ondaatje Theatre for one evening a year. This allowed the MEF to institute an annual fund-raising evening, which it has done ever since, sometimes linking up with other bodies, like the Himalayan Trust UK in 2013.

While I have thoroughly enjoyed my work for the MEF, I'm flattered to say that my efforts have not gone unnoticed. In 1999 I was granted honorary fellowship of the Royal Geographical Society and following nomination by the BMC, in 2002 I received a Torch Trophy Trust Award, which was presented by Princess Alexandra at a ceremony held in The Queen's Club. A few years later I was elected to honorary membership of the Alpine Club.

ANDY MACNAE

The Future of the MEF

Since its inception in the aftermath of Everest 1953, the Mount Everest Foundation has granted well over £1m to expeditions exploring and pushing the boundaries in virtually every mountain region on Earth. Key first ascents supported include new routes on Everest, Kangchenjunga, Annapurna, Shishapangma, Changabang, Nanga Parbat, Xuelian and the Ogre as well as many lightweight trips that have pushed forward the boundaries of modern mountaineering. Over 1,600 expeditions have benefited and many would not have happened without MEF support.

But it is always good for an organisation to occasionally take a look at itself and ask if it's doing as well as it could. Last year, when the MEF Committee of Management pondered this question, it appeared as though the answer might well be: 'not quite.' For one thing the number of grant applications was down on where it was at the start of the millennium; in particular we were seeing fewer applications from younger teams and first-time applicants. At the same time the MEF fund was growing and as a charity we needed to ask whether we were doing enough to get funding where it was needed. And then there were a number of governance questions around whether we were following best practice. So with all this in mind we did what any committee worth its salt would do and launched a review. And having been banging on about all this for some time I got the pleasure of co-ordinating it and along with some willing colleagues, pulled together everyone's views into some recommendations.

Importantly, the MEF committed to consider everything and anything; this gave us the licence to ask some challenging questions. Sometimes you need to play devil's advocate. One deliberately challenging question posed was: 'Does the MEF matter anymore?' It was revealing to see just how passionate responses were. On one hand we could point to the decline in application numbers and, most importantly, a general feeling among members of the committee that many expeditions would have happened with or without MEF support; at the same time policy limited what we could do for really ambitious trips. On the other hand we can always point to genuinely innovative and exploratory trips still happening today that epitomise what the MEF is all about.

So in asking questions like this we were trying to focus on what difference the MEF should be making in the future. We agreed we want to see MEF funding making the difference between expeditions going and not going, and helping climbers and scientists think about ambitious trips to places that they couldn't otherwise afford. And so the key review question to us was how we might adapt the grant system to deliver this? At the same time we wanted to address some parallel issues:

- Is the MEF well governed? Do we follow best practice?
- Are the objectives of the organisation appropriate for today? Here's a little known fact: the charitable objectives of the Mount Everest Foundation don't actually include the word 'mountaineering' but focus on exploration and science in mountain regions.
- Do enough people know about the MEF and the grants we offer? And do these grants feel accessible? Are they perceived as elitist? With fewer applications from younger teams this seemed a valid concern.
- In any case, can we make the grant information and application process more transparent and easy to use?

Focussing on the task, we could see our review was really about two things. First, the business of simply making sure how the MEF is managed keeps up with best practice and second, and more interestingly, ensuring the MEF continues to make a difference by enabling exciting, cutting edge and exploratory trips to happen when they would not otherwise have done so. I could fill pages with a blow-by-blow account of the review process and all the debates that underpinned it. But time is short, so let's skip that and see what we came up with.

Our work and recommendations were grouped into three areas: governance, publicity and grant policy. Taking governance first and quickly: we decided we couldn't see any need for a wholesale rewrite of the constitution or objectives. We recognised just how widely 'exploration' could be interpreted (i.e. not just in terms of geography) and also that we could and should be doing more to support science in the mountains. Particularly when it has positive repercussions for mountaineers. We recommended tweaking the committee membership to add the treasurer and honorary secretary as full members and looking at trustee retirement to maintain institutional memory. That was about it.

Onto the meaty stuff: we wanted to see a radical change in the way that the application process worked and the outcome in terms of what the grants made possible. The main change we recommended was that applicants be invited to request a grant amount and then be asked to justify this on the basis of need and fit with MEF objectives. And while total grants given in a year clearly need to be within limits of affordability, and applicants may well not get all they ask for, this opens the way for trips to expensive destinations to ask for significant sums. It also means that teams with very limited funding of their own can apply for a higher percentage of the expedition costs.

Alongside this we recommended expeditions be able to apply up to two years in advance and this new approach to be backed up by investment in much wider publicity and a more accessible application process. This will result in a new website and more MEF activity on social media and

The iconic image of Ian Clough jumaring on the south face of Annapurna in 1970.
The Mount Everest Foundation underwrote the expedition, covering expenses
and in return receiving expedition income from book and film rights and the
immediate post-expedition lectures, which all members of the team took part in,
receiving a modest fee. Bonington was paid a fee for writing the book and had
a budget for paying team members who contributed. The deal was brokered by
Bonington's well-connected agent George Greenfield, through his contact with
Douglas Busk, at the time chair of the MEF. The expedition made a reasonable
profit for the MEF. *(Chris Bonington Picture Library)*

at events. We want to target student and scientific groups in particular and make sure MEF support feels accessible to them. As well as direct publicity we also recommended that the MEF be more proactive in supporting events that disseminate information to potential expeditions and raise awareness of objectives and best practice: things like the BMC expedition seminars or AC symposia.

What does this new approach to grants mean in practice? I'll give two hypothetical examples, neither of which could happen under the old system.

A team of four really keen young climbers, who spend most of their time climbing and so don't have huge incomes, have spotted a great new line on an unclimbed 6,500m peak in Sikkim. The trip is genuinely exploratory and a long way from the road. They have done their best to minimise the budget but the cost of permits, porters and so on are still pretty high and so when the team add up the budget it looks unaffordable. At best they can manage about a third of the cost through their own funds and other likely grants (e.g. BMC) but this still leaves over £10,000 to find. In the past the team may simply have concluded that the trip was not on and opted instead for a good Alpine season. But under the proposed MEF system they can apply for this full amount on the basis of need, because the expedition couldn't go without it, and the fit with MEF objectives, being a highly exploratory trip in both geographical and personal terms.

In the second example, a team are looking at a world-class objective in a remote and hard-to-reach location. The trip might combine exploratory mountaineering with cutting-edge science. The budget would be pretty large (six figures) but the team reckon they have a good chance of getting sponsors and research funding for around 80% of the cost. But this will still leave them short and in any case they need to build funder confidence in the trip. Under the new system they could apply to the MEF two years in advance for what they think will be the funding gap. Let's say this is £25,000. If the team can make their case in terms of need and fit with objectives the MEF may choose to grant this amount provisional on the other funding being realised. This would then let the team go out and raise the rest of the cash with some confidence. In the case of such a big grant the MEF may well apply extra conditions in terms of acknowledgment, the level of report, use of images and support from the expedition members for future MEF fundraising.

I should stress that the larger grants, say £7,500, will remain the exception and that for very large grants, say £15,000, both the objective and team will need to be absolutely top class and able to demonstrate clearly that they have exhausted all other funding options as in the example above. And we will keep all this under review. But hopefully we will see British teams now looking differently at innovative, hard-core and exploratory objectives worldwide, both in terms of mountaineering and science, knowing that the Mount Everest Foundation wants to help make these trips possible.

For further information on the MEF and to apply for a grant please visit the MEF website *www.mef.org.uk*.

Science & Nature

The Junction of Lyon and Tay
John Warwick Smith (1749-1831)
1788. Watercolour over graphite on medium, slightly textured, beige wove
paper. 12⅛ x 17⅝ inches. Yale Center for British Art, Paul Mellon Collection.

JONATHAN BAMBER,
RICHARD ALLEY & DAN LUNT

The Response of Glaciers
to Climate Change

A photograph of Dig Tsho, the moraine-dammed lake in the Everest region
of Nepal. This breached in 1985 causing significant downstream damage,
including the destruction of a newly-constructed hydropower facility.
(Courtesy of Matt Westoby, Northumbria University)

Glaciers worldwide are shrinking because of global warming, which, since the latter half of the 20th century, has primarily been driven by carbon dioxide released by burning fossil fuels. Going further back in time, climate has always changed, albeit usually at a much slower rate than today, and glacier sizes have always fluctuated; knowledge of those past changes actually strengthens the scientific understanding that today's are primarily caused by humans, and could become much greater in the future.

The authors of this article are active scientists who have been working on climate and glaciological research for many decades, collectively just shy of a century. We have published some 500 peer-reviewed articles on these topics, which have been referenced about 24,000 times in other articles. We state this not to impress, simply to indicate that we have a deep understanding of the topics discussed and the current scientific consensus. This article does not represent the personal views of the authors. Our aim is to summarise this scientific understanding of past, present and future climate change and how it has, and will, impact glaciers around the world. It is not intended to be an exhaustive or comprehensive assessment and we

143

Jonathan Bamber, one of the authors of this article, on the White Spider, north face of the Eiger, August 1989. Today, the route is best climbed in November or spring, due to deterioration of the ice fields. *(Wil Hurford)*

have tried to avoid technical detail, which can be explored further in the references provided, many of which are subscription free. There are aspects of climate change research where open questions exist and a consensus is lacking. Here, however, we concentrate on what is well established and has high certainty.

The vast majority of glaciers worldwide are currently shrinking[1]. Careful monitoring programmes and satellite surveys confirm anecdotal evidence that mountain ranges are changing, affecting routes and creating hazards. In the summer of 2003, for example, local authorities, for the first time in the history of alpinism, 'closed' routes on Mont Blanc and the Matterhorn because of heightened rock fall hazards. Entire icefalls and crevasse fields have disappeared as their glaciers melted away. Landslides are increasing in some places as permafrost melts, and as shrinking glaciers no longer buttress steep valley walls. In other places, glacier retreat has left lakes behind unstable moraine dams, raising the danger of outburst floods[2].

1. D G Vaughan et al, *Climate Change 2013: The Physical Science Basis. Contribution of Working Group I to the Fifth Assessment Report of the Intergovernmental Panel on Climate Change*. T F Stocker et al (eds), Cambridge & New York, Cambridge University Press, 2013, pp317-82.
2. S J Cook et al, 'Glacier Change and Glacial Lake Outburst Flood Risk in Bolivian Andes', *The Cryosphere* **10**, 2016, pp2399-413.

Figure 1 Past CO_2 concentrations (blue solid line) and temperature (red line) recorded in an Antarctic ice core, going back 800,000 years. Also shown are recent observations of atmospheric CO_2 concentrations and the current atmospheric CO_2 concentration (c400ppm) measured since the 1950s from the Mauna Loa Observatory, Hawaii, often called the Keeling Curve. *(Data courtesy of NOAA National Climatic data Center, USA)*

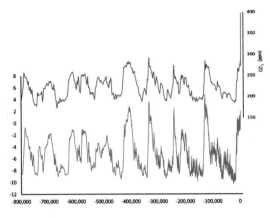

The photograph opposite was taken almost 30 years ago, in August 1989, from one of the most famous and iconic mountaineering routes in the world: the Eigerwand. The White Spider looks nothing like this today; the ice fields are so depleted and have deteriorated so much in just three decades that the route is best climbed in November or in spring. Is this due to natural variations in the climate system, or human-induced climate change? Glaciers have changed in the past, but what contribution, if any, are humans making? Here, we summarize some of the evidence on the long but clear scientific path leading from the observation of glacier shrinkage to the confident statement that humans are primarily responsible for current trends[3]. This path takes us through our understanding of glaciers, the physics of the climate system, computer climate models, recent observations, and much more.

First, it is useful to restate the difference between climate and weather. The latter is what happens in a particular day, month or season. Weather is inherently noisy and variable. Climate is the average state over a longer time period, often taken as 30 years by meteorologists. The idea is that taking the average over this period reduces the effects of variations in weather so that long-term trends can be identified. Glacier length variations act as natural thermometers for measuring changing *climate*, as discussed later, because they tend to average out year-to-year fluctuations due to weather and respond on timescales of tens to hundreds of years depending on their size and climatic setting[4]. The surface of a glacier can rise and fall in response to 'weather' (for example between the winter accumulation and summer melt seasons) but changes in extent are more gradual as the average glacier motion adjusts slowly to changes in climate. Typical Alpine glaciers have average speeds of about 100m per year.

3. Intergovernmental Panel on Climate Change, *Climate Change 2013: The Physical Science Basis. Contribution of Working Group I to the Fifth Assessment Report of the Intergovernmental Panel on Climate Change.* T F Stocker et al (eds), Cambridge & New York, Cambridge University Press, 2013, pp1-30.
4. W S B Paterson, *The Physics of Glaciers*, 3rd edn, Oxford, Pergamon, 1994, p480.

Climate and glaciers, including the great ice sheets that cover Greenland and Antarctica, have changed in the past, long before humans influenced climate, indeed, long before humans even existed (see *Figure 2*), but a 'four-legged stool' of evidence supports the understanding that recent warming, over the last few decades, and glacier shrinkage are primarily human-caused; these lines of evidence include physics, past climate and ice changes, recent observational data, and computer climate and ice models.

We'll now consider these four 'legs' of evidence, before addressing what they mean for future glacier and ice sheet changes.

The first leg: physics

Extracting and burning carbon-rich material such as coal, oil and gas increases carbon dioxide (CO_2) concentrations in the atmosphere. The human source is roughly one hundred times the natural volcanic source, and CO_2 concentrations in the atmosphere are currently increasing rapidly. Concentrations now exceed 400ppm, meaning that for every one million molecules in the atmosphere, 400 of them are CO_2 (see *Figure 1*). This is greater than at any time over about the last three million years[5]. The warming influence from this (i.e. the 'greenhouse effect') was first calculated by the Swedish chemist Arrhenius in 1896 and physics tells us that there is simply no known way to increase CO_2 concentrations and not have a warming influence, a signal that is routinely observed by satellites and terrestrial data, and also seen in ice cores drilled in Antarctica which go back 800,000 years (*Figure 1*). Without this warming effect of CO_2 and other greenhouse gases, simple physics tells us that our planet would be in a 'snowball' state, with temperatures about 30°C cooler than they are today.

The physics of glaciers is also well understood. Glaciers can change for many reasons, but they are most sensitive to temperature. Warming increases the melt rate on the warmest days and lengthens the melt season, and shifts the snowline higher to include more of the glacier in the zone of melting. It also switches some snowfall to rain. Conversely, warmer air can deliver more moisture when snowing, by roughly 7% per degree C, leading to occasionally heard speculation that warming should instead grow ice. However, across multiple glaciers, loss of ice due to melting increases about 35% per degree C, with some variations[6], meaning that the loss due to warming clearly dominates. In rare cases, changes in debris cover, or in supply of snow by avalanches, or other factors can cause a glacier to grow in a warming climate, and the tendency of some glaciers to surge or otherwise vary for internal reasons means you may need to monitor a glacier for a while to know what it is really doing. However, the great majority of glaciers shrink with warming, and glaciers are actually quite accurate thermometers for past climate, as discussed above[7].

5. M Pagani et al, 'High Earth-system Climate Sensitivity Determined from Pliocene Carbon Dioxide Concentrations', *Nature Geoscience* 3, 2010, pp27-30.
6. J Oerlemans and B K Reichert, 'Relating Glacier Mass Balance to Meteorological Data by Using a Seasonal Sensitivity Characteristic', *Journal of Glaciololgy* 46, 2000, pp1-6.
7. J Oerlemans, 'Extracting a Climate Signal from 169 Glacier Records', *Science* 308, 2005, pp675-7.

Figure 2 Global ocean oxygen isotope compilation from more than 40 ocean sediment cores shows several major climate transitions. Note the shift from 'greenhouse to icehouse' conditions at 34 Ma BP[8].

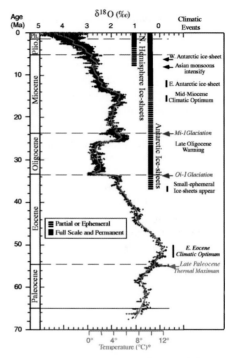

The second leg: past climate and ice changes

What about the big changes in climate and ice cover further in the past? These happened with no help from humans. However, as we shall see, they ultimately help confirm our understanding that human-induced climate change is important and becoming more important.

There are many ways of reconstructing past climate and ice changes. One of these is by examining the ratio of two isotopes of oxygen, with atomic mass of 18 versus 16, or ^{18}O and ^{16}O, found in the shells of ancient fossils layered in the sediment at the bottom of the ocean. These we can extract by drilling cores into the ocean floor. Tiny sea creatures called foraminifera live in the lowest layers of the ocean and their shells are made of calcium carbonate ($CaCO_3$). Next time you go climbing in Pembroke, the Dolomites or Julian Alps, remember those cliffs were all underwater millions of years ago and what you're hanging off are dead microfossils. The oxygen isotope ratio, $\partial^{18}O$, depends on the temperature of the oceans and the volume of ice on land and can be used as a 'paleo-thermometer'. Figure 2 shows this paleo-thermometer record for the last 65 million years, since the extinction of the dinosaurs, obtained from multiple ocean sediment cores[8]. About 35 million years ago, or 35Ma BP, there was a change from 'greenhouse to icehouse', or more formally the Eocene-Oligocene transition, when a relatively abrupt cooling of about 4°C took place. This is when extensive ice fields first started forming in Antarctica, at the same time as a decrease in atmospheric CO_2 and while South America and Australia were moving away from Antarctica, forming the Drake Passage and the Antarctic continent we know today (not as erroneously stated in *AJ* 2016, at 1Ma BP[9]). Extensive ice cover in Greenland is more recent, starting around 3.5Ma BP, with large fluctuations in extent since then[10].

8. J Zachos et al, 'Trends, Rhythms, and Aberrations in Global Climate 65 Ma to Present', *Science* **292**, 2001, pp686-93.
9. E Mearns and A Milne, 'The Shrinking Glacier Conundrum', *Alpine Journal*, 2016, pp195-207.
10. R B Alley et al, 'History of the Greenland Ice Sheet: Paleoclimatic Insights', *Quaternary Science Reviews* **29**, 2010, pp1728-56.

Clearly there have been dramatic shifts and transitions in the climate conditions of the planet in the past. We believe that these are driven primarily by changes in atmospheric CO_2[11][12], with contributions also from changes in the paleo-geography, the positions of the continents, variations in solar radiation reaching the Earth due to fluctuations of the Earth's rotation and orbit around the sun, and complex feedbacks between these and other parts of the climate system[8]. It is important to note, however, that the changes shown in *Figure 2* were slow compared to human timescales. The E-O transition, for example, took place in two stages over about 500,000 years. That is about two thousand times longer than the time since the start of the Industrial Revolution.

Once the ice began growing in the high latitudes and altitudes, it has waxed and waned, especially in the Northern Hemisphere, for reasons that at first had nothing to do with CO_2. Features of Earth's orbit and axis of rotation result in subtle shifts of sunlight around the planet, pole-wards or equator-wards, later in spring or later in autumn. For example, the North Pole does not point straight up from the plane in which the Earth orbits the sun, being tilted at about 23°, and as a result, the summer sun warms the pole. This 'obliquity' changes slightly over time, as the gravitational pull of other objects in the solar system tug at the Earth and cause the tilt to change, on a cycle of about 41,000 years. Higher obliquity – more tilt – allows relatively more sunlight at the poles, and relatively less at the equator. In addition, the direction that the North Pole points towards, known as the 'North Star' (currently Polaris), changes over 19,000 to 23,000 years. The 'North Star' was Vega 14,000 years ago. The shape of Earth's orbit becomes more and less elliptical over about 100,000 years as Jupiter tugs on us every time we pass it in the orbit. The great mathematician-astronomer Milutin Milankovitch calculated these changes in the early 20th century, predicting they would show up in ice-age records when geologists finally assembled good enough records.

And he was right! The Swiss-American scientist Louis Agassiz consolidated the idea of cycles in glacier retreat and advance. He noticed large rocks, known as erratics, like those used for bouldering throughout the Chamonix valley, that could only have been transported to where they were by glaciers that were no longer present. Thus developed the idea of ice ages, or glacial-interglacial cycles. During periods when summer sunlight has been relatively weak in the far north, ice has grown, whereas during periods when summer sunlight has been relatively strong, ice has melted. The Southern Hemisphere is less important for causing variations in ice sheets; ice has sat on Antarctica for tens of millions of years, and there isn't much land nearby for southern ice to grow, so the big northern landmasses have dominated. In addition, the vast ice sheets in the Northern Hemisphere

11. R M DeConto and D Pollard, 'Rapid Cenozoic Glaciation of Antarctica Induced by Declining Atmospheric CO_2', *Nature* **421**, 2003, pp245-9.
12. D J Lunt et al, 'Late Pliocene Greenland Glaciation Controlled by a Decline in Atmospheric CO_2 Levels', *Nature* **454**, 2008, pp1102-5.

during cold ice-age 'glacial' periods changed many other things in the climate. Sea level dropped over 100m, winds shifted, desert dust was blown around in different patterns, ocean currents rearranged – and some CO_2 shifted from the atmosphere into the deep ocean. During glacials, not only did the ice sheets covering Antarctica and Greenland expand but there were also ice sheets covering Eurasia and North America: the latter called the Laurentide Ice Sheet. At the Last Glacial Maximum, around 21,000 years ago, global average sea level was some 120m lower than the present day[13]. There isn't a single factor responsible for these dramatic shifts in ice cover, but many processes clearly contributed, and the evidence of the CO_2 decrease is very clear (see *Figure 1*). Furthermore, our computer climate models (the fourth leg of the stool) cannot reproduce the cold temperatures of the glacial periods without including the effect of decreased CO_2. Essentially the whole world cooled when sunshine dropped in the far north, and warmed when northern sunshine rose over ice-age cycles, even though large areas of the world had opposite trends in sunshine; the regions that cooled with rising sunshine and warmed with falling sunshine are explained by the trends in CO_2, and not explained otherwise.

The third leg: recent observational data
The last of the major deglaciations started after the Last Glacial Maximum, 21,000 years ago. The interglacial (i.e. relatively warm) period we are now experiencing began about 12,000 BP and is called the Holocene. It is during this period that civilisations and arable farming practices developed and it is characterised by a relatively stable climate compared to past glacials and interglacials. Nonetheless, there have been a number of periods of slight warming, such as the Medieval Climate Anomaly and cooling such as the Little Ice Age, both of which lasted several hundred years[14] (*Figure 3* over-leaf). Cooling from the sun-blocking effect of particles from large volcanic eruptions, and temperature changes from slight changes in the brightness of the sun, were instrumental in these small climate changes.

The average global temperature difference between these two events is estimated to be 0.24°C[14] but the effect in the Northern Hemisphere climate was more dramatic. In Europe, the Little Ice Age ended around 1850 and this roughly coincides with the Holocene maximum extent of glaciers in the Alps and elsewhere in the Northern Hemisphere. Since the late 19th century these glaciers have been receding in response to warmer temperatures. *Figure 3* shows the temperature anomalies, deviations from the average, for the last two thousand years for the Northern Hemisphere based on multiple indirect (e.g. tree rings) and instrumental records[15]. All these records show a marked warming trend at the beginning of the 20th century,

13. E Bard et al, 'Deglacial Sea-level Record from Tahiti Corals and the Timing of Global Meltwater Discharge', *Nature* **382**, 1996, pp241-4.
14. M E Mann et al, 'Global Signatures and Dynamical Origins of the Little Ice Age and Medieval Climate Anomaly' *Science* **326**, 2009, pp1256-60.
15. V Masson-Delmotte et al, in *Climate Change 2013: The Physical Science Basis. Contribution of Working Group I to the Fifth Assessment Report of the Intergovernmental Panel on Climate Change*. T F Stocker et al (eds), Cambridge & New York, Cambridge University Press, 2013, pp383–464.

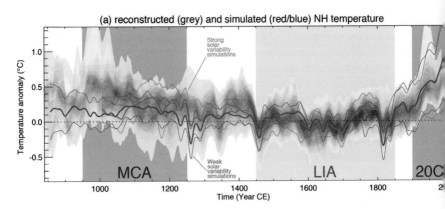

Figure 3 Reconstructed and modelled temperature variations for the Northern Hemisphere over the last millennium, adapted from Fig 5.8 of the IPCC Fifth Assessment Report, Chapter 5[15]. The grey cloud shows the spread of reconstructions from different 'paleo-proxies' such as tree rings, glacier length records, borehole temperatures etc. The thick red and blue lines represent multi-model mean reconstructions using natural (volcanic and solar activity) and human (greenhouse gases) with strong and weak solar variations.
The relative warmth of the Medieval Climate Anomaly and cooling of the Little Ice Age can be compared to the warming of the 20th century.

on top of a less intense warming coming out of the Little Ice Age. Not surprisingly, glaciers responded to that warming. It is apparent that the rate and magnitude of warming is unprecedented during the last two thousand years. Interestingly, the rate of sea level rise over the same time period shows a similar trend[16] and the rate over the last 25 years of 3.2mm per year is around twice the value for the 20th century[17]. Warming since the pre-industrial era, defined as pre-1880 when CO_2 concentrations in the atmosphere were around 280ppm, is 0.85°C, equivalent to over three times the contrast between the Medieval Climate Anomaly and the Little Ice Age[18]. Atmospheric CO_2 levels now exceed 400ppm (*Figure 1*).

The fourth leg: computer climate and ice models
So how much of the observed warming and glacier shrinking is due to natural variability in the climate system and how much is due to human-induced warming as a consequence of the increased concentrations of greenhouse gases? The most comprehensive synthesis of evidence addressing this question was undertaken by the Intergovernmental Panel on Climate

16. R E Kopp et al, 'Temperature-driven Global Sea-level Variability in the Common Era' *Proceedings of the National Academy of Sciences* **113**, 2016, E1434-41.
17. J A Church et al, *Climate Change 2013: The Physical Science Basis. Contribution of Working Group I to the Fifth Assessment Report of the Intergovernmental Panel on Climate Change.* T F Stocker et al (eds), Cambridge & New York, Cambridge University Press, 2013, pp1137-1216.
18. D L Hartmann et al, *Climate Change 2013: The Physical Science Basis. Contribution of Working Group I to the Fifth Assessment Report of the Intergovernmental Panel on Climate Change.* T F Stocker et al (eds), Cambridge & New York, Cambridge University Press, 2013, pp159-254.

Change (IPCC) and published in their Fifth Assessment Report (AR5)[19]. Electronic copies of individual chapters are freely available from the IPCC website: *https://www.ipcc.ch/report/ar5/wg1/*.

Their conclusions concerning the causes of recent warming were primarily based on comparing the results of computer climate models (known as General Circulation Models, or GCMs) with observations (*Figure 3*). GCMs encapsulate our understanding of physics in a numerical form, which can be solved on a computer. They produce remarkably accurate simulations of the Earth's climate, with storms riding the prevailing westerlies, a Gulf Stream in the Atlantic, a realistic Indian monsoon, El Niño events, and the other major features of our climate system that we know. These GCMs are used for weather forecasting as well as climate science, often the same model for both.

The AR5 was written by several hundred climate scientists, synthesising the results of several thousand publications and studies. We will not replicate that effort here! In summary, if the recent increase in CO_2 concentrations is 'turned off' in the models, then the simulated climate no longer matches reality, with observed recent warming no longer simulated by the model, contrary to observations. Applying GCMs to help understand the data shows humanity's fingerprint on recent changes[20].

The IPCC concluded from synthesising multiple studies that 'more than half of the observed increase in global mean surface temperature from 1951 to 2010 is very likely due to the observed anthropogenic [human-induced] increase in greenhouse gas concentrations.'[19] In this context, very likely means 90-100% confidence. There are other important conclusions in this and other chapters that are well worth exploring including a discussion of the role of solar forcing, the change in the average amount of solar energy absorbed per square metre of the Earth's area, on past and recent climate.

As well as climate models, there are also ice sheet and glacier computer models, which can similarly address the question of how natural versus human-induced warming has affected glaciers around the world, particularly over the last few decades? One thorough assessment of this question was undertaken in a recent study by Ben Marzeion at the University of Innsbruck and colleagues[20] in which they compared modelled and observed glacier mass balance, the balance between losses by melting and gains by precipitation, for both natural and 'full' (i.e. natural plus human) forcing (*Figure 4* overleaf).

The graphs in *Figure 4* are a little complicated but the key message is in panel C, which shows the proportion of glacier mass loss that is due to human-induced versus natural changes. In 1850 the percentage is close to zero, although human forcing had started, it was quite small compared to today. The year-to-year variations are large and noisy, but when smoothed

19. N L Bindoff et al, *Climate Change 2013: The Physical Science Basis. Contribution of Working Group I to the Fifth Assessment Report of the Intergovernmental Panel on Climate Change*. T F Stocker et al (eds), Cambridge & New York, Cambridge University Press, 2013, pp159-254.
20. B Marzeion et al, 'Attribution of Global Glacier Mass Loss to Anthropogenic and Natural Causes', *Science* **345**, 2014, pp919-21.

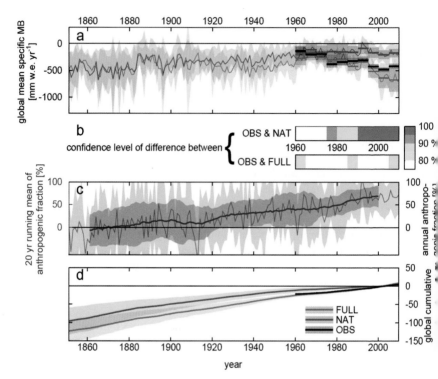

Figure 4 Attribution of glacier mass loss to natural and anthropogenic causes. Panel C shows the percentage of mass loss associated with human-induced climate change as a proportion of the total, while the top panel shows changes in the mass, and by inference volume, of glaciers around the world excluding the great ice sheets. The bars from 1960 represent five-year average values from direct and satellite-derived observations in black, modelled (natural and human) in red and modelled (natural only) in green. From about 1985 these two simulations diverge with 'natural only' being unable to reproduce the observations.

over twenty years, the solid blue line, a clear trend emerges. Over the whole period 1851-2010, 25% of glacier loss is due to humans. From 1991-2010, however, that fraction has increased to 69%[20]. So, while it is true to say that 'there is absolutely nothing unusual about glaciers melting during inter-glacials'[9], this statement is extremely misleading. What is 'unusual' in recent decades, are both the rate and the cause. As such, we think a more helpful statement is that 'there is absolutely nothing unusual about glaciers melting during inter-glacials, but the current rate (fast) and cause (human) is unprecedented in the entire period for which we have reliable observations.'

The future for glaciers and ice sheets?
So, that concludes the four-legged stool. What about the future of ice on the planet? Let's look briefly at some projections of glacier mass change over the next century based on several future climate scenarios produced

by the IPCC. Again, the most authoritative and comprehensive synthesis of projected climate change can be found in the IPCC report itself. Chapter 12 (*https://www.ipcc.ch/report/ar5/wg1/*) focuses on CO_2 scenarios and the response of parts of the climate system to these scenarios[21] while the reaction of glaciers and ice sheets is discussed in the subsequent chapter on sea level.

The choices we make now, and the effectiveness of climate action policy such as the Paris COP21 agreement will influence our future climate. There are several different pathways we, as a species, can follow. Which one we take will determine how the climate will evolve and the associated impacts. Various future emission scenarios were defined by the IPCC to explore how the climate system will evolve, called Representative Concentration Pathways (RCPs): the higher the number for the RCP, the greater the amount of CO_2 entering the atmosphere. The most pessimistic trajectory used was RCP8.5, which crudely equates to a business-as-usual scenario with emissions rising throughout the 21st century as a consequence of economic growth and minimal climate policy. For this pathway, the projections suggest that, by 2100, glaciers will have largely disappeared from central Europe, western Canada and the US, Svalbard, Caucasus, low-latitude areas and New Zealand. Other areas will experience significant volume losses but not as complete as these regions[22]. Whether this is a good or bad outcome of human-induced warming depends on what it is you're interested in. If you enjoy Alpine climbing or skiing the outlook is definitely bad for the European Alps[23]. Climate model simulations for the end of century indicate as much as a 50% reduction of snow cover even above 3,000m elevation. Remember also that, following a temperature increase, glaciers take a while to come into balance. If temperature were stabilized after warming, additional ice loss would occur for years to decades. We already are committed to more ice loss than has occurred, and similarly the warming projected by 2100 would cause additional mass loss beyond that date.

The IPCC, among many other organisations, summarised the strong scholarship that the negative consequences greatly outweigh the positive. (See IPCC Working Group 2 on impacts: *http://www.ipcc-wg2.awi.de/*) One particularly serious consequence of global warming is sea-level rise. Some 200 million people are at risk from a sea level rise of one metre, which for RCP8.5 could be achieved by the year 2100[24]. The Syrian refugee crisis that has so strained political stability and tolerance in Europe is 'only' about five million. Sea-level rise of this magnitude would be truly catastrophic. In a warming world, sea level increases through the dual effects of thermal

21. M Collins et al, *Climate Change 2013: The Physical Science Basis. Contribution of Working Group I to the Fifth Assessment Report of the Intergovernmental Panel on Climate Change.* T F Stocker et al (eds), Cambridge & New York, Cambridge University Press, 2013, pp1029-136.

22. B Marzeion, A H Jarosch, M Hofer, 'Past and Future Sea-level Change from the Surface Mass Balance of Glaciers', *The Cryosphere* 6, 2012, pp1295-1322.

23. C Marty et al, 'How Much Can We Save? Impact of Different Emission Scenarios on Future Snow Cover in the Alps', *The Cryosphere* 11, 2017, pp517-29.

24. J L Bamber and W P Aspinall, 'An Expert Judgement Assessment of Future Sea Level Rise from the Ice Sheets, *Nature Climate Change* 3, 2013, pp424-27.

expansion of the oceans and melting of land ice. During the last interglacial, called the Eemian, global average sea level was 6-9m higher than present[25], at a time when global ocean temperatures were 0.5°C warmer than pre-industrial and similar to the average for 1994-2014[26].

The Antarctic and Greenland ice sheets are huge. Anyone who has been to Antarctica will know how vast and humbling a landscape it is. These ice sheets contain enough water locked on land, to raise global mean sea level by 58m and 7.4m, respectively[1]. Antarctica covers an area larger than the lower 48 states of the US; the thickest ice is almost 5km thick in the interior. These are the 'super-tankers' of the climate system. In their slow-moving interior it can take thousands of years or longer to fully respond to changes in climate[4]. Around the edges, where the ice flows faster and, in particular, where it is in direct contact with the ocean, the response can be much faster. Once they have changed course, it will take a very long time to steer them in a different direction.

Projecting the response of these ice sheets to climate change is challenging because of complex linkages between the atmosphere, oceans and the ice and difficulties in observing and modelling processes that take place underneath 5km of ice. Nonetheless, observations from satellite data since 1992 indicate accelerating mass loss from both Greenland and the West Antarctic Ice Sheet[1], such that they are now contributing more than 1mm per year to sea-level rise. This may not sounds like much, but if the acceleration in mass loss continues it could soon become a serious threat to the stability of modern civilisation. The West Antarctic Ice Sheet, for example, is considered to be particularly vulnerable to changes in oceanic warming and has the potential to raise sea level by over 3m on its own[27]. Recent studies suggest it may have already passed the point of no return[28]. Other irreversible thresholds exist in the climate system and time is rapidly running out for us to implement affordable and palatable mitigation strategies[29]. We all have choices. Our future on the planet depends on those choices.

Note: The numbers presented in this article all have an error associated with them and, to aid readability, we have not included this error but note that they are all statistically significant to one standard deviation of the quoted uncertainty in the original manuscript.

25. R E Kopp et al, 'Probabilistic Assessment of Sea Level During the Last Interglacial Stage', *Nature* **462**, 2009, pp863-U851.
26. J S Hoffman et al, 'Regional and Global Sea-surface Temperatures During the Last Interglaciation', *Science* **355**, 2017, pp276-9.
27. J L Bamber et al, 'Reassessment of the Potential Sea-Level Rise from a Collapse of the West Antarctic Ice Sheet', *Science* **324**, 2009, pp901-3.
28. I Joughin, B E Smith, B Medley, 'Marine Ice Sheet Collapse Potentially Under Way for the Thwaites Glacier Basin, West Antarctica', *Science* **344**, 2014, pp735-8.
29. N Stern, *The Economics of Climate Change: The Stern Review*, Cambridge, Cambridge University Press, 2007.

MIKE PARSONS & MARY ROSE

Eiger Direct:
A Bareknuckle Fight

Equipment and men at the end of their tether. Top, Alexander Low's
publicity shot for the *Weekend Telegraph* featuring Layton Kor, Dougal Haston
and John Harlin with their equipment. Below, the successful summit climbers,
with Haston second from right in his shredded over-trousers.
(Chris Bonington Picture Library)

The high-profile first ascent of the Eiger Direct in 1966 was the subject recently of a widely praised book[1] by the journalist who covered the expedition, Peter Gillman, co-authored with Leni Gillman. This article looks at the clothing and equipment the climbers used, and how it compares with what we have today and what was available in 1938 for the first ascent of the north face. Parsons and Rose are the authors of Invisible on Everest: Innovation and the Gear Makers (Old City Publishing, 2002) and ran a research project on the garment textiles brought back from Everest following the discovery of George Mallory's body in 1999.

The 1966 Eiger Direct climb, like the first ascent of the north face in 1938, was a 'bareknuckle' fight: by today's standards clothing and equipment were primitive. While there had been some progress since 1938, the 1966 attempt was on the cusp of a revolutionary period involving both clothing and hardware. Not only were these emerging technologies not yet good enough, the polymer clothing was, arguably, worse than systems and products available in the 1920s. None of the branded textiles we know today had been created.

Furthermore, some of the latest equipment, which might have made a difference, wasn't used. Transfer of knowledge, techniques and products between different countries had been historically slow: before the Second World War it took decades. Language barriers, customs-duty borders and cultural differences all contributed to that delay. After the war the sharing of ideas began to accelerate and is now almost instantaneous thanks to social media. But the 1966 ascent took place at a time when tariff barriers across Europe were only starting to disappear. When, for example, Pete Hutchinson set up Mountain Equipment in the early 1960s, import duty on French down gear coming into UK was 40%.

Today the public perception is that leading mountaineers simply promote gear through sponsorship, but throughout 150 years of mountaineering development the key equipment innovators were not designers working for commercial manufacturers but climbers designing to achieve their own ends. We call these people 'lead users'. They have been responsible for around 70% of innovation in the history of mountaineering; the rest comes from 'commercial executions', changes made to boost sales. On the Eiger, mountaineers from different traditions met in the heat of action, shared equipment ideas and witnessed different techniques.

Eiger 1938
In 1922, Willo Welzenbach and his partner Fritz Rigele invented the first basic ice pitons, simple square bars with notches cut out by the local blacksmith, and used them on the first ascent of the Grosses Wiesbachhorn, where the steepest section was a 75° ice wall. This was the breakthrough that took the pre-Great War rope, karabiner and piton protection techniques of Hans Dülfer and friends in Germany onto steep ice faces in the Western Alps. Welzenbach put up another 11 major first ascents; for this and his creation of

1. P Gillman & L Gillman, *Extreme Eiger: Triumph and Tragedy on the North Face*, London, Simon & Schuster, 2016.

Left, the German leader on the Eiger Direct Jörg Lehne wearing a cotton over-suit and, right, the right-hand figure shoes what happened to it in bad weather: soaking up moisture and freezing. *(Chris Bonington Picture Library)*

the UIAA grading system he is sometimes referred to as the father of modern alpinism. These routes were just as steep as the Eiger; it was rock fall that differentiated that challenge, and publicity from the many deaths through the 1930s. Hinterstoisser's famous traverse was a function of the Dülfer technique using double ropes under tension, making retreat seemingly impossible.

Footwear in 1938 was nailed leather boots. German teams developed double boots for their 1930s Himalayan expeditions, but these were far too heavy and clumsy for Alpine use. Nail patterns were designed by selecting the most suitable nails for each section of the boot; Tricounis were arranged around the toe area and sides. Ropes were hemp, a natural fibre which absorbed water or snow and froze solid overnight. Clothing was almost all wool, either woven, 'loden', or knitted. Dachstein mitts were knitted and then felted to increase its density and windproof-ness. The climbers lacked down, even though it was used on Everest in 1922 and the 1930s. In 1933, Pierre Allain, best known for his rock boot, created a brilliant combined bivouac and clothing system incorporating the use of down, the cagoule and *pied d'éléphant*.

Of the four climbers, the two Germans, Heckmair and Vörg, were using 12-point crampons, still forged in that period, so they could climb facing inwards and move much faster than the Austrian pair, Harrer and Kasparek, who had one pair of 10-point crampons between them.

Eiger 1966

The two competing teams, German and Anglo-American, took the leading equipment of the day, influenced strongly by their own cultures and experiences and then modified after they found new methods and gear around the world. Both were drawing on Yosemite, that newly erupting volcano of innovative methodologies and translating them into an entirely different context. Sometimes the Germans compromised on cost, not wanting to pay for Angora wool as the leader suggested but opting instead for a cheaper wool and cotton mix. They didn't always understand the qualities of the new, and sometimes even the old materials as well as they might.

By the 1940s, nails had been replaced by the moulded sole, replicating the nail configuration, by Vitale Bramani: hence Vibram. The brilliant boot design for the Everest 1953 [Editor's note: See 'Hadow's Sole', *AJ* 2016] team was forgotten after 1955; had it been commercialised it would have led the world for perhaps two decades. However, in 1966, leather was still the only material for boots; the plastic shell was more than a decade ahead. Plastic boots were developed first by Bob Lange for ski boots in 1968 but it took another 10 years before Koflach developed a winning concept using a closed cell foam inner boot. This innovation had faded by the mid 1990s, such was the speed of transition to footwear that was gentler on the feet and more sensitive on holds. The closed cell neoprene over-boot, a Karrimor Whillans innovation and the vital bridge until the Koflach shell, was not developed until 1970 for Chris Bonington's Annapurna expedition. Even using leather boots, all climbers remained completely frostbite free. That wasn't the case on the Eiger.

As with clothing, the key factors were to prevent water ingress and provide warmth. Closed-cell foam, a key insulation material today, was just over the horizon. (There were no Karrimats either; these appeared in 1968.) Felt had been used in high-altitude boots since the 1924 Everest expedition. When highly compacted, it was a good material. But boot craftsman often used inner layers or even a separate inner (i.e. of a double boot) composed of thin leathers and open-cell foam, already in use for furniture, both of which absorbed water. Wool also holds lots of water, but when used as clothing it is always reckoned to retain warmth even when wet. After a bivy or two that would not be the case. The outer leather absorbed water from snow crystals like water into blotting paper. Within days this footwear would be sodden and then frozen.

John Harlin's teams chose to use only one pair of socks, rather than the two pairs usual for this period, presumably for the better footwork this offered. It may also have been a show of confidence in the new Le Phoque boot, which had the interesting modern feature of a rubber overlay to the laces. The 'bellows' tongue, which fully seals the boot across the top of the foot, did not yet exist, the tongue being semi-loose, rather like a modern ski boot inner today. It allowed lots of water in.

Le Phoque had been supplying Bonington with boots but he had never tried them in the hard conditions of an Eiger winter. When he got back to his hotel room after photographing the summit climbers, his assistant Mick

A pair of German feet emerging from a snow hole on the Eiger. The German company Salewa had recently introduced adjustable, pressed steel crampons. *(German 1966 Eiger Team)*

The Germans used plastic cylinders to transport supplies up the mountain. This was before the era of haul-bags. *(German 1966 Eiger Team)*

Burke was complaining of wet feet. Bonington boasted of having not had a problem, but then peeled off a sock to reveal five black toes. Both men fell about laughing and Bonington spent time in hyperbaric chambers in London as treatment.

The Germans had Lowa Eiger Triplex boots that were very heavy. Made of leather inside and out, and insulated with open cell foam, the problem was the inner boot, which never got dry. The leather kept the moisture trapped inside. As long as you were moving, you could warm the boot up but if you were standing still it froze. The Germans tried drying them over a stove, but it didn't really work and did more damage.

Layering

Layering has been in use since at least the Chalcolithic hunter Ötzi's time. It is not merely the use of multiple garments, but the technique of selecting and using them together and at different levels of activity and inactivity. Multiple layers offer flexibility as well as trapping warm air. The Anglo-American approach was based on multiple layers and stemmed from a century of polar exploration, experience translated into use on Everest in the 1920s. The German belief, until the 1960s or 1970s, was the fewer layers the better. This seems to have been reflected in their choice of less warm inner layers and more reliance on down equipment. For Anglo-Americans, the number one choice of the period was the Norwegian oiled wool sweater.

Dougal Haston and John Harlin wearing their PU shell gear. The pair had just descended from the face following a five-day bivouac during a storm. The lack of side zips meant they were eventually shredded by crampons. *(Peter Gillman)*

The German choice of a soft, non-waterproof cotton one-piece outer garment was unsurprisingly bad – 'We got wetter and wetter and froze.' – although one-piece shell suits and even down one-piece suits became standard for Himalayan expeditions by the early 1990s. Some of the Germans wore Angora underwear but this was costly and to save money others used knitted garments of mixed cotton and wool. Wool base layers today are often combined with polyester on the outer surface, which wicks away moisture.

The nylon outer layer selected by Harlin's team was equally unsuccessful, but in a different way. Condensation occurred of course, and the hydrophilic PU coatings we know today were still more than a decade away. 'We wore PU-coated outer clothing,' Bonington said. 'At the end of the day we were almost as wet as if we hadn't been wearing them.' Zips and Velcro were very well established, but photos reveal their over-trousers didn't have them. Trying to put these on over crampons results in tears; it's surprising this problem wasn't pre-empted.

It is perhaps too easy to make comparisons between the garments and fabrics available today. However, layering selection has always been as important as the technology. This is illustrated in the high success rates of Polish climbing teams in the 1980s, with the first winter ascent of Everest and other 8,000ers. Our research on the layers Mallory and Irvine used in 1924, tested to 25,000ft, showed they were good enough to go to the top on a good day, since the summit pair were moving together and not on terrain needing a belay. They were insufficient for a bivouac. The six clothing layers were tailor-made, alternating woven silk over wool over silk, with a final solid waterproof and totally windproof outer layer of Burberry cotton. The sequels to Burberry's fabric, Grenfell and Ventile, were never proven to be superior even though the garment designs were an improvement. They did not, however, use George Finch's great 1922 innovation, the down jacket.

These 1924 layers were probably superior to the Eiger 1966 layers because of the way in which windproof silk trapped air in the wool layers. However, conditions were much less wet than the Eiger. The great weakness of the 1920s system was the hood design: the poor closure around the throat and mouth area caused Somervell an almost fatal accident when his larynx froze. Mallory's boots were very good, high-density felt uppers with light leather reinforcement around the toes, and dried quickly but were totally unsuitable for use on steep ground and with crampons. By using nailed boots instead of crampons they avoided tight straps compressing the feet.

The Eiger 1966 men used wool but without windproof layering to trap air. This made them more dependent on their down outer layers, even when moving, in contrast to today's practice. The German one-piece outer layer made in basic cotton was nothing like as good as Burberry, and absorbed water. 'The Americans' equipment was much better,' one of the Germans said. 'As you can see from the photos we were wearing rags.' The outer fabrics of all the down gear did not have durable water resistant (DWR) finishes; snow and spindrift melted into the fibres and down very rapidly. The nylon PU outers would have prevented this, but condensation from sweat was then a problem.

Today we have much better layers, but the methodology is also different. This evolved step by step: the USA alpinist Mark Twight outlined his principles clearly in his book *Extreme Alpinism: Climbing Light, Fast & High* (The Mountaineers, 1999). Use only enough layers to keep you warm when climbing, but on belay use a big down jacket: thus the term 'belay jacket' was born, driven by the need to avoid changing layers when wearing a harness.

Today we have much better windproof layers. These emerged partly because of the need for much tighter woven nylon fabrics to stop increasingly fine down and micro-fibres of non-woven insulating polymer materials from leaking out. These fabrics still have good 'breathability' but with DWR finishes they have a degree of water repellency as well. Waterproof outer layers tend only to be used now when there is direct precipitation or much higher wind strengths. With this, hydrophilic coatings and ePTFE laminates allow sweat to pass through to a varying degree, not totally, but enough to make a huge difference to the drying of inner layers.[2]

Hardware, techniques and rope

How had technical climbing equipment in 1966 changed since the 1930s? In the early 1960s, new methods were evolving rapidly in Yosemite. This included the jumar rope clamp, used first in Europe for crevasse rescue and in Yosemite in 1964. Techniques were developed for multiday routes where loads were too heavy for the second man to carry. Jumars were used by the second to follow, rather than rock climbing. Harlin had introduced Bonington to jumars the summer before the Eiger and they allowed the climbers to climb back up fixed ropes quickly having resupplied or rested at Kleine Scheidegg.

Hermann Huber of Salewa, who supplied tubular ice screws, crampons and Hiebeler Prusikers commented: 'The jumars were more practical in use than the Salewa Hiebeler rope ascender, but these early jumars would not have worked on iced-up ropes. Jörg Lehne reported that only the smaller Salewa device could be used in any conditions. Later developments in Yosemite included large capacity cylindrical haul bags, although on the Eiger the Germans also used cylindrical containers attached to their harnesses.

Crampons in 1966 were mainly the new adjustable Salewa pressed steel model, although one of the German team commented that the front points of his forged crampons were bending out of shape and becoming useless. Crampons in 1966 were attached with straps, which compressed the boot and feet. Boots had much less internal structure then and so the risk of frostbite was much greater. The cable binding did not arrive until 1976 from Salewa, the same year that Lowe's Footfangs became available, a heel lever system that is essentially still in use today.

Ice axes had changed little since Whymper's time, save for the version with a hammerhead instead of the adze, although shorter lengths were becoming available in the 1960s. Yvon Chouinard's curved pick first appeared in 1969, although he was personally using shorter axes of 55cm from 1965. When the climbers were facing in, they used a short hand-held ice dagger in the other hand, which had limited penetration and little holding power. These could best be described as a psychological aid. Haston's final epic lead with only an ice dagger was incredible, needing an extra-

2. For further insights into clothing layers and technology see 'Keeping Dry and Staying Warm: Almost Everything You Need to Know about Outdoor and Mountaineering Garments and Usage Practices', *http://www.outdoorgearcoach.co.uk/publications/keeping-dry-staying-warm/*

Bonington pauses to snap Mick Burke shortly before flying up to the Eiger
to meet the climbers as they topped out from the Eiger Direct. Note the
old-fashioned axe head. *(Peter Gillman)*

ordinary level of physical and mental strength.

The new 'kernmantel' rope construction was invented in Germany and
became available from the early 1960s. The technology was a dramatic improvement over nylon hawser-laid ropes, let alone the hemp of 1938. Water
absorption was very low and they had much more stretch than hawser-laid

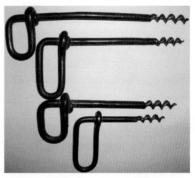

Marwa ice screws, affectionately and accurately recognised as effective bottle openers. *(Mike Parsons)*

An advertisement for the Le Phoque boots used by Harlin's team. Bonington suffered frostbite wearing them. *(Mike Parsons)*

versions, able to absorb more energy in a fall. Germans used a combination of what now would be called full weight and 5mm, a clear distinction, sort of a 'no ifs or buts' choice when climbing. The Anglo-American team, however, used full weight and 7mm, the latter for fixed ropes. It's assumed that jumaring this thinner diameter was the cause of Harlin's death. However, it is possible that the thicker rope would also have failed because of the way in which dynamic rope stretches under a load. Friction against the rock will cause abrasion and eventual failure. Today it is well understood that a rope used in a jumaring situation should be 'static', a rope without stretch, similar to those used for caving or on a yacht.

Harnesses were on the German equipment list: these were not the sit harnesses we know today but the Edelrid chest harness made from rope introduced two years earlier. This made it feasible for the Germans to suspend their plastic drums from their harness. It is unclear what the Anglo-American team used for harnesses but by 1964 the so called Swami belt using one-inch tubular nylon webbing had been developed in the US and something of this nature would have been used. Nylon webbing sit harnesses only appeared in 1970, developed by Whillans and Troll for the British Annapurna expedition.

Although the figure-of-eight abseil device was available, possibly as early as 1962, there is no evidence of its use on the Eiger Direct. Haston describes the rope burning painfully through his jacket near the hood: just what the classic method would do, using a karabiner clipped to the waist belt and running the rope over the shoulder to control descent.

The 1922 ice pitons of Welzenbach had gone, replaced by the Marwa ice screw, which looked rather like a bottle opener. The tubular ice screw, with many times more holding power, was invented in 1962 by Salewa.

The Germans carried 20 of the former, compared to 25 tubular screws. The Germans also took 100 rock pitons, of the original Fiechtl design, semi-soft to conform to cracks, unlike the American chrome-moly pitons that were hammered out, plus two drills and bolts, an indication of the terrain they thought they would encounter. Thanks to Layton Kor's technical brilliance, Harlin's team avoided bolts more successfully than the Germans. Both teams had decent helmets, an innovation of 1962. They also had headlamps: in 1938 candle lanterns were the only light. Candles were still used for bivouacs in the 1960s.

In the late 1960s, following an introduction from Graham Tiso, Mike Parsons, then with Karrimor, arrived in Leysin to talk to Dougal Haston about a successor to the famous orange Whillans pack, which had a capacity of only 27 litres. The resulting collaboration was the pack Dougal wanted on the Eiger in 1966: 60 litres, with a long extension sleeve for bivy protection and a long front zip to give easy access. This purple pack became known as the Haston Alpiniste.

A great deal more changed in the subsequent decade than had between 1938 and 1966, transforming margins of safety and techniques. The quality of ropes improved when UIAA testing began in 1967. Sit harnesses and belay plates meant falling, for so long anathema to climbers, became a way to test limits. Plastic boots and breathable fabrics made cold and bad weather less formidable threats. The consequent rise in standards drove more innovation, much of it led by technically minded climbers. By the early 1980s, in less than 20 years, mountaineering equipment had been transformed, and at a faster pace that at any time in the sport's history.

Timeline: the Road to 1966

1895 A F Mummery uses the first down sleeping bag on Nanga Parbat.

1922 George Finch invents the first down jacket for use on Everest, prompting some derision. They are not used in 1924.

1924 First recorded use of zips on mountain clothing. Sandy Irvine stitches zips into his outer clothing on for Everest.

1930s Austrian climbers experimented with making crampons rigid along their length to enhance performance, but it was not commercialised.

1931 Dr Karl Prusik of Vienna introduces a method of ascending the rope itself.

1932 Laurent Grivel introduces the first 12-point crampons.

1933 Pierre Allain designs and produces warm bivouac gear, like the *pied d'éléphant* down bag and *la grande cagoule* made of rubber-coated silk.

1934 Discovery of nylon polyamide fibres.

1937-9 Vitale Bramani developed, in conjunction with Pirelli, the first rubber sole, moulded to imitate the shape of nails.

1950s Pierre Allain's bivouac gear comes into general use in the Alps.

1952 French company 'Pile Wonder' produced first ever battery-operated headlamp.

1956-8 Marwa ice screws: the 'bottle-opener' type.

1960 First *Kernmantel* ropes become available in Germany.

1962 First fibreglass helmet, designed by Swiss climber Paul Hübel.

1962 Hermann Huber of Salewa achieves a design breakthrough producing the first easily adjustable crampons with increased strength for front pointing.

1962 First tubular ice screw developed by Huber of Salewa.

1962 An improved abseil device, the *Abseilachter* or figure of eight, was developed.

1964 Big wall climbers in Yosemite adopt the jumar, used first in Europe for crevasse rescue.

1965 Helly Hansen introduced a range of polypropylene underwear designed to wick moisture away from the skin.

1966 Chouinard persuades Charlet to make him an ice axe with a curved pick and a shaft of 55cm.

1968 The Karrimat, made from closed cell foam, becomes commercially available.

1970 The Annapurna south face expedition results in several innovations: the Whillans Box, the Whillans Harness, the down one-piece suit and neoprene over-boots for the single layer leather boots.

1978 Plastic shelled mountain boots introduced by Koflach of Austria. First available with felt inners and later with closed cell foam inners.

THOMAS KEIRLE

The Peak of Their Profession

Doctors on Everest 1921-53

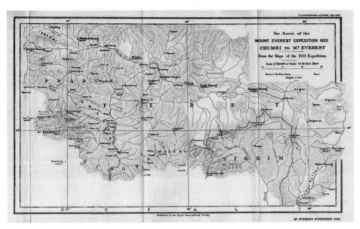

The road to Everest, as much physiological exploration as physical?
(Royal Geographical Society)

Until recently, the story of Mount Everest has been told predominantly
by climbers with attention focussed on mountaineering technicalities,
and scarce mention of medicine and physiology barring the occasional reference to oxygen apparatus.[1] The recent publication *Everest: the First Ascent*
by Harriet Tuckey changed all that. Tuckey is the daughter of Griffith Pugh
(1909-94), the physiologist and medical practitioner on the successful 1953
Everest expedition. She highlights how her father and experimental medicine were more instrumental in getting Ed Hillary and Tenzing Norgay
to the summit than hitherto realised. The subtitle to Tuckey's book – *The
Untold Story of Griffith Pugh, the Man Who Made It Possible* – is both true and
false. Pugh may be a neglected figure in mountaineering history, but he is
part of the wider story of mountain medicine, which involved many more
medical practitioners than Pugh alone. 'The man who made it possible' had
an important role but was one man in a larger network of doctors, climbers
and ideas in the history of medicine and physiology on Everest.

The doctor's role in high-altitude climbing is multifactorial; the doctor
is actively pursuing the same activity that is endangering the patient's life
and can suffer from the same maladies, including impingements on their

1. Edmund Hillary's autobiography makes little mention of doctors and scientists, and when mentioned it
is often done with a negative tone. Edmund Hillary, *High Adventure*, London, Hodder and Stoughton, 1955.

Alexander Kellas' grave at Kampa Dzong. Kellas, born in Aberdeen, was a crucial pioneer in high-altitude physiology. *(RGS)*

decision-making. They are responsible for declaring climbers fit or otherwise, have limited resources and have to tailor their interventions according to the environment or situation. One could crudely split historical medical tasks on Everest into four categories. Historically, some of these remain static whereas others evolve. First is assessing fitness of the climbing team. Second is experimental medicine. Third is involvement in oxygen equipment. Fourth is general medical consultation and intervention, the job that appears to change the least over the nine Everest expeditions between 1921 and 1953. This essay explores the changing role of medics and medicine in British Everest attempts in those years, demonstrating the emergence and reception of physiological work.

The first organised British visit to Everest was in 1921. This was a reconnaissance mission on the north side through Tibet and thus the team had no intention of reaching the summit that year. Chemistry lecturer Dr Alexander Kellas provides an early example of medical consideration for the Everest problem. Not a medical officer but nonetheless involved in high-altitude physiology, he accompanied the team with the intention of investigating this subject and the prospects of using oxygen on future attempts. Prior to the expedition, Kellas wrote an article entitled 'A Consideration of the Possibility of Ascending Mount Everest'. This summarised the prospective difficulties of climbing Everest and collected physiological data from air chamber experiments and explorers at altitude. He also defined altitude sickness (then termed 'mountain sickness') and addressed the question of acclimatisation.[2] The general effects of altitude were known of from the experiences of 19th century pioneers in ballooning, but now Kellas was using this knowledge to approach the Everest problem from a physiological angle. His conclusions mainly concerned theory: explaining the effects of altitude on blood and oxygen dissociation. But he also arrived at some practical conclusions similar to doctors on later expeditions, such as the importance of diet and acclimatisation.[3] Kellas died on the expedition of 1921 on the approach to Everest after he and several other members had been ill for days. His agenda remained dormant on that expedition and the publication of his paper was never pursued.[4] [Editor's note: for further information on the life and overlooked contribution of Alexander Kellas, see Ian R Mitchell and George W Rodway, *Prelude to Everest*, Luath Press, 2011.]

The next year saw the first serious attempt at climbing Everest, followed by another in 1924. In 1922 the team of twelve Europeans included three medically qualified men and a chemist: Tom Longstaff, Theodore Howard Somervell, Dr Arthur Wakefield and George Ingle Finch.[5] The medical officer on the expedition was Longstaff, a man who held a medical degree but was noted primarily for his extensive exploration portfolio and his abilities as a naturalist.[6] Despite being the medical authority on this expedition, he was sure to make it known that this was not his reason for being there:

I want to make one thing clear. I am the expedition's medical officer. And I am, as a matter of fact, a qualified doctor, but I feel it my duty now to remind you that I have never practised in my life. I beg you in no circumstances to seek my professional advice, since it would almost certainly turn out to be wrong. I am however, willing, if necessary, to sign a certificate of death.[7]

Additionally, Longstaff's diaries and memoirs demonstrate favour of naturalism over medicine with extensive notes on the fauna (particularly birds and butterflies) and little mention of his medical duties.[8] This demonstrates an important feature of the selection process for Everest expeditions during this period: doctors were chosen with their mountaineering ability taking priority over their medical ability.

Among the most able climbers, along with Mallory, was Somervell, present on both expeditions in 1922 and 1924, reaching altitudes of 27,000ft and 28,000ft respectively.[9] With much of his medical experience coming from his role in the Royal Army Medical Corps in France during the First World War, Somervell was a surgeon with experience in extreme environments.[10]

2. A M Kellas, 'A Consideration of the Possibility of Ascending Mount Everest', 1920, unpublished, Alpine Club Archives, C108.
3. A M Kellas, 'A Consideration of the Possibility of Ascending Mount Everest', 1920, unpublished, Alpine Club Archives, 50.
4. C K Howard Bury, 'The 1921 Mount Everest Expedition', *Alpine Journal* **34**, 1922, p201.
5. G Mallory, 'The Second Mount Everest Expedition', *Alpine Journal* **34**, 1922, p425.
6. P Lloyd, 'In Memoriam: T G Longstaff', *Alpine Journal* **69**, 1964, 322.
7. R Bayne, 'Arthur Wakefield on Everest 1922: No Passenger', *Alpine Journal* **109**, 2004, p224.
8. T G Longstaff, Everest Diary 1922, Alpine Club Archives D57.
9. N Odell, 'In Memoriam: T H Somervell', *Alpine Journal* **81**, 1976, p272.
10. N Odell, 'In Memoriam: T H Somervell', *Alpine Journal* **81**, 1976, p272.

Left: The sick parade at Kampa Dzong, doctor unknown.
(RGS) Centre and right: George Finch testing oxygen
equipment and the open-circuit set used in 1922. *(RGS)*

However, in his accounts of Everest expeditions, Somervell's medical role appears to be subordinate to his role as a climber. At 25,000ft on the North Col, Major Henry Morshead, acknowledged by Somervell to be a tough man, who, if he complained he was ill, most certainly was, complained of illness and was subsequently left alone by Somervell and Mallory who pressed on up the mountain, only to realise once unsuccessful that they should return to Morshead's aid and get him further down the mountain.[11] Additionally, in 1924 when the medical officer Major Richard Hingston accompanied the sick expedition leader back to India, medical matters were left to Somervell:

> *... so I have to do the medical job – a beastly nuisance but can't be helped.*[12]

It would be unfair to suggest Somervell was reckless, but this demonstrates a conflict in the doctor's role.

Following an illness lasting nearly a month, Longstaff's duties were entrusted to Wakefield and Somervell, though Wakefield's diaries seem to indicate that it was he who had most responsibility.[13] Despite the extensive medical stores supplied by Burroughs and Wellcome that each expedition took with them, the nature of high-altitude mountaineering and the remote environment meant that medical intervention was muted.[14] Additionally, Burroughs and Wellcome marketed their medicine chests as a multi-purpose product: for the military and navy, aeronauts, motorists, yachtsmen and explorers.[15] These medicines had no specific mountaineering use and most remained unused.[16]

Daily sick parades were standard, where members of the expedition, mainly porters, would present to the doctors of the expedition with minor complaints and receive what treatment was available, most of which were

11. T H Somervell, *After Everest*, London, Hodder & Stoughton, 1936, p55.
12. T H Somervell, *After Everest*, London, Hodder & Stoughton, 1936, p111.
13. R Bayne, 'Arthur Wakefield on Everest 1922: No Passenger', *Alpine Journal* **109**, 2004, p224.
14. T G Longstaff, Everest Diary 1922, Alpine Club Archives D57, 10, 12-13 April 1922.
15. Johnson, Tabloid Brand Medicine Chests, 250
16. Much of the medical equipment was reused from 1921 to 1924. R Hingston, 'Report on the Medical Supplies from Burroughs and Wellcome 1924', Wellcome Library Archives WF/M/I/PR/E16.

George demonstrates his oxygen system to cynical team members while the porters look on. *(RGS with IBG)*

wound dressings, sedatives, painkillers, salts for nutrition or purgatives.[17] Frequently, in accounts of expeditions, the European members would remark at the phenomenal ability of porters to carry such heavy loads at extreme altitudes with apparent ease. Considering that the porters vastly outnumbered the Europeans, the health of the porter workforce was extremely important.[18] Future expeditions were also contingent on approval from the Tibetan authorities, which might be unlikely if their people were subject to undue harm.

With several summit bids being abandoned within less than 2,000ft of the top, the term 'the problem of the last 1,000ft' began to emerge; most realised that the problem was a physiological one. Evidence of physiological testing long before Pugh on the 1953 expedition becomes apparent. Major Richard Hingston, medical officer and naturalist on the 1924 expedition, was an instrumental figure in dissecting the physiological problem of Everest. In an article published in the *Geographical Journal*, Hingston details his physiological observations. Importantly, the status of experimental medicine is distinctly different here in the 1920s in comparison to the 1950s.

17. Mount Everest Expedition Medical Stores, RGS EE/29/6.
18. G Mallory, 'The Second Mount Everest Expedition', *Alpine Journal* **34**, 1922, p435.

Irvine checking the oxygen cylinders at Base Camp; many were found to be faulty.

The primary objective of the 1924 mission was to summit Everest and scientific investigation was subordinate:

> *Elaborate scientific investigations were impossible, and anything involving complicated apparatus was altogether out of the question.*[19]

Therefore Hingston's work consisted mainly of anecdotes concerning the party's health and fitness, and simple experiments. At varying altitudes during the trip, he observed blood pressure, pulse, expiratory force and endurance and time that breath could be held.[20] Hingston's conclusions highlight the difficulty of the last 1,000ft in reference to Kellas' oxygen dissociation curve, where every 1,000ft becomes exponentially more difficult in terms of oxygen debt, and also stress the importance of acclimatisation.[21]

Remote experimentation, i.e. not in the field, is another feature not unique to the 1950s expeditions. Whilst Hingston's report made reference to oxygen

19. R Hingston, 'Physiological Difficulties in the Ascent of Mount Everest', *Geographical Journal* **65**, 1925, p4.
20. R Hingston, 'Physiological Difficulties in the Ascent of Mount Everest', *Geographical Journal* **65**, 1925, pp6-8.
21. R Hingston, 'Physiological Difficulties in the Ascent of Mount Everest', *Geographical Journal* **65**, 1925, p16.

use and debate, testing of oxygen was carried out in Britain under the supervision of Imperial College chemist George Ingle Finch.[22] A report by Percy Unna, Scottish mountaineer and environmentalist, details tests conducted in a vacuum chamber by Finch and Professor Dreyer of Oxford University whereby Finch would be observed carrying out tasks in a simulation of 21,000ft whilst carrying weight, with and without the assistance supplementary oxygen.[23] Analysis included taking pulse, subjective reports of how one felt in the chamber and objective observation of general demeanour. As well as Finch, Unna and Somervell made a journey to Oxford to participate in these experiments. Somervell was designated as the control and received no oxygen when in the chamber, expressing a blue face, hands and fingernails, faster breathing, quick pulse, mental confusion and a tendency to quarrel. He had to be forcibly given oxygen as his condition worsened.[24]

The oxygen debate is not new history. However it is important to give it mention as it usefully gives a snapshot of contemporary opinion concerning physiology, science and their place (or not) in mountaineering. Finch unsurprisingly was an advocate for the use of oxygen and dismissive of the old guard who saw use of oxygen as unsporting.[25] Mallory, whilst not a naysayer in the oxygen debate, was particularly scathing of laboratory experimentation into high altitude and oxygen and Finch's escapades to Oxford:

> I was told at Oxford last year, that the physiologists said it was impossible to climb to the top of Mount Everest without oxygen, the matter had been proved in a pressure reducing chamber. I told [them] that the physiologists might explode themselves in their diabolical chamber, but we would do what we could to explode their damnable heresy.[26]

Following the tragedy of the 1924 expedition in which Mallory and Irvine went missing, nine years passed until another British attempt on Everest. In 1933, Dr Raymond Greene was chosen to be the medical officer for Hugh Ruttledge's assault on Everest that year.[27] Greene's medical background was in general practice; he later became an authority on frostbite.[28] His role on the expedition that successfully climbed Kamet (7756m) in 1931 brought him to the attention of the Everest Committee.[29] Greene's autobiography, *Moments of Being*, contains numerous vignettes that paint a picture of the diverse roles of the medical officer. These include the attempted removal of an abscess from an elephant's back, removing a porter's tooth, which Greene stated was only his second dental operation since his student days, and tending to the wounds of a convicted murderer who received whipping

22. P Unna, 'The Oxygen Equipment of the 1922 Everest Expedition', *Alpine Journal* **34**, 1922, pp235-50.
23. P Unna, 'The Oxygen Equipment of the 1922 Everest Expedition', *Alpine Journal* **34**, 1922, p236.
24. P Unna, 'The Oxygen Equipment of the 1922 Everest Expedition', *Alpine Journal* **34**, 1922, p238.
25. G I Finch, 'The Second Attempt on Everest', *Alpine Journal* **34**, 1922, p440.
26. G Mallory, 'The Second Mount Everest Expedition', *Alpine Journal* **34**, 1922, p436.
27. H Ruttledge, 'Preparation', Everest 1933, London, Hodder & Stoughton, 1934, p31
28. C Warren, 'In Memoriam: Raymond Greene', *the Alpine Journal* **88**, 1983, p280.
29. R Greene, *Moments of Being*, London, Heinemann, 1974, p113.

as punishment.[30] Greene's flirtation with dentistry is an example of one of the few things that was learnt in terms of medical intervention, where in 1924, Somervell, lacking dental instruments, removed a porter's tooth with footprint pincers.[31] Charles Warren, the doctor present on the expeditions in 1936 and 1938 supported the importance of dentistry equipment.[32] Greene's account of the expedition shows that medical intervention was as limited and difficult as it had been in the 1920s. Greene highlights this himself, in reference to George Wood-Johnson he says:

> *George lay in his tent in great pain from his gastric ulcer which my primitive medicines did little to relieve.*[33]

Similarly, Ondi, a Sherpa who was suffering with what Greene retrospectively diagnosed as pulmonary oedema was given oxygen to stave off death whilst at altitude, and was then moved to lower altitudes accompanied by C G Crawford out of Greene's care.[34] This stasis in terms of medical intervention is demonstrated by the medical equipment, which was still supplied by Burroughs and Wellcome and was much the same as it had been on 1920s expeditions. Gordon Humphreys, the medical officer on Hugh Ruttledge's 1936 expedition remarks that the only medicines that were used up were throat sprays and paints to relieve the sore throat commonly associated with the altitude and dry air of the high Tibetan plateau.[35]

For the first time on Everest, in 1933 the medical officer took on the onus of coordinating the use of oxygen; previously this had been the remit of chemists Kellas, Finch and Irvine respectively.[36] Subsequent expeditions bestowed the oxygen work onto the doctors, including Charles Warren in 1936 and 1938, and Griffith Pugh in 1953.[37] Oxygen use was becoming increasingly medicalised. Though the oxygen equipment in 1933 was far less burdensome in terms of weight compared to the apparatus used in the 1920s, the 1933 expedition was hampered by bad weather and oxygen was subsequently not tested and abandoned somewhere on the North Col.[38]

After 1933, there was the 1935 reconnaissance, and full expeditions in 1936 and 1938. During this time, as in the 1920s, there is evidence of experimentation conducted in Britain on the use of oxygen equipment,[39] despite scathing comments from mountaineers on laboratory simulation. Greene

---

30. R Greene, *Moments of Being*, London, Heinemann, 1974, p123, p126, p128.
31. R Greene, *Moments of Being*, London, Heinemann, 1974, p123, p126, p128.
32. C Warren, 'Mount Everest in 1938: A Doctor's Account of the Adventure', *St Bartholomew's Hospital Journal*, 1939, p108.
33. R Greene, *Moments of Being*, London, Heinemann, 1974, p166.
34. C G Crawford, 'Everest Diary 1933', 21 April.
35. G N Humphreys, 'Health' in H Ruttledge *Everest: the Unfinished Adventure*, London, Hodder & Stoughton, 1937, p202.
36. R Greene, *Moments of Being*, London, Heinemann, 1974, p146.
37. It is important to note that on the 1938 expedition, both Dr Charles Warren and Engineer Peter Lloyd took charge of oxygen experimentation and use. Additionally, whilst Warren was medically trained, he was not the medical officer in 1936 but was in 1938. C Warren, 'Mount Everest in 1938: A Doctor's Account of the Adventure', *St Bartholomew's Hospital Journal*, 1939, p126.
38. R Greene, *Moments of Being*, London, Heinemann, 1974, p146.
39. Tilman wrote a letter to Warren telling him about his experiences using oxygen apparatus in the Lake District, 30 December 1937, Alpine Club Archives P46/6.

Left: Charles Warren taking the blood pressure of a disgruntled Eric Shipton. *(RGS)* Right: The medicine chest taken to Everest in 1933. *(Wellcome Trust)*

recalls having numerous discussions with physiologists J S Haldane and C G Douglas on the subject, and being the test subject in pressure chambers in Oxford:

> *Under their enthusiastic supervision I had spent long hours in a low pressure chamber at Oxford. Once a careless technician 'crashed' me from a simulated 20,000ft to earth in a few seconds. I had agonising earache and was deaf for 2 days.* [40]

Whilst not on the 1938 expedition, Greene was still consulting the organisers on the subject of oxygen, and was in contact with the physiologists who were dissecting the oxygen kit in the laboratory.[41]

The figure of Charles Warren perhaps best demonstrates the importance of experimental medicine in the pre-war Everest expeditions. Mentioned sparingly by Tuckey, Warren (along with Greene and Somervell) was praised by Pugh for his physiological work on Everest.[42] Warren's physiological 1935 notebooks contain details of red blood cell count, haemoglobin analysis particularly in comparing the Europeans and native porters and Sherpas, exercise tolerance, pulse and blood pressure, each element done at different altitudes.[43] In 1938 the list of inquiries expands, with analysis of urine pH, eye tests and observation of alveolar air content.[44] The sealed glass bulbs containing alveolar air were sent to the physiologist Douglas at Oxford and were subsequently analysed and reported in *Journal of Physiology*.[45] The *Alpine Journal* also featured an uncharacteristically scientific piece by Warren based on his analyses in 1938.[46]

40. R Greene, *Moments of Being*, London, Heinemann, 1974, p148.
41. C G Douglas sent a letter to Greene as to comparison of soda lime canisters used in closed circuit oxygen systems to convert exhaled carbon dioxide back into oxygen, 3 November 1937, Alpine Club Archives P46/6.
42. G Pugh, 'British Expedition to Cho Oyu, 1952', Alpine Club Archives, 16.
43. C Warren, Physiological Notebooks, 1935 and 1938, Alpine Club Archives D69.
44. C Warren, Physiological Notebooks, 1935 and 1938, Alpine Club Archives D69.
45. C Warren, 'Alveolar Air on Mount Everest 1938', *Journal of Physiology* **96**, 1939.
46. This article contained graphical representation of partial pressure of oxygen, red blood cells and haemoglobin change with altitude, as well as mathematical instruction as to how pressure of expired vapour was calculated. C Warren, 'Mountain Sickness and the Physiology of High Altitude Mountaineering', *Alpine Journal* **51**, 1939, p271-83.

Similar investigations had been performed by Greene on the 1933 expedition, and attempts at this were made by Somervell in 1924.[47] This demonstrates that experimental medicine was officially on the agenda before the 1950s. However, it existed on the agenda in what seemed a theoretical form as opposed to practically, as the main difference between the 1930s and 1950s is the allowance made for transporting scientific equipment. Despite lengthy passages concerning physiology and medicine being included in the expedition reports, on the expedition itself investigative physiology was not explicitly catered for in the 1930s.[48]

Paradoxically, whilst Warren's investigative work in the field was more extensive than those before him, the expedition leader in 1938 was probably the least accommodating of science and medicine of all expeditions up until this point. H W Tilman approached the Everest problem with minimalist tactics and a small team, unlike previous British missions, where the European personnel would range from 12 to 16. Tilman took only seven, arguing that because Everest is such a vast mountain, extra porters are needed to establish high camps, but teams needn't include doctors and other non-climbing members:[49]

> *The risk of serious illness developing is not great and is over-emphasised. The party are fit men when they start and presumably able to take care of themselves. Coughs, colds and sore throats seem to be inseparable from a journey across Tibet in the early spring, but their effects are not grave. Indeed, it seems better to face the possibility of serious illness than the certainty of having numerous mouths to feed and men falling over one another for lack of work.[50]*

Indeed, serious illness occurred only once, when Pasang, a porter, was left completely paralysed down one side at camp six at an altitude of 27,000ft.[51] Much like any other serious medical case on previous missions little could be done in such an extreme environment and he was simply lowered down the glacier on a rope and allowed to recover at lower altitudes.[52]

After the Second World War, having ruled out the possibility of a collaborative British and Swiss expedition, a British team set out to Cho Oyu (8201m) with the joint aim of climbing it and gathering useful experience and data for the forthcoming Everest expedition in 1953.[53] Medical supplies and hence remedial practice changed little from prior expeditions in the 1930s. However Burroughs and Wellcome did not supply the Everest

47. Unfortunately, Somervell collected his samples in rubber bags meaning much of the sample diffused out and reliable data could not be obtained. However, learning from this, Greene was the first to use glass ampoules. R Greene, 'Observations on the Composition of Alveolar Air on Everest 1933', *Journal of Physiology*, **82**,1934, p481.
48. Warren mentions that the primary objective of the 1936 expedition was to climb the mountain and hence no provision was made for scientific work which had to be done as a side issue. C Warren in H Ruttledge 'Physiology', *Everest: the Unfinished Adventure*, London, Hodder and Stoughton, 1937, p218.
49. H W Tilman, 'Introductory', *Mount Everest 1938*, Cambridge, Cambridge University Press, 1948, p6.
50. H W Tilman, 'Introductory', *Mount Everest 1938*, Cambridge, Cambridge University Press, 1948, p7.
51. C Warren in H W Tilman, 'The Everest Expedition of 1938', *Geographical Journal*, **92**, 1938, p492.
52. C Warren, 'A Doctor's Account of the Adventure', *St Bartholomew's Hospital Journal*, 1939, p127.
53. C Warren, 'A Doctor's Account of the Adventure', St Bartholomew's Hospital Journal, 1939, p127.

expedition of 1953. Much of their previous sponsorships of exploration of the poles, Himalaya and tropics were based on their economic interests in empire and a belief in western medical superiority over the colonies.[54] When India gained independence, effectively signalling the end of the British Empire, exploration could no longer be considered an imperial mission. Burroughs and Wellcome's economic and political stake in exploration was destroyed.

Whilst the Cho Oyu expedition was ultimately a failure, Pugh managed to conduct limited tests on three members of the team concerning alveolar air, the effect of breathing oxygen on capacity to work, oxygen consumption and food consumption.[55] Based on these experiments, Pugh identified five problems and posed solutions to each. For hypoxia, climbers should be given four litres per minute of supplementary oxygen using open circuit apparatus. For dehydration, climbers should drink three litres per day. Pugh suggested consumption of 3,000 calories to ensure adequate nutrition. As well as the suggestion of improved clothing, the solution to cold injury was supplemented by the solution to oxygen lack, as advantageous oxygen could increase climbing speed and hence heat production. Finally, to avoid deterioration it was necessary to use oxygen whilst sleeping.[56] However, not all of these recommendations were closely adhered to as is demonstrated by Michael Ward, the medical officer and hence assistant to Pugh in 1953. Ward felt it necessary to take histories of each member of the team once they had descended from the extreme altitude of the South Col, including Hillary and Tenzing following their successful summit bid. In the history Ward took of Hillary, he noted that whilst Hillary showed evidence of effective hydration, he was under-nourished and 'looked almost emaciated.'[57]

Many of those qualities identified by Pugh were not new to the climbing establishment. Open circuit oxygen used for the 1953 ascent was a technology first used 30 years prior and the problem of Everest had long been considered a predominantly physiological one. What had changed was the increased input from external medical organisations, namely the Medical Research Council (MRC), and the acceptance, reluctant or otherwise, of scientific medicine among those Lawrence Kirwan, organiser of the 1953 expedition, referred to as 'more die-hard colleagues in the mountaineering world'.[58] Now that international competition was clear and present, it was necessary to 'send out the most efficiently equipped expedition'.[59] To be efficiently equipped meant taking oxygen seriously, effectively killing the debate for the time being and ensuring that all members of the team are accepting of this 'advantageous aid':

54. Johnson, Tabloid Brand Medicine Chests, 249
55. G Pugh, 'British Expedition to Cho Oyu, 1952', Alpine Club Archives, 18.
56. G Pugh, 'British Expedition to Cho Oyu, 1952', Alpine Club Archives.
57. M Ward's Everest diary 1953, Michael Ward, 'The First Ascent of Everest, May 1953', Everest, A Thousand Years of Exploration, Glasgow, Ernest Press, 2003, p267.
58. Letter from L Kirwan to Dr Martin of the Royal Society, detailing Pugh's work and his importance for the upcoming Everest expedition, 11 June 1952, RGS EE/75/1
59. Letter from L Kirwan to Dr Himsworth of the Medical Research Council, 11 July 1952, RGS EE/75/1.

A breath of fresh air. Dr Griffith Pugh's determined research and development were critical factors in the success of 1953. *(RGS)*

Shipton indeed said to me the other day that any member of the Expedition who appeared unwilling to co-operate fully in oxygen indoctrination would lose his place in the party.[60]

The amateur approach was seemingly abandoned. The expeditions to Cho Oyu and Everest in the 1950s were the first to fully accommodate the transport of physiological hardware.[61] The problem was partially outsourced to organisations outside of the Alpine Club and Royal Geographical Society, which in the 1950s were perceived as elitist, with a reputation for stuffiness.[62]

The acceptance of investigative medicine in the 1950s was spurred on by the failure of the Cho Oyu expedition, the threat from Swiss climbers encroaching on what had previously been an exclusively British exercise and the success of the French in being the first to summit an 8,000m peak on Annapurna.[63]

Crucially, when the Swiss attempted Everest in 1952, they were the first team to do so from the newly opened south side, the side that is considered technically easier. The successful ascent was the first British effort on the south side. Should the previous expeditions have been granted access to this route, would they have made it to the summit given the equipment and knowledge they had? Likewise if the 1953 expedition team were forced to climb via the north route, would they have made it?

When Mallory and Irvine disappeared in 1924, they did so using oxygen. When Mallory was found in 1999, leg fractures suggested he had taken a fall, a theory supported by the discovery of an ice axe in 1933 some distance from any remains.[64] No physiological knowledge or medical ability could have prevented what appears to have been an accident. The expeditions of 1933, 1936 and 1938 were encumbered by bad weather and early monsoon; no stark organisational deficits were identified as causative of the lack of success. All expeditions from 1922 took oxygen with them, and although it

60. Letter from L Kirwan to Prof B Matthews of the Physiological Laboratory in Cambridge, 7 August 1952, RGS EE/75/1.
61. 1953 Medical Equipment, RGS EE/74.
62. D Walker, 'Evolution of Climbing Clubs in Britain', *the Alpine Journal* **109**, 2004, p192
63. S Harper, 'Other Annapurnas', *the Alpine Journal* **104**, 1999, p170
64. P Wyn-Harris found an ice axe later identified as Andrew Irvine's in 1933. Ruttledge goes on to say that it is extremely unlikely that any climber would abandon their ice axe. Ruttledge, *Everest 1933*, p158.

was only in the 1950s when debate was killed, and members were 'indoc-trinated' into the idea of oxygen, most climbers prior to this didn't oppose oxygen and didn't need indoctrination.

The combination of fortunate weather and access to the southern route via Nepal arguably played a vital role in the success of 1953. To say that science and medicine, and in particular one man made it possible isn't the whole picture. This is particularly poignant given that remedial medicine changed very little from 1921 to 1953. Barring the addition of antibiotics and several basic surgical instruments, the medical inventories look similar. (This does not mean that a lack of innovation was inhibitory, as therapeutic medicine in an extreme environment such as Everest has a limited scope.[65]) The physiological breakthroughs, which Tuckey credits to Griffith Pugh in the 1950s, had their origins in the eight Everest expeditions prior to 1953 where another untold story now lies.

65. 1953 Medical Equipment, RGS EE/74.

VICTOR SAUNDERS

A High-altitude Study of Age-related Forgetfulness

A riddle inside an enigma. The summit of Carstensz Pyramid,
also known as Puncak Jaya. *(All images Victor Saunders)*

It began in 2010 with an ancient copy of *New Scientist* magazine and a chance conversation in Sam's Bar in Kathmandu, a long-time Thamel favourite for climbers returning from the big mountains. Dr Rick had just got back from Everest where he had performed heroics in the rescue of Bonita Norris, bringing her down from the South Summit singlehandedly before he was joined at the Balcony by a team of Sherpas.

Slurping his Everest beer, Rick mentioned in passing that he wanted to climb the three highest peaks in West Papua, a province of Indonesia previously known as Irian Jaya. The three also happen to be the highest peaks in Indonesia, Australasia, Oceania, the Western Pacific rim and doubtless other undefined regions too. Consequently, they are a part of the seven summits lists. I don't usually go in for lists, certainly not long ones, because the seemingly endless reiteration of the same thing quickly becomes boring, like pornography. Yet this short list offered a good reason to travel to an unusual and interesting place with little in the way of repetition.

The three highest peaks in West Papua are Carstensz Pyramid (4884m), Sumantri (4820m), and the unpronounceable Ngga Polu (4817m). This last one used to be number two as late as 1999 before its glacial snow dome began to melt. Sumantri and Ngga Polu now share the remains of the fast disappearing North Wall glacier, which confusingly lies on their south sides. In 2006 I had climbed Ngga Polu, the second highest, now the third. This time our target would be Sumantri now the second, previously the third.

There are three ways to access the Carstensz group. The simplest, in theory, would take a few hours, through the Grasberg mine west of the peak, 'Grasberg' being the Dutch for grass mountain. The mine, leased and operated by Freeport, is now a mile-wide hole in the ground easily seen from space and the biggest producer in the world of gold and the third largest of copper. The mine has a recent operating history as environmentally controversial as it is profitable. At the time of writing, June 2017, a major strike is underway and the Indonesian government are hovering in the wings with threats to take back control. To keep out curious visitors, Freeport has prohibited travel through the mine to reach the mountain. This is a great pity because relations with native Papuans make it difficult and dangerous to approach the mountain by passing close to the mine from the short access south side.

A second route, from the north, involves a six-day jungle trek from the jungle village of Sugapa. This has many disadvantages, not least of which is the jungle. This is now the normal approach. The third route and the one we chose this time, is by helicopter, arranged through our excellent agent, less of whom later. Though expensive it would allow us to complete the entire expedition in two weeks instead of four. Like battles, all expeditions have a starting line and for ours there was a choice: Bali or Jakarta. Although when I say 'choice', what I mean to say is, we started from Bali.

Old climbers have a very short attention span. So, while having every intention of looking up Carstensz expedition reports in the library, I found myself leafing through a worn copy of *New Scientist*. Nothing unusual there. But something in particular caught my attention: the summary of a paper on laboratory rats. They had been given a popular asthma drug and somehow this had reversed what researchers had dubbed Age-related Forgetfulness (ARF). After six weeks they were finding their way through the laboratory maze as well as the young ones, showing that old rats can learn new tricks. The magic ingredient was called Montelukast, a leukotriene receptor antagonist, and is a longstanding anti-asthma drug.

I decided it didn't really matter that six rat weeks might be the equivalent of several human years; I just wanted to join the lab rats and regain

Dr Rick and the Temple of Doom: on the rope bridge to the summit of Carstensz.

my memory. On top of which, of course, I am an asthmatic. So, after several false starts and wrong turns, I eventually remembered the way to my GP. In my head I had various elaborate explanations for my newfound desire to become an experimental animal. I needn't have bothered. Dr Natalie is very talkative and long before I could get round to rambling on about why I wanted to try the new regimen, she had prescribed Montelukast for my asthma.

A week later I was on my way to Bali. The Qatar cabin crew were delightfully patient, serving endless rounds of drinks and cheered us with smiles when the children across the aisle refused to sleep. The man next to me snored. I can never sleep on planes, so I drank the weak beer and watched the screen. The best film was *42*. Not the Douglas Adams '42', but the true story of the first black player to break the baseball colour barrier. The film gave a rather ageing Harrison Ford and his lopsided grin a supporting role. It was great feel-good fare, but the reason I found it arresting is that my climbing partner, Dr Rick, can from a certain angle and in the right light appear almost the doppelganger of Ford, the doctor's lopsided grin sometimes giving me the curious sensation that I'm actually climbing with the Hollywood actor himself.

From Bali, Harrison Ford and I flew to West Papua where torrential rain delayed our flight to base camp by two days. Then, rather abruptly on the third morning, we found ourselves dumped by helicopter under the north face of Carstensz. The idea was to start with Sumantri, via Ngga Polu, and the move on to Carstensz itself. A pile of bags and boxes needed to be transformed into base camp, and we needed to get going on the first objective as soon as possible. The rain was threatening to return in force. Our cook, and sometime engineering student, Arleen made tea. Armed with a bar of chocolate, Rick and I, carrying umbrellas, hurried north for Ngga Polu. It was six years since I had last climbed Ngga Polu. First we climbed out of the Yellow valley, traversing the small ridge separating it from the Dabu Dabu. Splitting a pair of copper blue lakes – Dabu means lake, so Dabu Dabu is two of them – the path rose eastwards before turning north, then continued east for an hour or so, reaching a high col before following easy slabs back north to the summit. I had forgotten all of this so when a new trail led enticingly up into the mists I had a blinding moment of reverse ARF: reverse Age Related Forgetfulness being the condition of remembering things that have not yet happened. So it was that I recognised this path. And when features I didn't recall turned up, for example the lines of burly cliffs barring all upward progress, I assumed I was sinking back into normal ARF and had simply forgotten something I had never seen before.

The path continued to thread its way through large-scale karst scenery, deep intersecting canyons of limestone that were, in essence, a giant maze, one that I was going to find hard to learn. From the confusing central canyons, a deep yellow ravine led to the snout of a tropical glacier. In the mist we could not determine from which summit it flowed and it didn't seem at all familiar. Instinct led us to a scree slope to the west, our left, where we discovered a slightly smaller but equally confusing maze of limestone canyons, then a second glacial tongue. The glacier above us would lead to something, we were sure, but exactly what was hidden in the mists.

Crampons on, and staggering upwards in the fog, calf deep in wet snow, we passed over heat-weakened snow bridges, all the while marvelling at this equatorial glacier. And as we plodded uphill we became increasingly sure that we were nowhere near our target mountain.

Then, out of the clouds, rose a tower of rock.

'This isn't Ngga Polu,' I said miserably. 'Neither is it Sumantri.'

We poked round the back of the tower to see if there was likely looking route to the top. A moat-like canyon surrounded the tower like a castle, filled with clouds and doom, impassable with the small amount of equipment we had brought. We headed back down, following our tracks, hoping for better weather the next day, arriving back at base exhausted from the altitude. We had been to almost 5,000m from sea level without any prior acclimatisation. A less forgetful team would have prepared themselves with a little pre-acclimatising or Diamox. We were dehydrated and hungry, but Arleen fed us well, tea, rice and curry, and next day we left at dawn.

Being a good experimental rat I had taken my asthma drugs in the hope I would remember a bit more about the Carstensz climb than I had the one up Ngga Polu. And it went well: when dawn arrived we were already halfway up the big long slabs and fixed ropes that lead to the summit ridge. The Grasberg mine was now less than three miles away; we could hear the grinding machinery, with the occasional loud rumble, which, in other mountains, might have signified avalanches. It was turning into a blue-sky day. The limestone was dry and someone had replaced the frayed fixed lines with new static rope. It all felt very good.

The Carstensz summit ridge is a straightforward scramble with one awkward notch that used to involve a short rappel and stiff little climb up the other side. Then a few years ago the notch became a Tyrolean traverse. This year someone had set up a three-strand rope bridge. This was just as terrifying as the Tyrolean but much easier and quicker. We were on the summit of Carstensz in perfect weather in just four hours from base camp. Looking south the coast was concealed behind low-lying fog, the huge Grasberg mine was churning noisily to the west, in other directions the vastness of New Guinea's highlands and jungle stretched away to the blue horizon.

To the north were the peaks of Sumantri and Ngga Polu, with their glacial apron. The weather was so clear we could spot yesterday's tracks in the snow. And then it dawned on me. While looking for Ngga Polu, we had turned back just under the summit of our second objective, Sumantri. I felt sheepish.

'Rick,' I said, as if there was anyone else to speak to. 'You know how people are often mistaken about mountains?' I was thinking of the Cheshire cat; Alice says she has often seen a cat without a smile, but never a smile without a cat.

'Yes?'

'Well, I have often heard of people thinking they were on the right mountain when they were on the wrong one, but I have never heard of anyone thinking they were on the wrong mountain when they were on the right one.'

Nodding sadly, the good doctor took a last photograph of himself, posing heroically on the summit, and turned to descend. Hand rappelling the fixed lines, we were back in camp by midday. We had enjoyed perfect weather all day, a situation almost unheard of in New Guinea. Arleen had tea and soup waiting for us. We still needed to re-find the route to Sumantri, so next day, over breakfast tea, we agreed we would follow exactly the same route from two days earlier. Yet within an hour we had abandoned what little discipline we had after spotting a fine looking path that led off over some small bluffs and into a steep canyon in seemingly the right direction. When we joined the old path I failed to recognise the place we had been just 48 hours before. It took 20 minutes of abject confusion before I recognised where I was.

'Some bloody lab rat.'

'What did you say?' the doctor asked.

'Just talking to m'self,' I replied, feeling rather glum, and then plodded off up the next canyon. Rick produced one of his lopsided Hollywood smiles. I still could not work out what it meant. Was it amusement? Or pity?

With better weather it was easy to see the correct route through the rock tower. Easy scrambling soon brought us to the second-highest summit in

The limestone mazes of the Sudirman range and their fast-disappearing glaciers.

Australasia. A couple of kilometres to the east was the now rocky summit of Ngga Polu and north of us the jungle. Rick leant over the northern edge to photograph the steep north wall of Sumantri.

'First climbed solo, by Reinhold,' I said. And looking down into the abyss, we both shuddered at the thought.

Cumulus clouds were now billowing up the south side, our line of descent. Sliding down the glacier, the sky changed its mood. Hail, followed by thunder and then evil lightning, sent us scampering back to Arleen's cooking. Two days later we were in Bali sipping Mai Tais. A young Balinese on a bicycle stopped and stared at the doctor, then asked to be photographed with him.

'You are famous!' the youth said.

'Yes he is,' I told him, 'but please keep it quiet. We don't need to attract crowds right now.' I motioned a zip across the mouth and made him stand beside the good doctor. The youth took his selfie with Rick and went away happy, then we ordered another round of Mai Tais.

'I'm sorry,' I told him, 'it was the only way. He wasn't going to leave till he had his photograph.'

Rick relaxed back on his rattan chair and continued watching the tourists drift by. 'Still, I'm sure about one thing,' I added.

'Yeah?'

'The jury's still out on whether Montelukast works for Age Related Forgetfulness. In fact, on the evidence so far I'm sure it doesn't. But my asthma seems to have gone.'

Art & Photography

Ambleside
Francis Towne (1740-1816)
1786. Watercolour and brown and gray ink over graphite on
medium slightly textured cream laid paper. 9¼ x 6⅛ inches.
Yale Center for British Art, Paul Mellon Collection.

DONALD M ORR

Image and Reality: On Three Paintings of Mountains

'Der Watzmann' (1825) by Caspar Friedrich.

Mountains, as subject matter for painters, are exposed to all the theories and philosophies prevalent at the time of their conception as works of art. They are never accurate accounts of geology or topography nor are they simply artistic records of structure and scale, form and colour, and while they may occasionally be peopled to assist scale, emphasise vista or aid a narrative aspect it has always been the mountain's sheer bulk and dominance of the landscape that invited their inclusion into the world of fine art. The Romantic tradition broke from the fixed views of the Classical School's version of landscape as an idealised setting based on the Roman countryside and moved to a more naturalistic sense of colour, an emotional content and an occasional foray into the exotic, as mountains and wilderness were now seen as the work of the divine, and an area of research, meditation and contemplation; they were Ruskin's 'great cathedrals of the earth' and as such he believed they had a powerful influence on the human spirit.

189

Mountains also have an impact upon our senses whether it is the roughness of granite on our hands or the tether of an ice axe round our wrist, touch is important. Hearing too, especially the silence at altitude, and smell and taste add to the mountain experience but sight has an extraordinary effect on our awareness. Within the mountain environment there exists an enormous variety of scene, a great diversity of features in rock and snow, and an endless permutation of light and weather impressions that can make our mountain days precious and our memories of them enduring. The few paintings discussed here are a point of departure, not a final word: there can be no conclusive statements about the mountain world. We continue to explore it seeking again that which we have known and hoping for new revelations.

'Der Watzmann'

While mountain backdrops had been a continuing feature of the work of Caspar David Friedrich[1], especially in the contemplation pieces such as 'Gebirgslandschaft mit Regenbogen' – 'Landscape with Rainbow'[2], he had been drawn to specific rock formations as dramatic reflections of creation but still with the human element meditating on the grandeur of the scene as in 'Kreidefelsen auf Rügen' – 'Chalk Cliffs on Rügen'.[3] By the mid 1820s Friedrich had a serious interest in geognosy that took him further from his base in Dresden and generated the largest canvases of his career. This concern with the emerging notion of geological timescales inspired by the ventures in the mountains and exploration of the furthest parts of the planet saw the production of 'Das Eismeer' – 'Sea of Ice' also known as 'The Wreck of Hope'[4], motivated by Parry's expedition of 1819-20 to locate the North-West Passage. But it is in the paintings 'Der Watzmann' and 'Die Hochgebirge'[5] that a major change in the direction of Friedrich's work is revealed. Prior to this he had concentrated on the moonlit skies, empty shores and rocky coasts that had made him a central figure of the German School of Painting throughout the Romantic period. In his search for an extreme of nature as an alternative to the classical idyll he turned to the mountains of Bavaria 'although he himself had never visited the Alps.'[6]

The shift in attention was generated by an interest in historical geology then referred to as geognosy, a recently developed science that attempted to trace Earth's history and the place of mountains within that history. James Hutton, wandering in the Cairngorms in 1785, 'found fingers of granite penetrating the sedimentary rocks in a way such as to suggest that the former had been molten and forced themselves into the older rocks from below'.[7] This pattern of rock destruction and renewal became

1. Caspar David Friedrich (1774-1840). The most purely Romantic of the German landscape painters of this period, most of his life was spent in Dresden where the best collections of his works are housed.
2. 'Gebirgslandschaft mit Regenbogan' (1809-10). Oil on canvas, 70 x 102mm Museum Folkwang, Essen.
3. 'Kreidefelsen auf Rügen' (1818). Oil on canvas, 90.5 x 71cm, Museum Oskar Reinhardt am Stadgarten.
4. 'Das Eismeer' (1823-4). Oil on canvas, 96.7 x 126.9cm, Kuntshalle Hamburg, Hamburg.
5. 'Der Watzmann' (1825). Oil on canvas, 135 x 170cm, Alte Nationalgalerie, Berlin.
'Die Hochgebirge' (1823-4). Oil on canvas, 132 x 167cm. Formerly in the National Gallery, Berlin, destroyed in 1945.
6. W Vaughan, *German Romantic Painting*, New Haven and London, Yale University Press, 1980, p110.
7. V della Dora, *Mountain*, London, Reaktion Books, 2016, p148.

known as Plutonism but the opposite, Neptunism stated that the earth had originally consisted of water and such materials within it had sedimented over time creating the core of the planet. This latter theory was promoted by Abraham Gottlob Werner a professor at the Freiberg Mining Academy who was comfortable within the Biblical timescale endorsed at that time. 'Der Watzmann' was 'inspired by Werner's theories and classifications of rocks, landscape features as a sequence of geological layers each set on a different visual plane and devoid of human presence.'[8]

Der Watzmann (2713m), the peak itself, is situated in south-east Upper Bavaria in the Berchtesgaden National Park forming the central range of the Berchtesgaden Alps. Within the canvas, the movement, from boulder-field and tor-like blocks, sweeps across intermediate hills to the towering majesty of the twin peaks of the massif. The mountain is portrayed as greater than anything mankind can fabricate and will endure beyond anything constructed by humanity. 'Friedrich's painting is recognisable as a hymn to the universal laws of mountain formation'[9] – as those laws were then understood by Werner and his followers. What is rendered is not a snapshot of the mountain but a composite of several topographies encompassing an entire Alpine scene; a range large enough to warrant the scale of the canvas. 'Landscape is for him a mode of auguring a new Germany,'[10] where natural history was seen as an irreversible process, legible to all, which demonstrated the inevitability of the historical future as Friedrich always painted German landscapes and never indulged in the 'Claudian' or ideal landscape of Arcadia. The Classical landscape, marked by stability of form, intellectualisation and restraint, was rejected for a heroic stance that reflected exceptional courage, nobility or fortitude. His work displays an emphasis on feeling and content, and projects the notion of individuality as an exceptional quality. The light sky, snowy peaks and open aspect of 'Der Watzmann' are a direct invitation to contemplate the majesty of the Alps and to enter this arena, to strive within the mountain environment, relishing its purity and eternal nature. While the scene is devoid of people, as viewers, we are the ones contemplating the mountain, we are the ones challenged to strive for its clarity and wholesomeness and be at one in the eternal perfection of nature.

'Die Hochgebirge', tragically lost in 1945 in the bombing of Dresden, is a far darker, more challenging Alpine scene viewed through a notch-like col, whose precipitous sides hint at the chasms below and whose ice-filled gullies lead to a summit ice-field beyond, which stretch the seemingly untouched, untrodden aiguilles of the massif. Simply approaching this mountain is arduous and strenuous. This is not a place for the tourist, only the strong and resilient, the persevering and tenacious will travel this path and ascend these high peaks. His design for the canvas, with the mountain contained between two ridges, is 'literally a contraction of a sketch of Mont

8. V della Dora, *Mountain*, London, Reaktion Books, 2016, p150.
9. T Mitchell, 'German Romantic Painting and Historical Geology,' *Art Bulletin*, Vol 66, No 3.
10. J L Koerner, *Caspar David Friedrich and the Subject of Landscape*, London, Reaktion Books, 1995, p243.

Anvert by Carus.'[11] However the contraction emphasises the steep nature of the terrain and converts the distant snow-capped summit ridge into a remote lustrous spectre. Whatever may have been borrowed, 'the sense of unrelieved loneliness is his own.' For Friedrich, mountains were places of complete lifelessness and silent reserve, sacred places in an age, as he saw it, of soulless materialism. His work was an intricate balance of observation and symbolic meaning yet there is no contradiction here, no paradox nor ambiguity in his painting.

A fine series of mountain studies also exists of sandstone towers in the Elbesandsteingebirge now housed in the Neue Gallerie Kunsthistorisches in Vienna: 'Rocky Gorge in the Elbesandsteingebirge' (oil on canvas, 94 x 73cm) and in the delicate 'The Rock Gates in Neurathen' produced between 1826 and 1828 (a watercolour study over a pencil drawing 27.9 x 24.5cm) housed in The Hermitage, St Petersburg.

Friedrich's view of nature was theocentric: 'one saw God in what he had made, a diffuse and vast presence behind the screen of natural facts.'[12] The contemplative figures silhouetted in the loneliness of the mystery of nature are often linked to the highly allegorical elements where ships represent the journey through life and mountains the grandeur of God. Broadly speaking the 'Romantic conception of nature as the revelation of the infinite within the finite – of the divine creation in the world'[13] was central to Friedrich's work where his individual response to nature was to combine knowledge with feeling.

Friedrich's particular German philosophy had a great influence on the genre of Bergfilm, most popular in Weimar Germany and promoted and advanced by Arnold Fanck, which drew on the 'aesthetic conventions and iconography of nineteenth-century Romantic landscape painters, such as Caspar David Friedrich.'[14] The Alpine peaks, plunging gorges and eternal snows became projections and reflections of inner forces. In *The Holy Mountain* (1926), *The White Hell of Pitz Palu'* (1929) and in Leni Riefenstahl's directorial debut, *The Blue Light* (1932) sublime emotions and masculine heroic feats were set against the backdrop of the high Alps endorsing the greatest human virtues and named in the closing screen titles of *The Holy Mountain* as 'fidelity – truth – loyalty – faith.'

'Mont Sainte Victoire'[15]

This mountain in western Provence is in fact a massif extending over 18km, the highest point of which is Pic des Mouches (1011m). Its limestone ridge is clearly visible from Aix-en-Provence where Cézanne lived for many years. The mountain landscape of Provence is known as *garrigue*, low, open scrubland with a poor soil that maintains many evergreen shrubs, low trees, aro-

11. W Vaughan, *German Romantic Painting*, New Haven and London, Yale University Press, 1980, p110.
12. R Hughes, *Nothing If Not Critical*, London, Harvill, 1990, p90.
13. C Harrison, P Wood, J Gaiger. *Art in Theory* 1815-1900, Oxford, Blackwell, 1998, p12.
14. V della Dora, *Mountain*, London, Reaktion Books, 2016, p102.
15. Cézanne painted some 60 versions of this feature between 1882 and 1906 both in oils and watercolour. One of the most popular is from 1904-6, an oil on canvas, 29 x 36 inches in the Philadelphia Museum of Art.

'Mont Sainte Victoire' (1904-6) by Paul Cézanne. *(Alamy)*

matic herbs and bunchgrasses and popularised in the films *La Gloire de Mon Père* and *Le Château de Ma Mère*.

In his many paintings of this subject, Paul Cézanne[16] 'transformed a relatively minor peak in southern France ... into the most celebrated mountain in Western art.'[17] He presents a mountain as an interaction between the land mass and the environment it is located in. As such the context is everything and any notion of uniformity or stereotypical imagery is lost. Central to his painting of 'Mont Sainte Victoire' is 'a vast curiosity about the relativeness of seeing, coupled with an equally vast doubt that he or anyone else could approximate it in paint.'[18] The relationships of the landscape elements revealed under a shifting light are rendered in broken outlines where the motif of the mountain displays his process of seeing. The hesitancy of his vision is depicted in his invitation to us to look and ascertain exactly what a mountain is, how we perceive it and assimilate all its features.

---

16. Paul Cézanne (1839-1906) was one of the major figures in European art both as an Impressionist and Post-Impressionist. From 1886, on the death of his father, he lived near Aix-en-Provence.
17. E Bernbaum, *Sacred Mountains of the World*, San Francisco, Sierra Club, 1992, p232.
18. R Hughes, *The Shock of the New*, London, Thames & Hudson, 1996, p18.

Cézanne was never interested in the sinuous lines and decorative flatness of Gauguin as nature was never the same; the mountain was different every day. The changing sensations of landscape are rendered anew in the studies he made where the intensity of the landscape's sparse hillsides, the shifting light in the heat of the day and the limestone crags and arêtes are depicted afresh in each study. 'He never painted the same mountain twice'[19], as his scrutiny rendered every part of the canvas as a continually changing scene. To realise these changes meant that Cézanne needed to articulate the varying aspects of light and shadow that angled planes and deepened tones across the landscape to the bulk of the mountain. 'His goal was presence, not illusion.'[20] The enduring existence in the shifting angles of the sun, the altering hues of rock and foliage, the effects of mist or twilight, wind and weather. His paintings of Mont Sainte Victoire are examinations of space and depth and describe a sense of multiplicity as the governing element of reality where what we see is what we see today under these conditions.

His mountain canvases were an exploration of naturalistic truth and would later be developed into abstraction by the Cubists. His use of colour and tone, the telescoping of fore and mid-ground counteracted the enclosed space of previous artists. These paintings were about space itself, not merely as a decorative feature but as a new, stronger relationship between three-dimensional illusion and the painted surface where the faceted planes of the mountain may appear to oscillate back and forth between surface and image yet are bound to both. Thus, illusion and flatness, facet and stroke, space and movement seem to dislimn the picture then allow a re-incorporation of itself.

'He constructs a conventional but tense and highly concentrated landscape,'[21] an emotional yet stable treatment, a lyrical complex of broken features and jagged forms that maintains a spatial harmony and balance. Background and foreground achieve equal status and topographical features disappear from the plain before the mountain until an evanescent sea of colour allows one to sail to 'the heart of the geological drama, right to the undefined core, where apparent and imagined reality is one.'[22] The Classical concept of perspective was enhanced by a change in spatial awareness, observed colour and an emotional and spiritual dimension. Convergent lines and graded colour became obsolete yet there is no suggestion of a motionless world as his paintings seem to move and expand in an eternal interplay of shapes and colours.

'Glencoe, Argyllshire'

The paintings of Horatio McCulloch[23] exhibit a clarity and naturalness that was highly innovative in the 19th century. His many trips to the west Highlands and Islands of Scotland allowed him to render his canvases with an authenticity that maintained the landscapes' grandeur without the

19. R Hughes, *Nothing If Not Critical*, London, Harvill, 1990, p125.
20. R Hughes, *Nothing If Not Critical*, London, Harvill, 1990, p125.
21. F Elgar, *Cézanne*, London, Thames & Hudson, 1969, p216.
22. F Elgar, *Cézanne*, London, Thames & Hudson, 1969, p142.
23. H McCulloch (1805-67) was a Royal Scottish Academician, born in Glasgow, died in Edinburgh.

'Glencoe, Argyllshire' (1864) by Horatio McCulloch.

cloying sentimentality displayed by many of his contemporaries.

'Glencoe, Argyllshire'[24] is unique in is presentation of Buachaille Etive Mòr, the great herdsman of Etive, where Glen Coe meets Glen Etive. The modern view of 'the Buachaille' is characterised in many images taken from the main road from the south, the A82, as it rises over the Blackmount, where the peak of Stob Dearg rises sharply and the mountain ridge angles south-west, forming the northern side of Glen Etive. McCulloch's observation is clearly taken from the east, from the area around the Kings House Hotel. Built in the 17th century for travellers across Rannoch Moor, it was used as a barracks from 1746 but later in the 18th century had reverted to its former role. This watercolour sketch is less well known that the large canvas of the same year and title exhibited in the Kelvingrove Museum, Glasgow.[25] The view was well known to McCulloch as his earlier 'The Entrance to Glencoe from Rannoch Moor' of 1846[26] reveals.

In this study, he captures the bleak ruggedness of the mountain and its dominance of the landscape. While the sky is rendered freshly, the clouds shredding themselves over the ridges to reveal the clarity of the blue sky beyond, the weather overshadows the landscape, enhancing the sense of wildness and desolation; the cloud-filled Glen Etive is to be avoided. The small figures in the middle ground, one on horseback, are dominated by the landscape yet travel on using the mountain as a beacon or signpost

24. 'Glencoe, Argyllshire' (1864). Watercolour and body colour over pencil on paper, 13.60 x 21.60cm, National Gallery of Scotland, Edinburgh.
25. 'Glencoe' (1864). Oil on canvas, 1105 x 1829mm, Kelvingrove Museum and Art Galleries.
26. 'The Entrance to Glencoe From Rannoch Moor' (1846). Oil on canvas, 34.6 x 60.6cm, private collection.

on their journey. The treatment of the mountain is vague, in part to the weather and changing light but also, one senses, as a simplification of the many gullies and buttresses that seam the north face of the mountain. The painting is not just about the mountain but about being in the mountains of the West Highlands where changeable weather systems still make conditions difficult for the traveller on foot or the mountaineer. The image is at once an invitation to explore this wild environment and a warning that it is no easy tourist experience. Glen Coe is open and approachable but the traveller must be well prepared.

Whatever influences there may have been in his work his highly individual approach to Scottish landscape painting and, in particular, Highland and mountain scenery, with a truth and understanding that hitherto had been absent. During his lifetime 'he was fortunate that his fondness for painting the wilder parts of his country coincided with public taste'[27] but his legacy of mountain landscapes, so thoroughly explored, still exhibits the clear, cold blustery freshness any climber might meet in Glen Coe.

27. S Smith, *Horatio McCulloch 1805-1867*, Glasgow, Glasgow Museums and Galleries, 1988, p22.

JOHN CLEARE

1967: One Old Man
Recalls Another

The Old Man of Hoy

William Daniell visited the Old Man of Hoy in 1815 during his epic journey
around the coast of Britain, completed over the period 1813 to 1823. Daniell
(1769–1837) was an English landscape and marine painter, and printmaker,
notable for his work in aquatint. He travelled extensively in India in the
company of his uncle Thomas Daniell, with whom he collaborated on one
of the finest illustrated works of the period: *Oriental Scenery.*

It all began 51 years ago in a Holyhead pub. Alan Chivers, 'Chiv', head of
BBC TV Outside Broadcasting, joined a group of climbers and television
engineers refreshing themselves after the live broadcast from Craig Gogarth.

'Gather round, fellows,' he called, 'the DG's been on the blower. He says
well done and he wants another climb for next year. But where? Any ideas?'

'There's a bluidy great sea stack up in the Northern Isles,' suggested that
doyen of Scottish mountaineering Tom Patey. ''Tis 400ft high and virgin.
I'll do some research ...'

Come the autumn and the Old Man of Hoy was no longer virgin. In the
summer Tom had persuaded Rusty Baillie and Chris Bonington up to
the island of Hoy in the Orkney archipelago, where they had climbed the
slender 450ft rock pillar that stands off Hoy's intimidating western cliffs.

197

The rock – Devonian Old Red Sandstone – was poor, aid and Yosemite-style rope tactics had been used, and Rusty, who had led the crux, a bottomless, overhanging crack, had graded the climb XS/A3. The climb itself would go, and as Chris' photographs demonstrated, the location was indeed spectacular. The logistics appeared daunting.

Tom researched in depth, and in the autumn, after a few days in Ullapool, he entrusted me with the result to deliver to Chris Brasher at the Beeb. *Tom's Bumper Fun Book* was a foolscap-sized scrapbook, reinforced with pink NHS adhesive plaster, containing page after page of pasted cuttings from ferry timetables, information flyers, *The Orcadian* newspaper and photocopies of maps, ancient and modern, annotated by Tom's spidery handwriting. It detailed the history of the Old Man; an Elizabethan map indicated merely a fortified site at the tip of a narrow peninsula, but over the centuries caves had become tunnels and then arches, and in due course a free-standing stack was born, though it resembled more a horse than a man. By 1815, however, the horse's rump had fallen away and a recognisable Old Man had appeared, albeit with two legs. Only later did documented storms create the pillar we know today. Tom listed the name and phone number of every Orcadian who might be useful and every facility that might be required, notably Jack Rendell, the crofter at Rackwick, nearest habitation to the Old Man, who held the key to the old schoolhouse, now a primitive hostel for birdwatchers. There were even notes on Hoy birdlife: apparently the *bonxies* or great skuas could be troublesome. He suggested an engineering firm adept at moving heavy equipment to remote Highland construction sites. An historic document if ever there was, it became one of Brasher's prize possessions.

All very well, but was it possible to get a television signal back from the remote cliff-top? In January 1967 I flew up to Orkney with Alan Chivers, Brasher and several BBC engineers, where we met Tom and on one short, dark winter's day we crossed over to Hoy where he led us over the hills to the Old Man. I climbed down to the shore to take photographs while the engineers confirmed that if we could drive the cameras, they could get the transmission back into the national system. The wheels started to turn in earnest and a broadcast was scheduled for early July.

In April the BBC organised a climbing reconnaissance. We flew up from London in a chartered eight-seater de Haviland Dove, collecting Rusty Baillie en route in Glasgow and Tom in Inverness. Tom would be bringing his secret new rope-mate, rumoured to be a vivacious brunette. Among other tasks, we were to climb high on the Old Man so that I could shoot the necessary promotional pictures, and confirm my suggestion that two new routes should be attempted concurrent with the original one. Much of rock climbing can be painfully slow, and this would guarantee that the director could, in real time, cut to 'exciting action' on one route or another. With little room for baggage, we'd arranged that I would bring my cameras; Rusty, knowing exactly what was required, would organise the ironmongery, while Tom and his mysterious new friend would contribute plenty of rope.

Going, going, not yet gone: a view from sea level taken in 1967. *(All images John Cleare)*

At Inverness our expectations were dashed. Sydney was no lithe climbing lass but a lean, weather-beaten, rugged-looking clergyman with a wry laugh and an accent that melded East Lancashire with Aberdeen. As an Anglican missionary on Baffin Island, based at Great Whale River, he had done several new routes solo. As chaplain at Peterhead Prison he was indeed a hard man, and Tom took great delight in explaining how they had met. Perusing the *Press & Journal* while awaiting 'customers' in his Ullapool surgery, a report caught his eye telling how a certain clerical gentleman, a keen solo climber, had recently survived a fall of several hundred feet on snow-plastered Lochnagar and had walked away without a scratch,

Above: A tractor towing BBC TV equipment from Rackwick up to the cliff-top. Hamish MacInnes rides shotgun.

Left: Some of the climbers warmed up for the live broadcast on Hoy with the first ascent of Yesnaby Castle, off the west coast of Orkney Mainland. Rev Sydney Wilkinson making the Tyrolean back to shore.

Right: Dougal Haston on the south-east arête, left, with Chris Bonington on the long crack pitch on the east face.

attributing his survival to watchful angels. Ever ready to embrace new technology, Tom reckoned he'd be a useful rope mate, insurance as it were, and made contact. And now Syd was part of our team.

At the foot of the Old Man we broke out the gear: a limited selection of pegs and bongs, jumars, krabs, several bolts and a couple of *coins de bois*. Tom uncoiled two well-used 30m climbing ropes and from his sack Sydney emptied several hundred feet of orange 5mm fisherman's polypropylene line.

'That's not proper rope,' protested Rusty. 'It's string. I'm not climbing on that.'

'Och, it's fine fur abseiling provided yer dinna pause,' Sydney countered, 'Ah thought it better tae have too much rope than too little!'

I got my pictures, both on the spectacular crux of the original east face route, and also on the south-east arête, which we established was certainly possible. We ventured a little way up the south face and that too appeared viable. The climbing was essentially vertical, very strenuous and very fingery, the characteristic horizontal weathering providing plenty of rounded, sand-lubricated holds with frequent thin flutings that would snap off like digestive biscuit. The most reliable protection seemed to be horizontally placed bongs. No one actually trusted Sydney's polypropylene line so we caught no glimpses of angels.

Detailed planning now began: Chris Bonington with Tom Patey as his foil would repeat the east face, carefully rehearsed and timed. Simultaneously Pete Crew and Dougal Haston, who happened to be in training for their forthcoming attempt on Cerro Torre, would be pointed at the virgin south-east arête while Joe Brown with his foil, Ian McNaught-Davis, would attempt the blank wall of the south face. Everything would be visible to the half dozen outside-broadcast cameras placed at strategic positions around and below the grassy cliff-top opposite. Meanwhile, with portable radio cameras, Hamish MacInnes aided by Ian Clough and Pete Biven, would shoot close-ups from prepared stances on the east face, while Rusty and I would grab what close-ups we could on the arête and the south face. The live broadcast would run over two days as a sequence of 'slots', allowing the delights both of bivouacking and abseiling to be demonstrated. Sydney was appointed chief sherpa.

Logistically it was the most ambitious exercise the BBC had ever undertaken. Embarked on army landing craft, a convoy of large vehicles – the complete Scottish Outside Broadcast Unit – sailed from the Clyde up to the great Orkney anchorage of Scapa Flow, to come ashore at Lyness, an abandoned naval base on Hoy's gentle eastern shore. Some 12 miles of narrow lanes led to the sheltered bay of Rackwick, the almost deserted crofting settlement in the only gap in Hoy's western cliffs, where the trucks

Haston at work on pitch two of the south-east arête.

were 'gutted' and their contents loaded onto large sledges to be hauled by a powerful caterpillar tractor two miles up steep rock-strewn slopes and over a boggy 750ft col to the cliff edge. Here the BBC reassembled their equipment to create an editorial control room in several large tents, erected by the army and hopefully storm-proof. It was all very impressive.

We assembled in Orkney at the end of June, Ian Clough and I with our wives, and with Peter Gillman of the *Sunday Times* to keep the nation informed. We pitched our tents in the meadow beside the old school hostel at Rackwick. A platoon of Scots Guards, fresh from the Borneo jungle, had been loaned to the BBC, presumably disguised as an 'R and R' exercise, and they'd pitched a large mess tent where army cooks were to keep us fed and watered. Two young subalterns, resplendent in their tweed knickerbockers, went off rabbiting with their shotguns. Almost immediately the Old Man had two ascents, one by Joe and Pete who confirmed our earlier reconnaissance with an abseil descent of the south face, and one by Rusty and I to organise safe belays, a crucial task, for the untrustworthy rock was to see heavy and hurried traffic both up and down. The abseil points in particular required serious preparation and we fitted a strop of steel cable round the lower summit to replace loose blocks before placing one of Rusty's long three-eighth of an inch bolts at each stance.

While the planned new routes were correctly billed as unclimbed, so as to keep moving over the three spectacular small roofs at the start of the arête on the big day, Haston spent some time drilling the several points of aid required. Joe, however, having made his recce, was happy to leave the south face until transmission. The east face original route was to be the 'control', and consequently needed careful preparation; Chris and Tom were scheduled to be climbing certain moves at specific moments, so rehearsal and timing were essential. Chris repeated the overhanging crack crux several times, removing loose rock, organising decent protection and reducing Rusty's original A3 grade to a free E1.

With God on our side. The Anglican missionary Sydney Wilkinson belaying Rusty Baillie on the east face in April 1967 during a preparatory visit ahead of filming.

We'd recruited five climbing friends to join Sydney's sherpas, and they were kept busy, carving out camera platforms on the facing cliffs, fixing ropes down to the shore and laying cables. The day's work done, Sydney was keen to climb the Old Man himself but there was a peculiar reluctance to rope up with him. Eventually, the fell-runner Eric Beard, 'Beardie', took pity and offered his services, but as the day wore on his scepticism about angelic involvement overtook his valour; he confided his fears to Tom. Ever ready with a cure, the good doctor contrived a 'rock fall' and Beardie was despatched to Stromness hospital for a check-up.

After a week Alan Chivers was happy that we were ready to roll, so we all sailed off across Scapa Flow to Stromness – Tom Patey's *Venice of the North* – for a rest. But there was still work to do: Chiv's game plan required filming a trailer, although climbing elsewhere, for transmission on the evening prior to the weekend jollies on the Old Man itself. Thus we spent a leisurely day a few miles up the coast from Stromness at Yesnaby where the Castle, a spectacular virgin sea stack shaped like an inverted wedge, stood a rope-length off 100ft cliffs. Rusty led the assault, abseiling into the choppy sea and swimming across to the stack. Sydney joined him and they fixed a steeply sloping Tyrolean which Joe descended dry-shod to lead the climb. A Tyrolean from the summit delivered all three back to *terra firma*. The angels stood down and the hotel in Stromness ran out of beer.

Waiting for the final transmission, the stars of the 1967 broadcast, clockwise
from Dougal Haston, who is lying down looking a the camera, Tom Patey,
Ian McNaught-Davis, Joe Brown, Pete Crew, Chris Bonington and Pete Biven,
who was working on Hamish MacInnes' team. MacInnes and Baillie were down
below, de-rigging their camera position. Smoke is visible from the burning
heather that almost got out of hand.

Despite wind and damp, overcast weather, the live broadcasts on Saturday afternoon and evening went according to plan: it was almost an
anti-climax. On the east face Chris powered his way up the overhanging
crack, leaving Tom to repeat the spectacular swing far out into space of the
first ascent before jumaring up the hanging rope Yosemite-style, gushing
repartee the while. On the south face, linked by stiff co-axial cable and
weighed down with heavy radio-camera backpacks, walkie-talkies and
climbing gear, Rusty and I were thankful when Joe and Mac reached 'the
mouth', the shallow bivouac cave in the sandstone flutings on the far side
of the face, and we could abseil off and then trudge back up fixed ropes to
the cliff-top in the drizzly gloaming. Joined by Tom and Chris and Hamish's
camera crew, we watched the final floodlit shots of the Old Man as the two
bivouacked parties settled down for the night on their ledges, amply provi-
sioned, we knew, with goodies and plenty of scotch, before we left to enjoy
our own steak and chips, army-style, with appropriate refreshment.

Next day the sequence of live transmissions continued in better weather.
Despite the night's drizzle even the bivouackers were in good form, all
went according to plan and millions of television viewers sat glued to their
screens. By the time our radio camera broke down, the climbers had all
disappeared from view anyway, so we lowered off the gear and traversing

onto the east face joined the others on the summit. There was one final transmission to go and an hour to kill.

The Old Man has two summits separated by a small cleft where the final pitch on the east face – a perfect dièdre – meets the top of a chimney system on the west face. Sooner or later this is where the pillar will split in two and stepping across requires a steady head. The slightly higher summit is almost square, the lower considerably larger and slightly sloping; in 1967 both were still covered in grass, heather and wild flowers and on the latter the team were disporting themselves amid a tangle of ropes. Somehow the wherewithal materialised and Rusty soon had a stove going in a sheltered cranny, a brew on the way.

I'm not sure who first noticed the smoke or who caused it: Tom, Joe and Pete were all smokers. It drifted up from a heather clump and with ropes all over the place there was general consternation before Chris stamped out the flames.

'An old Hieland custom,' explained Tom, looking guilty. 'The clan warriors would celebrate a victory by firing the heather.' No one was amused.

The final transmission was billed to be a 400ft free abseil from the summit, claimed to be the world's longest ever, and Joe had been volunteered to brave it, a fact of which he seemed unaware. Hamish had supplied a special non-stretch mountain rescue rope for the purpose, and sherpas tied off the lower end to boulders some way out from the Old Man's foot. Fearing that friction from a regular device might melt the rope, Hamish had constructed a secret weapon which he now produced with a flourish from his rucksack. It resembled a sort-of overgrown block and tackle built of heat dissipating plates of some strange material.

Joe took a look at it. 'Yer want me ter go down on that?' he protested. 'It's almost as big as me.' Chris stepped in.

'That's okay, Joe, I'd like to do it.' Joe bowed out gracefully. It was nevertheless a very circumspect Bonington who stepped gingerly off the summit of the Old Man to slide slowly down and away into the Orcadian dusk. The Old Man of Hoy had claimed its first entry in the record books.

Twenty-three years later I repeated the climb with Mike Banks and was taken aback to discover that Rusty's three-eighths of an inch abseil bolts had rusted away to three-sixteenths. It happens to us all, even the Old Man.

DENNIS GRAY

'Hazard': The Life
of Tom Stobart

Alf Gregory's portrait of Tom Stobart. *(RGS)*

In 1959, I spent a month in the Dolomites working on the film *Hazard*, directed by Tom Stobart. I have been interested in his story ever since. He sprang to prominence as a member of the 1953 Everest expedition, responsible for the Oscar-nominated film *The Conquest of Everest*. But this was just one episode in a life brim full with adventure in the wilder regions of the Earth.

I first noted his name on a visit to Wharncliffe in the late 1950s, while climbing a Very Severe called *Himmelswillen*, which translates as 'for heaven's sake!' Tom had made the first ascent solo while a 19-year-old studying zoology at Sheffield University in 1933. I looked up a history of the university's climbing club, which describes Tom as their leading climber at that time, responsible for several other new routes in the Peak District. His father had been something of a climber and caver, and been on expeditions to Spitzbergen and climbed in the Alps. Noel Odell, the last person to see Mallory and Irvine alive on their fateful attempt on Everest's summit in 1924, was a close family friend in Sussex where Tom had grown up, inspired by these legends and wishing himself to become a Himalayan mountaineer.

Such aspirations lead climbers into career choices, and today there is a panoply of jobs within the sport: instructing, filming, photography, journalism, guiding, manufacturing and retailing. In the 1930s an adventurous spirit needed to be a pioneer to make a living out of wilderness activities. Graduating from Sheffield, Tom took up a scholarship to Cambridge, but found it was not taking him where he wished to be, so he made the brave decision to follow an interest he had developed in film. A film unit had been set up at the experimental education centre at Dartington Hall in Devon. Tom saw that it was making adventure films and he enrolled. He wrote later: 'In 1937 the film industry was one of the most difficult in the world to get into unless you knew the right people. Moreover what I wanted to do was not even something in the normal line of film work and it had never been attempted as a full-time job. I wanted to film original exploration and mountaineering expeditions – and that was not normal film work.'

While part of the Dartington Hall Film Unit he began work on his first film, *Physical Geography of Rivers* (1939). During filming he met the girl of his dreams, a raven-haired Romanian ballet student called Kara, whose mother was determined to bring her home as the clouds of war gathered; Tom decided to follow her and make a great film that would rescue Romania's rather poor reputation, and was consequently trapped in that country when the storm of war arrived. Tom was in trouble as Romania sided with Germany; he was seen as a spy and expelled with immediate effect. His route back to England travelling west was blocked, so he set out east through Bulgaria, Turkey, and Syria, travelling third class, roughing it. (Kara stayed behind, and Tom wrote of their parting: 'she would always act too late just as surely as I would always act too soon.') He must have made a memorable impression on those he met: Tom was six foot six, with a thatch of blond hair, deep blue eyes, and a big, generous smile, which is how I remember him from 1959. He covered the final section by ship, travelling deck class to fetch up stony broke in India, where, after living on the breadline working for Indian filmmakers, he joined the army and set up the service's first film unit on the sub-continent.

As soon as he could get away from his army duties he set out on a trek to the Nanda Devi range, and in 1945, at the end of the war in Europe, he organised a lightweight expedition to climb and film an attempt on Nun (7135m), then still unclimbed. With him was Roy Berry, father of the Bristol climber Steve. After setting up two camps on the mountain, the ascent ground to a halt due to the failure of their stoves; an over-strong and enthusiastic Sherpa called Saki stripped the threads off them. But Tom learned a lot about the difficulties of mountain filming on this pioneering trip.

The fox and the spy: Tom Stobart riding a camel in Jordan in 1962, taken by the zoologist and filmmaker Tony Morrison. Morrison was working for Stobart and the famous Daily Mail correspondent Ralph Izzard on a film for a David Attenborough series. On their way back to Beirut, Stobart bought a fox cub from a local man, which he put into the care of Morrison, since Stobart was returning to Italy to visit his wife Jane at their home in Bordighera. Morrison, having weaned and cared for the cub, in turn gave it to Kim Philby, then living in Beirut, who developed a deep attachment to the creature he named Jackie. It has been suggested that Jackie's death, found dead in the street, prompted Philby's final flight to the Soviet Union. *(With thanks to Tony Morrison/ nonesuchexpeditions.com)*

Returning to the UK after the war, Tom's career as a cameraman, thanks to his work in India, was firmly established and he was invited by what was to become the British Antarctic Survey to travel to the white continent as a documentary filmmaker. Again, this was ground-breaking work: Tom learned a lot about filming in extreme weather and cold conditions. Adventure documentaries and natural history programmes for TV developed apace during his career. At the forefront of these in the early 1950s was the wildlife cinematography of Armand and Michaela Denis, who funded their first film working on the movie *King Solomon's Mines*, Michaela performing as Deborah Kerr's stunt double. Tom worked on some of their documentaries as cameraman.

News of the British attempt on Everest in 1953 reached Tom as he was recovering from a severe liver illness contracted working in Africa, and he only just recovered in time to make it on the team, being the last appointed. With typical aplomb, he had cabled he was available to film the ascent if he was asked to do so.

Filming in high mountains is a thankless task. To get good results requires total dedication to the job and on Everest Tom Stobart was to find how difficult it was to work without hindering the climbing. He brought to the task know-how of filming in extreme conditions that few could match at that time. George Lowe recalled Tom's commitment in the *Alpine Journal* not long after Tom's death.

> *During the expedition his concentration on filming was total. He was there, bent over his tripod, his right arm and finger angled high above the camera button. We didn't see him as we walked and talked, for he was somewhere getting a long shot or close in on the local colour. At meals on the trek he wasn't eating, he was working.*

His main cameras weighed 8lb each, whilst his lightweight handheld ones were two and a half pounds. Unfortunately, perhaps because he had not sufficiently recovered from his African malaise, he developed pneumonia, and had to retreat from the high camps, descending below base to a yak-herder's hut. But not before he had persuaded other team-members – Alf Gregory, George Lowe and Ed Hillary – to continue filming with the hand-held cameras even near the summit. Fortunately he recovered his strength in time to capture the memorable scenes of the climbers returning from the summit. The Everest film was a huge success, being nominated for an Oscar, and shown in mainstream cinemas around the world.

Tom did not rest on his laurels, in 1954 leading an expedition backed by the *Daily Mail* to search for the yeti and learn more about it. The following year he spent in the Everest region, working on an anthropological film about the life of the Sherpa communities, *Tensing's Country* (1955). The following year, a drama occurred that would affect the rest of his life. Tom was a skilled raconteur and I remember this story the keenest of any he told in 1959. He returned to filming in Africa and in a remote area of Ethiopia, making a natural history programme, a local guide became mentally unstable and opened fire on Tom's party with his rifle. Several of the party were shot and Tom suffered injuries, which left him being partially disabled, with two direct hits to his legs that severed nerves and smashed one of his knees.

It took him quite some time to recover from this terrible event, but while he did so, he wrote his first book, the first of several, an autobiography titled *Adventurer's Eye* published to some acclaim in 1958. Despite his injuries he also returned to filming, making a documentary about the steelmaking community in Consett. This led to plans for a safety film for steelworkers titled *Hazard*.

This was for 1959 an innovative project, with a cast of well-known actors and a full professional film crew, and a budget to match. It was a story about two steelworkers from Sheffield who are keen climbers. One is a risk-taking daredevil, the other more reasoned and careful. The action begins in the steelworks and the fact of the different approaches to safety by the two main characters is established by some very dangerous actions leading to some near-misses by the daredevil. For their holidays they travel out to the Dolomites to attempt a new route, and inevitably the approach to this by the risk-taker leads them into serious difficulty and an accident with a dramatic rescue.

Joe Brown led our six-man climbing team and the action sequences were filmed throughout the Cortina region: Tofana, Tre Cime, Cinque Torre. We soon learned that film work is no rest cure. We acted as guides to the camera crews, led them up rock faces to good camera positions, carried heavy film equipment, built platforms for cameras and sound recorders, portered up to film locations 30 prepared dinners each day from local refuges. Among the more bizarre items we carried around were a 20ft ladder and sacks of straw to put underneath in case of a fall: essential to get some of the stars above ground level. It was a serious business but there were lots of laughs, especially when we doubled for the stars.

For me the most interesting part of all this was observing how Tom ran the show. He briefed the crew and the actors what he wanted from a shot, but he left the details – how to pose, for example – to his actors, giving them the freedom to interpret the brief as they saw best as professional performers. On occasion his patience was impressive; one of the actors had trouble remembering his lines and this led to dozens of takes balanced above the ground. Yet I never saw him even slightly annoyed or unruffled. *Hazard* was highly successful. Like Tom's Everest film, it was shown in mainstream cinemas and nominated for a BAFTA. It was screened at a Kendal Mountain Film Festival a few years ago and received an enthusiastic reception from a full house despite being more than five decades old.

Tom made more than a dozen films, and was awarded a BAFTA certificate of merit. In later life he became well known as a writer on cooking, herbs and food. He wrote two seminal books about these subjects, *The Cook's Encyclopaedia: Ingredients and Processes*, and a guide to *Herbs, Spices and Flavourings*. He also published a book about filming wildlife, *Tiger Trail* (1975)

Stobart in Beirut. Morrison stayed
with the Stobarts in Italy in 1963,
and Stobart returned to Jordan in
1964, filming with Joe Brown.
After a failed filming venture in India,
Stobart struggled financially at his
last home on Mallorca before his
early death in 1980. *(Tony Morrison)*

and an American edition of his autobiography, *I Take Pictures for Adventure*.

The last film he directed was about animal traders stealing monkeys in India, 1979's *The Great Monkey Rip Off*. Unusually, despite the serious subject matter, Tom produced it as a comedy; the film made quite an impression internationally. It was to be his last great effort; Tom died suddenly from a heart attack in 1980, at a railway station in West Sussex, on a visit to England from his home in Mallorca. He was 66.

Like so many in his teens he was enraptured by climbing, his early adventures as a student rock climber led on to a life fulfilled by an art form he discovered he was exceptionally good at. It complimented his adventurous approach to living. It seems to me that this is something you either have built into your psyche or not, and that Tom had this in abundance his life story confirms. He really did possess an 'adventurer's eye.'

History

Yewbarrow, Wastwater
Edward Lear (1812-88)
16 September 1836. Graphite with stumping and white gouache on moderately
thick, moderately textured, gray-green wove paper. 6¾ x 10⅛ inches.
Yale Center for British Art, gift of Donald C Gallup.

JONATHAN WESTAWAY

Eric Shipton's Secret History

Peaks north-east of Zug Shaksgam from the point reached by Eric Shipton
and Bill Tilman. *(All images courtesy of the Shipton family)*

E ric Shipton was notoriously circumspect about many aspects of his life
and there is much that remains unexplained about his career and his
motivations. Mountain travel books like *Mountains of Tartary* (1950) tell us
next to nothing about the political context of his time as consul-general in
Kashgar, Xinjiang in the years 1940-2 and 1946-8, indeed the text serves
quite deliberately to deceive. Enmeshed in the apparatus of the British
Imperial security state in Chinese Central Asia, Shipton became adept at
covering his tracks by directing his readers' attention elsewhere.[1]

   At the heart of the Shipton story is a missing decade. Leaving Kashgar
early in 1942 Shipton travelled through Soviet Central Asia, eventually
ending up working for the Foreign Office as a consular official in Iran in
March 1943, then under Allied-Soviet occupation. In the few lines he ever
wrote about this 20-month period, he described his job as that of an agri-
cultural adviser, a role he was singularly unqualified for. In his biography
of Shipton, Peter Steele asserts that he was almost certainly undertaking

1. J Westaway, 'That Undisclosed World: Eric Shipton's *Mountains of Tartary* (1950)', *Studies in Travel Writing*
special issue on Xinjiang, vol 18 (4), 2014, pp357-73.

intelligence work in Iran.[2] Leaving Iran in December 1944, by March 1945 he was working for the War Office as an attaché with the British Military Mission in Hungary. In May 1946 he was posted to Vienna working for the United Nations Relief and Rehabilitation Administration. After a second spell in Kashgar, Shipton accepted the Foreign Office offer of the post of consul-general in Kunming, Yunnan, one of the last anti-Communist bridgeheads in Nationalist China, a post he held from the summer of 1949 until expelled by the Chinese communists in the summer of 1951.

In his early thirties at the start of the Second World War, Shipton's wartime career is highly unusual. Far from joining the army in India or returning to England to enlist, he spent the war years and the start of the Cold War working respectively for the External Affairs Department of the Government of India, the Foreign Office, the War Office and the United Nations, always in geographical locations immediately adjacent to Soviet or Chinese communist spheres of influence. The Kashgar consulate was of prime geostrategic importance to the defence of British Imperial India, situated at the junction of the Soviet, Chinese and British empires. His posting was highly prized and usually held by Indian Army officers seconded to the political branch of the Government of India which ran the Kashgar consulate, or held by career civil servants, the 'heaven born' of the Indian Civil Service. The question of how Shipton landed this prize posting remains unanswered but it undoubtedly has a lot to do with his growing entanglement with the agencies of the British imperial security state in India from the mid-1930s, in particular his work with the Survey of India.

The Survey of India's role in compiling geographical intelligence on the un-demarcated border with Chinese Xinjiang had begun to assume a greater geostrategic significance in the mid-1930s due to a number of internal and external factors. Having ceded many government ministries to Indian National Congress officials under the 1935 Government of India Act, British imperial rule became increasingly concerned with the security of India's borders, fuelled by 'tribal' and Islamist insurrections in the North-West Frontier Province and the growing Soviet influence in Xinjiang. The increasingly problematized border zone of British India was also mountain frontier, running in a long arc from the Suleiman Mountains on the borders of Afghanistan, through the Karakoram and the main Himalaya ranges, to modern day Arunachal Pradesh and the Chittagong Hills on the borders of Burma in the east. This mountain frontier was a tightly controlled political zone. Various methods were used to control local populations and limit free movement within this zone. Both the North-West Frontier Province and the North-East Frontier Agency were extraterritorial political agencies where separate tribal law prevailed. Governed by political officers, the indigenous populations were kept in check by tribal levies and periodic punishment campaigns by the Frontier Force. An Inner Line of Control stretched along the entire frontier, outsiders requiring official permission to cross.

2. P Steele, *Eric Shipton: Everest and Beyond*, London, Constable, 1998, pp118-23.

A number of client states also secured the mountain frontier. Nepal remained nominally independent, its borders closed to outsiders, in return for allowing the British Army of India to recruit to Gurkha regiments. Access to both Everest via Tibet and to the Karakoram via the Gilgit road was through nominally independent princely states that were politically controlled by the British under a system of diarchy. North of Darjeeling, Sikkim was controlled by a British political officer with British sepoys periodically deployed deep into Tibet at Gyantse to protect the trade delegation there. The Karakoram were approached via Kashmir, British political interests being watched over by the British resident in Srinagar. No one gained access to travel in these regions without political oversight and clearance and by the mid-1930s there was a tightening of control. By 1936 the British had become so concerned about the potential for Soviet infiltration from Xinjiang that they ended the system of diarchy in the Kashmiri tribute state of Gilgit and assumed direct rule.

The year 1936 also seems to represent something of a turning point for Eric Shipton. The 1936 Everest expedition, a complete failure, had only served to heighten his disillusion with large-scale expeditions. In July of that year Shipton was planning on lecturing in Simla and hoping to interview the viceroy and get him interested in his plans for exploration in Kashmir when a request came through from the Survey of India.[3] Major Gordon Osmaston of the Survey had spent the early part of 1936 surveying the Gangotri and Chaturangi glaciers in the northern Tehri Garhwal when he was ordered by the surveyor-general to extend the survey to the east and include the Nanda Devi Sanctuary. In his privately published memoirs, Gordon Osmaston records that 'knowing that Shipton had been exploring round Everest, and was still in India, I wrote to him, asking if he would come and act as my guide to Nanda Devi.'[4] This seemingly informal request represented an extraordinary opportunity for Shipton. In many ways the Survey of India had already pioneered the model of lightweight expeditionary travel that Shipton had been increasingly advocating.[5] It put him in the pay of the Government of India and gave him unprecedented access to key individuals, such as the surveyor-general, Brigadier H J Couchman. It presented the possibility that he might gain access to the restricted mountain border zones of the Karakoram, where mountaineering skills, exploration and survey work were still required to fill in all of the blanks on the map. In 1936 Shipton was forced to make choices, always with his eye on the bigger prize. Unable to both go to Everest and also join Bill Tilman on the British-American Himalayan Expedition to climb Nanda Devi, Shipton chose Everest. Ascending the Rishi gorge on his way to the Nanda Devi Sanctuary with Osmaston, Shipton met members of the successful Houston party returning from Nanda Devi. Shipton would have had to console

3. J Perrin, *Shipton and Tilman: The Great Decade of Himalayan Exploration* London, 2013, p267.
4. G Osmaston, *Memories of Surveying in India 1919-1939*, T G Osmaston (ed), Windermere, 2005, p32.
5. K Mason, *Abode of Snow: A History of Himalayan Exploration and Mountaineering* London, Rupert Hart-David, 1955.

himself on missing out on the first ascent of Nanda Devi with the thought that he had set out on a course of action that would facilitate his ready access to restricted mountain zones beyond the Inner Line in northern Kashmir. That this was already uppermost in Shipton's plans in the summer of 1936 becomes immediately apparent in a set of documents from the former India Office Library, now held at the British Library in London.

In undertaking government survey work, Shipton became the subject of attention of the British imperial security state, the External Affairs Department of the Government of India, which opened a 'Travellers' file on him in 1936, maintaining it until 1944.[6] In many ways there is nothing unusual in this. All significant individuals who received permission to travel beyond the Inner Line of Control or to cross into Central Asia or Tibet had Travellers files held on them, containing the records of the complex diplomatic, political and security arrangements generated by all requests to traverse the frontier zone. Shipton's Travellers file starts on 30 July 1936 with the copy of a letter sent from K P S Menon[7], additional deputy secretary to the Government of India in the Foreign and Political Department (subsequently the External Affairs Department), to the British Resident in Kashmir. Menon notes that:

> I am directed to say that Mr Eric Shipton who was a member of the Mount Everest Expedition this year wishes to come out again next spring to explore the country between Shimshal (Hunza) and the Shaksgam (Leh). The Government of India are aware that while agreeing to the German expedition to Nanga Parbat the Kashmir Darbar expressed the hope that no other expedition would be allowed to visit the state in 1937. Mr Shipton, however, will be accompanied by only one European and four porters whom he proposes to take with him from Darjeeling.

Aware of the Kashmiri government's concerns about the economically destabilising effects of large expeditions on food prices and labour costs, Menon went on to assert that Shipton has pointed out that his expedition will not be a large expedition like the Visser's Netherlands-Karakoram Expedition of 1929-30 and that Shipton will bring his own food from the plains, only requiring twenty 'coolies' to carry to base camp. On 2 September 1936 the British resident in Srinagar replied that the Kashmiri Durbar had no objection to Shipton's visit, writing again on the 12 September to indicate that the political agent in Gilgit had also intimated he had no objection to 'Mr Eric Shipton's proposed expedition' and that Shipton should get in touch with the agent 'direct over details'.

These letters are evidence of the complex political interactions necessary to gain expeditionary knowledge and the importance of having friends in high places. They also suggest Shipton's philosophy of lightweight exploration was just as much a political necessity as an ethical standpoint.

6. 'Travellers: Northern Frontier Tibet. Mr Eric Shipton', British Library, IOR/L/PS/12/4324.
7. 'K P S Menon (senior)', https://en.wikipedia.org/wiki/K._P._S._Menon_(senior), [Accessed 20.05.17]

The colossal impact of large-scale expeditions, with men absent at harvest time and the inevitable toll of porter deaths, all meant that the authorities were extremely reluctant to provide access to multiple large-scale expeditions in any one year in economically and environmentally fragile mountain regions. The authorities were also at pains to point out to Shipton the politically sensitive nature of the border region. On 22 September 1936, Menon wrote to Shipton from Simla. With reference to their conversation of 28 July 1936, Menon informed him that permission had been granted 'to your proposed visit to Shingshal (Hunza) and the Shaksgam (Leh) in 1937', going on to point out that

> *You are doubtless aware that the Indian frontier in this area is un-demarcated. The Chinese authorities should not be approached for passports unless, for any unforeseen reason, you wish to travel beyond the mountain regions into undisputed Chinese territory, and in that case, your subsequent journey should not be connected with your exploratory activities in the Karakoram.*

Shipton's response survives in a series of Kashmiri government telegrams and letters forwarded to the External Affairs Department by the British resident in Srinagar on 30 April 1937. A copy of a letter from Shipton, dated 5 March 1937, Royal Geographical Society, London, starts:

> *Thank you very much for your letter and the extracts from "Notes for Visitors to Kashmir". I did not write before as my plans were somewhat vague. When I got home I was asked to take with me to the Karakoram (1) Michael Spender, who has the post here of research assistant, and (2) John Auden of the Geological Survey, Calcutta ...*
>
> *Brigadier Couchman, surveyor general of India, has very kindly taken an interest in the project and I hope to receive financial assistance from his department ...*
>
> *We will be a party of four Europeans and seven Sherpa porters from Darjeeling. Owing to this increase I have decided to tackle the work from a base to the north of the Baltoro Glacier instead of going to the Shaksgam via Hunza and Shingshal. In this way we will not encounter any people after leaving Askole (to be reached via Dras and Skardu) until we return. We will not go north into Chinese territory ...*
>
> *We will require about 40 coolies (or 20 animals) to transport our equipment from Srinagar to Askole, and we will require about the same number for a week or so after leaving Askole after which we will be self-supporting ...*
>
> *I hope this change of plan meets with your approval. I am sorry I did not communicate with you sooner, but it was some time before I was in the position to make final decisions about my plan ...*
>
> *The 40 porter loads which I have referred to include about 20 maunds of coolie food which I propose to take from Srinagar as I do not suppose that it will be available at Skardu or Askole ...*
>
> *PS The object[s] of this trip are purely scientific and it will receive no newspaper publicity.*

Having changed his itinerary, increased the number of European expedition members, added three more Sherpas to the proposed party and raised
the consequent porter loads required, Shipton is at pains in this letter to
reassure the British resident in Srinagar that he will address all the known
government concerns. He offered to supply the 'coolie' food from Srinagar
rather than rely on local resources on the Gilgit road, reminds the resident
of the support from the surveyor general and addressed political concerns by
indicating that there would not be any undue publicity that might come to the
attention of the Chinese authorities. Above all, Shipton promised not to go
north into Chinese territory. All of these changes had to be approved by the
Kashmiri government, the prime minister of Jammu and Kashmir sending
a telegram to the British resident, Kashmir dated 23 April 1937 referencing

> *Your demi-official letter D.1173, April seventh, Mr Shipton's expedition His
> Highness Government have approved change in composition of party and have
> issued necessary instructions to local revenue officers to arrange for requisite
> transport on payment.*

Immediately following this in the archive is a handwritten letter,
addressed to 'Sir F Stewart' from the India Office in London. It notes:

> *The frontier is un-demarcated in the neighbourhood of the Shaksgam.
> I understand we would probably claim the valley up to its northern watershed,
> but not beyond. Mr Shipton said he would not go north 'into Chinese territory'.*

This letter is stark evidence of British territorial 'maximal-ism' at the
time, which went hand-in-hand with concerns for border security. Most
British administrators in India would have considered the Karakoram
watershed the de facto border, although some British maps at the time
pressed the case for the northern border of Jammu and Kashmir extending
to the Yarkand river. Despite his assurances to the contrary, by crossing
the Aghil Pass in 1937, Shipton crossed the northern watershed of the
Shaksgam river and surveyed down to the banks of the Yarkand river,
clearly beyond the limits set by the India Office in London. This would
have been seen as an unauthorised infringement of Chinese territory by the
Chinese authorities in Urumchi and Peking. Whilst it was highly unlikely
that Shipton, Tilman and Auden would have encountered a Chinese patrol
on the remote upper reaches of the Yarkand, the consequences of such an
encounter would have been very serious indeed.

What are we to make then of Shipton's promise not to go north into
Chinese territory? Clearly the British Indian state increasingly problematized its geographical intelligence deficits in the Shaksgam and stood
to gain by this purposeful infringement into the un-demarcated border
region. Menon in his letter to Shipton of 22 September 1936 had only advised
Shipton not to 'travel beyond the mountain regions into undisputed Chinese
territory', which would require the acquisition of Chinese passports and

The Shaksgam valley.

raise questions about where he had come from and what he had been doing. We do not know the exact orders Shipton received from the surveyor-general but clearly, part of the draw of exploratory journeying for Shipton in this un-demarcated border region was exactly this thrill of extraterritoriality; of being neither 'here' nor 'there', of wandering in debatable lands with all the risks that that entailed.

Shipton's Travellers file also reveals a hitherto unreported attempt by Shipton to gain access to western Tibet, part of an intended extension of his Karakoram survey work in 1939 that was cut short by the outbreak of the Second World War. On 5 December 1938, G E Crombie at the India Office in Whitehall wrote to Sir Aubrey Metcalfe, foreign secretary of the Government of India:

> In Peel's absence on sick leave I enclose a copy of corr which he has had with Shipton about the latter's desire to enter Tibet from Leh during the summer of 1940. We assume that the GOI are already fully seized of Shipton's proposals for exploring in the Shimshal and Shaksgam valleys during the winter of 1939-40. As regards his subsequent plans we understand that he wishes to enter Tibet via the Indus valley and travel up the Indus as far as the

*mountain on the north side called Alling Kangri which he would like to explore
(see the Survey of India's new map of highlands of Tibet and surrounding
regions). From there he would make his way Gartok and return to India in the
autumn along the ordinary trade route. We should be grateful if you would let
us have the Government of India's views on the question of approaching the
Tibetan Government for permission for this project so as to enable us to reply
to Shipton's letter. The summer of 1940 is, of course, still a good way ahead.*

On 24 May 1939 the political officer Sikkim wrote to the under secretary to the Government of India in the External Affairs Department, Simla,
referring to Simla's 'demi-official' letter of 25 April 1939. Scribbled in pencil
at the top of this copy is the phrase 'for I O', indicating that the political
officers comments should be copied to the India Office in London. Basil
Gould, the political officer for Sikkim was also the Government of India's
representative in Tibet and Bhutan between 1935-45 and perhaps the most
influential member of the British Tibet cadre in the Indian Civil Service,
attending the installation of the 14th Dalai Lama in Lhasa on 22 February
1940. Gould, it is fair to say, determined much of British policy towards
Tibet. In his opinion:

*It is highly improbable that the Tibetan Government would view with
favour an application to visit Aling Kangri, which is north of the Indus; and
it is still more improbable that they would consent to anything in the nature of
a survey, if Shipton has one in view; and it is undesirable that any surveying
should be undertaken without prior consent of the Tibetan Government.*

*In view especially of the letter from the Tibetan Government forwarded with
my demi-official letter No 7 (9)-/38, dated the 24 May 1939, I feel that we shall
need, for some time at least, to confine our applications for permission to travel
off the trade routes to cases to which the GOI attach special importance, and/
or to cases in which there is reason to suppose that the Tibetan Government
will be willing to grant permission.*

*One has always to keep in mind the prospect of having to concentrate effort
on securing permission for a further Everest Expedition. In connection with
this matter it may be remarked that the fact that there has been no pre-monsoon
Everest effort this year is not to be regretted, as the whole of May up to date
appears to have been even wetter than May 1938 in the high hills.*

The letter from the Tibetan government that Gould mentions here
appears next in the archive and relates to another request to travel, this time
in eastern Tibet. The request appears to have been made by George Sheriff,
the former British vice-consul at Kashgar 1927-31 and a renowned Himalayan botanist who had already visited Tibet in the 1930s.[8] In granting
permission for Sheriff to enter Tibet, the Tibetan government made clear
its displeasure at continuing to receive such requests:

---

8. 'George Sheriff', *https://en.wikipedia.org/wiki/George_Sherriff* [Accessed 22/05/17]

Camp on the Aghil Pass.

Translation of a Tibetan letter dated the 7ʰ day of the 3rd Tibetan month [corresponding to 26 April 1939] from Minister of Tibet, to the British Trade Agent, Gyantse, Lhasa ...

Reference your letter requesting permission for Mr Sherriff, a friend of his and a doctor to visit Poyul, west of Yirong chhu, near Tongyuk Dzong to collect flower seeds, travelling via Gyantse, Nagartse, Tsetang, Tsegang and returning by Tsari, Sanga Choling, Chayul Dzong and Tsona.

In view of the great friendship existing between the British and the Tibetan Governments, permission is granted for the proposed visit for this time.

As granting of permission to visit various parts of Tibet will be followed by more applications from foreigners causing great embarrassment to us, the Government of India may kindly be approached with request not to let visitors apply for such visits in future and a reply to this may please be communicated to us.

Gould's opinion on the matter was final. Shipton's request did not meet the Government of India's criteria of 'special importance' and threatened to scupper the delicate negotiations required for future Everest attempts. The External Affairs Department of the Government of India wrote to the India Office in London in June 1939 advising them that the 'GOI are averse from approaching the Tibetan Government to obtain their sanction for Shipton to visit Tibet in 1940.' As befits British Indian bureaucracy, Shipton received an

K2 from the Aghil Pass.

emphatic official double negative from both branches of the Government of India. The External Affairs Department in Simla wrote to him 'C/O Officer Commanding 'A' Company, Survey of India, Muree' on the 9 June 1939:

Dear Shipton,

Will you please refer to your letter dated the 28 November 1938 to Mr Peel, regarding your desire to enter Tibet from Leh during the summer of 1940.

As you probably know the Tibetans are particularly sensitive regarding applications for permission to visit parts of Tibet which are off the normal trade routes and unfortunately they have recently adopted a more uncompromising attitude in the matter. The question of placing your supplication before the Tibetan Government has been carefully considered by the GOI in consultation with the Political Officer in Sikkim and we feel that to forward a formal application to the Tibetan Govt from you in the near future would merely court an immediate refusal and would give rise to difficulties in obtaining permission for the Everest expeditions in 1940 which are under consideration. In the circumstances we must, I am afraid, ask you to give up your idea of visiting Tibet next year.

Yours sincerely,
Sd/-C A G Savidge

Shipton received a similar letter from the India Office in Whitehall dated
15 June 1939 and addressed via the Royal Geographical Society. The door
to Tibet was firmly but politely closed.

Shipton's Travellers file also contains a series of letters from the early
1940s dealing with the survey data from the 1937 and 1939 Karakoram surveys, letters that demonstrate the close working relations between the Royal
Geographical Society and the India Office in Whitehall and the importance
placed by both on securing geographical intelligence. On 23 January 1940,
Arthur Hinks at the RGS wrote to the India Office:

Dear Mr Peel,

*As you probably know Eric Shipton led an expedition last summer to the
Karakoram where they made further important surveys, which Shipton is now
working up at the Geodetic Branch, Dehra Dun. He wrote on January 5 to
Michael Spender "At the moment we are plotting my photo survey of the
Panmah which is going to take a long time as I did 16 major stations and 5 sub
stations in the area. Where are Auden's photographs and angle-books. If they
are at the RGS, could you get them to send them out by Air Mail. It is very
important to have them as we want many intersections in areas covered by his
photos that I have not got".*

*I find that the weight I gave you by telephone this morning did not cover all
the material which they want at Dehra Dun, and the weight of the package is
now about one pound seven ounces. I do not think that the photographs and
map can be sent out of the country except in official bags: so that I hope it may
be possible for you to include this material in the next Air Mail bag to India as
it is for the Survey of India at Dehra Dun.*

Yours very sincerely,
Arthur R Hinks

At the bottom of Hinks's letter, written in a separate hand, are the instructions from the India Office to use official air mail as the 'package is required
in connection with Mr Shipton's work for the Indian Survey & that being
so, I think we should waive recovery.' There is then nothing in Shipton's
Travellers file covering the subsequent two years when he was consul-general in Kashgar. Having returned from Kashgar, a letter from 4 November
1942 indicates Shipton was still using official channels to transfer geographical data back to the RGS:

From The Secretary to the Govt of India in the External Affairs Department

To The Secretary, External Department, India Office, London

*Negatives of photographs taken by Mr Shipton on his expedition to the
Karakoram in 1939.*

Kun Lun from the Aghil Pass.

Sir,
I am directed to forward at Mr Shipton's request a packet containing
negatives of photographs taken by him of his expedition to Karakoram in '39.
If there is no objection, the packet may kindly be forwarded to the Royal
Geographical Society, Kensington, Gore, London, S. W.7.

I have the honour to be, Sir, Your most obedient servant
A, [K]oorhah

For Secy. To the Govt. of India

The final section of Shipton's Travellers file descends into high bureaucratic farce. On the 9 October 1943, the India Office in Whitehall wrote to
Shipton care of the RGS, clearly unaware of his posting to Persia, attempting to obtain information from him about rent owing on a theodolite used
in the Karakoram in 1939. They forwarded a letter from the Government
of India, Simla, dated 19 September 1943, who were similarly unaware of
Shipton's whereabouts:

Reference enclosed copy of express letter from the Custodian of Enemy Prop-
erty, Bombay, No P/Forms/G/91-4598, dated the 19ʰ August 1943 and its
enclosures, Photo theodolite obtained on loan from messers. Zeiss Aerotopo-
graph of Jena, Germany, by a representative of Mr. E. E. Shipton's expedi-
tion to the Karakoram. Mr. Shipton is no longer the British Consul General,
Kashgar, and his present address is not known here. It is understood that his
future employment was under the consideration of His Majesty's Government
in January last. The GOI would be grateful if the information regarding the

rent paid for the instrument by the Expedition could be obtained from Mr Ship-ton and communicated to this Department at an early date.

The issue of the above has been duly authorised.

V J Shiveshwarkar

Under Secretary to the Government of India

Attached to this is a copy of an express letter from the Custodian of Enemy Property, Bombay, dated 19 August 1943, addressed to the Department of Commerce in Simla. What this reveals is that the Zeiss Aerotopograph 'TAL' photo theodolite used by Shipton in the Karakoram in 1939 had been stored with the Survey of India in November 1939, subsequently becoming part of the technical equipment of the Survey Company in the 10th Army. The scrupulous Custodians of Enemy Property had then pursued the Director of Survey for either compensation or a rental equivalent to the amount they assumed Shipton had been paying, receiving the following exasperated response from somewhere in Persia or Iraq, where the 10th Army was stationed:

Copy of letter No. Svy-70/8/3/1310, dated the 27ʰ August 1942, from the Survey Directorate, Head Quarters, Tenth Army.

Refce:- Your letter No.P.Forms/G6059 dated 15 July 1942

Your proposal that I should pay the rupee equivalent of £300/- to the Reserve Bank of India, Bombay does not suit me. Will you kindly inform me what rent was paid by Mr. E. E. Shipton's Expedition to the Karakoram Himalayas as I am unaware of the figure. If you do not know I suggest that reference be made to Mr. E. E.Shipton who is I Under-stand His Majesty's Consul in Kashgar.

By 24 March 1944, the India Office in Whitehall had finally tracked Shipton down in Persia and pressed him for a response:

To: E S Shipton, Esq,
Consular Liaison Officer
c/o H B M.Consulate,
Korramshahr,
Persia.
22 mar 1944

Dear Mr. Shipton,
I enclose a copy of a letter, together with enclosures, which Clauson addressed to you last October, regarding a theodolite, and to which we have not received a reply.

[box] dated 9ᵗʰ October 1943 (with enclosures)

It is possible that the letter, which in ignorance of your location was sent c/o the Royal Geographical Society, has not found you, or perhaps you have replied direct to the GOI.
In any case would you be good enough to let us know so that we can satisfy ourselves here that there is nothing further we need to do.

(Signed) JR Blair

Copy to India by air mail.

[handwritten] Mr Blair This is rather out of date but it is only recently that I have been able to locate Mr S. I think we might try to clear it up. If you agree will you sign? 18/3/44

This is an important piece of evidence in attempting to understand Shipton's time in Persia as it locates Shipton in Khorramshahr on the Persian Gulf, the bridgehead of the Allied war effort to supply the Soviets via the Persian Corridor. Peter Steele, with access to Shipton's letters, only noted that Shipton was in Tehran as a consular liaison officer, with a subsequent posting to Kermanshah 'in the northern Zagros Mountains on the border of Persia and Iraq' where he was supposed to be undertaking 'Food Control Work'.[9] Further letters were to follow to and from the office of the Secretary of State for India on the subject of Shipton's theodolite, the correspondence ending wearily on 19 July 1944, the last entry in the Travellers file held on Shipton by the Government of India. It indicated:

Two letters have been addressed to Mr Shipton, of which copies are enclosed, but no reply has yet been received from him ...
So far as is known here, Mr Shipton is still serving as Consular Liaison Officer in Persia and it is suggested that the GOI might more conveniently reach him by addressing a letter to him direct C/o the British Embassy, Tehran, who will know his location.

(Sgd) J R Blair

Copy to FO

[handwritten] Mr Blair I am proving weary of chasing this theodolite!

It seems the very height of absurdity that during British India's deepest existential crisis, with the Japanese Imperial Army in India trying to fight its way beyond Imphal, that the organs of the British Indian state should go

9. P Steele, *Eric Shipton: Everest and Beyond*, London, Constable, 1998, p119.

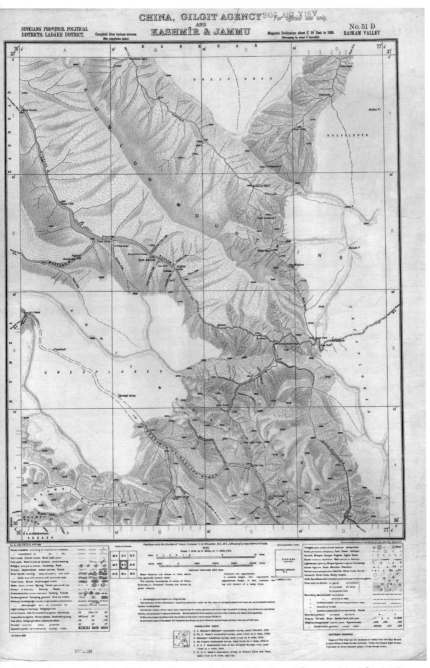

Shipton's map of the Aghil Pass. *(By permission of the Royal Geographical Society)*

to such lengths to secure the property rights of enemy aliens. Then again, perhaps this emphasis on rights and the rule of law is exactly what the Allied and Indian forces were fighting for. Shipton's Travellers file provides us with a rare glimpse of the British imperial security state at both its most effective and at its most banal and pettifogging. The same imperial security apparatus that maintained such tight control over the trans-Himalaya border regions was also seemingly unable to track down and locate one of its own across all of its various agencies in wartime. Shipton's Travellers file sheds further light about the ways in which he sought to negotiate access to the politically controlled border zone of British India, providing us with many more tantalizing details of his movements and motivations. It reveals, for the first time, his concerted efforts to explore in the remote regions of western Tibet and the power of British India's border cadres to deny access to anyone whose interest did not align directly with those of the Government of India. It somehow seems appropriate then that Shipton's Travellers file ends with the India Office awaiting a reply from Shipton, a reply one suspects that never came. Given to reticence, Shipton in the archive is elusive, always on the move, as befits a traveller. You have to wonder: if the Government of India couldn't find Shipton and get a reply from him, what hope has the modern historian or biographer got of finally tracking him down?

STEPHEN GOLDING & PETER GILLMAN

George Mallory and Francis Urquhart: an Academic Friendship

George Mallory was a keen oarsman, here rowing with Balliol College
members at Sandford on the Thames, 1 May 1911. From L to R:
Alexander Cardew, Arthur Kirby, Mallory, George Randolph.
(All images from the albums of Francis Urquhart)

On a plateau on the Prarion, one of the western foothills of Mont
Blanc, there is a large, traditional wooden chalet set among larch trees,
where summer walking and reading parties have been held since 1891.
The Chalet des Mélèzes, or Chalet des Anglais as it is now invariably
known, was built in 1865 by David Urquhart, a self-styled Victorian mover
and shaker. Among his eccentricities was his belief that the human brain
functioned better at low oxygen pressure, so when he moved to Switzerland
in 1864 he resolved to construct a summer home above 5,000ft.

David Urquhart's youngest son, Francis Fortescue Urquhart (known
universally as 'Sligger'), was born in St Gervais les Bains, the town in the
valley below the chalet in 1868, and spent his childhood summers there. By
the time Francis was admitted to Balliol College, Oxford, in 1890, his father

Above: Mallory sporting his pipe.
From L to R: Kirby, Mallory, Francis
'Sligger' Urquhart, Randolph.

Right: The only photograph of Mallory
rowing, with Arthur Kirby.

had died and the family were making little use of the chalet. So at the end
of his first academic year Francis invited a group of university friends to
stay there, beginning the tradition of summer reading parties from Oxford,
which has continued to this day, save for the interruption of two world wars.

Sligger was taken on to the staff of Balliol in 1893 and continued to
run the Chalet des Anglais parties until shortly before his death in 1934.
He was a keen amateur photographer, recording in particular his travels in
France and his activities at the chalet. These photographs were preserved
chronologically in albums, each carefully labelled with the date and place
and usually also identifying the individuals who were shown. They are
preserved in the Balliol College archives and study of them has uncovered
a close friendship between Sligger and Everest pioneer George Mallory
which has not previously been documented.

Mallory's first appearance in Sligger's albums occurs in a set of four
photographs taken on May Day 1911 which show Mallory rowing on
the Thames with Sligger and three contemporaries from Balliol: see illustrations. Mallory was a keen oarsman, having captained the boat for his
Cambridge college, Magdalene, so it was natural that, on what is presumed
to have been Mallory's first visit to Oxford, Sligger should give him a taste
of rowing there. Three shots show him in a static boat; the last is the only
action shot of Mallory rowing that has ever come to light.

In view of Sligger's association with the Alps, it was tempting to believe
that this was how his friendship with Mallory developed. Our research has
shown that this was almost certainly not the case. In the autumn of 1910,
Mallory was appointed a teacher at Charterhouse School, where one of his

George Mallory enjoyed being photographed, here in a wistful and camera-conscious mood at the window of Sligger's room, Balliol College, 1913.

responsibilities was to teach history to boys preparing for scholarships[1]. Sligger was history tutor at Balliol and it is likely Mallory was in contact with him to further his pupils's chances of entering Oxford. An introduction may well have been provided by Mallory's Charterhouse colleague Frank Fletcher, a close friend of Sligger, who went on to become headmaster in 1911[2].

We know from the 1969 biography by David Robertson, Mallory's son-in-law, that Mallory spent Easter 1911 at Geoffrey Winthrop Young's regular climbing party at Pen y Pass. He went on to visit his parents at Birkenhead, and then stayed in Oxford with Sligger[3]. By 2 May he was in London where he attended a meeting of the Alpine Club. These photographs, therefore, appear to document this Oxford visit.

Although Mallory had other links with Oxford – he visited the university mountaineering club in 1912 in the company of Geoffrey Winthrop Young, H O Jones and Claude Elliott[4] – his next appearance in Sligger's records is the album entry for 1913, where a single photo shows him sitting in wistful mood in the bay window of Sligger's room in Balliol: see illustration. Among Sligger's shots, this is the strongest suggesting Mallory's fondness for being photographed and his readiness to play to the camera, seen later in photographs taken by his Everest colleagues and – most celebrated of all – in the earlier sequence of nude photographs taken by the Bloomsbury artist Duncan Grant in 1912[5].

There is confirmation of his visit in David Pye's 1927 memoir of Mallory[6]. Pye records that after two years at Charterhouse, some time in 1913, Mallory wrote to an unidentified recipient reporting that he had recently spent five days in Oxford where Sligger had advised him to consider becoming a don. Sligger told Mallory that vacancies were arising from the departure of other history tutors but Mallory felt his position at

1. D Robertson, *George Mallory*, London, Faber and Faber, 1969, 2nd edn, 1999, p63.
2. D Robertson, *George Mallory*, London, Faber and Faber, 1969, 2nd edn, 1999, p78.
3. D Robertson, *George Mallory*, London, Faber and Faber, 1969, 2nd edn, 1999, p 71.
4. A Ross, '100 Years of the OUMC', *Alpine Journal*, vol 114, no 358, 2009, pp229-35.
5. P and L Gillman, *The Wildest Dream: the biography of George Mallory*, London, Headline, 2000, p96.
6. D Pye, *George Leigh Mallory: a memoir*, Oxford, Oxford University Press, 1927, repub Orchid Press, Bangkok, 2002, p68.

The familiar image of Mallory sitting on the loggia of The Holt, often attributed to Mallory's daughter Clare, but actually photographed by Sligger Urquhart in July 1915.

Charterhouse suited him best. Although Sligger did not for once specify which month his photograph was taken, its position in the album sequence suggests this was around April 1913. As in 1911, Mallory attended Geoffrey Winthrop Young's Pen y Pass party at Easter[7] and the 1913 photograph was probably taken during another visit to Sligger when Mallory passed through Oxford on his journey home.

The final set of Sligger's photographs dates from 1915 and records a visit to George and Ruth Mallory at their home The Holt in Godalming, a mile or so from Charterhouse, between 3 and 5 July. One of these, showing Mallory sitting on the loggia of the house, with the spires of Charterhouse in the background, has been widely published, usually attributed to the Mallorys's daughter Clare or an unidentified source. The sequence in Sligger's album now makes clear that he was the photographer and it appears that he sent a duplicate set of prints to George and Ruth after his visit, preserving the originals in his album.

Another photograph in this set is merely a view of the school from the loggia. A third, showing Mallory in an armchair, presents a very differ-ent aspect when compared to the loggia portrait, once again suggesting Mallory's awareness of the camera. There is also a very rare view of George and Ruth together; only one other is known, the familiar image of Mallory

7. P and L Gillman, *The Wildest Dream: the biography of George Mallory*, London, Headline, 2000, p102.

Mallory, also from 1915, but this time in schoolmaster mode.

in his army uniform in the foreground, a slightly out-of-focus Ruth behind him. The remaining photograph in Sligger's sequence is too faded to reproduce but shows Mallory in a shaded area of the garden in the company of a young man who could be Hugh Heber-Percy, one of his former Charterhouse pupils. Following Sligger's visit, Mallory went climbing in Snowdonia with Heber-Percy[8]. Although Urquhart's photograph shows the young man in profile, a comparison with the frontal image in Heber-Percy's Charterhouse class photograph strongly suggests that it is him, implying that he was either visiting or staying with the Mallorys at the time of Sligger's visit.

The remaining photograph of Mallory in Sligger's possession appears to have been a gift. In a separate album, Sligger preserved portrait photographs of young men of his acquaintance, and these include a signed portrait of Mallory. This is an expanded version of the portrait that appears as the frontispiece to the Robertson biography. A portrait in the same style and with Mallory wearing the same clothes was used as the frontispiece to the 1927 Pye biography and is attributed to Underwood and Underwood of New York. It is dated to 1923, when Mallory was undertaking a financially unrewarding tour of the USA[9], presenting a lecture about the first two Everest expeditions. That Mallory should have presented Sligger with a signed photograph from that period demonstrates that their friendship was still alive in the year before Mallory died on Everest – and more than ten years from the time when we can assume they first met.

8. P and L Gillman, *The Wildest Dream: the biography of George Mallory*, London, Headline, 2000, p127.
9. P and L Gillman, *The Wildest Dream: the biography of George Mallory*, London, Headline, 2000, p230.

The autographed portrait of Mallory in Sligger's collection, 1923.

Such a relationship would have been characteristic of Sligger. Almost certainly a celibate bachelor don, he had a penchant for surrounding himself with good-looking young men who were academically inclined and also skilled sportsmen, as he did at the Chalet des Anglais. George Mallory, whose personality and physique had attracted the homoerotic attention of men like Duncan Grant and Lytton Strachey[10], was mainstream material for Sligger's choice of companion. In that, Sligger was in good company,

10. P and L Gillman, *The Wildest Dream: the biography of George Mallory*, London, Headline, 2000, p77.

Although out of focus, this is a rare view of Mallory and his wife Ruth together, on the loggia of The Holt (1915). Only one other is known, the image of Mallory in his army uniform in the foreground.

as Mallory had inspired similar feelings in an impressive number of other older men, including the Winchester master Ronald Irving, who first took him to the Alps; his Cambridge tutor Arthur Benson, who confided his passion for Mallory at great length in a secret diary; and Geoffrey Winthrop Young, who sponsored Mallory's climbing career and recommended him for the 1921 Everest expedition. These relationships were nonetheless also genuine friendships, as was the case with Sligger, who was generous in supporting those who became his friends[11]. He was also an assiduous correspondent and maintained exchanges of letters that in many cases were lifelong and often intimate. The Robertson biography quotes a letter to Sligger from Mallory in March 1914, where Mallory unburdens himself of the emotions he experienced in teaching[12]. Happily for his biographers, Mallory too was a diligent letter-writer, loyally sustaining his relationships in this way.

In fact, there may well be other letters that shed more light on the relationship between Sligger and Mallory. In the source notes for his biography, Robertson referred to further letters from Sligger, which he had found helpful but had not quoted. Sligger directed that at his death all correspondence should be either returned to the writer or destroyed. For

11. C Bailey, *Francis Fortescue Urquhart, a memoir*, Oxford, Macmillan and Co, 1936.
12. D Robertson, *George Mallory*, London, Faber and Faber, 1969, 2nd edn, 1999, p 93.

Robertson to refer to Sligger's letters in 1969 implies that when Sligger died in 1934 his correspondence with Mallory was returned to Ruth. If so, this correspondence may survive today in the Mallory family collection, now lodged in New Hampshire.

One conundrum remains. Did Mallory ever visit the Chalet des Anglais? It would be delightful to know that he did, particularly as one of us was an undergraduate at University College, Oxford, one of three colleges which use the chalet, while the other, a fellow at University College, still organises the college's summer chalet parties. We feel we have established that the Sligger-Mallory friendship was based not on their shared interest in mountains but on the practicalities of academic life. Even so, is it not likely that Sligger would have thought to enhance their friendship with an invitation to the chalet, given that Mallory was climbing in the Alps around the time that they first met[13]? Sadly, we have found no evidence this ever took place.

In addition to the record from his photograph albums, so meticulously maintained, Sligger kept a diary at Chalet des Anglais in which each visitor noted the dates when they stayed. Mallory's name does not appear and it is highly unlikely that Sligger would have allowed a distinguished climber to be at the chalet without recording that fact. Whether or not an invitation was ever formally made, it may have been tacitly accepted by one or both of them that the study and hill walking Sligger offered at the chalet would have been too tame an environment for so accomplished a climber.

There is an intriguing footnote to the Sligger-Mallory friendship. On the chalet bookshelves are a number of books belonging to Mallory's Pen y Pass climbing partner Cottie Sanders, later Lady Mary O'Malley and the novelist Ann Bridge. They include *The Climbs on Lliwedd*, the 1909 Climbers' Club guide by J M Archer Thomson and A W Andrews. There is a note by Cottie on page 27 recording that she climbed *Central Route* (also known as *Route One*) with Mallory on 3 January 1911, which accords with the roster of his ascents in the various biographies. So, we speculated, were Cottie's climbing books passed on to Sligger by Mallory when Cottie was obliged to withdraw from the climbing community on the insistence of her husband, Owen O'Malley[14]? This theory does not stand up either, as some of Cottie's books date from after Mallory's death on Everest in 1924. By whatever route this lady climber's books arrived at the Chalet des Anglais, it was not through the agency of the friendship between George Mallory and Francis Urquhart.

Acknowledgements
We are grateful to the master and fellows of Balliol College for access to their archives and for permission to reproduce the photographs in this paper, and to Catherine Smith, archivist of Charterhouse, for information on Hugh Heber-Percy.

13. P and L Gillman, *The Wildest Dream: the biography of George Mallory*, London, Headline, 2000, p63.
14. P and L Gillman, *The Wildest Dream: the biography of George Mallory*, London, Headline, 2000, p106.

MICK CONEFREY

Filming the Summit of K2

Mario Fantin, expedition photographer and cinematographer, wearing an oxygen set at Rawalpindi airport before or after his flight around K2. Apart from summit day, this is one of few times the K2 team used oxygen, because their plane was not pressurised. *(All images courtesy of the Italian Alpine Club)*

At around 6pm on 31 July 1954, two Italians, Achille Compagnoni and Lino Lacedelli arrived at the summit of K2 after a long gruelling day. After shaking hands and taking off their oxygen sets, they set about recording their achievement on film. The results were spectacular but no one realised the strange role the film would play in the many controversies that developed after the expedition.

Almost all the previous K2 expeditions had also taken a film camera: Vittorio Sella in 1909, Charlie Houston in 1938 and 1953 and the hapless Dudley Wolfe in 1939. But in each case, most of the footage was shot on the approach march or low on the mountain. In 1954, the Italians wanted to do it differently. A year earlier, Ed Hillary and Tenzing had reached the summit of Everest, but a last minute packing crisis had forced them to leave their cine-camera on the South Col. All they came back with was a roll of colour stills. If all went well Compagnoni and Lacedelli would be the first to bring back moving images from the summit of an 8,000m peak.

It was never going to be easy though. In the first instance, commercial producers were reluctant to risk their cash on an expedition that had no guarantee of success. And even if the money could be raised, there were significant logistical problems of filming on K2, which everyone knew was going to be a hard climb.

The solution was for the Italian Alpine Club (CAI), the expedition's sponsor, to go into partnership with Marcello Baldi, a documentary maker

A photomontage illustrating how still photographs taken by Mario Fantin at base camp were subsequently hand-tinted for film posters: the oxygen bottles are blue in the German version, red in the Italian.

from Trentino. He would write and edit the film and shoot some additional material in Italy. Most of the expedition filming would be done by Mario Fantin, a well-known climber and cameraman from Bologna.

Predictably, like cameraman Tom Stobart[1] and John Hunt on Everest, Mario Fantin argued a lot with expedition leader Ardito Desio. Desio wanted the best possible outcome but he didn't want the filmmaking to get in the way of the climbing, and didn't want Fantin to go beyond camp four. In order to get footage higher on the mountain, Fantin trained several of the climbers and equipped them with a small, easy-to-operate 16mm camera.

The end product, *Italia K2*, was released in Italy in the autumn of 1954, and was a big success. As with *The Conquest of Everest*, which showcased George Lowe's cinematography on the Lhotse Face and the South Col, the high-altitude footage shot by Compagnoni and the others got a lot of attention.

Unfortunately, as with so many other aspects of the expedition, the film soon generated a lot of arguments. First off, Ardito Desio accused Mario Fantin of using some film stock destined for the geographical survey that followed the ascent of K2. Desio was wrong but he only retracted his accusation after Fantin began court proceedings to clear his name.

A second and much longer argument also went to court. The plaintiff in this case was Achille Compagnoni. He had suffered severe frostbite to three fingers and argued that his injuries were caused by filming on the summit; he should therefore be given a share of the profits. Some claimed Compagnoni had been put up to it by Ardito Desio, who by then had fallen out with the Italian Alpine Club and the majority of the team, but whatever the truth, Compagnoni lost his case.

These early controversies soured the aftermath of the expedition but were as nothing compared the bitter argument between Walter Bonatti and

1. See Dennis Gray's article on Stobart in this year's volume, pp206-11.

Three freeze frames from *Italia K2*. Above: Pino Gallotti surrounded by oxygen bottles and (above right) a pile of oxygen cylinders at base camp. Most were red Dalmine bottles, a smaller number were blue Dräger bottles. Each had a distinctive valve. The third freeze frame (right), from footage shot on the summit, shows that both Dalmine and Dräger bottles were taken to the top.

Achille Compagnoni, which ran for decades. Essentially Bonatti argued two things: firstly that Compagnoni had deliberately placed the top camp higher than had been agreed, and secondly that Compagnoni and Lacedelli's account of their oxygen running out on the way to the summit was false.

Bonatti's first point was impossible to prove conclusively, it was essentially one man's word against another's. Compagnoni insisted that it made sense to place the last camp as high as possible, Bonatti insisted that this was not what had been agreed, and that Compagnoni had deliberately endangered his life and the life of Mahdi, the Hunza porter who had helped him carry up the summit team's oxygen. Neither man ever conceded the point.

The second controversy was different. It was not a question of motivation but of fact, and if Bonatti was right, then the story that Lacedelli and Compagnoni told about their oxygen running out on the way up to the summit, was a lie. In the years that followed, the 'oxygen controversy' became a kind of proxy for the dispute about the positioning of the high camp. If Compagnoni had lied about the oxygen, it would destroy his credibility. This time though it wasn't just a question of one man's word against that of two others. There was independent evidence: namely the film and photographs taken by Compagnoni and Lacedelli on the summit.

In first post-summit press release, written on 2 August, before the summit pair returned to base camp, Desio had outlined the bones of the story:

'At six o'clock yesterday afternoon, two of us finally reached the summit of K2!!! They got back into camp at 11 pm and left two oxygen sets with two bottles on the summit. For the last hour they had no oxygen.'

In the official expedition book, *The Conquest of K2*, Compagnoni and Lacedelli explained that they had carried their empty sets to the summit because they thought it was so close and that it was too awkward to remove them. They were very vague on detail though, never specifying where or when the oxygen actually ran out. In statements to the press in autumn 1954, Compagnoni was consistently inconsistent: sometimes he said 100m below the summit, sometimes 200m. When he wrote his own personal account in 1958, he wrote 'at around 200m, perhaps higher'.

Bonatti rejected this, appealing to common sense and mathematics: why would any climber carry 19kg of empty oxygen bottles to the summit? Their Dräger oxygen sets, he argued, were designed to supply at least ten hours of oxygen. Compagnoni and Lacedelli had taken nine and a half hours to get from their oxygen dump to the summit, so there must have been at least half an hour of oxygen left.

After so many previous controversies, the Italian press was not that interested in this latest spat, but in 1994, one of Bonatti's supporters, Robert Marshall, published an article in which he argued that that he had definitive proof that Bonatti was right. He had found a photograph showing Compagnoni on the summit wearing his mask, proving, he claimed, that the oxygen had lasted all the way to the top. 'How ironic,' he wrote, 'that in the end their own photographs should provide the most damning evidence imaginable.'

Marshall's claim got a lot of publicity but the summit pair insisted he had misunderstood the photograph, arguing that Compagnoni had only temporarily put his mask on to warm the air he was inhaling. This claim was partially backed up by Erich Abram, the team's oxygen expert who said in a 2003 interview: 'It was almost habitual to wear a mask, with the tube separated from the cylinders and tucked inside the clothes to make the incoming air a little less icy.' It certainly was the case that it was possible to breathe through an oxygen set even when the bottled oxygen wasn't flowing. On Kangchenjunga in 1955, Joe Brown recorded an unlucky Sherpa who spent several hours climbing with an open-circuit oxygen set, not realizing that the oxygen valve was closed.

Though a lot of attention was paid to the stills, no one seems to have consulted the expedition film. This offered some striking visual evidence of a different kind: almost two minutes of colour footage shot on the summit. This showed something that the stills did not: that one of their oxygen sets was loaded not with Dräger cylinders, in factory blue, but with red Dalmine cylinders, which were prone to leakage and had a lower capacity.

When I wrote an article about this in 2014, it caused a minor storm in Italy. Luigi Zanzi, one of the 'three sages' who investigated the story for a CAI enquiry in 2004, said that the colour of the cylinders was insignificant and in last year's *AJ* Eric Vola suggested that the summit film footage was actually black and white and only subsequently colourised. So what's the truth?

Two images that show the colourisation process. The original is black and white. In the hand-tinted version, a poster for the film, the oxygen bottles are incorrectly coloured red. It is clear that these should be blue Dräger bottles by comparing this image to what's actually seen on film.

Vola's point is easily answered: the records of the CAI confirm the summit footage was indeed Kodachrome 16mm colour reversal, subsequently blown up to 35mm for cinema projection. Vola's confusion comes because some of the black and white stills were indeed colourised and used on posters for the film. It's extremely time-consuming to do this accurately for a single still, so to colourise 115 seconds of film, comprising 2,760 individual frames would have been unthinkable and particularly hard as everything on the summit was shot hand held.

Zanzi's point is more complicated to answer but has a much greater bearing on the controversy. The colour matters because it shows that at least two of the oxygen cylinders used by Compagnoni and Lacedelli should not have been there. Dalmine was an Italian company with no track record in climbing equipment. As Erich Abram, the team's oxygen expert revealed in 2003, their bottles had very poor seals, some losing up to 30% of their contents. Somehow in the confusion of the last few days on the mountain a number of these were taken up instead of Dräger bottles.

So does this resolve the controversy definitively? No, but if they took up cylinders which were prone to leak, it does add credence to Compagnoni and Lacedelli's testimony that their oxygen ran out early and at the very least shows two things: firstly that at the climax of the K2 expedition things did not go according to plan, and secondly just how difficult it is to recall precise details many years after an event. Today Compagnoni does not have many fans so it is easy to forget that immediately after K2, he spent over 14 weeks in hospital in Italy, being treated for frostbite and complications

An original black and white still of Compagnoni on the summit and the hand-tinted version. Note that his windproofs are incorrectly coloured blue: they were in reality khaki.

due to pneumonia and pleurisy. He hallucinated on the way up to the summit and had a breakdown when he got there, both signs of hypoxia. If it hadn't been for Lacedelli's cool head, he might never have returned.

In a way though, it's what the film doesn't show that is most significant. Bar a few shots of oxygen cylinders at base camp and porters humping them up the mountain, there is no footage at all of anyone climbing on oxygen, apart from a single shot at the climax. This is not because the editor wasn't interested, or because no one filmed them: it's because the Italian team simply didn't use oxygen for climbing, apart from on the summit day.

The 1953 British Everest team had tried out their oxygen sets in North Wales and on the march in to Everest and from the Western Cwm upwards. They were familiar with their faults and foibles and needed to be because the equipment frequently went wrong. Compagnoni and Lacedelli had no such training. The oxygen sets they used on the summit day spent the previous two nights out in the open and unlike Hillary and Tenzing, they were not able to check or prepare them. Is it really so hard to accept that they were telling the truth, that either equipment or user error caused the oxygen to run out early?

There's no film of the moment when this happened, but there is one piece of visual evidence, which offers a clue. In Lacedelli's memoir, *The Price of Conquest*, he recalls that some time after their oxygen crisis, the clouds cleared and they were able to see down into their eighth camp where Walter Bonatti and Pino Gallotti were stationed. Seeing his friends below gave him the courage to carry on. The same moment is recorded in Gallotti's diary, where he remembered being dragged out of his tent by Isakhan, one of the Hunza porters, pointing at two figures on the summit ridge. It was around 5.30pm, about half an hour before they reached the summit. This makes sense of Desio's first press release and Lacedelli's memoir, released many year's later where he recalled the oxygen running out between 50m and 100m from the summit. Gallotti burst into silent tears of joy, knowing that victory was assured. If he could have seen into the future, and all the angst that would surround the expedition, he might have wept differently.

ERIC VOLA

The First Ascent of
the Barre des Écrins

A portrait of French army surveyors: 'ingénieurs géographes'.
(All illustrations courtesy of Editions du Fournel)

During the 150th anniversary of the first ascent of the Barre des Écrins, climbed on 25 June 1864 by Edward Whymper and party, a claim was made that a French army officer had climbed the mountain 11 years earlier and the credit should go to him. Lieutenant Meusnier was one of the French army's cartographers who in 1853 were mapping the Briançon area. The new theory was based on a digitised document published by the Institut Géographique National (IGN) in 2012. It is a draft of the 1/40,000 Briançon map, which includes an abbreviation of the word 'Signal' beside the name 'Les Écrins', what we now call Barre des Écrins. In 1853, before the Treaty of Turin of 1860 sealed the French annexation of Savoy and with it Mont Blanc, 'Les Écrins' was the highest peak in France. The implication was obvious: if there was a constructed surveying station, a *signal*, marked on the map, then someone must have gone there.

On the basis of this detail two researchers from Vallouise, Olivier Joseph and Paul-Billon Grand, claimed the summit had in fact been reached more than a decade before Whymper and his companions. They presented the discovery as a revolution in the history of alpinism and, with the co-opera- tion of freelance cartographer Alexandre Nicolas from Pelvoux and boosted by the work of Eugenio Garoglio from the Centro Studi e Ricerche Storiche sull'Architettura Militare del Piemonte at the University of Turin, began questioning other first ascents in the Écrins and Viso areas, including those by Francis Fox Tuckett, William Mathews and W A B Coolidge.

Joseph and his group presented their theories at conferences and ques- tioned the established narrative of specialist historians, the French Alpine Club (CAF) and the Alpine Club. The controversy was picked up by the press and on social media. At a conference in Vallouise in August 2016, AC member Sue Hare was present, prompting Olivier Joseph to comment afterwards on his website: 'As far as Sue Hare, Alpine Club secretary, was concerned, she did not hide her enthusiasm at the end of our conference.' Sue was not the AC secretary, although she serves as part of the AC Photo Library team, and while she does admire Olivier Joseph's dedication, she did not endorse his theory.

My friend Claude Deck (GHM-CAF) who ran *La Montagne et Alpin- isme*'s chronicle for some 40 years until 2016 was first to react, asking me to contact the Alpine Club to fire up a joint response to what he judged was a questionable thesis. He also sent a series of questions to Olivier Joseph. Joseph's response was both adamant and surprising. Not only had Lieu- tenant Meusnier climbed Les Écrins by himself 11 years before Adolphus Moore, Horace Walker, Edward Whymper and the best guides of the time, Christian Almer and Michel Croz, but also the Pelvoux, the Ailefroide Orientale, Pic de Neige Cordier, Pointe Nérot and more.

Deck asked Joseph: 'Challenging ascents of the most famous British alpinists is a real thunderclap in the history of alpinism ... Have you obtained the Alpine Club's opinion?' Joseph's response was dismissive: 'this is of no interest whatsoever to us. The history of alpinism was written by a small circle largely unconnected to local and scientific archives, which show quite a different view of human presence on the high summits of the Alps. We work with military and scientific historians and archaeologists to reconstitute this human presence in the high mountains before the alpin- ists' arrival. For us, alpinism represents a minor episode of little interest in the human history of mountains ...'

Such a prejudicial response made us question the objectivity of these historians. However, since Claude and I are neither cartographers nor academic historians, we could not challenge the validity of their work. Luckily we did not have to wait too long. Two French historians, Michèle Janin-Thivos from the University of Aix and Marseille and Michel

Details from the draft released by the French Géoportail website illustration the abbreviations following the peak names for Pelvoux and Les Écrins.

An equivalent extract from the completed 1866 Briançon sheet for the 1/80,000 Carte d'État-Major keeps the reference to a *signal* for Pelvoux, but there is no abbreviation now for Les Écrins.

Tailland from Toulon University, soon published a comprehensive response: *Des Ascensions Oubliées? Les opérations de la carte d'État-major de Briançon au XIXème siècle* (Editions du Fournel, 2016). They opened their book thus:

> *Revisiting established history is a sound and legitimate enterprise provided it is based on the crosschecking of sources and a verifiable scientific argument. The methodological inadequacies of this theory led us to look at the whole issue and analyse the idea of a signal being located on the Écrins, to check the nature of the document used (a draft published on the Géoportail website) and match it to the sources of the ordnance survey map in the history department of the ministry of defence … Then we went to the IGN to see the draft they used … Those documents prove definitely that there have been no 'forgotten ascents'.*

On the 1/40,000 draft the well-known *signal* on top of Pelvoux is indicated by the abbreviation 'S^{al}'. On the same draft the Les Écrins also has an abbreviation after its name, but it is actually quite difficult to tell whether it says 'S^{al}' for *signal* or 'S^{et}' for *sommet*. Assuming it could be the former, as Joseph and Grand claim, Janin-Thivos and Tailland examined the table of geographical points on the side of the same draft, where they found the Pelvoux *signal* mentioned but no corresponding entry of a *signal* for

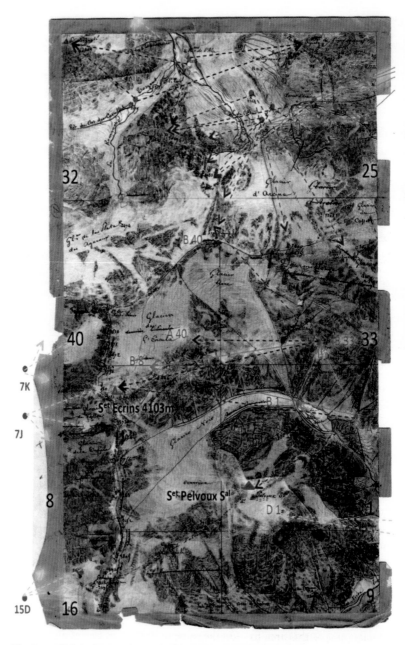

The beautiful draft map drawn by Meusnier featuring the north-west and south-west sections of the Briançon sheet. This shows the stations Meusnier used for his calculations.

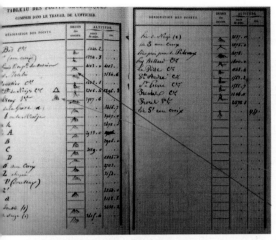

Signals could be geographical features, churches, bell towers, even trees or a remote chalet, or they could be built, like the one illustrated. But Meusnier, like other surveyors, differentiated between them. The blue line points to Meusnier's entry for Pelvoux, with a symbol indicating that this *signal* was built. There is no equivalent for Les Écrins, illustrated by the red line.

the Écrins: an obvious discrepancy between the table and the map itself. Officers doing the mapping drew 'pre-drafts' – *mappes* – that were the nearest documents to their field operations. When Janin-Thivos and Tailland examined Meusnier's field notes, they found no mention of a *signal* for the Écrins there either.

The digitised document that ignited the controversy was most probably a working document, just one copy of the true draft. The authors emphasise that 13 years passed between Meusnier's work and the map, during which many copies were made to link individual sheets together. These copies circulated through different hands before the final engraving. It is unfortunate that IGN only has one copy for this particular sheet but any mention of 'S^{al}' is undoubtedly a transcription error. Looking at the pre-draft of Captain Bourgeois, a colleague of Meusnier, there is a somewhat indistinct entry besides the name Les Écrins of 'S^{et}' for *sommet*. It seems more than likely that this was read in error as 'S^{al}' by one of many working on the document between survey and engraving. Janin-Thivos and Tailland concluded: 'The lack of critical analysis of this document has been used as a starting point to an erroneous interpretation … one source cannot be held as a proof.'

Furthermore, the authors could find no explanation for keeping a putative ascent of Les Écrins secret. There was no strategic problem attached to the mapping of this area to require secrecy. Far from being coy, surveyors documented first ascents of other peaks. General Louis Hurault, a former head of the IGN, made a significant contribution to the book *Les Alpinistes Célèbres* (1956), describing the well-known achievements of Adrien Durand, who began the Briançon mapping (1828-30). It was Durand who in 1828 erected the *signal* on the rocky summit of Pelvoux that now bears

Points trigonométriques de départ.

NOMS DES OBJETS PAR ORDRE ALPHABÉTIQUE.		HAUTEUR ABSOLUE DES POINTS TRIGONOMÉTRIQUES DE DÉPART.	
		Point de mire.	Sol.
		m	m
S^et des Écrins		4103.	4103.
Monetier C^er		1543.1	1493.
Bez C^er		1441.2	. . . . .
Pelvoux S^al		3937.6	. . . . .
lic A. St du Sablier		2933.	2933.
lic B. N^te Bouchard		2906.	2906.
lic C sur la crête de Combeynou		3089.	3089.
lic G. Croix de la Cucumelle		2703.	2703.
lic ... la crête du G^d Pelvoux		3854.	3854.
lic d		3118.	3118.
lic de Neige (1)		3615.4	3615.4
lic de Neige (2)		3537.	3537.
lic S^t avec Croix		2757.	2757.
Borel S^al		2572.1	
lic Signalé au f. de Dormilleuse		3660.	3660.
lic Signalé 4		3355.	3355.
.		. . . .	. . . .
		. . . .	. . . .
		. . . .	. . . .
		. . . .	. . . .
		. . . .	. . . .
		. . . .	. . . .
		. . . .	. . . .

Tableau N° 8 ter.

Meusnier's notes reveal entries for S^et, an abbreviation for *sommet*, des Écrins and Pelvoux S^al, short for *signal*.

his name. But there was no mention of the so-called first ascent of 1853. Durand didn't see the point of going on another 500m to reach Pelvoux's main snowy summit; his task was not to climb summits but map the area, and that was the case for the army cartographers who continued his work in the 1851-3 survey. They worked in difficult weather conditions and Durand himself suffered such strain that he died a few years after his work on Pelvoux at the age of just 48. Jean Puiseux made the first ascent of the main summit in 1848; it was known for a while as Pointe Puiseux.

Henri Beraldi (1849-1931), a writer and historian attached to the ministry of defence, also documented the ascent and mapping feats of Captain Durand on Pelvoux and those of his successor, Captain Davout, in his book *Balaïtous* and *Pelvoux* (1907), yet does not mention Meusnier or others as having climbed other summits. Later in his book, he does admire the 1864 ascent of the Écrins by Whymper, Moore, Walker, Almer and Croz. Why would a writer sometimes quite critical of alpinism ignore major ascents by his army colleagues, having had full access to the archives?

The many contacts between the French army, alpine clubs and alpinists like Tuckett and Anthony Adams Reilly, who actually climbed with some of those French army officers, rather proves the contrary. Janin-Thivos and Tailland mention a visit by Tuckett to the Dépôt de la Guerre, the military unit in charge of producing the Carte d'État-Major, showing the strong and open links between the French scientific community, French army officers in charge of mapping and Alpine Club members. This visit is described in a detailed article Tuckett published in the *Alpine Journal*[1]. He was given access to the Briançon map and 'the original memoranda of the officers of the État-Major'.

> ... *I met with the most courteous reception from General Blondel, director of the 'Dépôt', who gave me the freest access to maps and MSS including the original memoranda of the officers of the État-Major, allowed me the utmost liberty in making notes, and, besides permitting me to have printed copies of several unfinished and of course unpublished sheets, furnished me with a manuscript one, beautifully executed by draughtsmen of the 'Bureau' of the most important portion of the four MS sheets of the Feuille Briançon on the same scale as the original ... This last is partially engraved, being now, as it is termed, 'au trait'; i.e. the rivers, roads, names of places, heights and outlines (dotted) of mountains and glaciers are given, but no shading, nothing that represent relief. M le Commandant Brossard, head of the engraving department, informed me that this sheet would certainly be ready for publication in six years, and very probably in five. The superintendent of the topographical department, M le Colonel Bertrand, handed me over, after reading the general's order, to M le Commandant Loupôt, a most pleasant, polite, and intelligent gentleman, whose kindness I shall not soon forget. He seemed as though he could not do enough to meet my wishes, and*

---

1. F F Tuckett 'Explorations in The Alps of Dauphiné during the month of July 1862', *Alpine Journal*, vol 1, 1863, pp145-79.

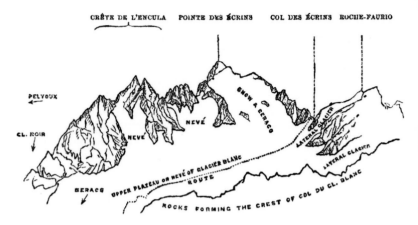

THE POINTE DES ÉCRINS COL AND NÉVÉ OF GLACIER BLANC, FROM
COL DU GLACIER BLANC.

A sketch from July 1862 of the Écrins massif by F F Tuckett included with his article on the region published in the *Alpine Journal* the following year.

most energetically seconded all my applications to his chef. The four original MS sheets, on a scale of 1/40,000, which form the basis of the future Feuille Briançon, are the result of the following labours:

Première Triangulation – 1828-9-30 … M le Commandant Durand.
Seconde Triangulation – 1851-2 … M. Davoût (Capitaine?)

La Topographie (détails) … MM les Capitaines Viroux, Valette, Taffin, Beaudouin, Bourgeois, Smet, Vuillemot, Courier, Cousinard, Versigny, and le lieutenant Meusnier [sic].

Of these gentlemen, MM Bourgeois, Courier, Cousinard and Meunier [sic] executed that portion which is included in the copy supplied to me, and of which a photographic reduction has been deposited at the rooms of the Alpine Club. From the large number of lofty summits ascended by them, I was led to anticipate a degree of accuracy which subsequent minute examination on the spot completely confirmed. With Commandant Durand the survey of this group of mountains was a labour of love to which he devoted all his energies. Indeed, to such an extent did he identify himself with the successful completion of his tasks cost him his reason … His successors appear, however, to have worked with equal intelligence and accuracy, and the result is a map which for faithful rendering of details will almost compare with those of the Swiss survey … I have reason to believe that the future Briançon sheet, N°189, will be a credit to the French engineers.

This is justified recognition for the work done by French officers but also clear evidence that he was told what summits they had climbed and not climbed, certainly none of the summits claimed by Joseph and Grand. The documentation allowed Whymper to climb the Écrins and this co-operation between alpinists and French army cartographers continued until all the Alps were fully and properly mapped, in particular the French climbers and topographers Paul Helbronner and Henri Vallot. French army officers and members of CAF came, in the 19th century, from the same upper-middle class as AC members and shared their work quite openly. Indeed a number of those army officers were members of CAF from its foundation in 1874. The notion of a 'plot' between the AC and CAF to hog the glory is laughable.

The presence of the British in early mountaineering can be irritating to some French, but it is a reality well established. It is also true that the mapping work undertaken by French army officers in difficult and often dangerous conditions was a feat significant enough to be remembered. This achievement deserves more recognition than it has received, but surely not at the expense of historical truth.

C A RUSSELL

One Hundred Years Ago

As the First World War continued into another year the opportunities for mountaineering in the Alps in 1917 were again severely restricted. Although few climbers were active in the principal regions during the early months of the year several expeditions of note were undertaken. In the Bernese Alps in February Hans Morgenthaler and Bernhard Lauterburg made the first ski ascents of the Schinhorn, Nesthorn and Lötschentaler Breithorn, completing their tour with a winter ascent of the Aletschhorn. Other peaks ascended for the first time with the aid of ski included the Aiguille du Midi and the Tour Ronde, both climbed by Aldo Bonacossa and his companions. Several months later in the Pennine Alps in June Arnold Lunn, accompanied by Josef Knubel, completed the first ski ascent of the Dom, making 'the first ski track up the highest snowslope in Switzerland.'

After a cold and unsettled period during the spring and early summer favourable conditions prevailed for much of the climbing season. In July Lauterburg returned to the Bernese Alps accompanied on this occasion by Fritz Egger to open a serious new route on the Agassizhorn. Starting from the Finsteraarjoch they climbed directly to the summit by way of the steep north-east rib – a remarkable achievement for the period.

At Chamonix J Monroe Thorington, serving with the American Ambulance Corps, was able to arrange a guided ascent of Mont Blanc during a brief leave of absence. The Col du Dôme and the summit were reached by way of the Grands Mulets, where the party enjoyed four litres of wine which had survived a traverse through the icefall of the Bossons glacier.

An exceptionally fine spell in September enabled Henry Montagnier, an American member of the Alpine Club resident in Switzerland, to undertake an enjoyable and rewarding ascent of Monte Rosa. Accompanied by the guides Siegfried Burgener and Julius Zumtaugwald he climbed the Nordend before descending to the Silbersattel and reaching the summit ridge above the Grenzsattel. The party then traversed the ridge to the Dufourspitze where they remained for nearly an hour 'in our shirtsleeves – a lighted match hardly flickered.'

In August ceremonies were held to mark the inauguration of the Solvay hut which had been erected two years earlier at a height of some 4000m on the north-east, Hörnli ridge of the Matterhorn. The inauguration had been delayed on account of bad weather and also in the hope that Ernest Solvay, the Belgian industrialist who had donated the funds for construction, would be able to attend. For the occasion three guided parties climbed to the hut and continued to the summit before descending to join a banquet at the Mont Cervin hotel in Zermatt. As M Solvay was unable to travel

Geoffrey Winthrop Young (right) with H O Jones and Josef Knubel in 1911.
(Alpine Club Photo Library)

from German-occupied Belgium the Swiss Alpine Club forwarded a letter
of thanks for his generous contribution.

During the year some climbing was reported in other mountain regions
not directly affected by the conflict. In South Africa members of the Mountain Club continued their exploration of Table Mountain (1087m). In April
W T Cobern and C W Campbell added to their list of successful ascents
with *Cobblestone Face* and *Sheerness Face*, two very severe routes for the period.

To the east in the Drakensberg range D W Bassett-Smith and R G Kingdon made the first recorded ascent of Cathedral Peak (3004m).

In the Southern Alps of New Zealand Samuel Turner, who had already completed the traverse of all three peaks of Mount Cook (3724m), was determined to make a solo ascent of the mountain. Although his attempts to reach the High Peak were defeated by bad weather he succeeded on his own in making the first ascents of the two Anzac peaks (2528m and 2513m) above the Grand Plateau.

In the Canadian Rockies V A Fynn completed a number of notable expeditions in the Lake Louise district. In August, climbing alone, he made the first ascent of the north ridge of Mount Aberdeen (3151m) and with a companion the first complete traverse of Mount Whyte (2983m). After climbing Mounts Lefroy (3423m) and Victoria (3464m) from Abbot Pass with the guide Rudolph Aemmer in single long day Fynn rounded off a successful campaign by climbing Mount Louis (2682m), the imposing rock tower near Banff, with Edward Feuz junior.

In January considerable interest was aroused by the publication in the *Geographical Journal* of a paper by Alexander Kellas entitled 'A Consideration of the Possibility of Ascending the Loftier Himalaya'. The paper was reviewed in the *Alpine Journal* where it was considered to be 'a most valuable contribution to our knowledge of the effects of high altitudes on the human body.' Another work of great interest was *Two Summers in the Ice-Wilds of Eastern Karakoram*, the account by Dr William Hunter Workman and his wife Fanny Bullock Workman of their final two expeditions culminating in the exploration of the Siachen glacier and an ascent to Indira Col (5776m).

During the year Captain Farrar, who had succeeded Lord Justice Pickford as president of the Alpine Club, paid tribute to members killed or wounded on active service including Geoffrey Winthrop Young, one of the outstanding mountaineers of the day. While in command of an ambulance unit on the Italian front Young was severely wounded in his left leg which was subsequently amputated above the knee. This account is concluded with the final verse of Young's famous poem *I have not lost the magic of long days* – a poignant reminder of the tragedy of war and an indomitable spirit in the face of adversity.

What if I live no more those kingly days?
their night sleeps with me still.
I dream my feet upon the starry ways;
my heart rests in the hill.
I may not grudge the little left undone;
I hold the heights, I keep the dreams I won.

Area Notes

Untitled (Gordale Scar?)
Joseph Farington (1747-1821)
Undated. Pen and ink and watercolor over graphite on wove paper.
18 x 12⅞ inches. Yale Center for British Art, Paul Mellon Collection.

LINDSAY GRIFFIN

Alps & Dolomites 2016

Stephan Siegrist on the third pitch above the central ledge
of *Metanoia*, on the Eiger. *(Archive Metanoia)*

Thomas Huber on one of the harder rock pitches of *Metanoia*. Note the hot air balloon up and left. *(Archive Metanoia)*

The highlights of 2016, the really major ascents during both summer and winter, largely took place on the some of the most celebrated peaks of the Alpine chain: Eiger, Grandes Jorasses, Piz Badile, Civetta, Cima Grande. In particular, rare winter conditions in the Bregaglia-Masino led to some truly remarkable ascents.

There were several outstanding ascents on the north face of the Eiger, but none that matches the second ascent of the legendary *Metanoia* by Thomas Huber, Roger Schaeli and Stephan Siegrist. *Metanoia* is a Greek word meaning 'a fundamental change of thinking, a new view on the world'. This is how it left its author, Jeff Lowe, after his nine-day solo ascent in February 1991. At that time Lowe was at a very tough time in his life, both personally and financially, but he came away from the climb with a new perspective, and one that has helped him in recent years battle his debilitating ALS disease. From his wheelchair in the USA he gave valuable advice to the trio, and monitored their progress on the face.

The three made a good effort in the week before Christmas, reaching the central ledge after two long days, but then retreating in bad weather, reaching the Stollenloch in eight hours on their third day. A second attempt was shut down early, so on their third attempt, commencing 29 December, they opted to start from the Stollenloch. They re-climbed a few ropes they had left in place, and continued for two long days, reaching the summit on the evening of 30 December. Lowe used no bolts, but the three elected to place

The line of *Amore di Vetro* on the north-east face of the Piz Badile. *(Marcel Schenk)*

one 8mm bolt on a belay, as a fall at this point would have ripped the whole party off the mountain. The climbers confirmed that the 1,800m route (VII, A4, M6) set new standards of alpinism at the time. Or as Huber said: 'what he [Lowe] accomplished is really just madness.' The climb, and Lowe's ground-breaking career, is celebrated in the award-winning film *Metanoia*.

On the left side of the wall Tom Ballard and Marcin Tomaszewski spent seven days, finishing on 6 December, climbing a new route on the north pillar, an area of the face Ballard knows well as he had repeated the 1970 *Scottish Route* and added a new line, *Seven Pillars of Wisdom* – and has now spent more than 100 days on the north face. Ballard and Tomaszewski started a little to the right of the 2002 Swiss route, *Griff ins Licht*, crossed it, and eventually joined *Seven Pillars*, finishing up the *Lauper Route* to the summit. They had left ropes on part of the route (and their portaledge), so descended via 40 abseils. One of the 1970 Scottish team, Kenny Spence, described his route as how he would imagine climbing on the prow of the *Titanic*, so the two named their new line *Titanic* (1800m, A3, M5, 6b). The pair carried a power drill and placed 26 bolts for belay anchors and 24 additional bolts on pitches. They hand-drilled bolts on the abseil descent of the upper *Lauper Route*.

Ephemeral climbing took on something of a new meaning in the Bregaglia when Simon Gietl and Marcel Schenk finally climbed the much sought-after line, now named *Amore di Vetro* (800m, M5, R), on the north-east face of

the Piz Badile. The start follows a logical, if somewhat wandering, winter line, crossing the *Cassin* and *Linea Blanca* to reach the central snow patch, from where a beautiful sliver of ice over compact granite led direct to the top, right of *Memento Mori*. The significance of the ascent lies in the letter R indicating scanty protection. Although conditions were outstanding, thinly iced granite slabs gave little option for gear placements, the two joking that for much of the time they free soloed with a rope. One pitch was 110m, the climbers moving together protected only by a single Pecker. Needless to say, retreat from the upper section of the route would have been extremely tricky. Perhaps because of this they completed the ascent in a single day, 16 November, then abseiled the north ridge and continued down to the valley the same night.

Schenk continued to watch the face, given the general lack of snow in the Alps at the time, and exactly a month later was back at the Sasc Fura hut, this time with David Hefti, the two reaching the hut in trainers. After changing into boots and crampons they followed the *Cassin route* all the way to the central snow patch, and then moved left to reach the central couloir and

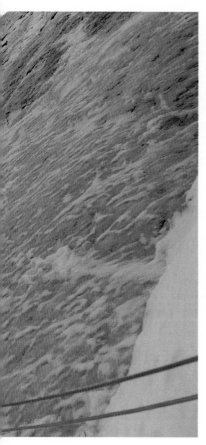

Above: Simon Gietl following a pitch of thin ice on *Amore di Vetro*, Piz Badile. *(Marcel Schenk)*

Left: Simon Gietl starting another run-out section in the upper part of *Amore di Vetro*. *(Marcel Schenk)*

the 1980 Czech route, *Memento Mori*. The next few pitches were relatively steep, badly protected, and required total commitment. Higher, there were difficulties of M7 but these were better protected than below. They reached the summit at 4.30pm, just as it was getting dark. Having previously seen from the Cengalo that conditions were good on the east side of the Badile, the two chose to descend to the Col di Cengalo, then climb down the Cengalo couloir below the north-east face. They regained their car at 9pm. The combination route has been christened the *Northeast Supercombo* (800m, M7, R), and a couple of weeks later was repeated by Luka Lindič and Ines Papert, who again found perfect thin ice all the way to the summit. While they were on the route, two other climbers were making a rare winter repeat of the *Cassin*: for a face that sees so little winter activity, to have two parties climbing at the same time is remarkable.

Hefti and Schenk are no newcomers to the range; as Swiss guides they take clients there frequently. In February 2015 the two made a rare winter ascent of the *Cassin*, after which Schenk came up with an audacious plan: the Bondasca Horseshoe. Although a continuous traverse of the peaks around the

The Bondasca Horseshoe. *(Vittorio Scartazzini)*

Val Bondasca, from the Pizzo Trubinasca, via the Badile, Cengalo, Gemelli and the Sciora Group to the Punta Innominata, had been completed once in summer (Jonas Gessler and Daniel Silbernagel, two long days in August 2008), it had never been done in winter. Conditions would be crucial: it would need to be relatively dry and require at least three days of perfect weather. In the final days of 2015 the stars seemed to be in alignment. On 26 December Hefti and Schenk walked up to the Sasc Fura hut, crossed the Trubinasca Pass to the upper Codera valley, and spent the night in the Pedroni del Pra bivouac hut. Leaving at 6am next day they crossed snowfields and soon reached the top of Punta Trubinasca. Making extremely rapid progress, they were on the summit of the Badile by 11am, the Cengalo at 2pm and, after crossing the Gemelli, they reached the Ronconi bivouac hut at the Passo di Bondo in the dark, a little after 5.30pm. They had allowed two days for this section, so were well pleased with their progress. Next day they met tricky climbing while crossing the Ago di Sciora, and unexpected difficulties before the Pioda, but they reached the Innominata that same day and descended via the west couloir to the Sciora hut, where they were surprised to find two cans of beer, deposited by a friend. The traverse crosses 17 summits, would involve around 200 pitches of climbing, difficulties up to 5+/6a in summer, and a ridiculous amount of total height gain given the many ups and downs on the crest.

In the Mont Blanc range two major routes were added to the Grandes Jorasses, both predominantly rock climbs, and were the first significant summer additions to the mountain in some years. The ascent of the Diamond Ridge

Punta Sertori 3195m
Pizzo Badile 3305m
Torrione del Badile 3140m
Punta Badilet 3171m
Punta Trubinasca 2998m
Pizzo Trubinasca 2918m

on the Tronchey Face by Simon Richardson and Micha Rinn, at 1,600m (5c, A0) one of the longest climbs in the massif, is recorded elsewhere in this edition of the *AJ*. The second new route was supplied by Russians. Left of the classic *Gervasutti Route* on the east face is a large left-slanting diedre, and left again is *The (Red) Pillar* climbed in 1988 by Paolo Cavagnetto and Enrico Rosso at around ED2, 6b, A2. These two Italians had hoped to climb through the final overhangs at the top of the pillar to reach the Tronchey Ridge at the Third Tower. In the end they were forced right, across the top of the diedre, to join the *Gervasutti* route. Roman Gorodischenskiy and Maxim Foygel studied the right wall of the pillar leading towards the diedre and found it to be quite wide, with a series of cracks and corners. Their initial ground, to a bivouac at the base of the diedre, is probably very similar to that taken by Cavagnetto and Rosso, but above they climbed six sustained pitches of 5c, 6a and A2, finishing direct through the overhangs to the Tronchey Ridge. After another bivouac they were on the summit of Pointe Walker around midday on 28 August, naming their route after the initial letters of their Christian names: *Via RoMa* (1350m, ED2, 6a, A2).

Arguably the most significant legacy left to the mountaineering world by the late Ueli Steck was his dedicated professionalism towards fitness, through nutrition, improved mental aptitude and a punishing training schedule. The result produced many astonishingly fast times over relatively moderate (for him) terrain. One such example occurred on 16 August, the day before he was due to attend an event in Courmayeur. He left the campsite in the Val Veni a little after 5am and in one hour had reached the

David Hefti climbing on the west ridge of the Badile during the first winter traverse of the Bondasca Horseshoe. Note the remarkably dry conditions. *(Marcel Schenk)*

Monzino hut, three and a half or more hours for average mortals. From there he covered the five to seven hour approach to the Eccles hut in 1h 45m, and the eight to 11 hour ascent of the *Innominata Ridge* (D+) in 2h 45m. A good track in frozen terrain allowed him to descend to the Torino hut in 2h 10m, from where he embarked on the long run down to the valley, returning to the campsite just 9h 25m after setting out.

In the Dolomites, a well known route on the north-west face of Civetta (3220m) is the classic *Solleder Route*, climbed by Lettenbauer and Solleder in 1925, generally acknowledged as the first grade VI climb in the Alps and Dolomites. A free ascent is now considered 6a. Following a logical line linking natural features to the right of this classic, over two days in August Tom Ballard and Marcin Tomaszewski created *Dirty Harry* (1375m, VII). The route has 29 pitches and was completed with one bivouac at the end of pitch 12, where the route arrives at the prominent snow patch on the face, and another on the descent. In common with nearby routes on this vast wall, the rock ranged from outstanding to atrocious, with everything in between.

Another big Dolomite wall to gain a new route was the north face of Monte Agner (2873m). On 3 September, after a tip-off by local resident Geoff Hornby, Simon Messner and Philipp Prunster climbed independent ground close to but generally left of the classic 1921 *Andreoletti-Jori-Zanutti route* (1500m, V) to reach the summit in 12 hours. Their new line was 1,500m and VI+ but lack of time and equipment forced them to exit via the right-hand variant of the 1921 route. A Polish team climbed a route in this vicinity during 1968 but Messner and Prunster found no traces of previous passage on their line after an ancient piton 100m off the ground.

Marcel Schenk on the Sciora di Dentro early morning of the second day of the Bondasca Horseshoe. Behind are the Gemelli and Cengalo. *(David Hefti)*

Beginning in the autumn of 2015 and climbing without a bolt kit, Simon Gietl and Vittorio Messini made several forays up the wall immediately to the right of the classic *Comici Route* on the north face of the Cima Grande (2999m) before emerging onto the Ring Band after 13 pitches. Given the number of routes now in existence on this historic face, it is surprising to find that after the initial pitch up the pedestal of the *Comici*, the route is entirely independent and does not cross any other. The two finished the climb in June 2016, having used a mixture of free and aid, but only natural gear. After a few more days of work, cleaning and attempting the pitches, Gietl returned in July with Andrea Oberbacher to free climb the route. The crux, pitch five, is 40m of very compact rock at 7b+. Here, it was not only difficult to place pegs for protection, but some of the small flakes and edges were snappy. The route was named *Das Erbe der Vater (The Legacy of our Ancestors)* (500m, IX-) as a tribute to Comici, Dimai, Cassin, Ratti etc, whose achievements on these Lavaredo walls were outstanding for the era.

On the left side of the same wall a notable achievement was the second free ascent of the 1977 *Spanish Route* (Carillo-Gallego-Gomez-Lozano, VI, A3) by Poles Lukasz Dudek and Jacek Matuszek. The route was climbed almost free in 2003 by Mauro 'Bubu' Bole at 8a+, but a wet roof eluded him. The Austrian Much Mayr eventually made the first complete free ascent in 2015 at 8b+. While Mayr was working the route, now arguably the hardest on the Cima Grande, Dudek and Matuszek were climbing neighbouring *Bellavista* (8b+) on the Cima Ovest. It was obvious to them what their next target on these walls should be.

The Spanish Route lies just left of the 1995 *Das Phantom der Zinne* (7c) by

Kurt Astner and Christoph Hainz, and it is good to see that more than 20 years after this ascent Hainz is still as active as ever. As part of a documentary on the Ortler (3905m) Hainz and a film crew were inspecting the southwest face, with a view to shooting footage of the 1976 *Messner* route up the central pillar. However, Hainz, then 54, spotted the unclimbed southwest pillar. He persuaded the film company that he could do a new route instead, but insisted he climbed it alone. The rock varied from outstanding to poor, but on 29 August Hainz completed the 750m line to the summit ice cap at c3500m in just 1h 55m, and has named it the *Golden Pillar of Ortler* (VI+, though mainly IV+ and V).

Now, if you've read this far, and are female, you might be disillusioned by what appears to be an entirely male dominated report. But take heart, as women also made highly significant repeats during 2016. Nina Caprez, perhaps best noted for her high-standard sport climbing, became almost certainly the first women to free climb, and on sight, *Divine Providence* (7b) on Mont Blanc's Grand Pilier d'Angle. With Robert Schaeli, New Zealand's Mayan Smith-Gobat completed the 1991 Anker-Siegrist route, *La Vida es Silbar* (900m) on the north face of the Eiger. Schaeli was able to make a redpoint ascent at 7c, only the second free ascent of this route (FFA by Siegrist and Steck in 2003). Smith-Gobat, who was recovering from a shoulder operation, managed to free climb all but a few sections. And on 17 July the Italian Federica Mingolla became the first woman to climb the famous 920m *Fish* on the south face of the Marmolada d'Ombretta (3230m), leading every pitch free (7b+). She took only one fall, not on the crux, but on a difficult 6c pitch. In addition Mingolla more or less made the first winter ascent of the legendary 1988 route *Delta Minox* (Fazzini-Gianola-Gianola-Riva, 460m, 7a/b, 6c+ obl) on the south-west pillar of the Cima Scingino (2502m) in the Bregaglia-Masino, considered by many to be one of the most difficult mountain slab climbs in the Alps. Whilst the belays are bolted and the granite is excellent, the pitches are sparsely protected, with hard climbing and 'classic' Masino smeary traverses more than 10m away from gear. Unfortunately, she was not able to climb the last few metres to the summit; the finishing crack of the final pitch was choked with ice and the party had no equipment to deal with it. Mingolla used some points of aid on damp sections, but free climbed up to an estimated 7b+. It was an enlightening experience for the 21-year-old from Torino who has redpointed 8b+. Despite having climbed and bouldered in Mello, this was her first time on the mountains of the Masino and also her first experience of using snowshoes.

SIMON RICHARDSON

Scottish Winter 2016-17

Iain Small leading the ice-filled corner on the second pitch of *The Ninety-Five Theses* (IX,9) on Church Door Buttress in Glen Coe. The double roof with its hanging icicle fringe can be seen above. *(Simon Richardson)*

Die-hard regulars agree they could not remember a poorer winter climbing season than the 2017 Scottish winter. The weather was often calm and settled but infrequent snowfalls were quickly followed by deep thaws that left the hills bare. There was no chance for a base to build, and low-angled terrain that would normally be covered in consolidated snow was often left as blank slabs or unstable rubble. Not only did the dry conditions prevent gullies and drainage lines forming ice, it made classic mixed climbs difficult and time consuming. A recipe of heavy snowfalls and devastating thaws meant the turf was rarely frozen, but it did provide opportunities for ascents of steep snowed-up rock routes for those poised and ready to climb immediately after the storms.

As might be expected for such a lean season, Ben Nevis saw the bulk of the pioneering activity, and eight significant new routes were added to the mountain. Iain Small led the way with *The Shape of Things to Come* (IX,9) and *Failure is Not An Option* (VIII,9), followed by myself. Both climbs are situated on the north wall of Carn Dearg and are major four-pitch outings climbed on snowed-up rock, although the second route also relied on transitory thin ice. Greg Boswell added one of the most aesthetic lines to the mountain in January when he climbed *Hanging Garden* (VII,8) with Jon Frederick (visiting from the USA) and Stuart Lade; the route is a direct finish up cracks in the soaring Babylon arête on Number Three Gully Buttress. Also of note was the first ascent of *Cloudjumper* (VIII,9) by Dave MacLeod and Helen Rennard. This steep route lies on the east flank of Tower Ridge, another venue that is becoming recognised for its speed to come into condition after a heavy snowfall.

In the Cairngorms, the big event was Greg Boswell's first ascent of *Intravenous Fly Trap* (X,10) with Scott Grosdanoff. This takes the very steep wall left of *Daddy Longlegs* in Coire an Lochain, and joins a very select group of Scottish Grade X routes (namely *The Greatest Show on Earth*, *Range War* and *Messiah* all ascended by Boswell in 2015), that have been climbed on sight. Elsewhere in the Cairngorms in early November, Steve Perry made the first ascent of the strenuous *Theory of Relativity* (VII,9) on Lurcher's Crag with Andy Nisbet and Jonathan Preston. Two weeks later the trio were joined by Sarah Sigley for the challenging line of *Wolfpack* (VI,7) that lies to the right. Deeper in the Cairngorms, Roger Webb and I made several additions to Braeriach such as *Shark* (V,7) on Sron na Lairig, but in general, opportunities for harder climbs were few and far between.

The warm weather restricted activity in the Northern Highlands, but Skye saw some good ascents during the winter festival that later culminated in the first winter ascent of *Canopy* (VI,6) on Blaven by Michael Barnard and John MacLeod. Also of note was the 235m *Silver Fox* (V,5) in Coire Lagan by Mike Lates and Sophie Grace Chappell. Dry easterly winds meant that the turf was often aerated and unfriendly in the Southern Highlands, although Stuart McFarlane and Brian Shackleton added the fine *Clockwork Orange* (V,4) to Beinn an Lochain, and Greg Boswell and Guy Robertson climbed the short but technical *Moral Compass* (VII,9) on Ben Vorlich.

Roger Webb above the awkward squeeze-slot on a new III,5 in Coire an Lochain on Braeriach. Although the rapid sequence of snowfall and thaws through the season rarely led to good build up of snow and ice, there was enjoyable climbing to be found on lower-angled turfy mixed lines in the high Cairngorms corries. *(Simon Richardson)*

In Glen Coe, activity focused on mixed climbing on the high crags such as Stob Coire nan Lochan where the difficult *Unicorn* (VIII,8) saw several ascents. The higher altitude Church Door Buttress on Bidean was also popular with an on-form Iain Small leading the way on the new route front. In January, he made the first ascent of *The Prentice Pillar* (VIII,8) on the lower front face with Helen Rennard. He and I returned in March, and Iain led the stupendous line of *The Ninety-Five Theses* (IX,9), which takes the impending groove-line and stepped roofs to the right of last year's addition *Gates of Paradise*. Few Scottish winter routes overhang from the first move to the very last, especially when much of the progress depends on thin ice, and there is little doubt that this climb has set a new level for Scottish icy mixed. Given the poor conditions through the season it was remarkable that any high standard climbing took place at all. Fingers are now firmly crossed for a more helpful and productive 2018 season.

TIMOTHY ELSON

India 2016

Marikula Killa's north spure with Peak 5780m on the left. *(Martin Moran)*

The big news for climbing in the Indian Himalaya, although only for 2017, was the reduction in peak fees on 81 selected peaks as a promotional scheme intending to encourage climbers to visit less frequented areas than the usual honeypots. There has also been a relaxation in the Protected Area Permit (PAP) regime to enable foreigners to visit the Nubra valley without a permit. In Sikkim 14 new peaks below 7,000m have been opened and there is an airport under construction in Pakyang, allowing flights into Sikkim for the first time. The FCO continue to advise against all travel to Jammu & Kashmir other than to Ladakh and the city of Jammu. More detail can be found on the BMC website, where they have the Indian Mountaineering Foundation's newsletter (not visible on the IMF website), APEX, volume 4.

Expeditions to the Indian Himalaya in 2016 were concentrated in the pre-and post-monsoon climbing seasons, as usual; below is a summary of the expeditions.

Indian East Karakoram
Between 25 August and 2 October, an Alpine Club team of Derek Buckle, Mike Cocker, Drew Cook, Gus Morton and Knut Tønsberg visited the remote Nubra valley in the Indian East Karakoram. From Leh they travelled over the Khardung La (5370m) to the Nubra valley and trekked for three days up the Tirit Phu, to the confluence of the Rassa and Phunangma glacier outflows where they established base camp (4756m). Over the next few days they established camps on the lower Rassa glacier. From a high camp the team made the first (10 September) and second (11 September) ascents of Peak 6222m, named Lak Kangri, via the south-east face (AD). On 19 September the team made the first ascent of Peak 6315m, dubbed Thrung-ma Kangri, via the south face (D).

Between 5 May and 12 June the Indian team of Rajesh Gadgil, Ratnesh Javeri, Vineeta Muni, Dinesh Korday, Roshmin Mehandru and Divyesh Muni attempted the first ascent of Shahi Kangri (6934m) in the Indian East Karakorum. The team were unable to reach the proposed base camp due to loose terrain and a bottleneck in the Chip Chap Nala. They changed their objective to the unclimbed Nya Kangri (6480m) and established base camp at Phoglas (4630m) on 28 May. They worked their way up the south-west ridge of Nya Kangri to within 250m of the summit before being turned back by bad weather on 3 June. After five rest days they made a second attempt but again were forced down by weather that was so bad it also shut the Khardung La road with heavy snowfall.

In August and into the start of September, Giorgos Margaritis, Petros Tolias and Nikolas Kroupis of the Hellenic Alpine Club of Komotini attempted the first ascent of Nya Kangri (6480m) from the north side. After acclimatising on the popular Stok Kangri (6123m) they travelled up the Nubra valley and started the trek in on 25 August. They climbed up to 5,810m on the south-southwest ridge, but after heavy snowfall on 29 August they retreated. They returned to Leh and climbed the Mentok group peaks in their remaining time.

Kishtwar
In October 2016, the American duo of Jeff Shapiro and Chris Gibisch made the third ascent of Brammah II (6486m) in the Kishtwar, via the south face. Approaching from the Kijai Nala drainage to the cirque below Brammah II and Arjuna (6230m), they took three days to reach base camp from the roadhead. Access to the peaks from this side was complex and it took days of exploration, with frequent rockfall and wet snow slides observed in the high temperatures; they focussed their attention on the most objectively safe route on the south face of Brammah II. Setting off early, they simul-climbed the lower section of the face to a bivy. The second day provided the crux and they reached the summit at 6.30pm before taking one and a half days to descend. They called the route *Pneuma* (1300m, VI, AI4, M5). The first ascent of Brammah II was in 1975 by a large Japanese team via the west ridge from the Brammah glacier; this route was repeated by an Indian team

in 1993. In 1975 a British expedition led by Rob Collister had attempted to approach Brammah II via the Kijai Nala but had not found a viable way in for the lightweight style of trip.

Between 8 and 9 June 2016, an Italian team comprising of Nicola Binelli, Luca Cornella, Silvestro Franchini and Tomas Franchini made the first ascent of the east pillar of Kishtwar Shivling, to the summit of the pillar (5780m). The team had made an initial attempt but were forced to retreat due to rockfall that damaged their ropes; during the night when back at their camp below the pillar, an avalanche narrowly missed their camp. In the morning Luca headed down to base camp. On 7 June the remaining three climbers re-fixed their ropes on the lower section and hauled their gear up. On 8 June, Nicola, Silvestro and Tomas set off in alpine style, attaining their high point of the previous attempt by 12.30pm and continuing to a cold bivy on top of a snow mushroom, dubbed the 'floating meringue', at 5,600m. On 9 June they started early and reached the summit of the pillar at 12.30pm, then abseiled the route, stripping their fixed ropes and those of a previous attempt (1992 Italian). They named their route *Via dei Trentini* (800m, VIII, A1, M4+). Kishtwar Shivling (6040m) was first climbed by Dick Renshaw and Stephen Venables in 1983 via the impressive north face. In 2015 the Swiss team of Stephan Siegrist, Andreas 'Dres' Abegglen and Thomas Senf made an ascent of a hidden couloir on to the left of the east pillar which they named *Challo* (WI5, M5) to the east summit (5895m); they described the route as reminiscent of *Supercanaleta* on Fitz Roy.

In September 2016 Jim Lowther (UK), Mark Richey (US) and Mark Wilford (US) made the first ascent of Gupta (5618m), a mountain in the Kishtwar. Approaching via the Dharlang Nala from Gulab Garh with 15 horses it took them four days to reach base camp, which unfortunately was on the wrong side of the river to the intended mountain; after a swim across the river a Tyrolean was set up. After some acclimatisation trips and a few days' rest due to illness, the team set off on 26 September to ascend the north-east face to the east ridge, summiting on 28 September and reaching base camp at 6pm on 29 September. The climbing was on generally sound granite with difficulties up to M5 and 5.9.

From 5 to 7 June, Max Didier and Cristobal Señoret (Chile) with the German climber Caro North made the first ascent of a rock peak south of Kishtwar Shivling which they named Monte Iñaki (5370m) after their good friend Iñaki Coussirat who died on Fitz Roy in early 2016. They climbed the south-east ridge in alpine style, hand-drilling two bolts on the ascent. They named the route *Namaste Dost/Arista de los Sueños* (700m, 17 pitches, 6c+/7a).

Zanskar

From mid-July to the beginning of September 2016, Anastasija Davidova and Matija Jošt (Slovenia) visited Rangtik Tokpo, Shimling Tokpo and Denyai Tokpo in the Haptal mountains of Zanskar. These are rarely visited valleys heading south-west from the Doda river (main Zanskar valley) which runs from the Darung-Drung glacier near Pensi La; the Doda river runs in a south-east direction towards Padum next to the Kargil to Padum road. The team's first visit was to Rangtik Tokpo, attempting Remalaye (6378m) where they reached the west summit (6266m), then followed it up with Phobrang (6193m). They then repeated *Rolling Stone* (500m, D+, V+, 65) on Shawa Kangri (5728m), which had been first climbed in 2008 by the Spanish team of Luc Pellissa and Sergi Ricart. They subsequently trekked up to near the head of the Shimling glacier, but were forced back by bad weather; they noted that there is no recorded climbing activity in this valley. Following this, they trekked into the Denyai valley where all the peaks are unnamed and unclimbed. At the start of September the weather improved and they went back to the Rangtik Tokpo where they attempted Peak 6193m from the east and north but were stopped at 6,100m.

In August 2016 the Japanese explorers Kimikazu Sakamoto, Akira Taniguchi and Toshio Itoh visited the Mulung Tokpo valley in Zanskar. This team has made several visits since 2009 to southern Zanskar to record unclimbed peaks: their results are freely available online. The Mulung Tokpo is northwest of Padam a valley north of the Haptal; the mountains are sub-6,000m and all seem to be unclimbed.

In June 2016 the Romanian climbers Cosmin Andron and Cristina Pogacean visited the Chhogo Tokpo valley in Zanskar after reading an article by Kimikazu Sakamoto. From Padum, they reached their base camp in two days from the road head. With their Indian friends Karn Kowshik and Prerna Dangi, the four first attempted the west ridge of T13 (6436m), turning back at 5900m. From T13 Cosmin and Cristina spotted a fine couloir running straight up the south face of T16 (6413m). Setting off from their high camp at 5200m the pair climbed snow up to 75° in the lower couloir, with a step of steep polished rock and rotten ice. They stopped above this and bivied as the sun had hit the upper face causing rockfall. The next day started with the crux icefall and then some difficult mixed climbing before a second bivi on the face. The following day they climbed some of the best rock either of them had climbed in the high mountains to a false summit and finally reached the south summit at 4pm. The north summit was over a kilometre away; it is not known which is the higher summit, and at 5pm they started their descent, arriving back at base camp at 3am. See 'Zanskar's Supercouloir' in this edition of the *Alpine Journal*.

In August, Taylor Maavara (Canada), Bharat Bhushan and Karn Kowshik (India) made an attempted to climb Z1 (6163m) in the Suru valley of the Zanskar Himalaya. This peak had been climbed in 1980 by a joint Indo-Japanese expedition. From the Kun basecamp they started their attempt on the west face but were forced back by avalanche conditions. They note the wealth of unclimbed lines on 6000m peaks.

In July Sergio Martín de Santos and Oskar Porras Aramendi (Spain) visited the Stok and Kang Yatze range near Leh. They acclimatised on the popular Stok Kangri (6150m) on 6 July, then climbed Sukhu Kangri (6005m) on 8 July via a likely new route they called *Animaren Oihua* (250m, D)

Raja Peak: Transcendence climbs the central gully with a dogleg right before trending left again. *(John Crook)*

('Cry of the Soul' in Basque) on the north-east face with very dry conditions. After some rest days in Leh they travelled to Kang Yatze base camp (5045m) and climbed Reponi Mallai Ri (6050m) on 15 July. On 19 July they climbed a new route on the north-west face of Dzo Jongo (6214m/6280m), calling their route *Elur* (350m, MD 80° M4+) after Aramendi's son.

Himachal Pradesh

From 6-10 June Malcolm Bass and Guy Buckingham made the first ascent of north-west ridge of Gang-stang (6162m) in the Lahaul district of the Himachal Pradesh. Original-ly the team were to attempt Rimo III in the Indian East Karakorum, however the permit was denied at the last minute so, with the help of Martin Moran, they chose Gang-stang as a suitable object; Martin had led an expedition to the area in 2007. Approaching from the Naing-har roadhead, they took two days to reach base camp (4200m). With their liaison officer Parmender Sharma they first acclimatised by climbing Neel-kantha (5324m). On 6 June, Malcolm and Guy set off camping at 5000m below the north face; the next morning they climbed a couloir up to the north-west ridge, which was predominantly rock and mixed climbing on blocky granite. They had two bivies on the ridge, and on the third day the weather deteriorated when they reached 6000m. They followed calf-burn-ing blue ice up to the small summit where they spent a short amount of time and bivied once more, 100m down from the summit. On 10 June they descended the south-west ridge back to base camp; they graded the route ED1, 5a, Scottish VI, 1500m.

In September and October 2016 aspirant guides John Crook and David Sharpe made several impressive assents in the Miyar valley in the Lahaul Himalaya (Himachal Pradesh) on a joint trip with Martin Moran (see below). They started by acclimatising on Pk 6036m; with continuing good weather they immediately began approaching the remote and committing Raja Peak (6267m). It took them three days from their advanced base camp to reach the north face of Raja Peak, crossing the Kang La and follow-ing the Temasa valley to the base of the face. They spent a day observ-ing the face then set off on 31 September, following mixed and ice pitches (crux) to a bivy half way up the face, and the following day making the first ascent of the peak. They named the route *Transcendence* (ED2, Scottish VI, 1200m) and they descended the south ridge. After a couple of rest days they made the first ascent of James Peak (adjacent to Marakulla Killa, see below) via its north face on 6 October, naming the route *Last Chance Saloon* (TD-, Scottish IV, 1300m).

From 26 September to 2 October, Martin Moran and Ian Dring made the first ascent of Marakulla Killa (5755m) via the magnificent north spur, in the Miyar valley of Lahaul Himalaya (Himachal Pradesh). They started from the Jangpur glacier at 4650m and spent the next six days climbing varying quality of granite, including a very blank pitch that required several bolts. The graded the route ED2 (perhaps only ED1 for a repeat), 1300m, with 21 pitches of III-VIa+. They descended via the unknown west face, making it back to base camp on 2 October.

The duo of Mick Fowler and Victor Saunders teamed up for the first time in 27 years to make the first ascent of Sersank Peak (Shib Shankar, 6050m) via the striking north spur from 28 September to 4 October. Approaching over the Sersank La (5000m) the pair accessed the bottom of the face; heavy snowfall prior to starting the face made for slow going on the lower face. On the third day they started up the north face proper, with the fourth day providing the crux with several ice pitches just within their limits. On day five they chopped through the cornice to reach the summit plateau, and climbed the 150m high summit block the next day (a Japanese team had climbed to within 40m of the summit in 2008, but had not reached the very top). They then spent two days descending the complex south and west face; the route is graded ED, 1000m.

Uttarakhand

The Russian team of Dmitry Golovchenko, Dmitry Grigoriev and Sergey Nilov made the first ascent of the north buttress of Thalay Sagar (6904m). They named the route *Moveable Feast* (ED2, M7, WI5, 5c, A3, 1400m). For this ascent they received both the Russian Golden Ice Axe award and the Piolets d'Or. The north face of Thalay Sagar has around five other routes, including the original Hungarian route (1991) and the New Zealand-Australian route that was the first to directly tackle the ominous shale band at the top of the face, and winning the 1999 Piolets d'Or. The Russians started on 9 September, summiting on 17 September and returning to base camp on the 19th. They bivied nine times on the face without a portaledge (all other direct routes have used one). The first 500-600m was steep snow and ice, and led to the first rock bastion that involved steep climbing on ice filled cracks; this led to mixed ground and a steep headwall.

In October the US team of Jason Kruk, Joel Kauffman and Tad McCrea made the first ascent of Chaukhamba III (6974m) via the 1,600m south ridge, to within 16m of the summit. The ascent has proved controversial as the team did not have a permit to climb the mountain, and as a consequence there is a lack of information on the ascent. The team spent six days

View looking south from top of Diwali Lho. Siniolchu Needles or Singyel Lhu (5712m) on the right. *(Anindya Mujherjee)*

climbing the route and 12 days on the mountain; they named the route *Sab Kuch Milega* ('No Fun Allowed') and graded it 5.10, A0, 90°.

In May 2016 Martin Moran led a commercial trip with seven others where they made the first ascent of Vishnu Killa (Vishnu's Citadel, 5968m); the sub 6000m height of the peak meant that this could be completed in a three-week visit. Facing a mass retreat of porters on the way to base camp the team ended up ferrying the 500kg of supplies to base camp themselves. On 20 May they started the summit push at 22:30 as three ropes of four. Crossing a col and then a complex glacier to the serpentine ridge, they broke through the overhanging cornice and finally the summit, where they were afforded magnificent views of the Nanda Devi range.

In May Susan Jensen (Scotland) and Anindya 'Raja' Mukherjee (India) travelled to Vishnugarh Darh (Vishnu's fortress) range of unclimbed peaks south of the Panpatia Glacier, which is to the south of Nilkanth. However, Raja contracted a lung infection and the expedition brought Raja down for medical attention.

Sikkim

In October and November an Irish expedition including Jack Bergin, Alan Tees, Richard Creagh, Sean Martin, Olga Joensuu, Damien Hawkins, Piaras Kelly, Mick Donnelly with support staff of Lakpa Sherpa and Anindya Mukherjee, travelled to Zumthul Phuk glacier; the team had visited this area in 2014. After three days of poor weather they established an advanced base camp. From there they made the first ascent of Diwali Lho (4886m), climbed on the first day of Diwali, by two different routes on the same day. Both the routes involved mixed climbing up to Scottish III. Following that they made the first ascent of a 5,000m peak which involved a pitch of British VS climbing. Meanwhile, two members climbed two cols (5064m and 5226m) in one morning exploring a possible passage to the Zemu glacier. After the first col (5064m, N27°43'34" E88°23'01.") they realised this col had been crossed by Paul Bauer's 1937 expedition. The other col (5226m, N27°43'38.27", E88°22'28.55") was a first ascent. They proposed to name it White Col after John Claude White. While, descending the second col, they came across unusual footprints that reminded them of the local legend about the Bon Manchi.

Finally there were several impressive repeats in the Indian Himalaya in 2016, including French ascents of the *Scottish Pillar* and the *Estrella Impossible* on Bhagirathi III (6454m). Also worthy of mention is Ueli Steck's fortieth birthday ascent of Shivling (6543m) with his wife in a remarkable seven-day trip.

• With additional information from Anindya Mukherjee, Lindsay Griffin and Nandini Purandare.

IAN WALL

Nepal 2015-16

The new Ukrainian route *Daddy Magnum Force* (2350m, ED2, M6, AI6, A3)
on the north-west pillar of Talung (7348m). *(Nikita Balabanov)*

The earthquakes that struck Nepal in the spring of 2015 continue to have a devastating impact on ordinary people and the region's infrastructure. Because of extensive damage to the border crossing areas, China closed the Tibet Himalaya and expeditions scheduled for Shishapangma, and the north sides of Cho Oyu and Everest had to relocate; many went to Mansalu. Then in September 2015, India closed its joint border with Nepal, allegedly due to hostilities in the Terai region of Nepal over the nation's new constitution. Many people publically expressed the view that India was annoyed about Nepal's apparent turn from a Hindu state to a secular one. The border closures further slowed Nepal's recovery from the earthquakes.

Autumn 2015
Foreign visitors likely noticed little difference to life in Kathmandu other than fewer vehicles being on the road. India's blockade manifested itself in particular in Kathmandu: there was no fuel, no medicines or raw materials and no cooking gas since Nepal gets 95% of these requirements from India. As might be expected, a thriving black market developed driving prices up. Domestic flight costs increased as there was limited aviation fuel and many non-tourist flights were cancelled, although that happens during more normal periods too.

Some expeditions did succeed during the autumn 2015 season. The first ascent of **Gave Ding** (6571m), by Mick Fowler and Paul Ramsden, in far north-western Nepal via its difficult north face was covered in *AJ* 2016. This difficult ED+ route took five days up and another two days for the descent. Hansjörg Auer, Alexander Blümel and Gerhard Fiegl climbed **Nilgiri South** (6839m) via the south face between 22 and 26 October. The route (1500m, M5, 90°) follows the previously unclimbed Nilgiri Spire to the right side of the south face, then the ridge to the summit. This was only the second ascent of the mountain since the Japanese made the first ascent in 1978. The technically difficult and unclimbed south-west ridge was followed in descent, but tragically Gerry Fiegl fell and died. The climb required three bivouacs for the ascent and one in descent.

Thulagi Chuli (7059m), Mansari Himal, west Nepal received a first ascent via the west face by the Russian team of Aleksander Gukov, Ivan Dojdev, Valeriy Shamalo and Ruslan Kirichenko. They set out from ABC at 5,759m on 24 September and reached the summit on 25 September, returning to base camp on 27 September. A snow cave bivy was used in ascent and descent. The team called the route *Happy Birthday* (1850m, TD+, VI (5c), AI4+, M4).

Justin Griffin and Skiy DeTray (USA) climbed **Tawoche** (6541m) in the Khumbu via the north buttress in November 2015 over five days. The climbers compared the route to the north face of Mt Hunter in Alaska with the added difficulties of altitude. Tawoche, also spelled Taboche, offers extreme alpine climbing on steep ice and steep granite; the west face is 1,524m high and the American route had consistent pitches of M5 and one very exposed pitch of AI5, M5R at 6,100m. The top of the buttress was reached on 14

What's in a name? Nepal Peak (7177m) in the Kangchenjunga region, first climbed by Erwin Schneider in 1930. *(Ian Wall)*

November but the true summit lay several hours off. The descent route was via the east face gully. Sadly, virtually at the foot of difficulties, Justin Griffin lost his footing on steep but technically easy ice and was killed.

The south face of **Ama Dablam** (6812m) received its first alpine-style ascent via the *Lagunak Ridge* (1200m, TD+, F5, AI5, M4, 90°) from French guides and aspirant guides Fleur Fouque, Sébastien Rougegré, Fanny Schmutz, Damien Tomasi. Between 22 and 25 October the climbers succeeded on the mixed route with pitches of F5 on good quality rock. At the steep barrier the climbers reported pitches of M4, the ice was grade V with a long 50° slope to the summit. Overall, Ama Dablam was attempted by seven expeditions; all other teams climbed via the south-west ridge and of these five succeeded.

In the Kangchenjunga region, the Ukrainian climbers Nikita Balabanov and Mikhail Formin climbed the much-eyed north-north-west pillar of **Talung** (7348m) between 18 and 25 October 2015, calling their route *Daddy Magnum Force* (2350m, ED2, M6, AI6, A3). It is reported as being long and very steep and similar to winter routes in Chamonix, but with the additional problems incurred with heavy sacks and altitude. The route mainly consisted of hard mixed climbing on thin ice, and the descent route was via the west side of the mountain. The technical difficulties began at 5,600m at the bergschrund followed by pitches of M6 and A3; the summit was reached on 23 October after five bivvys with another on the descent at 6,700m. Balabanov and Formin had previously made the first ascent of Langshisa Ri's north-west spur in 2014.

On 17 October, Julien Dusserre and Mathieu Détrie (France) made the first ascent of the north-east face (700m, TD+, WI5-) of **Dzasampt-se** (6293m). On 18 October Pierre Labbre and Mathieu Maynadier (France) summited via the same route. This was not the initial objective for the expedition, however. Several days of bad weather and the condition of their original objective forced the team to look at other possible lines in the Nangpai Gosum massif. The climbers likened their route to that of the north face of Les Droites.

Matej Mučič and Luka Stražar (Slovenia) climbed **Chugimago** (6258m) in Rolwaling. Starting on 15 October from ABC they climbed a direct line in the centre of the west face of, arriving on the summit at

The line of the American route on the north buttress of Taboche (6541m), which ended in tragedy. *(Skiy DeTray)*

8am the following morning. They took a line to the right of the *Hennessey-Kastelic*, reaching the summit ridge a very short distance north of the highest point. The pair then climbed down the south-west ridge a short distance before descending the west face. Their route (800m, WI4, M5) was thought to be about the same overall difficulty. **Chhopa Bamare** (6109m) was attempted by a French team via the south-east ridge but bad conditions caused the party to retreat before the summit.

Also in Rolwaling, Mingma Gyalje climbed the west face of **Chobut-se** (6686m) in October 2015. The 1,200m route starts in the valley under Chobutse before ascending the west ridge. Before the ridge steepens Mingma descended 60m to the foot of the snow face and from here the route was on steep snow. Mingma climbed solo and after being stranded for two days and nights on the summit without food or shelter he was evacuated by helicopter. As part of the same expedition Tashi Sherpa, Dawa Gyalie and Nima Tenji Sherpa climbed three new routes up previously unclimbed mountains in the same area: **Thakar-Go East** (6152m); **Langdak** (6220m); and **Raungsiyar** (6224m). All of the ascents mentioned were undertaken as private expeditions and are breakthrough ascents for the Sherpa of Nepal. Mingma Gyalje, Tashi Sherpa, Dawa Gyalie and Nima Tenji Sherpa were all on a Nepal Mountain Guide training course.

A French team attempted the east ridge of **Annapurna** (8091m) but experienced bad snow and avalanche conditions. A Japanese expedition climbed the north-west ridge of **Annapurna IV** (7525m) while another French team attempted the east ridge of **Annapurna South** (7219m) but again experienced bad snow and avalanche conditions. **Baruntse** (7152m) received attention from three expeditions all attempting the south-east ridge; it is believed that only one team achieved success on the main peak whilst the others struggled with storms and high winds.

Among the more regularly visited peaks, **Everest** (8848m) was attempted by a Japanese team via the South Col but was beaten by high winds and storms. **Himlung Himal** (7126m) was climbed via the west ridge by a combined Swiss, Austrian, German and Italian team, and then by a second expedition made up of French, Italian, Belgian and Swiss members. An Anglo-American expedition attempted **Makalu** (8468m) but was defeated by bad weather and snow conditions. **Manaslu** (8163m) was successfully climbed by 19 expeditions, all via the north-east face route. **Chamlang** (7319m) was climbed via the south-west ridge by a Spanish team. **Nuptse** (7855m) was attempted by two expeditions, one of Swiss and USA members while the other was an all-French expedition. Both teams were attempting the 1961 route on the south face but both experienced less than favourable conditions.

Among the lesser known peaks that received attention in the autumn season of 2015 were **Aichyn Peak** (6055m) in west Nepal. Yuki Senda, Shintaro Saito, Kaya Ko, Yuto Tamaki and Yuma Uno, members of the Doshisha University Alpine Club in Japan, made the first ascent via the south-west ridge on 3 September. A Spanish expedition reached **Ombiga-ichen** (6340m) planning to climb the south-west face but conditions were so bad they did not attempt to climb. **Jabou Ri** (6666m) received its first ascent from the American pair Eric Larsen and Ryan Waters, via the north-east face and north ridge, which they described as being 'not technical and we simply kicked our way up step after step.' The west ridge of **Kangchung Shar** (6103m) west ridge by a UK expedition but poor conditions prevented any major progress.

The high-profile duo of Conrad Anker and the Austrian David Lama, accompanied to base camp by two photographers Martin Hanslmayr and Menk Rufibach, attempted the west ridge of **Lunag Ri** (6895m), currently the highest unclimbed peak in Nepal. After climbing a steep rock wall to gain the north-west ridge, they started their summit attempt before dawn on 13 November. After spending 12 hours climbing a very exposed ridge the pair realised that the 300m headwall that stood between them and the summit would prove too risky in -25°C and strong winds, especially with no bivy equipment or sleeping bags. The expedition was abandoned but the pair was determined to return, which they did in the autumn of 2016. Anker suffered a heart attack and was evacuated home to Montana. A Romanian expedition attempted **Tsartse Peak** (6343m), north of Dhaulagiri, via the south-east ridge but bad weather and a high risk of avalanche made progress too dangerous.

Spring 2016

Over the last three years there have been various well-publicised events on **Everest** that shocked not only the mountaineering world but also Nepal and the rest of the world: the fight in 2013 between Sherpas and climbers, the avalanche in 2014 that killed 16 high-altitude workers and then the earthquake in 2015. Initially the number of expeditions requesting permits for Everest in 2016 was low. At the last minute, the Department of Tourism honoured their pledge to accept those expeditions who had permits for the 2015 season but had been cancelled due to the earthquake, announcing these would be accepted for both 2016 and 2017 seasons. At the same time it was announced that permits issued in 2014 that were not used due to the avalanche would be honoured through to 2019.

Various public sector organisations offer incentives for their members who summit Everest; the Indian armed services acknowledge an Everest summit with instant promotion, which includes a wage and pension increase. The stakes are high and at the end of the Everest 2016 season a story emerged that two police officers from the Pune police force used allegedly doctored photographs to prove to Nepal's Department of Tourism as proof of their success. The fraud was recognised by other expedition members who verified that the husband and wife team had been wearing red and black down suits throughout the expedition. In the summit photos they appear to be wearing yellow and black suits and their boots had also changed. A complaint was filed at Maharashtra police commissioner's office. Ultimately the Nepali authorities recommended a 10-year ban on Dinesh Chandrakant Rathod and his wife Tarkeshwari Chandrakant Bhelerao from climbing in Nepal and the cancellation of their summit certificates.

This scandal prompted an investigation into the role of liaison officers (LOs) in the expedition industry. LOs are allocated to all expeditions attempting mountains over 6,500m, with a remit to assist the expedition and resolve local issues, and provide evidence of summit bids and successes. Further, according to tourism regulations, they must stay at base camp for the duration of the expedition. On Everest they get nearly $3,000 for this task. During the spring 2016 Everest season nearly 50% of liaison officers, representing 33 teams, never reached Everest Base Camp (EBC) to carry out their duties. The majority of LOs who trekked to EBC vanished within minutes after taking a few 'selfies'.

Weather conditions also had an impact on some expeditions in the spring 2016 season. Two German nationals along with their 18 Nepali staff were stranded in the Saribung Himal following a snowstorm on 13 May, and had to be rescued using helicopters and long-line techniques. Everest witnessed the death of five climbers including three from India and one from Australia, all above higher camps. Over the last few days of May, areas of the Himalaya experienced very unsettled weather with strong winds and rapidly dropping temperatures.

The Peak League Table: Spring 2016			
Region	Mountain	Expeditions	Foreign members
Khumbu	Everest (8848m)	34	289
	Lhotse (8516m)	11	78
	Nuptse (7855m)	8	45
	Ama Dablam (6814)	3	36
Western	Saribung (6346m)	6	38
	Annapurna I (8091m)	5	26
	Annapurna III (7555m)	1	3
	Annapurna IV (7525m)	1	4
	Dhaulagiri I (8167m)	4	40
	Manaslu (8163m)	3	29
	Makalu (8463m)	5	51
	Tukuche Peak (6920m)	4	39
	Thapa Peak (6012m)	4	36
	Chamlang (7319m)	2	4
	Tilicho Peak (7134m)	1	2
	Thorong Peak (6144m)	1	1
	Himlung Himal (7126m)	1	8
	Khan Tari (6100m)	1	2

On Everest, 289 climbers from 29 foreign countries in 34 expeditions attempted to summit. By the end of the season a total of 456 mountaineers of whom 199 were foreign had succeeded. On 19 May alone 209 expedition members reached the summit. Just across the valley **Lhotse** (8516m) hosted 11 expeditions with a total of 78 members; **Nuptse** (7855m) had eight expeditions with a total of 45 members and one death. The Italian team of Hervé Barmasse and Daniele Bernasconi planned to attempt the south face in true alpine style but did not get to base of the route due to poor conditions. **Ama Dablam** (6812m) received the attention of three expeditions with a total of 36 members.

In the western district, the 'new' peak of **Saribung** (6346m) is proving a draw for commercial expeidtions. The fabled south-east ridge of **Annapurna III** (7555m) was attempted again, this time by David Lama, Hansjörg Auer and Alexander Blümel from Austria. They reached a similar altitude to the British team from 1981. Of the four expeditions on **Dhaulagiri I** (8167m), the 2016 Medical Research Expedition from the UK led by AC member Adrian Mellor climbed **Tukuche West** before continuing to summit Dhaulagiri I in alpine style via the north-east ridge on 20 April 2016. The expedition carried out several ground-breaking medical experiments. On **Chamlang** (7319m), the two expeditions trying the mountain via the north ridge included Andy Houseman and Jon Griffith and the Italians Marco Farina and François Cazzanelli. Both teams were beaten by the weather. **Khan Tari** (6100m) was summited by Spaniards Ángel Salamanca and Javi San Miguel, with technical sections of M6.

Danfe Sail (6103m) is situated in Dolpo on the northernmost point of the border with Tibet providing a strenuous 16-day walk to base camp. An expedition from UK, Australia and Nepal comprising Ian Wall, Alasdair Lawrence, Bill Crozier, Alex Cramb, Michael Salmon, Chirring Bhotia and Wongchhu Sherpa were beaten by a combination of strong winds, poor conditions and ultimately a lack of time. Attempts were made on **Chumbu** (6859m) and **Om Tso Go** (6332m). Brian Jackson was prevented from reaching the summit by a combination of weather and a dangerous and complicated glacier. Attempts were also made on **Dhechyan Khang** (6019m) and **Gorakh Khang** (6254m).

Despite the fact the mountains were fairly busy it seems that in the 2016 spring season trekkers stayed away, with a reported decrease of 40% from the previous year, hurting hotels, restaurants and taxis in Kathmandu, as well as the teahouses, guides and porters throughout the trekking areas of Nepal. Trekking brings more money to Nepal than climbing, so the backlash from the bad publicity centred on the earthquake and Indian embargo did have a major impact.

Expeditions had problems of a different kind. During the first week of July local people stopped two foreign mountaineers from entering Upper Mustang. The expedition to **Arniko Chuli** (6039m) was told they could not progress through Upper Mustang during the 'growing season' because this might precipitate bad omens, from hailstorms to storms. Despite paying all the taxes and obtaining the required permissions for mountaineering, local people elected to impose the ban on foreigners entering the area from the Tij festival in April until September. Upper Mustang residents can fine foreigners who breach this law. After receiving a complaint from the climbers, the Department of Tourism's director Laxman Sharma told expedition members that the department would look into the case.

After years of denying requests from international guides and local mountain workers, in 2016 Nepal's Department of Tourism finally granted permission for a helicopter to transport rope-fixing gear from Everest Base Camp to camp one on Everest's South Col route, bypassing the treacherous Khumbu Icefall and thereby sparing mountain workers some of the exposure. On 23 April, a helicopter made six trips to camp one (6035m) in the Western Cwm to deliver ropes, anchors, and oxygen for Nepali workers: a total of roughly 2,870lb of equipment: roughly 84 loads out of a thousand or more. It is estimated loads could be further cut by 50% or more via a mix of helicopters, storing gear at camp two and restricting all the luxuries and other clutter from camp two like carpeting, chairs, tables, huge kitchens and kitchen staff, and solar panels.

On 19 July 2016 it was reported that the Department of Tourism was to propose a set of new rules for climbing in Nepal. These will include a ban on solo ascents of 'climbing' peaks, a restriction on people who are completely blind, double amputees, and climbers over 75 years of age; the younger age limit is already set at 16 years. It is also proposed that people attempting to scale Everest should be assigned at least one mountain guide, while a guide should accompany two climbers on other peaks. The criteria for being issued with an Everest permit is that a climber should have previously climbed a 7,000m peak.

Autumn 2016

Much has been written over the last decade or so about the hundreds of people attempting Everest on commercial expeditions each season. However, the low number of expeditions to other Nepali 8,000m peaks is causing Nepali officials to ask why there isn't so much interest in the other big mountains. The answer must rest in a combination of time commitments and the high cost of permits, as well as the draw of the world's highest mountain.

With the internet and access to other information sources, more mountaineers are focusing on lower-altitude mountains with greater technical difficulty that are less expensive and often with fairly straightforward access. The internet also provides those with the desire for self-promotion the opportunity to stand out from the rest by proclaiming a first ascent on a technically hard route.

The Nepali authorities, mainly with the aim of keeping the coffers full, opened 104 'new' peaks for mountaineering in 2014. However, there were several major problems with this. Although Nepal has been open for climbing since the 1950s the peak permit system only really came into existence in the mid 1970s. When that happened there was no vigorous monitoring of what had been attempted or what had been climbed: record keeping was virtually non-existent. Without a transparent and robust monitoring system it was difficult to keep track, not only of financial transactions but also of which mountains had been climbed and which had not.

In more recent times mountains have been re-named from local or traditional names to something, in the eyes of the authorities, to reflect modern times or honour personalities: Baden-Powell Peak, Nepal Peak, Pasang Lhamu Chuli, Tenzing Peak, Hillary Peak, Peak Hawley – and so on. With the lack of robust systems it is likely that in 2014 officials did not have either the ability or inclination to research all 'newly' opened peaks to find out what these peaks are actually called and whether they had been climbed. Ascents were not always recorded by the first waves of mountaineers in pre-permit times. Other peaks have been climbed 'illegally', either because of lack of information or on 'the spur of the moment'. In some cases people were not prepared to abide by Nepali law to pay the fees, either as a matter of principle or because of their own economic situation.

The resulting confusion of newly opened peaks created a media frenzy in the autumn season of 2016 compounded by Nepal's push to open up remote areas with the inducement of waiving peak fees: climbers were still required to get permission however. During the autumn of 2016 Sean Burch (USA) fell foul of this situation when he claimed to have climbed 31 closed peaks in 21 days in the Humla region as part of his traverse of the Nepal Himalaya. His claims not only raised eyebrows within the mountaineering community but also within the Department of Tourism, which was stated that Burch

The Spanish climber Oriol Baro high on Numbur (6958m). The expedition was unapologetic in not paying for permits.

did not have the appropriate permission to attempt any of these mountains which were not deemed by the Nepali authorities open for climbing. Burch stated that as the peaks were all below 6,500m he did not need permission from a higher authority but had obtained what he considered the relevant permission from local authorities. According to the Nepal Tourism Act permits should still have been obtained to climb mountains that were normally closed to mountaineering activities (regardless of height) even if fees were not due.

Similarly three Spanish climbers made successful (but illegal) ascents of **Karyolung** (6530m) and **Numbur** (6958m) in the Rolwaling without obtaining permission from the Department of Tourism. Santi Padros, Oriol Baro and Roger Cararach claimed the new routes in the media admitting that they did not get official permission and that they climbed independently and without Nepali support. Again the Department of Tourism issued a statement: 'It is illegal to climb mountains in Nepal without obtaining Government permission ... according to Nepal's mountaineering regulations a three member expedition to any mountain below 7,000m must obtain a permit from the Department by paying the Government's royalty of $700 per mountain along with a garbage deposit, the expeditions must have the service of a liaison officer and employ high-altitude workers to support climbing activities.' On **Karyolung** the Spainards named the new route *Pilar Dudh Khunda* (1400m, 6a, AI4, M4) and on **Numbur**, *The Nepal Sun* (1000m, V, M4).The Department of Tourism has threatened legal action against the above-mentioned climbers.

So as a potential mountaineer in Nepal, how do you cover the bases? The Himalayan Database would be the best place to start, and most of the Himalayan and Alpine clubs have good records of Himalayan ascents. It doesn't help that many mountain names also have different spellings. First ascent or not, to save stress in the future always offer information to the Himalayan Database via their website so an accurate record can be kept. Also check thoroughly with the Department of Tourism in Nepal; failure to do so could not only be very expensive but could result in being banned from climbing in Nepal for the foreseeable future, or worse.

'Fake news' seems to be a buzz phrase at the moment and why should Nepal miss out? During autumn 2016 **Manaslu** received a reported 150 ascents but initially only three climbers were given 'summit certificates' (another thorny issue previously mentioned in this year's *Journal*) stating that there was insufficient evidence from the liaison officers of climbers actually reaching the true summit at 8,163m, and consequently the Department of Tourism would withhold the certificates. Clear summit images should be submitted as supporting evidence; it is the responsibility of the liaison officer to verify these facts. Interestingly 90% of the Manaslu liaison officers failed to accompany their expeditions to base camp despite being paid (out of expedition funds) $2,000 per expedition. Four did arrive at base camp, but according to base camp officials they only stayed a day or two. This is a recurring issue but 2016 was the first time that the Department had responded in such a stringent way, and to the detriment of the climbers. The true Manaslu summit is a fine snow cone and, according to Mingma Sherpa of Seven Summit Treks, one of the largest Nepali operators, the normal window is too short to allow all climbers to stand on the actual summit. In the past it had been agreed that there should be an alternative summit option some five to 10 metres below the actual summit. It was reported in December that certificates would be issued to all getting 'near' to Manaslu's summit! As an aside, Mingma David Sherpa, Tashi Sherpa and Krishna Thapa Magar became the first to complete a ski descent on Manaslu, from 7,500m.

The two Indian police officials, Dinesh Chandrakant Rathod and his wife Tarkeshwari Chandrakant Bhelerao of Maharashtra who falsified their Everest summit claims were investigated by the Punjabi police and having been proven guilty, were dismissed from the force and any enhancements provided by the police at that time had to be returned. The Nepali Government also enforced a ten-year ban on the climbers and imposed a $4,000 fine on Makalu Travel for aiding and abetting the couple. However, no action was taken against the liaison officer.

In December 2016, Reinhold Messner, interviewed by the *Himalayan Times*, stressed that 'the traditional art of mountaineering should be preserved and promoted as it was a direct exposure to nature'. He went on

When is a summit not a summit? Climbers gathering on a fore-summit of Manaslu to avoid congestion on the real thing.

Masha Gordon on the first ascent of Khangchung Shar (6063m).

The line of the new Austrian route on Gimmigela East (7005m) near Kangchenjunga.

Maya Sherpa, left, who climbed K2 in 2015 along with two other Nepali female climbers, was the only Nepali woman to climb Everest in 2016; she then went on to climb Himlung Himal (7126m) in the Manaslu Himal, the first Nepali woman to do so. Maya is also the first Nepali woman to have climbed Ama Dablam, Baruntse, Pumori and Cho Oyu and the first Nepali climber to summit Khan Tengri in Kyrgyzstan. Maya, along with Dawa Yangzum Sherpa, centre, and Pasang Akita Sherpa, right, are planning an expedition to Kangchenjunga in the autumn of 2017. *(Ian Wall)*

Left: In October 2016 the French ambassador to Nepal, Yves Carmona, presented the *Légion d'Honneur* to Ang Norbu Sherpa in recognition of his contribution in saving the lives of French tourists during the earthquakes of 2015.

to add that traditional alpinism and tourism were two factors that created a huge division in the Alpine community. He likened the present trend of commercial expeditions to 'climbing indoors' while traditional alpinism is all about 'climbing on the rocks'. Referring to the Everest fraud incident during spring 2016 and the Manaslu autumn 2016 incident, Messner said it was a result of prioritising tourism over alpinism; he went on to reinforce the fact that Nepal needs tourists now more than ever. With regard to recent comments made by the Nepali government on amputees and people with hearing or visual impediments attempting to climb Everest, he stressed that those people had paid thousands of dollars into the Nepali economy to make that happen, and that was tourism not alpinism. His views on the way 'expeditions' are run in today's' world: 'this is tourism and Nepal needs that, the Nepali agents are perfectly capable of running those themselves, now there is no need for the American or British companies to operate such ventures in Nepal.'

A 5.6 tremor on 28 November, rated as an aftershock of the 2015 earthquake, triggered an avalanche on **Ama Dablam**, which killed Lakpa Thundu Sherpa and injured British climber Ciaran Hill.

In October 2016, **Cho Oyu** was climbed twice over two consecutive days but within 24 hours by Australian guide and expedition agency owner Rolfe Oostra, together with his clients. In Rolwaling, **Khang Karpo** (6704m), situated near the source of the Ripimo glacier on the border with Tibet, was climbed by eight mountaineers including three women: Squash Falconer (UK), Alison Levine (US), Kath Staniland (UK) along with Gopla Strestha, Phurba Tenjing Sherpa, Tsering Pemba and Lakpa Nurbu Sherpa, all Nepali guides. In the same valley Mark James Pugliese and Nikolas Ryan Mirhashemi (USA) climbed new technical lines on **Chukyima** (6289m).

In November **Khangchung Shar** (6063m) in the Mahalangur Himal received a first ascent from Ben O'Connor-Croft (UK), Joshua Jarrin (Ecuador), Masha Gordon (UK), Ang Phurba and Pasang (Nepal) via the Khangchung La, situated between Khanchung and Cholo Peak. Although not technically difficult, the rock required careful handling while there were stretches of exposed steep snow slopes.

Austrians Alex Blümel and Hansjörg Auer made the first ascent of the north face of **Gimmigela East** (7005m) a subsidiary summit of **Gimmigela Chuli** (7350m) approximately four kilometres east of Kangchenjunga in November 2016. The team set up base camp just above Pangpemba and acclimatised on Dhromo's south ridge. The route, climbed in alpine style, required two bivys but the 1,200m face of approximately 85° ice was in perfect condition and, according to Auer, presented no serious difficulties although the bivys were exposed.

TAMOTSU NAKAMURA

Tibet

The north face of Nyel Japo (6150m) rising immediately south of the Yarlung Tsangpo. *(All images Tamotsu Nakamura)*

In November 2016, the well-known mountain explorer Tom Nakamura with his regular companion Tsuyoshi Nagai, both now in their eighties, travelled along the Yarlung Tsangpo east of the ancient and strategic Tibetan city of Tsetang, 183km south-east of Lhasa and transcribed on Chinese maps as Zetang. The S306 road follows this section of the river, which becomes the Brahmaputra downstream. Nakamura writes that this area is now heavily restricted because of its proximity with the Indian state of Arunachal Pradesh. This sensitivity has only increased following China's attempt to drive a road into Doklam, a high narrow plateau Bhutan claims as sovereign territory, prompting Delhi to send troops to Bhutan. Nakamura's journey saw him photographing the Bobonung glacier, rock peaks in the Nyel Japo massif further west along the S306, and north-east of Tsetang, north of Mt Worde Kangge. Nakamura writes that special permits are required from Public Security Bureau and the People's Liberation Army. This gallery of photos from his trip shows the mountaineering potential of the region.

296

The holy mountain of Worde Kangge (5996m), also known as Ode Gungyel.
The great reformist monk Tsongkhapa (1357-1419) spent a six-year retreat
here, meditating in a cave and founding the monastery of Olka Choling.
The sixth Dalai Lama is said to have climbed the peak, burning juniper on the
summit. Ode Gungyel is the patriarch of nine deities, among them Nyenchen
Tanglha, a mountain more familiar to mountaineers.

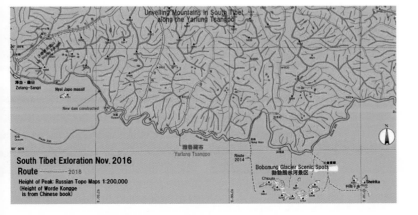

The equally impressive east face of Nyel Japo. Its altitude is taken from the Russian 1:200,000 map of the area.

The north face of peaks of c6,000m surrounding the Bobonung glacier valley.

A closer detail of the same north face.

A 6,000m peak north-west of the Bobonung massif.

Chipula (6152m), the north-east face of the west end of the Bobonung massif.

TIMOTHY ELSON

Pakistan 2016

The unclimbed west face of Chiring I (6861m). *(Christof Nettekoven)*

In 2016 there were 33 registered expeditions plus the Nanga Parbat winter expeditions; permits are not required in Pakistan for mountains under 6,500m, so this only includes those above that height. Of the registered expeditions, 25 were to 8,000m peaks. Various reports indicate that the summer of 2016 had constant south-westerly airflows with no high-pressure centres, leading to unstable weather through the whole summer season: August 2016 was particularly wet in the Karakoram.

The security situation seems to have improved, however the Foreign and Commonwealth Office is still advising not to travel on the Karakoram highway between Islamabad and Gilgit; this can be circumvented by the regular daily flights from Islamabad to Gilgit or Skardu. Some issues around permits were encountered in 2016, including entry denied to a climber due to Sherpa team members, as there is informal insistence on using Pakistani high-altitude porters on 8,000m peaks in Pakistan. There are also still some inconsistencies around requirements for a liaison officer; in theory only the Line of Control, Baltoro peaks and Afghan border need a liaison officer but that wasn't always what was enforced in practice.

Five of the magic 8,000m peaks are in Pakistan, and these attracted the vast majority of registered expeditions for 2016. In the summer of 2016 over 100 climbers attempted **K2**, a record number, none of whom were successful due to a major avalanche on 23 July that swept around camps three and four. There were reports of queues on the mountain, leading to the question of whether K2 is going the same way as Everest in terms of commercialisation. **Nanga Parbat** (8126m) received one winter ascent by three people, and one summer ascent by three people, all via the standard *Kinshofer* route. **Broad Peak** (8047m) received only one ascent by a pair of climbers. **Gasherbrum I** (8080m) saw one ascent by eight climbers on 4 August, and on 26 July a different group of eight climbers topped out on **Gasherbrum II** (8035m).

Nanga Parbat Winter
The biggest news of the year in the Karakoram was the first winter ascent of Nanga Parbat (8126m), ninth-highest mountain in the world, leaving K2 as the solitary 8,000er without a winter ascent. On 26 February 2016, Simone Moro (Italy), Muhammad Ali Sadpara (Pakistan) and Alex Txikon (Spain) reached the summit via the *Kinshofer* route on the Diamir Face [Editor's note: see *AJ* 2016 for Moro's account]. Over the official 2015-16 winter season (21 December to 20 March) six separate teams attempted the first winter ascent, with two teams on the Rupal side and four on the Diamir side. Initially Simon Moro, undoubtedly the maestro of winter Himalayan climbing this century, having already made the first winter ascents of Shishapangma (2005), Makalu (2009) and Gasherbrum II (2011), and Tamara Lunger (Italy) were attempting the *Messner-Eisendle* route on the Diamir face but switched targets to the *Kinshofer* after deciding the route was in an unsafe condition. At the start of the winter, two teams were attempting the *Kinshofer* route: Txikon, Sadpara with Daniele Nardi (Italy) and Adam Bielecki and Jacek Czech (Poland). The teams worked together, fixing ropes and setting camps in January. At about 5,800m Bielecki fell some 80m, and the Polish pair and Nardi decided to abandon their climbs. In January the team of Tomek Mackiewicz and Elisabeth Revol reached 7,500m on the *Messner-Eisendle* route but retreated due to extreme cold. On 29 January Txikon and Sadpara were partially buried in an avalanche on their attempt. Following this, Txikon, Sadpara, Moro and Lunger teamed up to climb together.

During the course of February, the climbers kept the trail up to camp one clear but were unable to proceed higher on the mountain due to high winds. On 22 February the team of four took advantage of a weather window to climb the fixed ropes up to camp two and on 25 February made it up to camp four, at 7,200m. On 26 February, the team set off for their summit bid, starting at around 6am which is late for a summit bid on an 8000m mountain; the thinking was that in winter on a west-facing slope, any earlier would be a waste of time. After a while Lunger was feeling unwell and descended back to camp four while the others continued; the team of three reached the summit at 3.37pm. They arrived back at base camp three days later. Prior to the summit, the highest any of the summiteers had been on the mountain was 6,700m, and that was only once.

Nanga Parbat has seen 31 known winter attempts from 1988 onwards, including a nearly-successful attempt by Txikon and Sadpara in the winter of

Gasherbrum IV from Concordia. The north-west ridge is the left-hand border of the Shining Wall. (*Stuart Holmes*)

2014-15. One of the chief difficulties on Nanga Parbat is the absolute height gain of 4608m from base camp, making acclimatisation even more difficult than normal and needing a particularly long weather window. In addition to the extreme cold, strong winds, short weather windows and short days that affect Himalayan winter climbing, the relative pressure in winter is lower meaning there is even less oxygen at a given height than in the standard climbing seasons.

Gasherbrum I

Eight climbers from a Dreamers Destination expedition made it to the summit of Gasherbrum I on 4 August, via the normal route; they had switched their attention from K2 following the large avalanche. The main news from Gasherbrum I, however, was the unsuccessful, alpine style attempt of a new route on the south-west face by Czech climbers Marek Holeček and Ondra Mandula. This was Holeček's fourth attempt of the route, which starts up the *Afanasiev-Babanov* couloir (2009) before heading out on mixed ground to gain the main south-west face and from there directly to the summit. The pair had acclimatised on the normal route to 7500m, and then set out on their attempt on 9 August. They bivied at 6000m on day one, 6800m on days two and three (due to bad weather) and bivied again at 7000m on day four. On 15 August they reached 7700m where they were pinned down by bad weather for several days before making a difficult retreat back to basecamp, arriving on 22 August.

The unclimbed Gasherbrum VI showing the line attempted by Dujmovits and Hansen. *(Nancy J Hansen)*

Gasherbrum IV & Broad Peak

In July, Aleš Česen and Luka Lindič (Slovenia) made the season's only ascent of Broad Peak (8047m) and then went on to repeat the north-west ridge of Gasherbrum IV (7925m). The original goal of the expedition was a new route on the magnificent west face, the 'Shining Wall', of Gasherbrum IV, but they did not get a weather window long enough to make an attempt. The Shining Wall was first climbed in 1985 by Wojciech Kurtyka (Poland) and Robert Schauer (Austria) in what is consider one of the most import ascents in Himalayan mountaineering both in terms of its pure alpine style and difficulty. A second route on the face, the central spur, was climbed by a Korean team in 1997. The north-west ridge was first climbed by Greg Child (Australia), Tom Hargis (US) and Tim Macartney-Snape (Australia) as part of an eight-member team in 1986 and has subsequently been repeated by Korean (1999) and Spanish (2008) teams; the ridge was also descended by Kurtyka and Schauer after their ascent of the Shining Wall.

Česen and Lindič first acclimatised on Broad Peak, summiting on 12 July after a battle with deep snow that had stopped all other teams. On receiving news they would have only a short weather window of a few days, they switched plans from the Shining Wall to the north-west ridge; escape is easier on the ridge and they would move faster on the less difficult ground. They bivied at 5,500m before the 6,500m col that marks the start of the proper ridge; the second bivouac was at 6,700m. Their third day on the route was a long one; they were slowed by deep snow, as on Broad Peak. The third bivouac was at 7,500m, and the weather broke that night. On the fourth day they set out into the snow and continued upwards in poor visibility, making it to the north summit of Gasherbrum IV where they fortunately had a good break in the weather. They did not continue onto the main summit, descending in three days back to base camp. On the route they found many abandoned fixed ropes from previous expeditions.

Also of note was the activity of Frenchman Antoine Girard, who set the paragliding height record of 8,157m above the summit of Broad Peak on 23 July.

Gasherbrum VI and Praqpa Ri

In June and July 2016 Nancy Hansen and Ralf Dujmovits (Canada) attempted to make the first ascents of Gasherbrum VI (7004m) and Praqpa Ri (7156m). Gasherbrum VI had been attempted four times, three of those via the south-east face (including one fatality) and once by the north-east face to east ridge. Hansen and Dujmovits attempted the south-west ridge, reaching the south-west col but were turned around by the rock band above, which consisted of compact marble covered in shallow, faceted snow. They then turned their attention to Praqpa Ri, south of Skilbrum, which seems to have had no previous attempts. They approached via the Khalkhal Pass (5705m) from the Savoia glacier which was horribly crevassed; the Khalkhal Pass is at the start of the east-south-east ridge that was their intended route. They reached 6300m but turned back due to the poor snow conditions that were not freezing overnight and became isothermal when the sun hit them at 04:00.

Gulmit Tower and Pregar

In June Aiden Laffey (Ireland) and Peter Thompson (UK) went in to attempt Gulmit Tower (5810m) from the Bulkish Yaz glacier above Gulmit village in the Hunza valley. On 11 June, shortly after arrival, a large rock fall hit their base camp; with no other suitable sites they abandoned their attempt. Gulmit Tower has seen five previous attempts and yet remains unclimbed. Laffey and Thompson moved around to the Moorkhun valley and on 23 June attempted Pregar (6200m) via the south face but were stopped by crevasses at 5,500m. On their second attempt, starting 26 June, they became separated by a large crevasse. Laffey waited at 5,700m while Thompson went on to attempt the summit, retreating just 20m below the top. They had believed the mountain to be unclimbed, but on their return home noted a report by an Austrian team where, in addition to their first ascent of Karun Koh in 1984, they had climbed a 6,200m peak west of Karun Koh that was probably Pregar.

Judl Peak

In May, and following a visit in 2011, Simón Elias and Gerald Boess (Spain) returned to the Honboro valley that lies north-west and west of the Hushe valley between the Hushe and Thalle valleys. On skis they travelled up the

Kande and then went to the first Kande cwm; from a camp in the cwm they climbed the north-east facing glacier slopes to the north-west ridge of Peak 5871m, which they named Judl Peak, then made a ski descent from below a large crevasse under the summit.

Mirshikhar, Maiun Chhish and Shispar

In June 2016, Nicolas Preitner (Switzerland) and Bruce Normand (UK) travelled to the Hunza with the aim of climbing a new route on Shispar (7611m). Although they had received clearance for Lupghar Sar (7200m), by a strange ruling of the Pakistan Army they would have required a liaison officer despite the entire Hunza and Hispar being open zones. Their first acclimatisation exercise was Mirshikhar (5486m), the peak separating Rakaposhi north base camp from the main Hunza valley, where they camped high on the peak. Next they climbed Maiun (Mayun) Chhish (5880m), a peak at the western end of the main Hunza valley which had seen one previous ascent: in 1993 Peter Thompson (UK) soloed from the Muchuar and Mandosh glaciers to the north face and north-east ridge. Preitner and Normand approached from the Hussainabad Nallah, starting at the bridge on the Karakoram Highway just below Aliabad to reach a small glacier below the east face, which they climbed to join the north-east ridge at 5600m for a low-angle traverse to the summit. A subsequent acclimatisation and reconnaissance visit to the glacier cirque east of Ultar was treated to particularly unstable and showery weather, which was the theme of summer 2016 in the region. At the end of the month, they hiked in to the beautiful but very low (3900m) meadow which serves as the base cam for the south and west sides of Shispar, from where they identified an objectively safe route. However, Preitner began to suffer mild HACE symptoms at 6100m, which caused them to break off their bid.

Porok Ri and Nera Peak

The German team of Matthias Bohe, Harry Kirschenhofer, Philipp Moser, Chris Romeike and Christof Nettekoven explored the Maedan glacier, a side valley off the Panmah glacier, in July and August. The four-day approach from Askole reached the Skinmang meadow at the junction of Chiring and Nobande Sobande glaciers. On 30 July, Bohe, Moser and Romeike made the first ascent of Peak 6020m via the west ridge; encountering a raven on the summit gave rise to the name Porok Ri ('Raven Mountain' in Balti). On 3 August, the whole team made the first ascent of Nera Peak (6143m) via the west flank and face, finding ice up to 80°. The team noted further potential for first ascents in this area with peaks S1 (6024m) and S2 (6000m) on the south side of the Maedan glacier, and unclimbed granite spires on the west side of the glacier. In the vicinity is the Chiring range that has several unclimbed peaks up to 6,861m, as well as granite faces of up to 1,400m.

Ogre II

On 22 August, US Alpinists Kyle Dempster and Scott Adamson were last seen part way up the north face of Ogre II (6969m). On 23 August a storm moved in and on 28 August a rescue was mounted; on 3 September the weather was finally good enough for two Pakistan military helicopters to do a proximity search of the mountain. Sadly, no evidence of the climbers could be found. In 2015 the same pair had made it to within a hair's breadth of the summit (about 6,600m high on the face), when Adamson broke his leg on a long lead fall. They then retreated down the face, and had a 90m fall at the base of the face when a v-thread pulled out during the abseil. Dempster and Adamson were well known alpinists with a string of hard first ascents between them, and will be missed by the climbing community.

Latok I

In August Thomas Huber, Toni Gutsch and Sebastian Brutscher (Germany) along with Jim Donini, George Lowe and Thom Engelbach (US) headed to the Choktoi valley. On 23 August they heard that Kyle Dempster and Scott Adamson were high on the Ogre II north face, and after six days of bad weather their concern for Dempster and Adamson took them to the base of the north face of Ogre II to help with the search, finding the pair's skis at the icefall at the base of the face. On 3 September, the two Pakistan military helicopters that flew in to search for the missing climbers picked up Thomas Huber to utilise his knowledge of the area; unfortunately no sign of the climbers was found. Shortly afterward, Huber, Gutsch and Brutscher attempted the north-west ridge of Ogre II (6969m), reaching 6,200m. Their main aim was an attempt at the north face of Latok I, but the team left without trying the face as the snowy conditions rendered the face too cold and dangerous. Remarkably, only three months prior to this trip, Thomas Huber had taken a 16m ground-fall in which he had fractured his skull.

Lailia Peak

The Italian team of Leonardo Comelli, Carlo Cosi, Zeno Cecon and Enrico Mosetti arrived in the Karakoram in May with the intention of making the first ski descent of Lailia Peak (6096m) via its north-west face. On 9 June the team reached a point 150m below the summit and set off down. Leonardo Comelli died in a fall on the descent and the other expedition members retrieved his body. Lailia Peak is the stunning pointed peak above the Hushe valley and was first climbed in 1987 by the British team of Andy Cave, Simon Yates, Sean Smith and Tommy Curtis; it has seen several unsuccessful ski attempts.

Muztagh Tower

The German team of Felix Berg and Matthias König attempted the first ascent of the full south-east ridge of Muztagh Tower (7276m). The French 1956 route takes the upper part of this ridge, joining at 6700m next to the black tooth; Berg and König intended to climb the south-east ridge *integrale* from a col at 5000m; this gives the whole ridge a distance of 7km. They reached the top of the rocky step (ca 6000m) but bad weather forced them down. They descended 700m and five abseils to join the French route, and a further two days to descend the broken and dangerous Dre glacier to their basecamp.

Muztagh Tower received its first and second ascents within five days of each other in 1956. On 6 July John Hartog, Joe Brown, Tom Patey and Ian McNaught-Davis (British) made the first ascent via the north-west ridge, followed by the French team of Guido Magnone, Robert Paragot, André Contamine and Paul Keller via the south-east ridge on 11 July. The British route has been repeated twice, whereas the French Route is unrepeated; the only other route completed to the summit was Russian in 2012, via the north-east face. The Russian team received the 2013 Piolets d'Or for this ascent.

Tirich Mir

A small French expedition of Jérôme Chazelas and Thomas Quillet climbed Tirich Mir (7708m) in the Hindu Kush in July. The peak is accessed via Chitral, and located close to the Afghanistan border, and this seems to be the first ascent of the highest peak in the Hindu Kush since 2001. The team made a variation to the normal 1967 *Czech* route that ascends the north-west face from the Tirich glacier.

• With additional information from Bruce Normand, Christof Nettekoven, Felix Berg and Lindsay Griffin.

HUGH THOMAS

Central Asia 2016

The hard new Russian route on the north-west face of Pik Piramidalny (5509m).
(Kirill Belotserkovskiy)

On the lower pitches of the
north-west face of Pik Piramidalny.
(Kirill Belotserkovskiy)

Kyrgyzstan

Kyrgyzstan saw the most activity in the ''stans'', mainly due to increasingly good access and cheap flights from Istanbul.

Robert Taylor and John Proctor went to the Jiptik valley, near the Kyrgyz-Tajik border and attempted the north face of Muz Tok (5066m) but unfortunately were blocked by a difficult rock barrier at 4971m. The other two in their party, Ciaran Mullan and Phil Dawson attempted Kara-Eet (4900m) but were also unsuccessful.

Two teams headed to Pik Piramidalny (5509m) in Pamir Alai. Kirill Belotserkovskiy and Max Ten made an acclimatisation ascent of the northwest face of Lomo (4750m), completing a new route up the northwest face in a 19hr round trip (WI4, M4). They then started up the 1,000m north-west face of Piramidalny after a complex approach and reached the summit on day four. This impressive ascent involved difficulties up to Russian 6A (WI5, M5), and some 'entertaining' loose rock pitches (see photo). A second team, young Germans about whom there is no other available information, ascended another new route on the same face up the buttress right of centre.

Kyzyl Asker (5842m) also saw significant action from two strong teams. First up was a Russian team consisting of Oleg Khvostenko, Vasya Terekhin and Alexander Parfyonov who headed to the southeast side of the mountain. They reported unstable weather in July but put up *Spear Route* (6a, A3, M8) over five days.

Ines Papert and Luka Lindič then put up another new route also from the south-east side of the mountain in September. This was an ice-mixed route, which Lindič described as one of the best lines he has climbed on a big mountain with lots of ice to the summit. They named the route *Lost in China* (1200m, ED, WI5+, M6). The line is to the left of the 2007 route in the picture, up the couloir. The pair also made what is believed to be the first free ascent of *Border Control* (650m, ED, WI5, M7) as an acclimatisation route on the Great Walls of China formation: see 'Lost in China' in this edition of the *Alpine Journal*.

Nearby, on the Great Wall of China (5120m) another Russian team put up a new line on the second ascent of this mountain. Vladimir Sysoev, Olesya Babushkina, Marina Popova, and Denis Prokofyev climbed *Tears of*

Routes on Kyzyl Asker (5842m): the red line shows *Lost in China*.

the Dragon (Russian 6B, A3 M5, 1150m) over three days in July 2016 with a portaledge.

Also in the Kokshaal-too range, in August, the Austrian Young Alpinists group put up two new routes on the east side of Pik Gronky (5080m): *East Buttress* (800m, UIAA, IV+, M5), and a rock route which they named *A Bang for the Buck* (350m, 6b+, WI5, M6). The group also climbed the northeast face of Pik Zuckerman (5045m) on a route they called *Pizzeria Komarovan* (600m, M4).

The International School of Mountaineering (ISM) made their annual visit to Kyrgyzstan, this time to the eastern end of the Trans Alai mountains in the Eastern Zaalay range. A team of 13 made numerous first ascents: Pik 4318m was named Pik Curperluk (Kyrgyz for 'butterfly'), Pik 4629m was named Pik Tereze ('window'), Pik 4736m was named Pik Chogurlush ('coming together'), Pik 4760m was named Pik Kanzaada ('the prince'), and Pik 4685m, which is awaiting a name.

A British expedition explored the Djenghi-Djer range in southeastern Kyrgyzstan, due south of Issyk Kul. This team, consisting of Calum Nicoll, Neil Smith, Struan Chisholm, Sandy Fowler, Mark Chonofsky, and Sam Newmark, explored on horseback and made four first ascents on peaks up to 4,346m. A full report is available from the MEF. In the Kuiluu valley Andy Wick and Miles Gould made several first ascents of c4500m peaks from the Kindyk glacier.

Tajikistan
Two Czechs, Michal Kleslo and Stefan Matuska, carefully 'interpreted' the restrictions around the Sarykol range on the border between Tajikistan and

Perfect granite cracks on the west
face of Point Samba in Tajikistan,
one of several new routes climbed
by an all-female teams from the DAV.

China, and approached from the Buzchubek valley, setting up basecamp
at 4,500m. Their main goal was Karasak (5747m), which they climbed via
a straightforward glacier approach of nine kilometres, suggesting that the
ascent was similar to Elbrus, but lacking a cable car.

A Polish team from the Krakow Mountaineering Club explored the Dara
Darshai valley in the far west of the Shakhdara range in the southwest Pamir in July. After two days of trekking from Darshai village in the Wakhan
Corridor, Mirosław Burzyński, Daria Mamica-Gałka, Radosław Stawiar-
ski, Monika Wałaszek, and Jakub Gałka, set up base camp at 4,200m. They
made what they believe to be the second ascent of Pik Imast (5954m) via
the north-north-west ridge. They also climbed Pik Kolgasonrnyi (5604m)
via the east ridge. They noted that although most summits in this area are
climbed, there remains plenty of potential, particularly Pik 5722, immediately south-east of Pik Mayakovsky.

The German Alpine Club's (DAV) young female alpinists' team, comprising Esther Baum, Franzi Wiele, Maria Pilarski, Susi Süßmeier, Vroni
Krieger and Marie Hofmann, travelled to the south-east of Tajikistan to
visit the Shadzud valley in August and September. Remarkably, in those five
weeks they had consistently perfect weather, but did recommend visiting
earlier in the year when there would be more snow, as the area's glaciers are

The north face of Muz Tok showing the high point reached by John Proctor and Robert Taylor. *(John Proctor)*

rapidly receding due to climate change. Nevertheless, they put up a mixture of rock and ice routes. On Peak 4977m, which was named Point Samba and which has a real altitude of around 5,100m: *South Ridge* (250m, much scrambling, with two pitches of French 4); *West Face* (250m, six pitches, 6c A0, great rock and some scrambling to the summit). On Peak 5411m, which was named Farihta (Shugni for 'the goddess', 5437m): *East Face* (500m, 80°, descent required ten 60m rappels). On Peak 5595m, which is the highest peak in the valley and was named Safed Haikal (Shugni for 'white giant', 5498m) *South-east Face*, a long glacier with a short summit headwall (120m, 60°). On Peak 5210m, which was named Azhdar (Shugni for 'dragon peak', 5264m N 37°83'49", E 72°29'47"): *North Ridge* (300m, F3, 60°).

Finally, in April a mixed team consisting of Anna Bushe, Stefan Jachmich, and Derek Buckle headed to the Bazar-Dara valley in the northern Alichursky range to explore on skis. This team succeeded in making first ascents of Pik Perestroika (4952m), Pik Glasnost (4918m), and Pik Druzba (5021m).

Kazakhstan

There is limited information on climbing in Kazakhstan. However, Kirill Belotserkovskiy and Max Ten were active again. Before heading to Pik Piramidalny in Kyrgyzstan (described above), the pair headed to Sairam (4238m) in the western Tien Shan approximately 150km northeast of Tashkent. They climbed a new variation on the north face of Sairam in April which they graded Russian 5B (WI5, M7, A0).

ANTONIO 'SEVI' GÓMEZ BOHÓRQUEZ

Peru 2015-16

The *Anzac* variation of the *Guides'* route on Taulliraju (5830m). The mountain saw sustained activity from a largely New Zealand team in June 2016.

Cordillera Blanca

On the granodiorite east face of **Cerro Parón** (5325m), known today as The Sphinx, Roger Schaeli (Switzerland) and Simon Gietl (Italy) opened *Chappie* (600m, 7b+max) over five days from 1 July 2015. The route lies between *Intuition* and *Dion's Dihedral*. The team also climbed the routes *Cruz del Sur* (800m, 7b) and the 1985 classic *Bohórquez-García* on the eastern side. They used pitons and Friends and 8mm para-bolts at the belays. Allow one to two days for the ascent and carry two sets of Camalots up to No2 and a set of wires.

Italian brothers Tomas and Silvestro Franchini camped at the foot (4450m) of the steep south-west face of **Nevado Churup** (5495m), to the left of the central buttress. At first light on 2 June 2015 they reached 4,850m and moved to the right of the buttress on 75° snow and ice. Their route *Divine Providence* (Peru) (650m, M7) continued with mixed climbing (M5) via a crack-dihedral on good rock. Above the buttress was more ice and snow (80°) to reach and overcome a rock band. They then climbed an overhanging section, followed by delicate ice (M7), to the left of a large dihedral in the spur that comes down from the summit. They continued mixed climbing (M4+), then 75° 'Andean snow', more M4+ mixed and finally rock (V) to the top of the spur. There is no indication about whether they summited via the south-south-east spur.

The line climbed on the west ridge of Taulliraju climbed at 5.8, M4 and AI5.

At the end of May 2016, a group from New Zealand arrived for a five-week trip to the Cordillera Blanca. The climbers (all NZ except where noted) were Ben Dare, Steven Fortune, Pete Harris, Daniel Joll, Alastair McDowell, Reg Measures (UK), Claire Measures (UK), Jaz Morris, Rose Pearson, Lincoln Quilliam (Australia), Matthew Scholes (Australia) and Stephen Skelton (USA).

On 1 June, McDowell (NZ), Quilliam (Australia), Skelton (USA) and Dare (NZ) camped at the head of Laguna Parón and paired up into two ropes to climb separate gullies on the 400m south face of **Caraz III** (5720m). On 3 June, McDowell and Quilliam climbed the *Khesghi-Bell* route (1987), in the fluting located right of the central gully that goes directly to the top. They found snow and ice of moderate difficulty (WI2) and mixed M4 terrain. Skelton and Dare climbed the *Wolf-Erickson-Knoll* (1997) route, located to the left of the central gully, 'following a steep, névé-filled gully broken by a series of thinly iced rock slabs. The climbing was engaging although never difficult, with completely unprotectable ice up to WI3.' The two teams reached approximately 30m below the menacing cornices of the upper edges, 'one of which collapsed on Skelton and I as we neared the top, fortunately without serious damage other than a smashed helmet.'

On 6 June, Dare climbed the south-west face of the **Pyramid of Garcilaso** (5885m) via a new route. Starting by a small avalanche cone to the left of the *Wolf-Clarke* route, he continued about 500m across mixed terrain and thin ice to the west ridge, almost two-thirds the height of the peak. Discouraged by the unstable ice mushrooms, he abseiled down the same

The route climbed on the south ridge of Taulliraju South (5400m).

line without continuing to the summit. After activity in Quebrada de Parón, where teams of this group climbed the east face of **Cerro Parón** (La Esfinge 5325m), they returned to Huaraz and on 15 June established base camp in Quebrada Santa Cruz: see notes below.

On 16 June 2016, Steven Fortune, Daniel Joll (NZ) and Matthew Scholes (Australia) set off for **Taulliraju** (5830m) from base camp at Taullipampa (c4250m) in the Santa Cruz Gorge. They planned to climb the south-south-east ridge, first climbed by Chamonix guides in 1978. A variant was opened on 3-4 July 1988 by Bruno Prom, Jean-Marc Gryska and Dominique Gleizes of the Groupe Militaire de Haute Montagne (GMHM), through the central gully (400m, MD, 80°) of Taulliraju's Third Buttress, on the right side of the south-west face. The 2016 trio of Antipodeans found the buttress lacking in ice, so they climbed the ridge left of the corridor: 'nine new pitches of sustained and often run-out mixed ground (M6) to reach the south-south-east ridge. Here, ice conditions improved and they were able to follow the upper section of the *Guides'* route (1978) to the summit.' They encountered overhanging ice steps to AI6 on the final pitches and dubbed their new line the *ANZAC Variation*.

On 21 June, Steven Fortune, Alastair McDowell and Rose Pearson (New Zealand) climbed the south ridge (450m, TD-, M5) of **Taulliraju South** (c5400m). The trio encountered sustained mixed climbing on the lower ridge (M5). After a short diversion onto the north-west face, they regained the ridge, climbing moderate, blocky ground to the summit.' On the same day, Quilliam and Dare attempted **Pucahirca South** (6039m) by the south face. For more information on attempts and ascents of this peak, see *AJ* 2009, pp294-6.

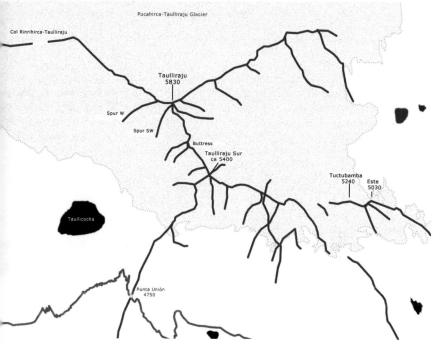

A topo map of the Taulliraju massif. *(Sevi Gómez Bohórquez)*

On 23 June 2016 Rose Pearson and Alastair McDowell travelled from base camp to the Rinrihirca (Rinrijirka) Pass, climbing a fair way up the unclimbed north-west edge of **Taulliraju**. A day later Reg Measures and Steven Fortune did the same. Soon, both teams were weaving their way along the ridge crest confronted with vertical unconsolidated snow, overhanging ice, thin mixed climbing and compact dry granite (5.8, AI5, M4). On the afternoon of their fourth and third days respectively, all four climbers reached the summit. In total there were three bivouacs on the ridge and one on descent, on the col where the south-south-east ridge meets the Third Buttress. They continued to the west shoulder of Taulliraju South and descended by its west face. Rose Pearson was the first woman on the summit of Taulliraju.

On 18 June, Ben Dare and Stephen Skelton left base camp for the far side of the peak, in search of a new route on the east face. They started up the first five pitches of the Chamonix *Guides'* route, and after a camp on the crest of the lower south-east ridge, abseiled into the lower glacier below the face on 19 June and soloed 300m of easy snow and ice. Once on the face they climbed 12 pitches of immaculate granite, with difficulties up to 5.10c, taking them directly to the upper north-east ridge, where they bivied. The morning of 20 June saw them traverse onto the upper north face to climb another four ice and mixed pitches (M5/AI5) directly to the summit; the entire route was some 950m of climbing. Descent was via the south-east ridge, with an overnight stop where they had left their tent, returning to base camp on 21 June.

Cordillera Huayhuash

On 8 August 2015, Lorenzo Festorazzi and Silvano Arrigoni reached the secondary summit of **Jirishanca Chico Oeste** (5270m) of Jirishanca Chico (5467m or 5446m) by a (likely) new route; most of the climbing on *Via del Ragni* (400m, D+) was 65-70° with a short stretch of vertical climbing. This minor peak is given 5270m on the DÖAV 1936 map, and was named Jirishanca Chico Oeste when it was climbed by a Japanese expedition in 1967 (*AAJ* 1968 p194). It seems that the Italian route climbed on the north-east side of this minor peak, possibly a little to the right of the *Iwatani-Furuhata* route, to arrive at the col between Jirishanca Chico and its west peak. It is difficult to know which sections of the Italian route coincide with those of the Japanese. Festorazzi and Arrigoni continued from the western summit on the west ridge toward the summit of Jirishanca Chico (5467m) but this 'final ridge presents certain problems due to the thinness of the ice', so they returned by the same route.

On 15 August 2016, Arnaud Bayol, Antoine Bletton, Cyril Duchêne and Dimitry Munoz, members of the GMHM, set up an advanced base camp at Suerococha (4818m). (This lake is called Suiro-kocha on the original map from the DAV, but the correct name of Suerococha and correct height are given on the 2008 map of Österreichischer Alpenverein.) In the subsequent days, mainly using aid and fixed ropes through the first 200m of the north face of **Puscanturpa East** (5410m), as it was difficult to protect. The team climbed as two ropes: the first prepared the route with the second intending to climb as cleanly as possible. Cleaning cracks and adding some bolts for belays or run-out sections, the climbers took seven days to reach the summit. The French quartet named the route *El Juego Sumando*, incomprehensible to Spanish speakers being an extrapolation of French to Spanish. Bayol added that although in situ stations reduced overall seriousness, the climb was still quite hard, with long passages of 6b climbing lacking protection.

Max Bonniot and Didier Jourdain, members of the GMHM, set up base camp in the Siulá Lagoon (4290m) and spent several days studying the 1,300m unclimbed east face of the **Nevado Siulá Grande** (6356m). They crossed the eastern glacier complex to access this limestone wall and started climbing on 21 August 2016. Difficulties started from the first pitch, but the weather worsened that afternoon. They waited overnight, and in the morning returned to base camp. Returning to the wall on 24 August, they climbed 200m of rock, then surmounted a collapsed snow and ice formation they called 'La Casquette' and bivouacked above it. Seeing a logical line that seemed to lead to the summit. Next day the difficulties increased, and they had another precarious bivouac on a platform. On the morning of 26 August they climbed excellent limestone with good protection to reach the end of a rocky triangle (c5700m) at noon, with half the route finished. About 100m of rappelling took them to the south-east ridge, which began with snow and bad ice, giving laborious climbing. On 27 August they climbed without rest because a storm was forecast for the following afternoon; they arrived at 9pm at the base of the mushroom top and found a good bivouac (6200m). Continuing at 5am, three hours later they reached a windless summit, after almost 1,500m of climbing: 750m on rock to La Casquette (6c) and another 750m of snow and ice up to 70° in pure alpine style for five days with four bivouacs and without placing bolts. They descended by the same route, bivouacked before the rocky wall and arrived at the base camp at 2am on 28 August. They named their route *Le Bruit des Glaçons* (1400m, ED, 6c, WI5), which means: 'the sound of ice cubes', a reference to seracs around base camp.

Cordillera Carabaya

On 29 June, 2016, Vahi Beltrami, Yasu Beltrami, Germán Silva (Chile), Nathan Heald (USA-Peru), Duncan McDaniel, Aaron Zimmerman (USA), and Derek Field (Canada) travelled to the Cordillera Carabaya. This seldom-visited range, with impressive snow and rock peaks rising to 5,780m, is located about 200km north of Juliaca in the Puno region of south-east Peru. The potential for new rock and ice routes is significant.

The team drove north from the town of Macusani, capital of Carabaya province, establishing a first base camp (c4600m) in the moraine basin of the Antajahua valley, below **Allinccapac** (5780m; 5837m GPS). On 30 June, from a high camp directly below the glacier at 5,000m, they climbed the gentle north-east face of **Japuma** (c5550m), identifying a potential route on a fluted ice face below and slightly east of Pico Carol (5715m), a pinnacle described as 'a prominent gendarme on the east ridge of Allinccapac' by the 1960 Oxford Andean expedition.

On 1 July 2016 at 3am, Heald, Zimmerman and Field set out from their high camp towards the ice face, with the intention of reaching the eastern edge of the Allinccapac from the col (5700m) just east of the Pt5715m. Heald: 'After crossing a penitente plain, slogging through deep snow, and overcoming a pitch of AI3 on the lower face, we crossed two significant crevasses and arrived at the base of the main headwall (c5500m). This presented four pitches of steep, hard, and blue ice (80°). On the fourth lead, we traversed 20m left across a steep, unstable snow slope to gain the col. We continued along the east ridge of Allinccapac, bypassing Pico Carol on its north flank, but were unable to find a safe route, so retraced our steps to the col. As a consolation prize, we climbed 15m of easy mixed ground up the northeast ridge of Pico Carol to the summit. We descended north down a snow slope, crossed a glacial plain at around 5,600m, and wrapped around the west shoulder of Allinccapac, making two rappels from its west ridge down to the base of the glacier. We made it back to base camp at 5pm, concluding a circumnavigation of the mountain. Our route up the south face of Pico Carol is 700m, D WI4.'

On 3 July, Zimmerman and Field traversed the **Papaccapac** (5460m) and **Mamaccapac** (5450m) tops from the south, via a tributary of the

Huayllatera valley. They knew that in 2007 a British group had climbed the Papaccapac by its north side (see *AJ* 2008), but they believed Mamaccapac remained unclimbed. From a camp at 4,700m, they climbed 400m of scree to a small rocky crest and down 100m into the adjacent Chambine drainage to access the tongue of ice extending southward from the col between Papaccapac and Mamaccapac. By dawn the same day they navigated lower crevasse fields, then climbed the right side of the main (south) face (200m, 70-80°) to the col between the two peaks (c5350m). The complex east face of Papaccapac was taken via a rock gully on the right of the summit, plus three pitches of grade 5.5-5.7 to the gendarmed summit.

The route was called *Mom and Pop Shoppe* (350m, D, 5.7, AI3). They note that Papaccapac is definitely taller than Mamaccapac, by about 10m but it is difficult to tell which gendarme on Papaccapac is the true summit. Rappelling down to the col, they ascended the west side of Mamaccapac's summit tower (called the south-west ridge by the 2007 British expedition), which is more of a blocky buttress than a ridge, and generally faces west. Difficulties included 50° ice, and 5.7 rock climbing; at the summit there was a cairn and abseil anchor from the 2007 team; they descended via abseil to the col and the lower glacier.

On 5 October Nathan Heald returned to Carabaya, travelling from Cuzco with his Peruvian friends Luis Crispín and Jorge (Coqui) Gálvez Aramburu. Next day they travelled by taxi from Macusani Lodge to the lake below **Nevado Allincapac** (5837m GPS). That afternoon they reached 5,200m on the western shoulder. At 2am next morning they started up the west shoulder (WI3), gaining a lower-angle platform that led to a prominent rock band. A series of easy pitches and a traverse took them to the summit ice cap, then WI2/3 pitches to the large summit plateau where they walked 300m to the highest point. They summited at 9.30am on 8 October; GPS indicated 5837m. They descended by the same route. Local climber Rafo León later reported he had climbed Allinccapac with Ángel Pérez on 19 June 2008 by the same or similar route; their ascent is confirmed with a photo on the summit.

Cordillera Vilcanota

The **Cayangate** massif lies 10km north-west of Apu Ausangate in the remote Vilcanota range south-east of Cusco. This chain of five high peaks is aligned and numbered I-V, north to south, on a 4.5km ridge. In 1953 three Austrians led by Heinrich Harrer made first ascents of the big peaks on the western front of the range. First Ausangate, then Colque Cruz, then the highest, Cayangate IV. They climbed the north-west icefall to bivouac on the col between Cayangate III and IV, finishing up the north-east face. The Japanese expedition of 1962 made first ascents of Cayangates II, III and a sub-peak of Cayangate I they called 'Pico de Victor', though I believe this to be the 'Horrorhorn' of subsequent expeditions. It seems they climbed the north-west sides of these peaks. The southernmost and last peak to be climbed was Cayangate V in 1966. The DAV named it 'Chimbaya', also the name of a couple of more remote peaks in the Vilcanota range. On the Peruvian IGN map it is labelled confusingly as 'Colque Cruz', not to be mistaken for the actual Colque Cruz chain to the north.

Subsequent ascents of this chain are few and far between. In 1972 a French team made it to within 200m of the highest summit but had to turn back because of a storm. Their report claimed a new route but they seem to have gone more or less along the line of the first ascent. In 1985 four Polish climbers reached the summit by a new route: the technical rock buttress to the right of the north-west ice fall. They bivouacked on the col from Cayangate III, as did the Austrians and French before them. The most recent ascent, and the only one on the eastern side of the mountain, was in 2006. Three AAC members, Chris Alstrin, Andrew Frost and Mark Hesse, climbed the technically difficult 1,000m eastern rock ridge, and finished on the north face to make the third definite summit.

Nathan Heald and Caleb Johnson, having met Luis Crispín and his brother Adan in the village of Marampaki on 18 April 2015, followed moraines south of Laguna Armacocha for a few hours and next day moraine ridge on the west side of the icefall coming down from the west face to where it finishes in the shadow of the west ridge that descends **Cayangate IV** (6120m). Being early in the season, crevasses were covered or had good snow bridges to cross on the glacier below the face. Leaving about midnight on 20 April, Heald, Johnson and Luis Crispín followed the most direct line up the face, climbing over avalanche debris from seracs higher up. One pitch of WI3 gave access to snow slopes; the rest of the face was 60-70° snow and ice, followed by a 70° snow runnel, to the summit at 11.20am. Due to avalanche hazard, they descended down easier slopes on the upper mountain to the right of the route. They arrived at base camp at dusk.

The name Huayna Ausangate applies to two different peaks on the western side of the Cordillera Vilcanota. One of them is a sub-peak of **Nevado Ausangate**, located two miles west of the main summit on the west ridge. It was probably first climb in 1953 by Austrians on their way to the first ascent of the main summit. The other **Huayna Ausangate** (5600m) is a pointy, prominent summit at the western end of the Colque Cruz massif. Although not as high as its neighbours, it is steeper on all sides and requires mixed climbing to reach the top. There are only a few references to the peak in past expedition accounts and I believe it to have been climbed three times previously. The first was by Fritz Mörz, Heinz Steinmetz, Jürgen Wellenkamp and Heinrich Harrer in 1953. Comparing photographs from then and now, Huayna Ausangate used to be covered with much more ice.

Nathan Heald's interest in Huayna Ausangate was raised during attempts on Colque Cruz in 2014, as they had established base camp below the south face. This face seemed dangerous low down due to a rock wall topped by a large serac, so Heald decided on an approach from the north. On 27 September, Heald, Alexis Trudel (Canada) and Luis Crispín (Peru) reached base camp on the north-west side of Huayna Ausangate at 4,900m, a flat moraine next to a clear lagoon the size of a football field near the circular stone camps of an old expedition.

On 28 September, the three carried gear up a moraine ridge to the glacier icefall that comes down from the north-west side of the peak; it seemed to have the easiest access of the three glaciers. Next morning at 1am they crossed the crevasse field to reach the north face of the west ridge and climbed 300m of easy mixed ground at 60-70° to the west ridge at about the exact spot where the Austrians of 1953 had taken their photo. Trudel, suffering from altitude, decided to wait on the ridge. The ridge had much less ice than previous years and was difficult to follow because of cornices, so Heald and Crispín abseiled 20m off the ridge, down soft snow to the glacier below the south face, and traversed east under the south face looking for a line. One pitch of poor snow, then several pitches of mixed climbing at 70° with good rock but poor ice and six inches of loose snow brought them to the summit at 9.30am (600m, D, AI3, M4). They descended by abseil down the south-west face to avoid rock fall that threatened them on the way up. They met Alexis on the ridge and descending in bad weather reached their tent at 4pm.

Starting on 29 May 2016, Nathan Heald and Derek Field (Canada) took five days to reach the summit of **Hatumhuma** (6127m GPS) via a new route on the east face. They left their high camp (c5300m) shortly after midnight on 1 June, arriving at dawn at the base of the main wall, climbed several hundred metres up 70° snow slopes to reach the summit ridge and continued towards the north, taking extreme care on the corniced arête. At 9am they reached the summit where Heald's GPS recorded 6127m. Heald and Field are correct in believing that their new route is near but left of that of the Yugoslav expedition of 1980, which started from a camp on the south-west side.

Cordillera Vilcabamba

Ever since Nathan Heald and Edwin Espinoza (Peru) climbed **Tucarhuay Este** (5700m) in 2013, Heald has been interested in the west summit. 'The climbing history on this peak,' Heald explains, 'is short since it hadn't seen a summit bid since 1968. After making the second ascent of Salkantay in 1956, Lionel Terray, Tom DeBooy, C G Egeler and Raymond Jenny made the first ascent of Tucarhuay from just over the Salkantay pass on the less steep north face, but in good alpine style.' The second ascent in the late 1960s involved a siege-style Japanese expedition that used 5,000ft of fixed rope. Heald continues: 'There is a large glacial lagoon at the foot of the south face that many tourists go to visit. A local rancher named Antonio Huari told me that he had to recover the bodies of two climbers who had tried the south face above the lagoon many years ago.'

Heald climbed to the south face of Turcahuay with Duncan McDaniel, an American living in Chile. Having warmed up on **Cerro Soray** (5428m) on 28 April 2015, the pair descended to the cabins of his friend Edwin Espinoza in Soraypampa. Next day they climbed 600m to carry equipment up to a camp (4800m) on ledges at the end of a spur of the south ridge of

Tucarhuay (5943m). That same night, about 11pm, they left for the summit with a stove, but no bivouac equipment. The terrain was easy up to the glacier ice formed by the south ridge, but they had to overcome huge seracs, steep slopes of hard ice, and roping up to cross crevasses and snow bridges. Above the seracs they traversed west (left) below the face, looking for runnels that would lead directly to the summit.

The first 60m were 70° ice, increasing to 80° and 90°. They alternated 30m pitches, and the slope eased to 70° in a series of mixed pitches. In the afternoon it began to snow hard, and the accumulating snow avalanched down onto them as they climbed runnels with large slabs of unstable snow. At 4pm they realised they would not reach the summit before nightfall. They climbed another 15m to a ledge of ice beneath a roof of rock (5800m), which they upholstered with ropes to fend off the cold. The night was clear and they shivered through it all. At dawn on 1 May they melted water for tea as soon as they could – the sun's warmth wouldn't reach this face – and left the ledge at 6.45am. They climbed mixed ground covered with fresh snow and two pitches later they were under a huge, hanging cornice where the face met the south ridge. Fragile snow and ice conditions gave Heald some of the most dangerous climbing he's faced in the Andes, as the pair moved together on ground 'full of loose snow, brittle ice-mesh traverses, on top of airy cornices that felt and looked to me like I was standing on clouds.' They reached the summit at 9.45am in time to see Salkantay disappearing into cloud. The final 150m took three hours. Now in cloud, the pair descended on v-threads, although the ropes were jammed after the first abseil, as they melted in and then froze again. After 10 abseils and a convoluted descent they reached their tent at 7pm: *South Face Direct* (1000m, TD+ AI4).

Before climbing Turcahuay, McDaniel and Heald , with Coqui Galvez Aramburu, left Urubamba for Yanahuara, turning up the valley that leads to **Pumahuanca** (5350m). Heald and Aramburu had tried the mountain's east ridge in November 2013 but found it too broken with rock towers, judging it easier to approach via the south or north-east faces. On this attempt they would climb the south face.

A three and a half hour trek took them up to a large lagoon and around its right side to gain altitude up to moraine where they could access the glacier. They bivouacked (5050m) but during the night it started snowing lightly and became windy. They climbed good snow at 45-60°, traversing up and right across the south face to reach the ridge, following it the final 50m up to the summit. It was a complete, frosty whiteout and the climbers stayed only a few minutes before going down at 6:15am. They were back in Cusco by late afternoon. 'It is quite accessible,' Heald write, 'in between Halancoma and Chicon, but is a minor peak in the Cordillera Urubamba and does not have a big pull as an objective: on Malcolm Slesser's 1964 map, this area has a question mark instead of a name; I could not find any information on the peak.'

Nevado Palqay (5422m) is north-east of Salkantay, whose east ridge drops down to the Palqay Pass before it swings north to form the peaks of Chuyunco and Palqay at the northern end. Further along, in the cloud forest to the north, this ridge ends in the famous site of Machu Picchu and the peak Huayna Picchu before dropping steeply to the Urubamba river. According to Nathan Heald, there is no record of it being climbed, but Tom Hendrickson, who climbed the south-west ridge of Veronica and has lived in Cusco since the 1970s, said he climbed one of these peaks in 1978. He and his New Zealand partner approached from the large, flat area north of the Palqay Pass, but when they reached the summit there were too many clouds to see anything. There are a few glaciated peaks in between Chuyunco and Palqay on the mountain ridge. Heald's route went direct to the northernmost, highest peak.

Heald and Waldemar Niclevicz (Brazil) left Cusco on 8 May 2015 for Soraypampa and next day, with horses, reached the base of the north-east ridge of Nevado Salkantay at 4,200m. The 22km trek crosses the Inkachiri-aska and Palqay passes. The following day they headed to the east side of the river and north to a pasture below the west ridge of Nevado Palqay. They climbed a scree chute to the ridge then traversed to the other side for 100m. They found a protected site on a shelf next to the glacier. Leaving tent at 2am on 11 May, they started traversing the glacier below the ridge. After a tentative approach up a rock chute, they returned to the glacier and kept traversing steeper snow until they gained a snow rib that led to the upper glacier. The climbing was on good 60-70° snow. They gained the west ridge proper as daylight arrived.

Seracs on the west face kept them to the north side of the ridge but route finding remained tricky until they climbed a short steep pitch of ice. Then they could see the ridge leading to the fore-summit. Continuing up this for 200m, they traversed the easy angled face under the fore-summit to the col between it and the rocky main summit. The final ridge was two rope-lengths of 60° snow and rock traverses with fun exposure. They were on the summit at 7:30am: *West Ridge* (500m, D). It was a beautiful day and they stayed on the summit for almost an hour taking in the views of Nevados Veronica, Salkantay and the airspace above the Inca Trail and Machu Picchu.

Later in the year, Edwin Espinoza (Peru), Roger Gasser (Switzerland), Duncan McDaniel and Heald repeated the 1968 Fritz Kasparek Memorial Expedition route on **Salkantay's** north face, via the direct north face of the east peak in perfect weather. Gasser later had the pleasure of finding Bruno Klausbruckner, one of the members of this expedition, in Switzerland, sharing information and photos.

On 23 May 2015, Basque alpinists Odie Girado and Kepa Berasategi travelled from Huaraz to Collón (3400m), a centre of population in the Taricá-district. They trekked the Quebrada Ishinca and carried on past Jatunpampa, crossing to the right side of the river before reaching a water-fall. They followed the tributary Jangya Uran, called Uran Mangya on the old German maps, to the right (west) and after six hours and 1,200m of altitude, set up base camp (c4500m) on a pampa just before the moraine leading to **Jangyaraju I** (5675m). Next day they followed the moraine for two hours, and camped at (c4900 m) near a glacial stream. On 25 May they climbed heading rightward, toward the north-west ridge, to avoid the glacier. They climbed easy passages of UIAA III, reaching the base of the rocky northeast wall in two and a half hours, spending the rest of the day to reach the summit, abseil back to the glacier and return to camp: *Libre* (655m, MD+, 6a+ A2, 60°, M5). This is likely to be a different route to that climbed by Australians Chris Turner and Mary Ambrose in 1993.

Nevado Panta (5680m GPS) is the last major ice-covered massif in the western Cordillera Vilcabamba. Its only known ascent was in 1960 by a Swiss Mapping Expedition on the north face. On 15 August 2016, Nathan Heald, Duncan McDaniel and Waldemar Niclevicz (Brazil) travelled from Huancacalle and its archaeological sites of Ñusta Hispana and Rosaspata to the south side of Panta on 4WD roads. From a large bend in the road, southeast of the peak and by a bromeliad forest (*Puya raimondii*), they walked to base camp, following a good path along the left side of the valley (4800m). At 1amn on 16 August, they climbed the glacier below the wide southern ridge. Once at the very edge they went through a labyrinth of seracs and crevasses, with some sections of WI4. Once on the summit plateau, they post-holed to the top, reaching it at 10am. They were back at their camp by 5pm having completed the peak's second ascent and a new route: *South-west Face* (850m, D+ WI4). Panta's summit was give as c5840m in the note on the Swiss expedition of 1959, published in *AAJ* 1960 p141.

The Vilcabamba remains one of the least climbed areas in Peru with great new-route potential, not just on glaciated peaks but also on large granite towers like those in Quelcamachay. Nowadays there are many roads offering easier access to these areas.

Cordillera Urubamba

On 9 March 2016, Nathan Heald (USA-Peru), Yjeguel Camasa and Eduardo Baca (Peru) climbed **Nevado Bonanta** (5319m): a large, rounded glacial summit on the ridge extending west from Nevado Veronica (5893m). Heald recorded in *AAJ* 2017 that their 'route up the east ramp had a short, easy, but very exposed fifth-class rock section to gain the glacier. Here, I found an old Charlet Moser ice axe; I believe it is from the 1958 Italian expedition that made the first ascents of Bonanta, Huakeihuilqui, Marconi, and the Chicon peaks farther east (*AAJ* 1959). The climb onto the summit plateau was straightforward on 120m of 50° ice, after which we post-holed up knee-deep snow until the summit (300m, PD+). There were no views, as it was still the wet season, but they would be spectacular on a clear day.'

On a photo Heald published online with the names of the Nevados ('Bonanta, Wakaywillka and Veronica'), the Bonanta summit (5300m) seems to coincide with that of the (unofficial) Nevado Bonomia (5110m), as named by the Italian expedition of 1958 led by Luigi Binaghi. This P5110m was later named 'Nevado Bonanta' (5319m) in the Urubamba sheet of the Instituto Geográfico Nacional (IGN) of Peru, where its summit is to the south-west of the 'Huajayhuillca Nevado' (5361m), that is, 'of the

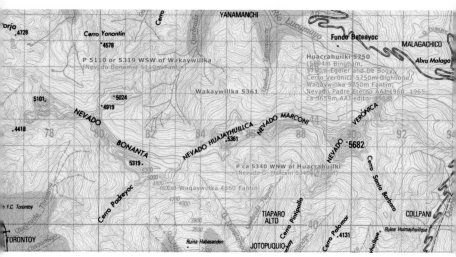

When oronomy and topography collide. Complex naming history in the Cordillera Urubamba.

Wakaywilka'. This could be confusing, because the publications of Mario Fantin, Binaghi's companion, give the name 'Waqaywilka (Veronica)' to the main snow-capped mountain massif itself.

John F Ricker, a scholar of the Andes and Quechuan oronomy, Huacrahuilki is the correct local name of what is today called Nevado Veronica. The *AAJ* 1960 article on the re-naming of mountains: 'The editor deplores giving foreign names to Andean peaks, rather than Quechua or at least Spanish names.' Perhaps we should not use the names Bonomia or Bonanta, names that H Adams Carter, John F Ricker or Evelio Echevarría (among others) would consider 'unacceptable and worse, tactless and offensive' and instead should use 'P5110' or 'P5319 west of Huacrahuilki' until the Peruvian geographical authorities decide on another name. Hirishi Furuhata and Tomoaki Kato (Japan) were the second to ascend P5110, on 30 August, 1967, with two bivouacs.

On 5 April 2016, Nathan Heald, Jorge (Coqui) Gálvez Aramburu, Eduardo Baca and Yjeguel Camasa (Peru) approached from the north-west via Maucau (Pampacorral Community) and in five hours reached the eastern slopes of the Chainopuerto (5650m). This, according to Heald, is an outlying peak of **Nevado Sahuasiray** (5818m). They left camp at 2am on 7 April, crossed the eastern glacier and from the col with the Nevado Can Can climbed ice of up to 70° on the south side of the Chainopuerto pyramid. Clouds from the jungle reduced visibility to 40m. They had to take turns standing on the unstable summit ledge. They returned via the same route (600m, D AI3). This was probably a new route and the second overall ascent.

Nevado Chainopuerto was first attempted in 1964 from its south-eastern side by a Scottish team; they came up 200ft short of the summit (*AAJ* 1965).

In 1968 an Irish team made the first ascent. It was attempted by Club de Andinismo Cusco a few times in the early 2000s without success. Heald believes the route up the east side of the peak to the col is new, but they likely climbed the summit cone via a similar route to the Scots and Irish.

On 28 June 2016, Brad Johnson (USA) and Andrés Marín (Peru) travelled from Ollantaytambo on paved road 28B, up switchbacks to the Abra de Málaga (4316m), with the idea of climbing the Halancoma. They started their approach at the largest left-turning switchback beyond the 117km marker, at about 3900m, followed a steep, grassy valley, from which they climbed a steep hillside on the right for c700m to gain a ridge crest (4570m), where they could view the west face of Halancoma. They traversed for some time, reaching a lake camp (4650m) below the west face. Starting next morning at 4am, down moraine and slabs to a glacial ramp of 50° ice, they reached the summit ridge about four hours after leaving camp (700m, 50° AI2 5.5). The last 20m of summit ridge was mixed climbing. The main summit of Halancoma was a few hundred meters to the south, but poor rock convinced them to descend from where they were, having settled for **Nevado Halancoma Sur** (5367m).

The Halancoma south summit, less frequented than the north, was reached in 1981 by Tom Hendrickson (Club Andino Bariloche, Chile) and John E Saunders (Alpine Club of Canada); In 2015 the Peruvians César Cahuana and Alfredo Zúñiga traversed the north-to-south ridge between the two peaks; and in 2016 the Peruvian Jorge (Coqui) Gálvez Aramburu opened a route (PD 55-65 °) by the south face. The easy normal route to the north summit (c5300m) of Halancoma is now the habitual route of local groups.

MARCELO SCANU

Argentina & Brazil

The line of *Qhapac Ñan* (330m, 6c+) in the Chañi group, Argentina.
(Facundo Suárez Zapiola)

Province of Jujuy

Morro Von Rosen (5450m) is part of the Chañi group, named for one of the first climbers of the mountain in the early 1900s. In April 2016, Matías Cruz and Facundo Suarez Zapiola set up a base camp in the hut on the slopes of **Chañi**. They warmed up on a nearby dihedral, opening a new line on mostly good rock. They climbed about 100m of 6a, with moves of 6a+, before giving up because of rotten sections of rock.

Windy conditions kept them to a very vertical spur on Morro Von Rosen. They approached by a creek to the south-east of the mountain, which then steepened to become a rock gully that delivered them to the base of the route. The first couple of pitches were 5+/6a followed by 4. The next three ropes lengths were of a dihedral and a crack with a few small roofs, all 6a to 6c+ climbing. The final pitch, slightly overhanging, took them with no further difficulties to the summit, on 24 April at 4pm. *Qhapac Ñan* (330m, 6c+) is the name of the ancient Inca road; one of the roads went to Chañi for the purpose of child sacrifice on its summit.

326

Above: The top of the cableway on
Cumbre General Belgrano (6097m),
behind, once the longest in the world,
serving the massif's gold mines.
(Pedro Strelin)

Right: The 400m Tabuleiro Wall in
Brazil. The line of Para Temprano es
Tarde is just left of the waterfall, going
through the right-hand side of the roof.
(Horacio Gratton)

Province of Catamarca

A large Argentine expedition was active in the **Volcán Antofalla** massif,
in the north of Catamarca, on 9-20 January 2017. The group consisted of
Julieta Balza, Sergio Cerutti, Adrián Gandino, Gerardo Casaldi, Martín
Giraudo, Emilio González Turu, Javier Echenique, Gastón Vitry and Christian Vitry. The approach was by miners' tracks, then across open, unmarked
terrain. Together the group ascended the virgin Cerro Negro (4905m) on
12 January. The next day Echenique and Casaldi made the second ascent
of **Cerro Colorado de Antofalla** (5775m). Other members climbed an
unclimbed peak (5450m), naming it Cerro Gringo Cerutti. The group set up
a high camp (5600m) on 15 January and the following day Turu, Christian
Vitry, Gandino, Echenique, Balza, Giraudo and Casaldi reached the top of
sacred Antofalla (6440m), first climbed by the Incas who erected a stone,
open-air temple. They then traversed to a virgin peak they called Pico Peñas
Coloradas (6320m). On 17 January both Vitry and Echenique arrived at
the west summit, called Huamán (6335m), finding evidence of a previous
ascent. Echenique continued to the unclimbed south summit (6404m).

During the last days of February, Argentines Andrés Zapata and Marcelo Scanu explored the area north of the giant **Volcán Galán**, the world's
biggest caldera. They found an interesting landscape with vicuñas and
other wildlife, and a thermal river with trout and leeches. Constant vigilance
was required to deter the innumerable spiders that tried to crawl into their
nostrils and ears at night. From a camp in the Río Aguas Calientes, Scanu
reached the top of an unclimbed mountain (c5100m) via the long north-east
ridge. It was christened Cerro Cóndor Solitario.

Province of La Rioja

The highest summit of the Famatina range, the Sierras Pampeanas and all the extra-Andean Argentine region is **Cumbre General Belgrano** (6097m), which can be seen from many provinces. It also has several ancient gold mines and at one time held the highest and longest cableway in the world, now in ruins but active between 1904 and 1929 for transportation of minerals to Chilecito.

In 2009 Pedro Strelin ascended the Pico Riojano (a lower summit) from Villa Castelli, via a new route and began thinking of a west-to-east Famatina traverse, from Chilecito to Villa Castelli. In December 2016, Pedro, his brother, Alejandro, and Sergio Velázquez left the second station of the cableway (1080m) near Chilecito. Five days later they arrived at La Mejicana, the highest station ruins. They camped by the lagoon (5000m) and at 4am on 20 December they headed to the summit. Alejandro had to give up, and returned alone to Chilecito. The other two continued past another lagoon, one of the world's highest at 5,800m, and were on Cumbre General Belgrano's summit at midday; they reached 4000m on the western slopes the same day. The next day they descended 17 hours, reaching the Villa Castelli cemetery at 9pm to complete the first traverse of this massive mountain.

Province of Mendoza

Cordón de los Clonquis is part of the Cordillera Principal. Sedimentary mountains, they consist of five principal summits that separate Quebrada Chorrillos to the south, and Potrero Escondido to the north. This area is almost completely unexplored; access is via a 10km trek from Punta de Vacas along the Río Tupungato, followed by another 8km in the Río Blanco to reach the Potrero Escondido. During 2016, four of its principal summits were ascended. Only Clonquis Oriental (4400m) remains unclimbed, defended by its vertical, rotten rock.

At the extreme south of the range towers **Cerro Horqueta** (4565m), so called because of its resemblance to a forked tree. It was climbed with no great difficulties by the north-west face in March 2016, by Argentines Glauco Muratti and Adrián Petrocelli. They found some exposed rotten rock steps of grade III, the longest of them about 25 meters. In the same month they climbed the west face of Cerro Tropa (4530m) with the occasional exposed grade III step; the summit rocks resembles a herd or troop. **Clonquis Central** (4576m) was ascended by Argentines Diego Molina and Pablo González, approaching from the Quebrada del Potrero Escondido in October 2016. They reached the summit, 1300m from base camp, by a snow gully with easy if exposed rock steps.

Brazil

In 2016, two very interesting routes were opened in Brazil. In July, Argentine Horacio Gratton teamed with Brazilians Lucas 'Jah' Marques and Gustavo Fontes. They focused on a new route on **Tabuleiro**, in the Bahai state of Brazil. Tabuleiro is a 400m wall with 250m of overhang and a

Sangre Latina
Piedra Baiana | Nova Belém | MG | Brasil
800m - 8b

60m – 4º
60m – 5º
60m – 6º
60m – 6º
50m – 8a/+
50m – 8a+/b
40m – 7b
30m – 6º
55m – 8a+/b
45m – 8a/+
50m – 8a/+
55m – 7c+
Buraco Vivac
35m – 6º
30m – 7a
35m – 7b
40m – 8b
50m – 7c+/8a

waterfall in its centre. Both Brazilians were familiar with the wall; they had previously climbed the most difficult of its routes: *Smoke on the Water* (350m, 8a+). On this trip they climbed the first pitches of *Smoke on the Water* to reach a shelf, which made an excellent first camp as it is the beginning of the overhang that leads to a huge roof. They opened the first two pitches in the first couple of days, the first pitch being the harder (8b/8b+) on 45m of overhanging but solid quartzite. They aren't sure that the second pitch, crossing the 30m PacMan roof (8a), can be climbed free.

A topo of *Sangre Latina*, the hard new route on Pedra Baiana *(left)*, also pictured with a handsome cloud cap *(top left)*, a view looking down on the 8b+ second pitch *(top right)* and a view of the unusual landscape *(above)*. *(Gabriel Tarso/Edson Vandeira)*

They then left their gear on the shelf and went to a bouldering festival in Ouro Preto for a couple of days. Returning to conclude the climb, they connected to the last pitch of *Smoke on the Water*, a nice 7a, followed by a short traverse to finish the climb in a fresh water lake that is the beginning of the waterfall. Their climb has been named *Para Temprano es Tarde* (400m, 8b/b+, 8a, 8a, 8a+) and as with the other route established by Gratton, *Sangre Latina*, see below, some pitches weren't climbed free. They have plans to return to sort that out.

Pedra Baiana is located about 20km south-east of the better-known Pedra Riscada, between the towns of Itabirinha and Nova Belem. In August 2016 Argentinian Horacio Gratton and Brazilians Ed Padilha, Valdesir Machado, Wagner Borges and William Lacerda opened a 17-pitch route, nine of the pitches at 8a or above. They called it *Sangre Latina* ('Latin blood') because of the wounds inflicted during the ascent. The team was granted access from the coffee growers that own the land, and set up base camp 20 minutes from the east wall. The route begins with a slab at 7c+/8a. The second pitch, a dihedral with a finger crack, was climbed at 8b/8b+, finishing in a roof that the climbers say resembles the Great Roof of El Capitan's *The Nose*. They climbed these first three pitches (the third being another finger crack-to-offwidth, 7b+) over two days, and saw that they were aiming for a heart-shaped pocket. They reached that on the third day, and found easier terrain (pitches of 7a and 6c).

On the fourth day they climbed over 7c+ ground towards what looked like a bivouac shelf, but the shelf didn't exist. Fortunately, 15m to the left they found a perfect cave with level ground that could sleep three or four people. From there the rock was overhanging with more pitches of grade 8. The 8b/8b+ pitches were climbed with aid, over a succession of days with teams bringing equipment, water and food to the climbers. Finally on the tenth day the route relented, they reached the top by the easiest pitches of the route and enjoyed the magic of being the first people to explore the summit.

The team left roughly 160 bolts on the route, including abseil-belay points, but left no bolts on the crack pitches. Gabriel Tarso and Edson Vandeira filmed and photographed the ascent. They plan to return soon to climb it free in its entirety.

KESTER BROWN

New Zealand 2015-16

The north-west face of Mt Aspiring. This photo was taken
on the day of the first ascent of the face. *(Ben Dare)*

Good winter ice conditions for **2015** meant there was considerable new-route activity in the Southern Lakes and Fiordland regions this year. Climbing existing routes has been popular in the Southern Alps regions but development of new routes was minimal, with just a few minor lines being added. Some significant first ski descents also occurred in the Mt Cook region.

Winter climbing activity in the Darrans was invigorated by the annual NZAC Darrans winter meet, held over the week of 10-19 July, and it just so happened that the first few days of that week coincided with the best conditions for ice climbing in the Darrans since the winter of 1992. This of course meant some good routes were done, including new climbs and some fine repeats.

Alastair Walker and Stephen Skelton found a new line on the left-hand buttress of **McPherson** cirque. *The Key* (IV, 4+) is a 650m gully just right of *Comshingaun*. Steve and Al had released their swanky new 74-page guidebook *The Darran Mountains in Winter* just the day before, ensuring the guide was current for less than 24 hours. The guide is available as a PDF download from *www.alpineclub.org.nz*.

Steven Fortune and Ben Dare trudged up Gomer to access the upper McPherson cirque area and climbed a water-ice line that Steve had been patiently waiting to touch down for some years. *Crystal Ship* (IV, 7; WI5+) is a beautiful freestanding pillar that is probably the most technically difficult pure ice line in the area.

Steven and Ben followed that ascent with another impressive new route the following day on the lower McPherson cirque wall. *Ether* (IV, 5) follows the striking left-angling groove line between *Rabbit Run* and *Stirling Moss*. The grade somewhat belies the difficulties of that route, which was climbed on mostly thin névé and ice. The barely-there protection and difficult-to-find belays made the route committing and scary.

Alastair McDowell and Lincoln Quilliam completed a new route in the lower **Cirque Creek** valley, left of *Mama Says It's Alright To Dream*. The new line, *Freycinet*, ascends to the snowfields below Mt Crosscut (600m, WI3).

After the dream start to the week, warm temps came, along with rain. Steven Fortune and Reg Measures climbed a new single-pitch route on Marge's Crag just below Homer Saddle, on the Hollyford side. *Canyonero* has a casual commitment grade (I), but a relatively heavyweight technical grade (6). Ben Dare and Danny Murphy added a new line late in the week in the Cirque Creek valley. *Na Fianna* (IV, 4+) climbs the rock buttress to the right of Squealing.

Some notable repeats also occurred during the first part of the meet, before the warm-up. *Squealing* (IV, 6+; WI4) was climbed twice in two days, first by Steven Fortune and Ben Dare, then Graham Johnson, Matthias Kerkmann and Johan Maillol. *Squealing* was put up in 1993 by Dave Vass and Paul Rogers and despite offering four pitches of fine ice climbing had only seen one other ascent before this year. Allan thought the route so good he went back and climbed it again later in the winter with Lionel Clay and Milo Gilmour. Milo said it was the best ice route he'd ever climbed in New Zealand, so now that the rodent's out of the stuff-sack, it might get climbed more often.

Stirling Moss is another one of those almost-mythical Darrans winter routes, put up in strange fashion in the big winter of 1992 by two parties over two days, who each climbed separate parts of the route. Al Mark and Pete Sykes climbed the whole thing in one hit shortly after, chucking a bolt in at the top, as the snow was soft and sketchy. The first couple of pitches of *Stirling Moss* rarely form, which might account for the 23-year gap in ascents. Reg Measures and Alastair McDowell found the initial ice in fat condition, so took the opportunity to nab the third ascent.

While climbing in the Cirque Creek valley during the meet, Ben Dare took note of the stonking ice line that had formed just to the right of *Squealing* and the following week day-tripped back down from Queenstown and rope-soloed the first ascent. *Tempest* (IV, 6+; WI5-, R) is the same length as *Squealing* but is thinner and the climbing more technical.

As the seasons rolled on and spring came around, attention shifted to the slightly loftier heights of the upper Cirque Creek area. On 21 September Milo Gilmour and Allan Uren climbed the line everyone had been eyeing, on the buttress to the right of Hotel Caribbean, on the south face of **Mt Crosscut**. Gilmour and Uren called their route *Up Cirque Creek Without a Shovel* (400m, VI, 6).

Inspired by this, Ben Dare and Steven Fortune sought adventure on the upper Cirque Creek ice a few weeks later. Starting from the base of the famous Cyclops project, Dare and Fortune angled up and left to climb the first ascent of *Tramadol Dreams* (V, 4+). Notably, both parties that completed new routes in the upper Cirque Creek area this year abseiled back down to the base of the climbs by way of V-threads, and returned to the Hollyford via Cirque Creek. It is unusual for the ice to be in good enough condition for this, and most parties descend by walking off the back of the headwall, traversing the ridge to Barrier Knob and then into the Gertrude valley.

The good winter conditions also extended to the **Remarkables Range**, where a number of significant new ice and mixed climbs were established. Early in July, Steven Fortune and Stephen Skelton put up *Stease* (M6, 4p) on the Wall of Evening Light. On the same day, Ben Dare and Danny Murphy added *Miss Adventure* (M4+, 4p) on the same wall. Later in the winter Steven Fortune returned to the wall and made the first winter and first trad ascent of *Once* (M7).

In early August Ben Dare and Tom Brownlie climbed a new mixed route above Lake Alta, *Highland Park* (80m, M5, WI4) starts up *White Jism* then branches right after the crux of that route into a steep chimney system. Daniel Joll pulled off the first winter ascent of *Can I Sit On It* (M7), a testing long corner on the west face of the **Telecom Tower**. Kester Brown and Steven Fortune climbed a new, direct corner line above the first pitch of *State of the Nation* (M5).

Danny Murphy and Stephen Skelton climbed *Old Guard* (M5), a new line near *Sumo* on the west face of **Double Cone** in August. Steven Fortune and Daniel Joll did an alternate start (M5) to *Naturalisation*, on the same face. Ben Dare and Kester Brown found a new line on the Telecom Tower to the right of *The Clearances*. *Royal Blood* (M5) has good corner climbing over five pitches. Lincoln Quilliam and Rene Provis climbed a possible new line at Wye Creek, *VB and Vegemite* (WI3) is a nice flow above and left of the main area. Jono Clarke made the first onsight of a grade M8 trad route when he sent *Under Pressure*. Karl 'Merry' Schimanski followed suit shortly after.

Merry then swapped to the east side and set to work on *The Fly* project at **Terminator Crag**. After a couple of days of effort, Merry redpointed *The Fly* (M10), thus establishing New Zealand's most difficult trad mixed line – by two grades. Jin Cong scored the FA of *Learning to Lead* (M3), on the Telecom Tower, for which she received the Macpac Hardest New Route Award at the 2015 Remarkables Ice and Mixed Festival.

Summer in the Darrans was a productive time for a number of parties seeking new climbs. In January, Richard Thomson, Rich Turner and Dave

Vass completed the first new line on the north-west wall of **Nga Mokopuna**, a subsidiary peak to **Mt Te Wera**. The wall is a continuation of the Statue Wall on the north-west flank of Karetai Peak: *Kilroy Wuz Here* (250m, I, 21). Rich Turner returned to the wall in February, this time with James Spears, and the pair climbed *Brothers in Arms* (325m, II, 22). Following that, Rich and James were sucked up the *Katabatic Gravity Well* (300m, II, 23) on the Statue Wall of Karetai.

American climbers Kyle Dempster and Jewell Lund ventured to Te Puoho area in March and climbed a new line on the east face of **Karetai**, the seven-pitch *Tabula Rasa* (22) is just to the right of last summer's new route *Rising High*, which was done by a visiting German team.

Troy Mattingley and Zac Orme completed an audacious and fine first ascent on the east face of the Mighty Dur, in **Te Puoho** basin: *Yeah, Nah, Dur* (24, 5 pitches) follows an amazing line straight through a steep, golden shield of rock. On 11 February, Mike Buchanan and Kieran Parsons made the first ascent of *Weigh a Pie* (19, 7 pitches) on a buttress of **Mt Tuhawaiki's** south-east ridge, above Rainbow Lake.

Two parties ventured onto the upper south face of **Barrier Peak** on the same day in late February. Both teams accessed the face from the Gertrude valley via the Barrier Face and a traverse in on ledges from the Barrier-Crosscut col. Michael Eatson and Jaz Morris made the first ascent of *Jaz Hands* (310m, 18), while Pete Harris and Daniel Joll climbed *Peaking Pete* (440m, 20, A2).

Max Olsen and James Thornton ventured into the Fiordland wilderness south-west of the Darrans to make the first ascent of the *Poison Dagger* (Pt1714) via Diamond Creek and the peak's north ridge.

Outside of the major climbing areas, the following new routes have been recorded: Ben Dare completed the first ascent of the *South Ridge* (17) of **Amphion Peak** (1965m) on the range between the Rock Burn and Beans Burn in Mt Aspiring National Park on 27 February. Dare had spied the line the previous summer while climbing Somnus.

Nina Dickerhof, Neil Sloan and James Thornton made the first ascent of the west ridge of **Mt Enderby**, on the divide between the Hunter and Wills valleys. Andrew Finnigan and Sam Spector climbed a new ice line on a previously unclimbed face of **Pt2016** in the Glacier Burn, near Glenorchy, in July. The unnamed route includes three pitches of steep climbing (WI3-, M4), then a 200m stretch of easy snow, then a 100m, 50° snow-ice ramp to the top, with an easy walk-off descent. Andrew notes there is scope for more winter routes on the face.

On 10 January, Peter Joynt and Alastair McDowell made the first ascent of the 250m south face of **Mt Euclid**, a granite peak in the central Paparoa range. Peter and Alastair's climb, including approach and egress, was completed over two days thanks to the discovery of a direct approach via a flagged track through the bush on the north-west ridge of Mt Fleming. That track is not shown on topo maps, perhaps explaining why the peak is seldom visited. A detailed description of the approach can now be found on

Kieran Parsons on the upper reaches of *Oma Rapeti* (600m, MC4+, 17), Mt Huxley.
(Steve Fortune)

climbnz.org.nz. The route takes a direct line up a series of cracks and corners in the centre of the face, offering thin face climbing on quartz edges, engaging chimneys and steep corners. The first five pitches consist of sustained grade 16-19 climbing on solid granite, after that, two easier pitches lead to the summit of the lower peak. Descent is a straightforward scramble down the west ridge. McDowell comments that there is potential for more good routes to be unearthed in the **Paparoa**, and that the western aspects of the central buttress on the south face of Euclid look particularly good.

On 10 August, Wanaka chopper pilot Bill Day flew Lionel Clay and Allan Uren in to the head of Eyre Creek, in the **Eyre Mountains**, Southland. The next day, Lionel and Allan climbed four water-ice pitches on a 120m high cliff. The climb is very steep the whole way, with the top 50m section being vertical to slightly overhanging. The pair accessed the climb by abseiling in, which, Uren said, 'gave the route a strong feeling of commitment and air of seriousness … There is another line to the right that looks just as good and hard.' *Bill's Way* (120m, WI6) is the first climb of this grade in New Zealand.

Dean and Glen Aspin discovered a good water-ice climbing venue in the Marlborough region, somewhere near Hanmer. More than 10 new climbs were added, including at least one multi-pitch ice route. The location is still under wraps, but if nothing else, this proves there's plenty of unclimbed ice out there, waiting for climbers willing to venture off the beaten path.

A few notable ski-mountaineering descents have occurred in the Mt Cook region. Snowboarder Shane Orchard made the first descent of the Montague Spur from the West Peak of **Elie de Beaumont**. Chamonix-based skiers Tom Grant and Ross Hewitt made the first descent of the Right Flank on the Spencer Face of Elie a short time later. Grant and Hewitt also skied a new, involved line on the south face of a sub-peak west of **Mt Darwin**. Tess Carney and Shane Orchard snowboarded the Central Couloir on the southeast face of **The Warrior**, in the Armoury Range, in September.

The **2016** New Zealand alpine climbing year has been 'business as usual' in most respects. Plenty of NZAC members have been active in the mountains here in Aotearoa. Most mountaineering activity has taken place at the established popular locations, like the Grand Plateau, the head of the Tasman, Arthur's Pass, Mt Ruapehu, and the Darrans.

NZAC's instruction programmes, both at the national and section level, are continuously over-subscribed, suggesting a healthy and on-going appetite amongst New Zealanders to learn the skills required to climb, ski and travel safely in our mountains. The New Zealand Mountain Guides Association also reports a strong demand for guided ascents of the classic routes on our highest peaks. Ski mountaineering has been booming in popularity in recent years, with 2016 being no exception. However, we have no major first descents to report this year.

The popularity of the better-known peaks and routes does not seem to have resulted in over-crowding of the more remote alpine areas of New Zealand. That is perhaps a blessing for those interested in a more explorative style of mountain adventure. There is still plenty of opportunity in the New Zealand mountains to find new routes and peaceful situations, that is if you can find a valley free of scenic helicopter flights.

An adventurous spirit does remain amongst Kiwi mountaineers, as evidenced by the reports in this journal of new alpine climbs completed over the last year.

Festivals and meets continue to be a staple of the alpine year, and have proved successful in motivating groups of climbers to seek out new climbs, as well as link up to enjoy established climbs. The Remarkables Ice and Mixed Festival, organised by the Expedition Climbers Club, had its highest ever turn-out in 2016. The NZAC Darrans Winter Meet endured poor conditions this year, but still saw a number of climbs done.

The most significant ascent of the year, in terms of difficulty, was Ben Dare's winter solo of a new route on the east face of **Fastness Peak**. On 30 January, Ben Dare, Danny Murphy and Stephen Skelton made the first ascent of the curiously overlooked north-west face of **Mt Aspiring**, via what is, by their reports, a route of reasonable quality and moderate grade.

Over a stunning week of fine weather, Rich Thomson and Rich Turner ventured once more to the Central Darrans, adding 30 pitches of new routes on superb quality rock. From a camp in Te Puoho, the *North-west Pillar* of **Taiaroa** (450m, 22) climbs the striking pillar that drapes the end of the west face above the glacier lake. Even better was the oft-eyed right arête of the

Mighty Dur, which *Dur-rich-t* tackles head on (350m, 22). The third pitch was a daunting proposition and situation, but turned in at a very reasonable grade of 22, giving excellent gear, glorious holds and sequences in a breathtakingly exposed setting. Best. Pitch. Ever.

Moving operations to the Eyrie, the pair then climbed another line (the seventh) on the pinnacled wall running between Te Wera and Karetai. Starting up the enormous corner-roof system just left of the base of *Lindsay's Ledges*, 21+ (300m, 21+) soon breaks right and straight up the steep black streak. Cutting back around Karetai of a misty morning, they climbed a line on the south-east face, a continuously steep and technical wall with well-featured rock. *Hugs not Drugs* (290m, 22) starts just left of the Jones-Jones line and heads more or less 'straight up bro' with a leftward lean. Climbed in low-visibility shmoo, it's pretty hard to say exactly where the line went, but the whole face seems to be climbable almost anywhere with consistent high teens and unavoidable low 20s cruxes.

On 22 January, Michael Eatson and Tawny Wagstaff completed a new route on the Outlier Peak of **Mt Arrowsmith**, in the Arrowsmith Range. *The Outlier* has six pitches on compact sandstone with excellent protection. Also in January, Pete Harris and Alastair McDowell made the first ascent of the west ridge of **Mt Percy Smith** (MC4-). Kieran Parsons and Steve Fortune climbed *Oma Rapeti* (600m, MC4+, 17) on the south-west face of **Mt Huxley**. Janette Heung and Lukas Kirchner climbed a new route on the south face of **Mt Aspiring** called *Thales*, with no further information available. In the Darrans, as part of the last bit of the winter meet, Kieran Parsons, Conor Smith and Steve Fortune climbed a five-pitch new route on **Mt Talbot** called *Tears of Papatuanuku* (IV, 7).

Karl Schimanski on-sighting *Under Pressure* (M8), Telecom Tower, Remarkables.
(Daniel Joll)

Mount Everest Foundation Expedition Reports

SUMMARISED BY GLYN HUGHES

The Mount Everest Foundation (*www.mef.org.uk*) was established as a registered charity following the successful ascent of Everest in 1953, and was initially financed using surplus funds and subsequent royalties from that expedition. It is a continuing initiative administered jointly by the Alpine Club and the Royal Geographical Society.

Surprisingly the word 'mountaineering' does not appear anywhere in its Memorandum and Articles of Association, the prime object being the promotion of 'exploration' in mountain areas: this is mainly geographic, but can also include the application of other exploratory disciplines in these areas, such as geology, botany, zoology, glaciology and medical research.

The MEF has now distributed well over £1m to more than 1,600 British and New Zealand expeditions undertaking such exploration. Most of the grants have been awarded to ambitious young climbers who help to maintain Britain's reputation as one of the world's leading exploratory nations. In return for supporting an expedition, all that the MEF requires is a comprehensive report. Copies of these reports are lodged with AC and the RGS, who make them available to all interested parties. The AC have organised the scanning of all the existing MEF reports, and these will be accessible on-line on the AC website by the end of 2017.

Donations to the MEF are always welcome and help us meet the continuing demand for support. If you have benefited from MEF support please consider including a bequest to the Foundation in your will.

The following notes summarise reports from the expeditions supported during 2016, and are divided into geographical areas.

NORTH AMERICA

West Face of Celeno Peak 2016 – Graham Zimmerman and Chris Wright (May 2016).
Celeno Peak (13,395ft) is located in the Wrangell-Saint Elias range in Alaska. The objective was the first ascent of the W face, and the second ascent of the peak overall. They flew to Anchorage, and then to the small town of McCarthy, where Jay Claus, who had made the first ascent of Celeno in 2012, flew them to Canyon Creek glacier. A storm at base camp was followed by a forecast for a weeklong weather window, so after allowing two days for conditions to clear they set off up the face, starting with 2,000ft of snow and ice un-roped to a mixed spur leading to the summit. This started with mixed climbing generally M4/M5, but with an M6 crux. The next day they tackled a rock band, which included the route crux at

5.10X A2+, where dislodged rocks cut their rope. From the top of the band they continued on steep snow and ice to the top of the spur. A rightward traverse led an iced gully, which was followed to a bivouac just below the summit. The following day they reached the summit, with spectacular views, and descended by the first ascent route, starting down the NW ridge, and then a couloir giving access to the glacier below. They described this as 'a fruitful and enjoyable expedition'.   MEF ref 16-14

British Hunter Foraker 2016 – Ben Silvestre, Pete Graham and Will Harris (May 2016).
The primary objective was a new route on the S face of Mt Hunter South. They flew to Talkeetna, and then to Thunder glacier, where they scouted new routes, and attempted a route on Pt 9000 (Lightning Peak). They completed about half of this route, but aborted because of deep fresh powder snow. These conditions were typical in the Thunder glacier area, so they decided on a change of plan. They flew to the Kahiltna glacier where they acclimatised on the west buttress of Denali, turning back at 17,000ft in freezing cold wind. They then transferred to their secondary objective, the first British ascent of the Infinite Spur on the S face of Mt Foraker, which they completed in three days, and descended in declining weather with heavy precipitation. The view of the Thunder cirque from the summit of Foraker showed much drier conditions than they had experienced, and possibly good mixed climbing potential.   MEF ref 16-16

British Juneau Icefield 2016 – Tom Bide, Carl Reilly, Anita Holtham, Jake Phillips, Mandy Tee and Rachel Bell (April 2016).
Objectives were first ascents in the Juneau Icefield area of SW Alaska, specifically the Devils Paw (2616m) and surrounding peaks, and Taku Towers. Unfortunately they experienced poor weather for most of the three weeks duration, and were unable to achieve any of the climbing objectives. However, they did complete a 70km N-S traverse of the icefield on skis, from Atlin on the Canadian side of the range to the Taku glacier on the US side, from which they were flown out back to Juneau.   MEF ref 16-20

Team BMG East Buttress of Mount Laurens – John Crook, David Sharpe and Gavin Pike (May/June 2016).
Initial objective was the first ascent of the east buttress of Mt Laurens on the Lacuna glacier. They flew into Kahiltna base camp, and started by reconnoitring potential routes. They attempted the west face of Pt10022, but found it far too warm, and conditions too dangerous for climbing at this altitude, so flew to Denali and acclimatised by climbing up to 6,000m on that mountain. They then climbed Kahiltna Queen in a single day alpine ascent, and then moved on to attempt the Infinite Spur. They reached 11,000ft, before a persistent snowstorm forced them to retreat. (Presumably this was the storm experienced by 16-16 during their descent from the Infinite Spur.)   MEF ref 16-29

GREENLAND

British Renland Expedition 2016 – Geoff Hornby, David Barlow, Rob Powell and Paul Seabrook (July/August 2016).
This expedition was to an unnamed and unexplored glacier near the Mirror Wall area of south Renland. From Iceland they flew to Constable Point and from there made a 12-hour overnight passage in a RIB (hard boat recommended for future trips) to the drop-off point and base camp. Climbs were done from an advanced base a few hours from here. Four new routes were completed, including first ascents of two mountains, Cerro Castillito and Mount Hannes. The routes were: the first ascent of Cerro Castillito by the SE ridge, 1300m at alpine AD/D; a 400m rock climb, E2 5b named *Arctic Monkeys*; *Double 00 Couloir*, an 800m snow couloir at alpine AD, and an alpine arête on mount Hannes, a new route of approximately 1,400m, Alpine TD-/TD.   MEF ref 16-25

INDIA

Nubra Valley – Derek Buckle, Andrew Cook, Michael Cocker, Gus Morton and Knut Tønsberg (August/September 2016).
The expedition acclimatised in Leh before travelling to Tirit and a three day trek to base camp at Arganglas. This is near the bifurcation of the Rassa and Phonglas glaciers, from which they planned to explore one of the southerly arms of the Rassa glacier. They established two further camps at 5,585m and 5,675m, from which Buckle and Cook made the first ascent of Pk 6222 (Lak Kangri) via its SE face at Alpine AD. The route was repeated by Cocker and Morton. The same four climbers then made the first ascent of Pk 6315 (Thrung-ma Kangri) via its S face, at Alpine D. Tønsberg unfortunately suffered a serious medical condition, and had to be evacuated to Leh, and via Delhi to home, where he made a full recovery.
                                                             MEF ref 16-06

British Sersank Expedition – Mick Fowler and Victor Saunders (September/October 2016).
Sersank (6050m) is at the head of the Sural valley in Himachal Pradesh. It was approached over the Rohtang Pass from Manali to Sural Butori, followed by a two-day trek through the Sural valley to base camp (4390m) below the South Sersank glacier. The pair spent five days climbing the N face of Sersank, and a further two days completing the route to the summit and descending to base camp via the S ridge. The route included rock buttresses covered in powder snow, steep ice climbing and easier mixed climbing, at up to Alpine ED2 and some pitches of Scottish V. They experienced poor weather during acclimatisation, but exceptionally good conditions during the ascent.   MEF ref 16-10

Jangpar Wall Expedition – Martin Moran, John Crook, Dave Sharp and Ian Dring (September/October 2016).
The main objective was to make an alpine ascent of the N spur of the unclimbed Pk 5755 in the Miyar valley in Himachal Pradesh. The approach was via Manali and the Rohtang Pass to the roadhead at Khanjar. From ABC (4320m) Moran and Dring made the first ascent of Pk 5755 (named Marakula Killa) via the N spur at Alpine ED2 and with pitches up to VIa+, and descended via the W face. Meanwhile Sharpe and Crook crossed the Kang La Pass to set up their ABC (4860m), and made the first ascent of Raja Peak (6267m) at Alpine ED2, Scottish VI, descending via the S Ridge. After returning to base camp (a round trip of 60km) they made the first ascent of James Peak (5780m) via its N face at TD-. MEF ref 16-19

Vishnugarh Darh Expedition – Susan Jensen, and Anindya 'Raja' Mukherjee (May/June 2016).
Aiming for unclimbed peaks up to 6,000m around the Panpatia glacier in Garhwal, they approached via Josimath and a two-day walk-in. Base camp was established at 3,815m and an ABC at 4,199m for acclimatisation. Soon after this camp was set up Raja started to experience breathing problems. Jensen continued reconnaissance alone up to 4765m, but as Raja's condition did not improve they decided to terminate the expedition and get medical care for him. The problem turned out to be a lung infection related to a condition during a previous expedition when he had a tapeworm in his lung. MEF ref 16-30

Gangstang 2016 – Malcolm Bass and Guy Buckingham (May/June 2016).
After permission was refused for their first objective (Rimo III) they changed target to the NW ridge of Gangstang (6163m) in the Lahaul district of Himachal Pradesh. They drove via Manali to the road head at Naingarth, then made a two-day trek to base camp. Bass and Buckingham acclimatised with the second ascent of Neelkantha (5630m), accompanied by liaison officer Parmendar Sharma. The pair then completed the ascent of the NW ridge of Gangstang over four days, 1,500m at Alpine ED1, 5a and Scottish VI. They were blessed with good weather, which meant that they could acclimatise and achieve their objectives in short order. MEF ref 16-31

NEPAL

Khumbu Glacier 2016 – Cameron Scott Watson, Owen King and Darren Jones (May/June 2016).
This was the second of a series of three campaigns studying supraglacial pond development and melt at ice cliffs on the debris covered Khumbu glacier. An ascent of Lobuche East (6090m) gave them a good vantage point over the Khumbu glacier. They completed 11 photographic surveys of ice cliffs, which will be processed to generate 3D point clouds, from which melt data can be calculated. They surveyed 19 supraglacial ponds to derive

area-volume relationships, enabling the estimation of surface water storage from satellite images.   MEF ref 16-01

Khumbu New Routing – Will Harris and Jon Gupta (October/November 2015).
The original objectives were to attempt an unclimbed line on Pharilapcha N face and a secondary target of Chhuphu in the Thame valley. They acclimatised on Lobuche East, and then, finding the N face of Phalirapcha in poor condition, attempted a route on Kangshung (6061m). Here they were thwarted by unseasonable and unstable new snow. Next they tried the unclimbed NE face and north ridge of Kyajo Ri (6186m), reaching 5900m before a dropped rucksack forced retreat. They found some compensation with good icefall climbing in the Machhermo Khola. They were unable to attempt their secondary target of Chhuphu because of permit problems.
                                                                MEF ref 16-02

British Services Dhaulagiri Medical Research Expedition – Adrian Mellor, John O'Hara, David Woods, Matthew Barlow, and Mark Cooke (April/May 2016).
This was part of a much larger joint-services expedition to the Dhaulagiri region, and involved the establishment of mechanisms associated with the development of acute mountain sickness (AMS), and assessing the effectiveness of pre-acclimatisation strategies in reducing the occurrence of AMS. The occurrence of AMS among the military deployed at high altitude can affect military performance. A total of 129 personnel took part in the expedition, and were invited to consent to a variety of studies investigating adaptation to high altitude and diagnosis of altitude illness.
                                                                MEF ref 16-03

British Chamlang 2016 – Andy Houseman, Jon Griffith (April/May 2016)
An attempt on the first ascent of the unclimbed N ridge of Chamlang (7319m). They started with an ascent of Ama Dablam by the normal SW ridge route. This was a work project, but provided perfect acclimatisation for Chamlang. The whole Everest region was very dry, and the view from Ama Dablam was not promising, with bare rock where there should have been névé. Consideration of options for the approach to Chamlang led them to opt for a helicopter, for reasons of cost as well as time. Conditions on the N ridge of Chamlang were very poor, and the forecast weather window failed to materialise; there was consistent snow from lunchtime every day. They made a brief tentative attempt on the route, but judging conditions were too dangerous they aborted the attempt at about 5,800m.   MEF ref 16-18

TIBET

British West Nainqentanglha Expediton – Paul Ramsden and Nick Bullock (September/October 2016)
The initial objective was the N buttress of Naiqentanglha Feng (7162m) in the West Nyainqentanglha range, to the NW of Lhasa. Their approach was from a road head between Damshung and Guangbajian, and involved a one-day walk in to base camp at 5000m using ponies. Although the original objective was on the main peak, exploration along the N face revealed a hidden face with a huge buttress on the N side of Nainqentanglha SE, which only became visible when they were directly below it. They decided to make this their target instead. Heavy snow halted their first attempt, when their tent almost blew away. Returning after a few days, they started ploughing through deep snow to an uncomfortable bivouac. A steep rock band with enough ice runnels allowed progress to the next bivouac. Further progress up a ridge led to more deep snow, finally summiting on day five. They started their descent down the E ridge with difficulty in poor conditions; these improved the following day.   MEF ref 16-07

PAKISTAN

Gulmit Tower expedition – Peter Thompson and Aiden Laffey (June 2016). An attempted first ascent of Gulmit Tower (5810m) in the Hunza region of Pakistan, via the E face and SE ridge. The approach was by road from Gilgit to Gulmit village with base camp at 4,100m.The attempt on Gulmit Tower was abandoned when a major rockfall hit their camp at 4,480m, and no other suitable safe site could be identified. They moved to the nearby Moorkhun valley and attempted the first ascent of Pregar (6026m) by the S face. Their first attempt reached 5,500m before being stopped by crevasses, and in a further attempt from a bivouac at 5,075m Thompson was within 20m of the summit when he was turned back by dangerous snow conditions.   MEF ref 16-24

CENTRAL ASIA

Alichursky Mountains Ski Expedition – Alex Reid, Derek Buckle, Anna Bushe and Stefan Jachmich (April 2016).
Exploration of the North Alichursky region of the Tajikistan Pamirs in the vicinity of the Bazar-Dara Pass, visiting remote unexplored side valleys, and unclimbed mountains near the Bazar-Dara lake. After being responsible for organising the expedition, Alex Reid was unable to take part and Derek Buckle took over leadership. The team flew to Osh in Kyrgyzstan, and drove via Sary-Tash and the Kyzlart Pass into Tajikistan and the town of Alichur. Three camps were established at 4,057m, 4,349m and 4,525m, and these were used for exploration over 14 days. From camp two Jachmich soloed Pk4982m via its S ridge, almost entirely on skis, and named it Pik

Perestroika. From camp three all three explored a side valley, and Buckle and Jachmich skinned up the S face of Pk 4918m to an awkward traverse to a rocky summit at Alpine PD. They named this Pk Glasnost. Returning to camp two the party skinned to a col (4856m), from which Buckle and Jachmich climbed Pk 5021m, and named it Pik Druzhba. At camp one they found snow cover had deteriorated, and they left for home.

MEF ref 16-08

Djenghi-Djer Expedition Kyrgyzstan – Struan Chisholm, Calum Nicholl, Sandy Fowler, Sam Newmark, Mark Chonofsky and Neil Smith (July/ August 2016).
Exploration and climbing in unexplored valleys in the Djenghi-Djer mountain range in SE Kyrgyzstan. Travelling was by horseback for reasons of speed and flexibility: only one of the participants had previous riding experience. They travelled by taxi from Bishkek to Kara-say via Tamga, and here picked up their horses: one each plus four for the baggage. They rode west to their first base camp in the east of the range. They then set up a series of three further base camps along the north side of the range, the furthest 80km from Kara-say, and generally about one hour from the start of their peaks. Climbing in pairs they made five ascents, four believed firsts. These were Mt Trident (4436m), Mt Stann Chonofsky (4412m), An Trus (4168m), Clachan Niall (4135m) and Pointsystem (4157m). Routes were generally PD or AD, with one D. They identified numerous more unclimbed peaks.

MEF ref 16-15

QUBMC Kaindy Expedition – Owen Largey, Stephen Rooney, Michael Campbell, Kevin Cheing, Thomas O'Hagen, Matthew Boyd, Kora Przybyzewska, Aleksey Przbyzewska and Vladimir Zholobenko (August 2016).
New routes and unclimbed peaks from the basin of the Kaindy glacier, south of the Inylchek glacier in central Tien Shan. They flew to Bishkek, travelled by road via Karakol to Maydaadyr, and from there by helicopter to base camp. After several days of heavy snow they were able to explore side valleys and establish higher camps. Successful ascents were made of Peak Oskal by the W face (A Przbyzewska, O'Hagen, Largey, Rooney and Campbell), and Peak Svyatoye Mesto (A Przbyzewska, Boyd, O'Hagen and K Przbyzewska). Several other peaks were attempted, but abandoned, usually due to unfavourable conditions.   MEF ref 16-21

Jiptik 2016 – John Proctor, Robert Taylor, Ciaran Mullen and Phil Dawson (July 2016).
An attempt on the unclimbed N face of Muz Tok (5066m), part of the Pamir Alai range in SW Kyrgyzstan, and with three other unclimbed peaks as possible secondary objectives. The approach was from Osh to the road head at Sary Zhaz via Batken by 4WD, followed by a two and a half day walk to base camp. After acclimatisation a number of attempts on Muz Tok failed early on due to bad weather and poor climbing conditions.

A further attempt was made by Proctor and Taylor, and they succeeded in climbing the face of the pyramid which jutted out of Muz Tok to the North, but were unable to surmount the short final headwall that linked this to the true summit. They descended by abseil down the ascent route. Taylor and Mullen each separately climbed a subsidiary peak of Kara-Eet. The three secondary objectives remain unclimbed.   MEF ref 16-22

Tortoisebutler Kyrgyzstan Expedition 2016 – Miles Gould and Andy Vine (August 2016).
First ascents of peaks surrounding the Kindyk valley, Kuiluu massif, Kyrgyzstan. They flew to Bishkek, and continued by road via Karakol to the Kuiluu valley. They established base camp (3200m) in the Kindyk valley and an ABC at 3,800m. Over the next week they made the first ascents of four peaks: Pk 4605m, Pk 4714m, Pk 4554m, Pk 4444m, all at Alpine PD or AD. Further possibilities were identified.   MEF ref 16-27

Reviews

High Tor, Matlock
Henry Moore (1898-1986)
Undated. Watercolour and graphite on medium, slightly textured, cream wove
paper. 13⅞ x 20⅜ inches. Yale Center for British Art, Paul Mellon Collection.

Reviews

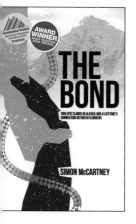

The Bond
Simon McCartney
Vertebrate Publishing, 2016, pp346, £24

Simon McCartney is a lucky man. The 'bond' of the title of this absorbing tale is that commitment often referred to as 'the brotherhood of the rope'. There is, you'll realise, an element of tribal conceit here: the unfathomable depth of altruism that prompts humans to imperil life and limb for the sake of others, often strangers, is by no means peculiar to climbers. But whatever, the image of the rope, linking those climbing brothers forever in existential struggle goes beyond metaphor when on a mountain. And Simon McCartney stretched that rope to a very tenuous thread indeed.

It is well towards the end of the book before McCartney acknowledges what has been apparent to the reader for some time: were it not for 'the bond' this cocky young man would be dead. He is alive thanks to the goodness of partners, strangers and the rescue services of Switzerland and Alaska. That McCartney disappeared from the climbing scene for 30 years after his denouement on Denali probably has a good deal to do with shame. He certainly admits to such a feeling in the immediate aftermath of his last ordeal.

McCartney has also benefited from a big stroke of luck as an author. The two most important players in the Alaskan dramas that form the meat of *The Bond* – partner Jack Roberts and good Samaritan Bob Kandiko – both kept excellent diaries. Chunky extracts from these provide a lot of the real-time climbing detail, insights and anguish that enrich McCartney's story.

Mark Westman, the embodied encyclopaedia of Alaskan climbing, describes McCartney and Roberts's first ascents of the hazardous north face of Mount Huntington and the massive south-west face of Denali as 'the greatest story never told in the annals of Alaskan climbing literature.' Westman too played a big part in bringing the book about, not least piecing together details of the route on the south-west face for those days when McCartney's throbbing head was elsewhere.

McCartney quit climbing following the Denali epic in 1980, settled in Australia and eventually became a successful businessman, in architectural lighting, in Hong Kong. In cruel irony Jack Roberts fell to his death from frozen Bridal Veil Falls at Telluride in 2012 just as McCartney had tracked him down through the internet and was looking forward to making contact after decades of unknowing.

Pam Roberts, Jack's widow, became another friend and ally in piecing together the story that was to become *The Bond*. Indeed by now McCartney was rediscovering a bond, becoming part of the climbing community once again. Heartened, he was then able to track down Bob Kandiko who, for me, emerges as the true hero of this extraordinary tale.

So far I've deliberately peppered this review with tasters but precious little detail of the Alaskan climbs as such and nothing at all about other locations – the Eiger, Mont Blanc, Yosemite, Cheddar even – or characters such as Dave Wilkinson and Smiler Cuthbertson that feature here. That's for you to discover.

Even so, I'd like to ruminate a little longer on Bob Kandiko, still adventuring from his home in Washington State, who led McCartney back to life in a gruelling descent of the Cassin ridge. McCartney describes it neatly:

> *The nightmare Jack and I had on the descent of Mount Huntington is being relived, this time with Bob. The same game is afoot: a first ascent, followed by a descent of a classic route. I am seeing a lot of quality Alaskan climbing in spontaneous disasters.*

Was the disaster on Denali so spontaneous? Only a couple of days into the climb McCartney suffered headaches and nausea. He'd had altitude problems before. Was awareness of acute mountains sickness that much less in 1980, or was youthful ambition over riding common sense? By day 11 McCartney is helpless, though somehow, with great perseverance from Roberts, who has frostbite, they've climbed the face and reached the upper part of the Cassin.

Enter Kandiko, climbing the ridge with fellow American Mike Helms. He volunteers to look after McCartney. As wind and snow batter the tent, and without food for days, Kandiko reflects gloomily on his decision to forsake summit and safety to help a total stranger:

> *I had deep, fond thoughts of my family and how tragic the scene would be to die in these frozen heights without seeing them again. Why was I here? I could go over the top by myself and leave Simon but my humanity wouldn't allow it. He was a dead man unless we got some assistance. Is it courageous to choose to die?*

Fortunately Kandiko is addicted to life. And so too must be some inner depth of McCartney. Though at his worst he is unable to take more than three steps at a time, weeps like a child and accidentally pees over the inside of the tent and Kandiko, his body defies what seems an inevitable total collapse. As the incredulous surgeon at Providence hospital, Anchorage, tells McCartney later: 'Climbers with cerebral oedema who continue to ascend usually die.'

So *The Bond* is the story of a very lucky man, of a climbing partnership pushed to estrangement, and of heartening humanity and self-sacrifice.

Quite a combination. No wonder that Simon McCartney – the arrogance of youth long shed – carried off the 2016 Boardman Tasker Award for Mountain Literature.

Stephen Goodwin

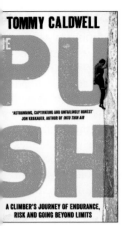

The Push
A Climber's Journey of Endurance, Risk, and Going Beyond Limits
Tommy Caldwell
Michael Joseph, 2017, pp352, £20

The best climbing books often tell us about other things than climbing. They lift the lid on life, even if it is a life that revolves almost exclusively – as Tommy Caldwell's does – around climbing.

Caldwell needs little introduction. His Yosemite big wall ascents – not least his free ascent with Kevin Jorgeson of the Dawn Wall, which fixated international media attention – is only rivalled by his kidnapping with a group of US climbers on a expedition to Kyrgyzstan which led to Caldwell, in extremis, pushing one of his abductors off a cliff to what Caldwell believed was the man's death.

There you have it. The push: a play on words that goes to the core of Caldwell's memoir. It encapsulates the interwoven themes of that moment when he thought he had killed another human being but also the impetus behind his climbing, and finally the push itself on the Dawn Wall.

It is not always comfortable reading. In an era when elite, and non-elite climbing, has become mediatised by video and Instagram feeds, to present an idealised picture of top-end climbing, like the endless summer of first surfing films, Caldwell suggests the worm in the apple.

Caldwell leaves little out of his account, even at the risk of portraying himself in an unflattering light: in the depiction of his failed relationship with Beth Rodden; in the unkind letter written to his father; even his uneasy relationship with Kevin Jorgeson as they try the Dawn Wall over seven years.

And oddly, for a book about climbing, it is the story of Caldwell and Rodden's relationship that is the most striking, of two elite climbers, unequal in their love for each other, thrown together by the fatal and life-altering events in Kyrgyzstan.

Rodden has described her own side of the story that chimes with Caldwell's insecurity around their relationship. 'I was realizing that, for me at least, the romantic part wasn't really there,' she wrote in a long piece for *Outside* earlier this year describing how they prepared for the fatal trip that would lead to the kidnapping.

'A week before we left, at the North Face's corporate headquarters, I tried to break up with Tommy. I told him I thought we should just stick to being friends and climbing partners. He laid his dirty-blond head on the floor. Neither of us was particularly strong and brave about emotions. He asked if we could please just go on the trip and see how we did. I hated conflict. I said yes. I was 20 years old, and Tommy was 21.'

What would emerge, after the disastrous trip to Kyrgyzstan, judging by Caldwell's account, would be an excruciating co-dependency as Rodden struggled with symptoms of something like PTSD.

'One minute Beth was crying,' writes Caldwell, 'then she would be trembling in fear or staring blankly out the window. She felt certain that the IMU [the group that kidnapped them] was going to hunt us down ... I had the discomfiting sensation that as bad as the abduction had been, it had finite starting and end points. How long was our recovery going to take?'

Through it all and beyond, through Rodden's affair that will split them up, the couple continue climbing, not always joyously, sometimes almost obsessively.

For Caldwell it is something that not only motivates but helps him through the hardest times, not least his pursuit of free ascents of Yosemite's big walls. Until it doesn't.

After the break up of his relationship with Rodden and the rupture with his father he finds himself on the Dawn Wall. 'In the past I'd always experienced an overarching sense of connection while on El Cap. But this time I felt estranged from the world ... For the first time in my life climbing felt self-glorifying, even pointless.'

Losing a finger in a carpentry accident that threatens to end his climbing career, Caldwell evokes something of what had driven him for so long up to that point.

'Had I done something to deserve this? I was so used to living a life bound by this equation: Effort equals results. Luck didn't play a part in climbing. You got what you deserved. Did I deserve this?'

Then it strikes you. So many books about climbing evoke, or try to evoke, the intimacy of the rope, Forster's admonition to 'only connect.' Caldwell has a subtly different story to tell, often underlined by either a lack of intimacy or a shortfall: the distances between even in the midst of climbing a big wall.

His relationship with Jorgeson has echoes, sometimes explicitly described, of his relationship with Rodden, as they try to piece together the Dawn Wall, conscious of their differences, of a different level of commitment. Despite being a professional climber himself, Caldwell is bothered at one point as Jorgeson talks about climbing as a 'business'.

> Then one day Kevin made a comment that made me squirm. 'Wouldn't it be badass if the first route I climbed on El Cap was the Dawn Wall.' Suddenly I wondered if Kevin was really interested in learning, or if the Dawn Wall was merely an avenue to gain recognition and up his value as a professional athlete.
>
> When Beth and I divorced, I bitterly thought that her attraction to me might have had to do with creating a desirable career path than actual love. Was

Kevin using me the same way? Or was he just becoming collateral damage from the baggage of my failed marriage? After all, in a sense I was also using him.

It is the honesty, coaxed out of Caldwell by co-writer Kelly Cordes, who Caldwell describes as confidant, therapist and best friend that distinguishes *The Push*. In a pursuit where egotism, self-doubt, obsession and competition are sometimes brushed under the carpet, Caldwell is not afraid to confront head on what some might see as his own personal shortcomings and put them under the spotlight. And in the end he grows through it, learning how to love in a different way and becoming a father. Finding a place, at last, that he feels comfortable to call home.

Peter Beaumont

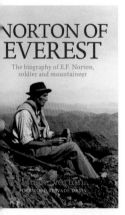

Norton of Everest
The Biography of E F Norton
Hugh Norton
Vertebrate Publishing, 2017, pp181, £13

Edward 'Teddy' Norton was a stalwart among mountaineers; this tribute to him by his son, Hugh, gives wider perspective to his life beyond the Everest attempts in 1922 and 1924 and the dramatic shadow cast by the disappearance of Mallory and Irvine. He emerges as a willowy, six-foot-four-inch professional soldier with no acknowledged skills as a climber but with phenomenal stamina, natural leadership qualities and a dry sense of humour; toughness and determination demonstrated by reaching more than 28,000ft on Everest without bottled oxygen, a record that remained unbeaten for 27 years, and by surviving every major battle of the First World War during which he was three times mentioned in dispatches for bravery and awarded the Military Cross.

Norton was born in Argentina where his father was a successful investor in shipping. An early enthusiasm for mountains was encouraged by Alfred Wills, his maternal grandfather, a founder of the Alpine Club and conspicuous as the judge who sentenced Oscar Wilde to two years' hard labour for gross indecency, a man remembered for his austere integrity. Norton and his formidable grandparent made guided ascents from their summer home near Sixt in the French Alps but his was a relatively thin record to justify a place on an expedition that would carry such national prestige.

Hugh Norton describes how after an unhappy time at public school his father rejected academe and opted for a career in the army. Aged 16 he sat the entrance exam for the Royal Military Academy at Woolwich. A commission in the Royal Field Artillery followed with service in Ireland and seven years to postings in India where he transferred to the Royal Horse Artillery, the elite wing of the gunners, which allowed him a colourful

The talented Messrs Norton.

full-dress uniform jacket. It amused him on one ceremonial occasion when he turned up in full lieutenant-general fig, an elderly lady, thinking he was from the Salvation Army, pressed a coin into his hand and whispered 'for the cause'.

His time in India saw the Raj in full swing and Norton with his battery commander shared a passion for big game hunting, fishing and pig sticking, the sport of slaughtering wild boars that were a menace to crops by spearing them from horseback. Occasionally the wild life fought back and he narrowly missed being caught by three male boars he had failed to shoot. They were four yards off his heels and catching up so he swung round a tree trunk and the notoriously short-sighted pursuers cantered past. Alongside these soldierly activities Norton also developed gentler pursuits of painting in watercolours and noting and observing a wide spectrum of natural history, all of which became a life long passion.

Thus far Norton's activities as a sportsman had featured more prominently than his work as a professional soldier, but the 12 years of 'honeymoon' as a lieutenant were about to end with the First World War and four and a half years of continuous action in France in every major battle, with the artillery at times closely involved in the thick of the fighting. In the German offensive of March 1918 Edward and his brother Dick were serving in adjoining batteries when Dick was killed in action. There was little time then to mourn. Edward commanded his battery of guns with distinction and post-war became a student at the staff college at Camberley: an essential precursor to reaching high rank. The invitation to Everest then arrived 'as a funny little slice out of my life' but also as a 'crowning glory' of his enduring fascination with mountains. Any concern that an eight-month absence from military duty might jeopardise his career proved unnecessary. He stuck to his belief that no game was ever worth a rap for a rational man to play into which no accident, no mishap, could possibly find its way. While not actually courting danger, he liked 'to get a good fright.'

In 1922 Everest obliged. The route had been reconnoitred the previous year, but now the base camp was swept throughout the day by freezing, blistering winds. Three weeks were spent surmounting the North Col and establishing camps for a summit attempt. Mallory, Norton and Somervell reached just under 27,000ft without oxygen. A second attempt by Finch and Geoffrey Bruce, using oxygen, reached 27,500ft, but as they descended from the North Col an avalanche swept seven porters to their death.

Norton returned two years later and that attempt, leading to the loss of Mallory and Irvine, and Norton's heroic climb without oxygen to 28,126ft, have been well recorded, not least in Norton's own account *The Fight for Everest 1924*. It was an epic fight, with Norton taking over the leadership. He and Mallory had already rescued four Sherpa porters trapped by heavy snowfall at the North Col. In the next push for the summit Norton climbed on alone towards what became known as the Norton Couloir after Somervell turned back, suffocated by his own swollen throat. Hugh Norton records the great distress the loss of Mallory and Irvine caused his father who was convinced that their deaths resulted from a climbing accident and not from any determination to press on regardless of the consequences. Norton resisted much of the praise and invitations from the climbing establishment that followed and he did not go on to attempt a string of other great Himalayan or Alpine climbs. According to Hugh Norton, his father remained first and foremost a soldier. Mountaineering was not for him an end in itself, but a highly enjoyable pastime, to be savoured whenever possible in his leisure time.

At this point and with a third of his story still to come, Norton, aged 41, married Joyce Pasteur, aged 25, and a shade short of 5ft 9in. They shared a keen interest in horse riding and similar build, but whilst Joyce played the piano well and had studied at the Royal College of Music, Edward was tone deaf.

Norton was posted as a general staff officer at the War Office, the family moved to London and their first son, Dick, was born. They engaged a young live-in 'Nannie' who stayed with the family for 28 years and followed them throughout their travels. For Edward, appointments followed to what became the Royal College for Defence Studies and a course for handpicked high flyers, rapidly rising from student to senior instructor, taking the change in his stride. Promotion to major-general came with command of the Madras District in southern India, which involved ceremonial and social duties. Among them was a visit to the Nandidroog gold mine at Kolar, reputed to be the deepest in the world, thus giving him the distinction of being the first human to have stood at two points on earth separated by the greatest vertical distance in altitude. He told this to an audience of schoolboys, adding that whilst the mine had a lift to take him to the depths, Mount Everest lacked a similar amenity.

Hugh Norton provides a fine account of his father's extraordinary life from modest mountaineering hero to high-flying professional soldier and acting governor of Hong Kong. A thoroughly excellent read.

Ronald Faux

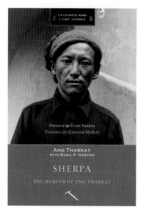

Sherpa: The Memoir of Ang Tharkay
With Basil P Norton
Translated by Corrine McKay
Mountaineers Books, 2016, pp192, £17

Before Tenzing Norgay's meteoric rise to a fame that endures today, Ang Tharkay was perhaps the best known of the Sherpas, not least for his role as sirdar in the 1950 ascent of Annapurna. Before that he worked on four Everest expeditions in the 1930s and was a much-admired hired hand for the mountain explorations of Eric Shipton and Bill Tilman. The latter described him as 'a sort of Jeeves, Admirable Crichton, and Napoleon rolled into one,' a judgement some might dismiss as a little patronising and written to meet the expectations of his audience, but is actually shrewder than it looks: Crichton takes over in the wilderness, Jeeves regards his employer as a naïve dimwit to be gently steered and Ang Tharkay, not a tall man, could be a towering, even despotic figure in a bad mood, and one who wouldn't back down easily.

For those, therefore, with an interest in the history of the Sherpas, both as an ethnic group and as mountaineers, this book is unearthed treasure from a lost age, a glimpse of a world that has passed about which we know far less than we might like or indeed should. Mountaineers Books and those enthusiasts around the project should be congratulated on bringing this book to wider attention, winkling it out from the dusty shelves of obscure libraries.

But how far should we trust it? First published in 1954 in French, and nowhere else until this welcome first edition in English, it was necessarily ghosted, by Basil P Norton, a man about whom we know next to nothing. Writing Tenzing's biography, and having laboriously read his book in French, I looked hard and ultimately almost in vain for any trace of him, hoping to find his manuscript in English to judge how much it differed from the published version. (One researcher has even speculated that Basil P Norton was actually Eric Shipton.)

Norton himself acknowledges that Ang Tharkay had no English or French and he had no Nepali. Norton did have some Hindi, but since Ang Tharkay's own Hindi, his third language, was limited, they conversed through an interpreter, one Mohan Lal Mukerjee. And so we have a book ghosted through an interpreter, written in English, translated into French (by Henri Delgove, who also translated Alan Sillitoe and Upton Sinclair) and then translated back into English, by Corinne McKay; it's a book that also draws heavily on sources the subject of the book would not have known: Christoph von Fürer Haimendorf, for example, an anthropologist who is viewed more equivocally in modern Nepal than he once was. 'This is a sincere, unaltered story,' Norton tells us. Sincere it may be: unaltered it is not.

Why does this matter? One example: in a famous moment in Himalayan mountaineering, at the French high camp on Annapurna, Maurice Herzog, a man referred to in this book, somewhat ominously, as 'the great leader', offers Ang Tharkay the chance to come with him to the summit. This is what Ang Tharkay says:

> 'Excuse me, Bara Sahib,' I said to him pitifully. 'But I am not worthy of this great task. I am profoundly grateful to you for the honor you have given me, and in all my life I will never forget this moment. Allow me to return to Camp IV-A, and may God protect you, you and the valiant Lachenal Sahib!'

Compare this Uriah Heep-like speech to Herzog's own account of the exchange, in *Annapurna*, which, as Herzog explains, was conducted in basic English.

> 'Thank you very much, Bara Sahib, but my feet are beginning to freeze …'
> 'I see.'
> '… and I prefer to go down to Camp IV.'

These two accounts are roughly similar, as you would expect, given that Norton clearly read Herzog. Yet the difference in tone is revealing: why did

Ang Tharkay speak 'pitifully'? He was anything but as a man. And why has such a convoluted, ingratiating speech been put into the mouth of someone at extreme altitude who speaks little English? It is certainly not the true voice of Ang Tharkay. There's an agenda here, and it's one unconnected, I suspect, to the life of this exceptional Sherpa. It might be instructive to compare the original English manuscript with the published French one, but we can't do that, as we don't have it.

If whose story this is isn't always clear, the book is still a valuable trove of detail about Ang Tharkay's life. The earlier sections in particular, those parts that aren't simply Norton's version of Sherpa anthropological learning, are revelatory. Although their origins are subtly different, both Tenzing and Ang Tharkay came from impoverished backgrounds, a familiar pattern even now: those Sherpas with means don't need their children to be climbing for a living. Tenzing's family had known status but lost their position; Ang Tharkay's was simply dirt poor. His mother was Tibetan, and Ang Tharkay spent a portion of his childhood in Tibet living with his aunt because his parents didn't have enough to support him, a period he regarded as idyllic. As a young teenager, he was working as a day labourer to help meet his father's debts, taken on during a period of ill health. The fragility of living standards in the high mountains is one of the many lessons of this book.

Ang Tharkay's life changed, as it did for so many Sherpas and Bhotias, when he discovered Darjeeling's bright lights. It wasn't just the relative sophistication; here was a world where a humbly born young man, away from the stratified society of his homeland, could, with a bit of gumption, advance his stars, which is precisely what Ang Tharkay did. Stripping out the context and borrowed narrative of his ghost or French translator, these sections of the book are the most moving, revealing glimpses of a high-altitude world, of cultural kinship, of trade, of religion, that is priceless. There are glimpses too of Sherpa life on the road, familiar to anyone who has explored remote places with them. I especially enjoyed the Annapurna team's puzzlement at their rapidly disappearing wine cellar.

The publisher has included explanatory notes, which are immensely useful if occasionally wayward: Tenzing was not born in Thame, and most likely not in 1917, for example. There is a list of Ang Tharkay's expeditions, useful for his post-1954 life, and a quietly affecting note from his son Dawa about his later life. 'Forget about going to the mountains as a Sherpa on expeditions,' he told Dawa. 'Life as a Sherpa is not a joke. It is real hard and you would not earn a good salary.' At least climbing was there to stave off the ever-present threat of extreme poverty long enough to give Dawa that chance. But you feel that the debt owed to men like Ang Tharkay was never fully met.

Ed Douglas

1865
The Golden Age of Mountaineering
Gilles Modica
Translated by Deke Dusinberre
Vertebrate Publishing & Editions Paulsen, 2016,
pp400, £39

We British have always understood that we invented
the game of alpinism, and that those who did so
during the so-called Golden Age were the same
chaps who in 1857 formed the Alpine Club. While the AC was indeed the
world's first such organisation, the invention of alpinism by our founding
fathers is by no means the complete story. This excellent, superbly illustrated
book looks in considerable detail at the Golden Age, the years 1856 to 1865,
at its leading protagonists and their doings, having first examined the lead-
up to those years over the proceeding century. Unusually it is written from
a European perspective.

Not only is the author a much-published journalist specialising in the
history of mountaineering – his research has been exhaustive – but as a
member of the GHM with a proud international climbing record, his
personal experience of the subject is monumental. French he may be, but
he's obviously an anglophile, giving credit where credit is due, while the
translation is excellent and usually idiomatic, with but few literals.

Before the Golden Age it was mostly the Swiss who were the pre-eminent
peak-baggers, and not always for the sake of science. Between 1744, when
monks from Engelberg Abbey climbed Titlis, and 1865 Swiss travellers
claimed more than fifty summits of more than 3,000m. But then 'the
English turned [it] into a game played for fun, devoid of scientific purpose.'

The titles of the 23 chapters will give some idea of the ground covered,
each one seen by the author as a sort of stepping stone in the development
of what eventually became known, with the arrival of those English, as
alpinism. Although chapter one covers 'Early Ascents' and chapter two
'James Forbes and Albert Smith', the subjects follow in logical, if not necessarily chronological order. Chapter four, for instance, covers the chequered
early history of the Chamonix guides, who in the years before the Golden
Age operated a closed shop and strict rota on Mont Blanc, and were occasionally prone to abandoning their protégés high on the mountain, leaving
them to attempt the summit on their own. Later the author traces the advent
of guideless climbing to the first ascent of Mont Blanc du Tacul and the
subsequent first ascent of Mont Blanc from St Gervais by Hudson's party in
1855, when guides from both flanks of the mountain refused to accompany
them. Hudson later wrote 'We have ourselves found guides to be an encum-
brance rather than an assistance,' an ironic statement considering the events
of ten years later.

Indeed, chapter seven is devoted to Charles Hudson, of whom it was
said, 'He's as good as a guide,' and surely one of the most important figures

Above and opposite: 1865: the triumph and tragedy. John Ruskin's perspective on the Matterhorn from 2 August 1849 and Gustave Doré's vision of the first descent, the dramatic climax to the Golden Age.

of the Golden Age. The following chapter is entitled 'The Alpine Club', and apparently from its inception, the AC was highly regarded by European climbers. In 1872 – by which time the Club had some 300 members – the French philosopher Hippolyte Taine pronounced '… difficulty, trouble and danger are incentives. Many English take delight in … forcing themselves to surmount obstacles. The Alpine Club is proof of this.' Unlike the mass-membership continental clubs, which subsequently appeared, election to the AC depended on a climbing qualification, which of course it still does. Nevertheless rare exceptions are still made for those making major contributions to mountain literature or art, first of whom was the Romantic traveller John Ruskin, who having expressed disgust at the 'acrobatics and unseemly antics' of AC members, found himself elected to membership in 1869 on the strength of his essay 'Of Mountain Beauty'.

More meaty chapters follow: 'Conquering the Weisshorn', 'John Tyndall', 'Shaggy Natives' and 'Gentlemen Travellers'. We learn how crystal gatherers and chamois hunters gradually morphed into guides and then professional mountaineers, we read what shoes they wore and why, anticipating the advent of the PA by often climbing with bare feet rubbed with resin. We read what sustenance they preferred on the hill and how fresh chamois blood was a sure cure for altitude sickness. Several pages cover the development and use of first the plain *bâton* or staff, then the alpenstock – actually quite a useful bit of kit if used intelligently – and then of the

ice axe itself, finally giving Hamish MacInnes credit for the first all-metal axe. Nailing patterns are discussed and the use of – or lack of – ropes and belays. London-made manila rope, as made for the Royal Navy, was much prized, ideally in hundred foot lengths at half-inch diameter. The guides' own ropes, typically of Italian hemp and likely to have been used around the farm, were not to be trusted.

Individual chapters on Stephen, Tuckett and Moore follow, and abound in further fascinating insights: here is Moore cogently arguing against artificial aids, fixed ropes, ladders and even huts, and Tuckett amassing a total of a thousand climbs by the age of 57. Especially illuminating are the various discourses on pedestrianism. While appreciating that our forebears were, of necessity, great walkers, the speed of the regular shuttles between Zermatt and Chamonix that the pioneering alpinists seemed to accomplish has always seemed to be exaggerated. But here is Whymper himself, aged 17, pounding along at 5mph for 27 miles without a pause. A full-page map illustrates his incredible, convoluted itinerary back and forth between Lauterbrunnen, Zinal, Zermatt, Chatillon, Courmayeur, Chamonix, Aosta, Breuil and Zermatt again, via summit after summit and pass after pass, during the hectic four weeks of his 1865 campaign. Years later, on the eve of his expedition to Ecuador at the age of 40, he was still timed at 5½mph over seven miles. It seems that Hudson too was a great pedestrian, a 50 miles a day man who once walked from Geneva to St Gervais and back, a distance of 82 miles, in under 24 hours. A good walker today is pleased to reach 3¾mph carrying a light sack on flat ground.

The book progresses towards the race for, and eventual ascent of the Matterhorn. The complete story of the many attempts is contained within no less than five chapters, but unlike other masterful accounts of that particular campaign – notably Whymper's own book and Alan Lyall's *The First Descent of the Matterhorn* – that successful yet fateful climb is seen here in perspective with another climb made on Mont Blanc the very next day.

The 'Brenva Spur' is the final chapter. It covers an ascent the author considers of even greater importance than that of the Matterhorn. A line 60 years ahead of its time, the 'Old Brenva' was a glimpse into the future in both concept and difficulty. Himalayan in style, it was, claims the author, the greatest exploit of the Golden Age, 'yet the least well known to the general public, that ignorant vulture who has feasted on the corpses of the Matterhorn for these past 150 years.' That's fighting talk, yet those of us who have intimate knowledge of both climbs are likely to agree.

For any serious student of mountaineering this handsome volume is not only a fascinating, enlightening and entertaining read but an essential source of reference: useful appendices repeat Coolidge's 1913 list of the major Alpine first ascents between 1358 (Rochemelon) and 1907 (Dames Anglaises) and include a table detailing the 65 important first ascents of 1865 that rounded off the Golden Age. Many of the prolific, beautifully reproduced illustrations – paintings, engravings, sketches, photographs and maps – were new to me and are thankfully so placed so as to complement the adjacent text. This lavish book was a great pleasure both to handle and read; congratulations are due to Vertebrate for bringing it to the English-speaking reader.

John Cleare

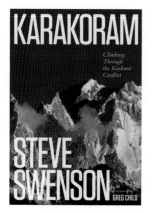

Karakoram: Climbing through the Kashmir Conflict
Steve Swenson
Mountaineers Books, 2017, pp315, £20

If a civil engineer could play God and be given the chance to construct a major mountain range, and if that engineer happened to be Steve Swenson, then I suspect that range would be the Karakoram. Over a period of nearly 40 years, Swenson has made many, many remarkable climbs in the Karakoram, seeking out well know mountains such as K2 and Gasherbrum IV, but also uncovering and exploring 'blanks on the maps' among the twisting complexities of glacier and river valleys that bind the range together. In those difficult to access corners he has uncovered an untouched architecture of granite faces and spires such as the south-west face of Saser Kangri II and the spectacular Changi Tower. His dramatic ascent of the former on his second attempt nearly killed him, but it was awarded a Piolets d'Or. Swenson knows the Karakoram intimately, and through the meticulously chronicled detail of each expedition, the range has become a giant mirror revealing his persistence, strength, mountaineering acuity while at the same time some very human foibles.

There are over 30 expeditions recorded in this book, but it is much more than opportunities for first ascents that have drawn Steve Swenson back to the region so many times. Two complementary themes run strongly through many of the chapters in the book to reveal his interests both in people and politics. The first theme is that of friendship and an examination of exactly what that means: the need for trust, understanding and mutual care and respect. For Steve, that embraces all the team: climbers, porters, LOs and base camp staff. His long term relationship with his cook Rasool and his family from Hushe is well told and includes visits from Steve's own family to Rasool's Pakistan, and support and care for the health and education of Rasool's children.

He examines his relationship with his climbing partners with a keen eye for the need for the right team. This ensures safety and efficiency. He writes honestly and openly about his partners, analysing the chances of success on their strengths and weaknesses. As the years pass and Steve's age advances, he begins to invite ever younger partners. He continues to achieve some remarkable ascents with these young guns, while he reciprocates with mentoring, exceptional hard work as part of the team and excellent expedition management. Steve describes this as 'passing the torch', and no doubt there are many who feel indebted to Steve. His expedition leadership and personal management skills are perfectly described by his friend Greg Child: 'while all around him could get wound up or possessed by their neuroses, Steve remained calm and objective. He was a bit like a counsellor acting on behalf of the mountain, which needed climbers to keep sane if they were to climb it.' It worked in 1990 when with Child he made oxygen-less ascent of the north ridge of K2.

This is the Steve Swenson we get to know through his writing. His application of engineering project management serves him well on his expeditions. As a successful engineer, he knows that nothing ever goes quite as planned. If there is a solution to a problem, then pragmatism supported by option analysis based on hours of careful planning for all contingencies is likely to reveal that solution. Many modern climbers have adopted this approach, assimilating and using modern technology to their advantage, technologies that a romantic might have shunned as somehow cheating. Hours spent examining photos and satellite maps create the mental picture needed to work out, and climb through, those blanks on the map.

Swenson reveals a no-nonsense emotional pragmatism that matches his mental and physical pragmatism. In this passage, he is reflecting on the death of his friend Alex Lowe: 'I realised at a young age that climbing is my life's calling. I've spent many years intimately experiencing the powerful forces of nature in the mountains. I wouldn't trade it for anything. I find greater happiness when I embrace this, which isn't always easy. Climbing is hard and dangerous, and it takes me away from the people I love. After a friend dies, it never gets any easier. It is extremely difficult to get motivated, to return to the mountains, to work hard on a route again. But doing so helps me process and grieve, which is what my lost climbing friends would want me to do.'

The other underlying theme is revealed in the subtitle for the book. The regional tension that began with the Kashmir war in 1947 has been stoked by 9/11, the conflicts in Afghanistan and the Swat valley and finally the terror attack at Nanga Parbat base camp in 2013. Especially for Americans, this continues to create doubts about the safety of some parts of the Karakoram. Steve is critical of the behaviour of both India and Pakistan in the continuing Siachen war, especially when the expenditure on the military is put into context of the woeful health and education facilities. But Swenson is not tempted to expand this subject to the detriment of the mountaineering stories he tells.

One element of the book I feel is a strength others may find hard to take. Swenson is relentless in his detailed descriptions, totally immersing us in the processes of obtaining permissions, organising transport, managing loads and porters, setting up camps, hauling gut-busting loads in deep snow, setting up miserable bivys and doing it all over again when bad weather forces a retreat. It isn't exactly a light read but it takes us into the hard realities of expedition climbing. If it doesn't sound like much fun, the reality is that much of the time it isn't. But it is the complete expedition experience, succeed or fail, and that is the point. Most of what truly fulfils life is hard work, and the outcome will always be in doubt.

John Porter

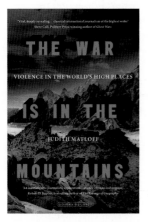

The War is in the Mountains
Judith Matloff
Duckworth Overlook, 2017, pp272, £20

Judith Matloff isn't a climber, or a hiker, or a mountaineer. In the introduction to *The War is in the Mountains* she describes herself as 'a plains person who suffers from vertigo. I favour coasts with endless horizons and the predictability of pavement and elevators.' That is not to say she hasn't led an adventurous life. Twenty years as foreign correspondent for Reuters and the *Christian Science Monitor* has seen to that. Journalism has taken her to some of the world's most intractable conflicts, spanning five continents and 39 countries, requiring boots and tablets for altitude sickness as well as a notepad and pen. 'The thin air of Kashmir became even harder to breathe when mixed with riot tear gas,' she writes. 'I cancelled a trip to Peru after Sendero Luminoso thugs from the mountains kidnapped a colleague.'

Her first book, *Fragments of a Forgotten War*, a damning account of Angola's slide into civil war in 1992, was based on first-hand reporting and let's be honest, Angola at that time wasn't a place for the faint hearted. In this new book she reflects on her most appalling memory from Africa 'of a church in Rwanda that had been desecrated by dozens of skulls of genocide victims. Just beyond it lay emerald green hills, tightly terraced because there wasn't enough arable soil for all the farmers.'

When she eventually moved back to New York she bought a run-down brownstone in West Harlem, a former crack den in a street run by drug dealers, in one of the biggest drug zones in the US. The process of redeveloping the house became her second book *Home Girl: Building a Dream House on a Lawless Block*. I think it's safe to assume that Matloff has a relationship with adrenaline to match any mountaineer.

She was at home playing Risk, the board game of world domination, with her son when he raised the question of where conflict was actually taking place in the world. She rolled out a map and pointed various places out to him. On noting the altitude key he pointed out that most occur in mountains. 'Why?'

Matloff's efforts to answer her son's question took her to many of the world's least hospitable environments, where 'the obdurate terrain is matched only by the obstinacy of its inhabitants.' She visits eight locations across nine chapters and the complexity of the conflicts escalates as the chapters pass. First off is the intimate matter of Albania's blood feuds that have been going on for centuries, and explore the social obligation to commit murder in order to salvage honour brought into question by an earlier murder or humiliation. If a male member of your family is due to have to 'pay' then they'll remain hidden. 'These days, men on the run often enjoy the creature comforts of modern homes, but the psychological stress remains constant. An estimated 6,000 Albanian males, including 650 children, were stuck at home.'

Next up is Mexico's southern mountains where local lives are hampered by landslides and narcotics traffickers, then it's a forlorn army outpost in Colombia in a mountain range that has seen half a century's worth of fighting. 'Since WW2, the average guerrilla insurgency has lasted ten years. That's forty years less than the FARC's.' The ins and outs of the conflict are explored and Matloff pays a visit to the region to obtain a greater understanding of the issues, meeting various characters en route, some deliberately, some not:

> *Suddenly a man appeared from the trees beyond, a jittery gargoyle who ran towards me and grabbed my sleeve. He wore the plastic sandals of peasants and a sneer. FARC, I thought.* He wants to kidnap me. *Gonzalez backed away, and darted across the bridge to the car, waving vigorously for me to follow … I shook my arm and galloped toward the vehicle.*

This reportage is the great strength of the book; it's not an academic study of every conflict on a hillside but a carefully chosen selection of issues that reflect the problems faced by those that live at altitude across the globe, and each area is visited to balance the research with boots-on-the-ground analysis.

Next up is Nepal, and the conflict over water and the damning of valleys to power India's industrial might.

> *'Is that …' I asked Deepak under my breath*
> *'Hashish,' he answered quietly.*
> *'Five hundred dollars a kilo!' Ganesh marveled. 'We started cultivating this year. Grows beautifully in the mountain climate. We're saving the profits in case the dam displaces us.'*

And then to the north Caucasus range whose fragmented clan society nurtured Islamic jihad. Matloff's light touch and humour keeps you riveted to the analysis as she describes being constantly followed by the security police with Beatles haircuts. Eventually 'The Beatles' haul her in.

> *The men commandeered our taxi and marched us at gunpoint into the dreaded 'Department Six' anti-terrorism headquarters. We were taken into an interrogation room whose sign above the door read, 'For the Wanted'. A particularly aggressive soldier barked that we'd never get out.*

Evidently he hadn't counted on the wit of a seasoned conflict journalist whose charm resulted in one of her interrogators quoting Pushkin and exchanging business cards before releasing her. We then head to Kashmir and the dreadful psychological effects of that conflict on its people, as Matloff spends time in a Srinagar clinic. 'I intended to observe the psychic cost of repressed and denied autonomy. But I hadn't adequately prepared myself for such an unfathomable degree of crisis.' This from a veteran of Angola's brutal civil war.

Matloff visits the US Mountain Warfare School in Jericho, Vermont, and NATO's Arctic training facilities in Norway before, as it draws to a close, heading to the playground of Europe: Switzerland. There she begins to look for answers and solutions, can Cantonment lead to contentment? After a short civil war in 1847 the Swiss realised they had to transcend the infighting amongst their religious and linguistic factions to avoid being swallowed up by the neighbours.

Many of the issues in this book are under most people's radar, but that doesn't make them less worthy of our attention, particularly if mountains are our playgrounds. There are a myriad of books to be found that spin yarns of derring-do, that inspire or enlighten us in some way or another. What *The War is in the Mountains* does is illustrate that all is not well in our playground, and that there is more to mountain literature than coffee-table gloss. Judging by Judith Matloff's boldness, adept dealings with objective danger, and handling of high-pressure moments, if she was a mountaineer she'd probably have a golden ice axe. As it is she has a very good book to her name.

Henry Iddon

Distant Snows: A Mountaineer's Odyssey
John Harding
Bâton Wicks, 2016, pp352, £20

In *Distant Snows: A Mountaineer's Odyssey* Harding recalls his life-time's travels, climbs and adventures in, on and through the mountains. From Scotland to Tasmania, Jotenheim to Rwenzori, the Pyrenees to Bhutan, Harding has covered over half the globe during his 60-plus years of mountaineering. His obvious love of the mountains, combined with a perceptive

and sympathetic description of landscape, people and action, serve to effortlessly transport the reader of this book to the 'distant snows'. It is packed with adventures exciting, amusing and informative. Harding writes with honesty, his achievements often hard won and valued regardless of the difficulty or conditions. His partners have a prominent part in his stories, highlighting the important role of companions in influencing both the experience and the outcome.

The book starts with Harding, a student at Cambridge, being invited to join the Cambridge North Persian Expedition to the Elburz. This proved to be a baptism of fire into the logistical, social and political complexities of mountaineering known only too well to those who climb outside the confines of the western world. With these early exploits involving such unlikely figures as Colonel Katchpiss and his 'mythical peaks', Harding's much needed sense of humour is apparent from the beginning.

From 1959, as a political officer and administrator in Aden, Yemen, Harding was able to use his periods of leave to explore Mount Kenya and the mountain ranges of Greece, Turkey and Rwenzori. Most were revisited, many as ski mountaineering destinations. Insights into the politics of the times enrich his accounts, and I particularly enjoyed the passages on Mount Kenya, empathising with the capriciousness of the weather and the problems of navigating some of the routes.

Harding's willingness to climb at times with relative novices and people unknown to him reflects his generosity of spirit and a genuine enjoyment of being in the mountains, rather than the self-obsession that motivates some hard-driven mountaineers. On occasions he recalls the way just about everything can, and does, go wrong. Most times this leads to discomfort, an exchange of harsh words and an amusing tale to tell after the event. Once such episode was on a visit to the Snowys, Australia. On a portentous Friday the 13th, in 1970, he and Terry Birtles went to climb the Townsend Spur. Although they had never climbed together before, Harding believed himself to be with a knowledgeable and competent companion.

However, after bushwhacking for miles and wading through an ice-cold river Geehi getting nowhere very fast, the pair realised they had no option other than to retreat. On the return journey the river had swelled even further making the crossing treacherous; a flagging Birtles was almost swept away. Sitting down on the bank to rest, he then got bitten by soldier ants. As he leapt up in protest, he trod on a venomous snake, slipped and sprained his ankle, dropping his expensive sleeping bag down the mountainside in the process. The night was spent in the car removing leeches from various body parts. Unlucky or what?

Fortunately such failures were rare; thrills were not. In New Zealand he recounts an ascent of Mount Aspiring, using a guide for the first time. On the

recommendation of a friend, Harding approached New Zealand's 'mountaineer of the year', Nick Craddock. In true Kiwi style Nick announced,
'Yer know mate, I've never climbed with anyone as old as you before ...'
Harding was a mere 54 years old. Despite a lack of synergy between the
two, and a potentially disastrous situation arising from poor navigation
on the part of the guide, Nick grudgingly congratulated Harding on their
successful ascent – and escape – with a 'Well done mate!'

It is almost impossible to live, and particularly to have a life of mountaineering, without some misfortune, disaster and loss of good friends. Harding
has had his share and these are sensitively woven into his stories. Merci-
fully there is little reference to the technicalities of mountaineering or ski
mountaineering, and thus there are none of the annoying footnotes that
explain climbing jargon to non-climbers. If you don't climb or ski, you don't
need to know and if you do, it doesn't take much to imagine the skill, knowledge and determination that have undoubtedly been required for many of
Harding's adventures.

Stories of the Alpine Club, Alpine Ski Club and the Eagle Ski Club are
touched upon as Harding held office in them all. His attempts to unite the AC
and the ASC are enlightening, especially as the proposition came following the
combining of the AC and the Ladies' Alpine Club. Harding was instrumental
in changing Arnold Lunn's rule that no women should be admitted to the
ASC, and he notes that the male objectors who threatened to resign if ladies
were admitted to the AC did not in fact do so, but that 34 of the ladies did.

Harding's numerous achievements, and the fact that he is still alive to tell
the tale, are proof that much can be attained through determination, some
degree of prudence and an open mind. Not only is this book a good read
for anyone interested in mountains, Harding's knowledge of the history and
culture of the places he visits, so eloquently woven into the narrative, brings
a dimension to mountain adventure that will appeal to a wider audience
than the mountaineer.

Adele Long

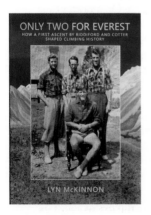

Only Two For Everest
How a First Ascent by Riddiford and Cotter Shaped
Climbing History
Lyn McKinnon
Otago University Press, 2016, pp352, £30

'Permission obtained for two of your members,'
was Eric Shipton's offer to the 1951 New Zealand
Himalayan Expedition, happily remembering Dan
Bryant from the 1935 Everest Reconnaissance. Yet in
making it, he sparked antagonism that festered for
decades. A day and a half of bitter dispute rent the
party asunder. Which two should go to Everest?
What if all four New Zealanders, Earle Riddiford,

Ed Cotter, Ed Hillary and George Lowe, had ignored the specified number, as Ed Cotter suggested they might, and all turned up at Shipton's rendezvous? Perhaps the outcome would have been very different. Shipton himself certainly wished that all four had come, given the bitterness the telegram caused.

In 1949 Riddiford had had the idea of an expedition to the Himalaya, which, at its most ambitious, was a proposal to attempt Kangchenjunga involving eight mountaineers, with names such as W B Beaven and Norman Hardie, as well as Ed Cotter and that great legend of New Zealand climbing Harry Ayres. Jim McFarlane was another and being aware that Hillary and Lowe were already considering their own expedition, Riddiford invited Lowe, who, in turn, wrote to Hillary who was at the time climbing with two other New Zealand mountaineers in the Bernese Oberland. Eventually, they settled on the unclimbed Mukut Parbat in Garhwal.

This book describes how Riddiford set up the expedition's dress rehearsal, along the magnificent Maximilian Ridge on the first ascent of Elie de Beaumont, and then the main production, his expedition to Mukut Parbat, which he climbed with Ed Cotter and Pasang Dawa Lama, how this led, via Eric Shipton, to the attachment of Hillary and Riddiford to the 1951 Everest Reconnaissance, and the furore that followed.

Journalist Lyn McKinnon was invited to write the biography of Ed Cotter by his son Guy, who had found his father's diary of the 1951 New Zealand Himalayan Expedition in the rubble of Cotter's home after the Christchurch earthquake of 2011. Other letters and family papers persuaded McKinnon to 'set the record straight'. Comprising three more or less equal parts, the book is 'an attempt to give credit where credit is due.' She has obviously carried out some excellent research and ably sets out her case.

There were certainly deep differences in the account of the summit day on Mukut Parbat, as McKinnon puts it: 'A major discrepancy that readers can ponder.' Hillary and Lowe leave the tent first, to be caught by the others while warming their feet at a fore-summit at 22,500ft. Yet in a letter home, Riddiford wrote on 27 July 1951 that his rope took over the lead after only half an hour. 'I had to lead all the way for nine and half hours.' At 5.45pm he, Cotter and Pasang Dawa Lama reached the summit. This was corroborated by Cotter's diary entry for 11 July, written some days later. But Lowe writes in his diary for 11 July:

> Earle, Pasang and McCarthney climbed Muket [sic] Parbat 23,760ft. ... We left – Perc [Hillary] & I a little ahead of the others. ... We cramponed steep ice for a few hundred feet – then stopped in shelter of a rock out of the biting gale & removed our boots to massage our feet. ½hr stop. Earle asked to lead & we set off ... At 12 noon we reached prominent peak (height about 22,500 ft.) & caught Earle who was cutting green hard ice.

Lowe and Hillary considered the prospect of reaching the top so hopeless they turned and reached camp three at 1.45pm. The summit pair returned to camp at 8.30pm. George Lowe wrote a letter dated 14 July to his Here-taunga Tramping Club: 'They were too intent to see my light. In half an hour they were within shouting distance. "Are you all OK?" "Yes!" – a laconic reply. "Did you climb the bugger?" "Yes!" – another laconic reply. "Bloody good show!" replied the search party.' Lowe rubbed Riddiford's frozen feet back to circulation and gave castor oil and cocaine drops to Cotter's snowblinded eyes whilst Hillary cooked a meal.

Having discovered Earle Riddiford was the main driving force behind the 1951 New Zealand Expedition to Mukut Parbat, the author's original subject, Cotter, ends up paying second fiddle to what develops into a sturdy defence of Riddiford. The book comprises three more or less equal parts: an overview of the expedition, a short biography of Cotter and another of Riddiford. She concludes with a consideration of Hillary and Lowe's part in the drama. Yet without George Lowe's diaries, his version of events during that evening of 24 August 1951 has not been taken fully into account. Here is that entry:

> *Telegrams from Shipton & N.Z.A.C. re 2 joining Everest reconnaissance party. Decided that Earle & Ed Hillary would join him in Katmandu & that Ed. C. & I should return home. Rest & eating. Arrival of 4 poines – tired.*

The entry for Saturday 25 August picks up the issue:

> *Actual decision was made this morning – i.e. party. McCarth. [Cotter] & I withdrew our desires & ambitions & so avoided a ballot system of choice – which I still feel would have been most fair & with least bite in the disappoint-ment.*

Hillary and Lowe were always the leading pair in Garhwal and this rankled with Riddiford, who announced that he would be going and that Lowe had no drive, accusing him and Hillary of giving up on Mukut Parbat. There is no deep animosity evident in Lowe's diary, no hint of a score to settle. Yet resentment remains strong among some factions of the New Zealand mountaineering community. It is a simple matter of fact that only two of the four had the time and the money: Lowe and Cotter didn't.

The reconnaissance led to Cho Oyu in 1952, but it became 'a personal nightmare' for Riddiford. His health was poor and he expressed doubts about Shipton's leadership. Having never forgiven Riddiford's previous self-selection, matters boiled over and Lowe apparently treated Riddiford very poorly. It was his last Himalayan expedition. The bitterness, however, remained. Although Riddiford was very gifted in logistical matters Hillary wrote of him in his autobiography *View from the Summit*: 'I can't say that I liked him – none of us did,' a statement that devastated Riddiford's widow Rosemary and which Hillary later regretted.

After Cho Oyu, Riddiford pursued a law career, developing 'a genius for friendship' and determination to 'put the family back on the map';

the former Riddiford property Orongorongo Station became the centre of much lavish entertaining of distinguished guests, including in 1971 Sir Edmund and Lady Louise with Tenzing and his wife Daku. In 1976 Riddiford was pushed out of the NZAC for not paying his subscriptions, arguing afterwards that 'the Club owes me more than I owe it.'

The third section of the book follows the life of Ed Cotter. He appears the gentleman throughout as McKinnon outlines his topsy-turvy life. He was introduced to the mountains whilst still at school being involved with his father in the Canterbury Mountaineering Club during the early 1940s. He later ventured into tourism and photography, but not having the business acumen of his friend Riddiford, failed to make money on both counts. This section of the book is a little tragic, almost sad, but also at times hilarious as Cotter goes from job to job. He was a very strong and accomplished mountaineer who was at his peak in 1951 and could have been an excellent choice for Everest; he was a valuable member of the 1964 New Zealand Andean Expedition. In later years Cotter returned to the Himalaya on several trips with his family.

With limited mountaineering knowledge or background, the author has done very well to familiarise herself with the facts, vividly describing the climbing situations, picking her way through with the help of one of her guides: Norman Hardie. Weaving together the stories of others, deciphering their handwritten diaries, isn't easy but McKinnon has succeeded. The book's layout is a delight, with over a 150 wonderful illustrations and four colour maps, strategically placed throughout and richly enhancing. Most are drawn from the Riddiford or Cotter collections, although credit should go to Lowe the photographer for many of the early shots. One in particular captures Ed Hillary looking longingly into the eyes of a female passenger as they lie together on the deck of the P&O ship *Orion*.

In the conclusion there is much criticism of Hillary and Lowe. I found this unbalanced, especially without reference to Lowe's version of events. McKinnon suggests 'readers need to make up their own minds,' but they can't without all sides of the argument. Is all this ultimately the proverbial mountain made out of a molehill? Her contention that Riddiford has been written out of history is overstretched, but while I am not one for re-heating old controversies, had she not done so I would not have had the pleasure of reading so much about Riddiford and Cotter.

Tony Astill

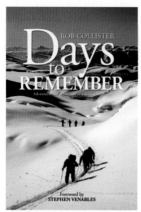

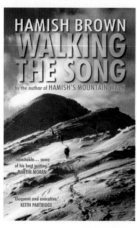

Days to Remember
Adventures and Reflections of a Mountain Guide
Rob Collister
Foreword by Stephen Venables
Bâton Wicks, 2016, pp160, £13

Walking the Song
Hamish Brown
Sandstone Press, 2017, pp320, £9

In the foreword of *Walking the Song*, his new collection of articles and essays, Hamish Brown turns to the Scottish man of letters Neil Munro, influential journalist and author of the gently comic Para Handy stories. Since his death, Munro has been rather disparaged, not least by the poet and Scottish nationalist Hugh MacDiarmid, for an overly retrospective view of the Highlands. But Hamish Brown quotes from Munro's best novel, *The New Road*, set in the Jacobite period, a powerful critique of the blinkered romanticism with which people see Highland culture. The hero, Aeneas, near the end of the book, his naïve outlook in tatters, has been left in a 'black mood' because the world is evil. 'So it is!' says his companion Ninian cheerfully, 'but man, there's blinks.'

Both these collections offer 'blinks', brief glimpses of something – heaven, freedom, fulfilment, nature, all at once if you like – that a mountain life provides in abundance. Both are woven together to create a kind of autobiography, or memoir, tracing two enviable mountaineering lives: from the fresh idealism of youth to Ninian's acknowledgement that while the world may well be evil, there are still fragments left to shore against our ruin. The well-known mountain guide Rob Collister has collected his various writings under three headings to reflect his life at home in north Wales, climbing and ski mountaineering in the Alps and greater ranges, and the ethical issues that exercise him, principally the state of the environment and our impact upon it. The first part gives the book its considerable charm, the latter its bite. He quotes the view of Satish Kumar, the former Jain monk and editor of *Resurgence* magazine, that we are all either tourists or pilgrims. One would expect, Collister writes, mountaineers to be pilgrims, and yet a consistent patter of exploitation has emerged.

Respect, reverence even, has been replaced by a view of mountains as commodities to be marketed for the benefit of local communities and as trophies to be collected by visitors. It is an attitude to be found at all ends of the mountain spectrum from Everest to Snowdon.

This is the paradox of the mountain life, expressed so adroitly by the French alpinist Jacques Lagarde, he of the couloir, which Collister quotes:

> *Ever since man has been drawn to the mountains by a love of wild nature, rigour, solitude and the unknown, all of which he found in that final refuge, he has done everything to eliminate precisely what he sought.*

It is this paradox, and his own role in it, that Collister seems most compelled by, how to acknowledge its implications and still live the life of your choice. He excoriates himself as well as the lazy, accumulative ways of our species, while at the same time remaining someone whose company you appreciate, because while there are flashes of anger and frustration, his sheer pleasure at being alive and still in love after so many years is affecting and rather inspirational. I enjoyed too some of the pieces from the middle section, particularly those drawn from his early years as an alpinist, especially his view of Cambridge in the 1960s.

Hamish Brown is a week younger than Chris Bonington, a useful comparison since they represent two contemporaneous worlds that sometimes intersect but run mostly in parallel. Both their careers, it might be argued, reached their apex in the 1970s, Brown's with his epic continuous round of the Munros and the inspirational book he wrote about it, *Hamish's Mountain Walk*, one of the great classics of British mountain literature, although, like Neil Munro, perhaps not properly understood in an era that doesn't set a premium on the quieter joys of the mountain life. A modern Brown would be tweeting their progress as they went: fun, but like boiled sweets, not the most nourishing.

This late collection of Brown's work is an absolute gem, the writings of a man who has experienced and thought deeply, remains fiercely curious, understands his own limitations, in the words of the poet, making the most of all that comes, and the least of all that goes. His style, practised over decades, manages to be both evocative and dynamic, never stuck but equally never rushed. He looks hard at the world around him, reads voraciously, quotes judiciously, is tolerant and mostly open-minded but knows the value of his own hard-won perspective. I found his recollections of the outdoor life at Braehead School, where he worked between 1960 and 1972, especially powerful, moving even for all that youthful wonder. I grew up under similar influences and understand my luck. I'm sure it wasn't always an idyll, but it was an experiment you'd like to see repeated, especially in an era when children's view of the natural world is mostly through a screen.

A sizable fraction of the book covers his many visits to Morocco. Brown must have spent fifteen years or so of his life there over the past half-century and the contrast with the soft wet mists of the Highlands is very welcome. There are glimpses of his past, his exotic origins, his Scottish childhood and national service. At times he's laugh-out-loud funny, watching hares career into each other on a mountaintop. He clearly adored his dogs, although the footnote to a section on Storm, his Shetland terrier, on how the 'show ring and stud yard' ruined the breed was dispiriting. The same is true for people, I suppose. Brown quotes Salman Rushdie elsewhere in the book: 'Adventure is nowadays the province of the determined, the curious and the idiosyncratic.' Hamish Brown, and Rob Collister too, qualify on all counts.

Ed Douglas

THE VALENTINE HOUSE

Emma Henderson

AUTHOR OF THE ORANGE PRIZE-SHORTLISTED
GRACE WILLIAMS SAYS IT LOUD

The Valentine House
Emma Henderson
Sceptre, 2017, pp338, £18

This is a novel in love with place. From the lascivious descriptions of the French Alps in the startling open pages to the lingering evocations of the high farms and pastures of Haute Savoie, it is clear Henderson relishes these landscapes. It is in Arete, the Valentine mountain holiday retreat that a story spanning a century plays out.

The story begins in 1865 when Sir Anthony Valentine, a keen mountaineer, has Arete constructed. It is his erotic prose which begins the book and it is his reputation for bedding local women which results in only 'uglies' being employed as female servants, as they were thought unlikely to pique his interest. This allows clever, misshapen Mathilde to enter the story. 'I was sturdy and squat, a bit squashed, with features uneven, I knew,' and there she remains: the working woman amongst the wealthy, privileged Valentine family: the *rosbifs*. For this is a novel, too, of class distinction: in work; in leisure: the Alpine Club; in family entitlement: a child from an extra-marital affair cast aside, unacknowledged.

The Valentine House is a family saga, spanning five generations, shot through with undercurrents and secrets. Things are never quite what they seem and the Valentines preserve their mysteries: a daughter who is no longer in the family circle, a wife who conducts a long-term affair with a local farmer, a streak of madness disguised as eccentricity.

Through it all, there is Mathilde. Initially, as a 14-year-old, she is tantalised and excited by her incursion into this strange new world and, as the book progresses, her frank narration makes sense of family intrigues for the reader. She is the observer, the commentator and the lifelong employee, accepted and trusted as a necessary part of life at Arete. The narration is shared: Sir Anthony's great-great-grandson George comes to Arete in 1976 for a long stay after the deaths of both his parents in a car crash. Whilst this dual, interleaved narration keeps the reader apprised of the generational changes in the family, it also asks heightened concentration of the reader in keeping a tally of the many family members, particularly some of the younger, more forgettable ones.

Indeed, the most convincing and memorable characters are, with the exception of George, those who have lived in the area all their lives: Costa,

Madame Tissot, Mathilde. They allow the reader to become familiar with local legends and traditions and consider the impact of development and its accompanying political manoeuvring on such a tranquil, unspoilt area. These factors have the potential to wither traditional communities until they die, just as the mountains themselves can bring death to the unwary or foolhardy.

Life at Arete is claustrophobic: crowded and isolated from the outside world. It provides an atmosphere in which deception flourishes and frailties in relationships are brutally exposed. Henderson's use of legends of the ibex and hidden gold not only provide a reminder that Arete has been a childhood home for many of its inhabitants but prepare us for the unlikely unravelling of closely guarded family secrets at the end of the novel.

Val Randall

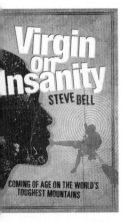

Virgin on Insanity
Steve Bell
Vertebrate Publishing, 2016, pp240, £20

Steve Bell was something a mountaineering prodigy. Growing up in Devon in the 1970s, he became hooked on climbing during a visit to the Dartmoor Expedition Centre, run then by John Earle. At 18, the day after leaving school, he hitched to Chamonix where, after ascents of the Chardonnet and the Flammes de Pierre, he and his partner Chris Gibson climbed the Bonatti Pillar. As Bell tells it, they made an accomplished ascent, with the worst moment a jammed abseil rope as they descended to the start of the route. He also describes being overtaken by Mick Fowler and Phill Thomas, who 'cruised on up the wall as if they knew every hold by heart.'

So far, so good. A day or so later, Bell took a minor fall and retreated from the north face of the Requin. Then came a much more serious fall from the crux ice pitch on the north face of the Triolet, but this time he and Gibson made it to the top. Over the next two years, the routes came thick and fast: in January 1978, north face of the Matterhorn; summer 1978, the Petit Dru and Grandes Jorasses; February 1980, a six-day ascent of the Eiger Nordwand with Roger Mear, followed by the first ascent of the east face of Huntingdon, again with Mear. Along the way he climbed in Yosemite and in the Scottish winter, and in 1981 failed on Annapurna III, along with Nick Colton and Tim Leach. By the time the book ends, Bell is still only 22.

Impressive though his climbing curricula are, we are on familiar mountaineering territory. Even so, Bell writes with a freshness and at times poetic intensity that makes the climbing come alive. His account of his leader fall on the Triolet, when he was convinced he was about to die, is tense and gripping. Bell had previously acknowledged that he had been chasing the near-death experience without wanting to die. Now this contradiction looked like being resolved: 'As I plummeted towards a certain end, two thoughts rose in my head, silent thoughts beneath the screaming: *Dead at eighteen. Sorry Chris.* I'd killed us both.' After a 100m fall, their belay held, and they overcome their injuries to continue. As in this passage, Bell's detailing is evocative and the narrative well paced. They also speak of their time, when vital improvements in technique and equipment were still being introduced, and ascents even of these well-trodden routes still had a naïve and epic nature.

There is another dimension to Bell's account, alluded to on the cover blurb which makes clear that this is also intended as a coming-of-age narrative, one of 'youthful insecurity and immature love', and presumably pitching the book beyond an immediate mountaineering audience. The book's rather gauche title gives us further clues; Bell weaves his quest for the summits with one for sexual gratification: in other words, to lose his virginity. Here, the confident mountaineer becomes the insecure post-adolescent, shying away from opportunities for fear of failure or the unknown. It has the potential to be embarrassing but Bell's writing wins you over. Bell finally achieves his goal with a vivacious New Zealand woman who worked in a climbing shop, leading him to conclude that falling in love is even better than the Eiger. All of this happens within a dozen pages of the end of the book – and a few pages later, Bell reveals his decision to spend nine months with the British Antarctic Survey, effectively ending the relationship.

It is a credit to Bell's writing that he leaves you wanting more. His climbing apart, Bell's main claim to fame is as founder of two successful and respected mountaineering travel and guiding companies, Himalayan Kingdoms and Jagged Globe. Before then he spent four years as an officer with the Royal Marines, all of which took place long after the period related in the book. Bell's subsequent climbing career was seriously affected by a back condition, already evident in his childhood, which came close to disabling him and is now just about controlled by drugs. Bell emigrated to Australia with his wife and three children in 2004 but later divorced and is now in his second marriage, pursuing a career in business as well as writing and lecturing. He has been writing a second book, *The Everest Business*, about the commercialisation of Everest, which he is exceptionally well placed to relate.

Peter Gillman

The Pen y Gwryd Hotel: Tales from the Smoke Room
Compiled and edited by Jonathan Copeland
and Peter O'Neil
Introduction by Jan Morris
Gomer Press, 2016, pp259, £15

The rich story of mountaineering features several mountain inns. Perhaps first to mind comes the Monte Rosa, immortalised by Whymper in his well known engraving 'The Club Room of Zermatt 1864' in which AC members disport themselves outside the still recognisable hotel. As iconic

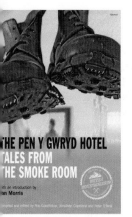

and equally celebrated, several British inns too have figured in the history of the game at home. The Old Dungeon Ghyll is one, the Wasdale Head another, the Kings House perhaps, but arguably the most celebrated of them all is the Pen y Gwryd Hotel.

Although it seems the Romans had some sort of military camp at this strategic location, the Gwryd itself dates back only to 1810 as a lonely squatter's cottage before becoming a travellers' hostelry. My own first visit came nearly a century and a half later when my schoolmaster mentor insisted we stopped by for afternoon tea on the long hike back to Gwern y Gof from a climb on Lliwedd. The young bloods of the CC were in residence, the talk was of the Pass and Very Severes, and for a desperately keen 14-year-old the ambiance was awesome.

Forward a decade and the 'PyG' had become a familiar watering hole and Chris Briggs a revered and much appreciated local figure: indeed, he ran the mountain rescue. Once he knew you by name and where you fitted, you might occasionally be invited into the smoking room to avoid the crowds of youthful hikers who'd recently discovered the public bar. Once we skied over the Pass from Nant Peris to lash out on a proper Christmas dinner, and there was the night when a highly respected instructor returned to Plas y Brenin after closing time with only three wheels on his Citroen. Then from time to time I actually became a resident myself, usually on an assignment for clients who expected you to live and behave like a gentleman. Chris Briggs even bought several of my rock climbing pictures. Or did I donate them?

Such are my personal memories of the Gwryd but what of this rather unusual book? Essentially it's an anthology of similar personal memories, reminiscences and anecdotes from some 60 contributors ranging from erudite writers such as Jim Perrin to famous climbers such as Joe Brown. Among other AC types, Anna Lawford, Rebecca Stephens, Tony Astill and Jim Milledge have their say, along with foreign folk such as Ed Webster and Norbu Tenzing. One or two pieces are posthumous, such as those from John Disley and Chuck Evans, but I found myself searching unsuccessfully for something from Chris Brasher, a PyG aficionado who secretly purchased the petrol station opposite in order to clear the ground, and who would surely have written something evocative and memorable. But despite the prolific name-dropping, I was unfamiliar with many of the worthy contributors, girls who'd worked at the Gwryd for instance, barmen who'd pulled pints, chefs who had cooked and local mountain-oriented folk who've drunk there for years.

Some writers lavish praise, others are more objective: about the plumbing for instance or Chris Briggs' favoured Worthington E. But what I found especially interesting were the historic contributions: I've always wondered who was Lockwood, he of the strenuous chimney? Where did Bodwyn fit: the black-clad, octogenarian Welsh lady who was a sort of *maîtresse d'* in the 1960s? What of the PyG before Chris Briggs arrived in 1947? Here was Mathews in 1865 holding the first AC domestic climbing meet: if only Whymper had made an engraving of 'The Snowdon Club Room'. Then at the PyG in 1870 Mathews, Moorshead and Adams-Reilly founded the Society of Welsh Rabbits, the germ that eventually took flower in 1898 as the CC. And so on. It's landmark stuff.

Given that this is a rather self-indulgent book and that the Gwryd is inordinately proud of its links to the 1953 Everest team, I do feel the book tastes overmuch of that mountain. A forgivable fault perhaps for the PyG is the only pub in the world that can legitimately claim that particular flavour. If you've ever been to the Gwryd it's worth reading. Anyway, I'm off next week to stay there, my first visit for all of 30 years, so we shall see.

John Cleare

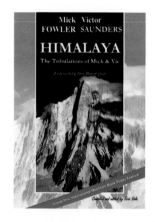

Himalaya: The Tribulations of Mick & Vic
Mick Fowler and Victor Saunders
Edited by Eric Vola
Lulu.com, 2017, pp270, £15

Compiled by Eric Vola, this book brings together extracts from existing works from these well-liked authors, with new material at the beginning and end. A shorter version of the book, published in French, won the *grand prix* at the Passey International Mountain Book Festival in 2015; it was following this success and the resulting alcohol-fuelled conversations in the pub afterwards that led to their reunion on Sersank, recounted in this English edition. The book's organising principle is that in bringing together Mick and Vic's experiences of climbs in the Himalaya, it will shine a light on how different personalities result in contrasting perspectives and recollections of the same experiences. Four Himalayan climbs are covered: Bojohagur Duanasir in 1984, Spantik in 1987, Ultar in 1991 and Sersank in 2016, with some additional stories that take place nearer to home, usually in pubs. Mick and Vic were climbing partners on Spantik and, 29 years later, Sersank.

In terms of a sub-genre of mountaineering literature, this book falls between *Touching the Void* and *The Ascent of Rum Doodle*. It has the nail-biting moments of the former, without the same level of disaster, fortunately, and I don't think I have laughed out loud as much since reading the latter. It is an indication of the stature of the authors and the respect they have for each other that they can write with such candour and self-effacing humour. Perhaps, as Andy Parkin suggests, they are just a little bit 'touched'.

Vola is to be congratulated for the novelty of the concept and his efforts in bringing out the idiosyncrasies of these top-notch mountaineers. Perhaps it needed a Frenchman to highlight the eccentricities of two *rosbifs*. Yet although it's an enjoyable read, the premise of a compilation didn't quite work for me. In places, the accounts by each author of the same period of time or event, included to demonstrate their unique approach and style, didn't always come across as different enough and at times were even repetitious. In other places, there was an account from just one author, which, although it made great reading, didn't fit the concept of the book as a whole. Even so, the book captures the 'tribulations', the camaraderie and joys, of expedition mountaineering from two of its best practitioners.

Adele Long

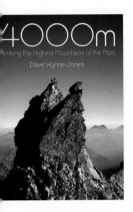

4000m: Climbing the Highest Mountains of the Alps
Dave Wynne-Jones
Whittles Publishing, 2016, pp240, £25

'This is not a guidebook,' writes Dave Wynne-Jones and it's soon obvious that his absorbing account of his long campaign, begun in 1981 and completed in 2007, to climb the Alpine 4,000ers is a great deal more than that. But anyone considering setting themselves on the long and winding road to emulate his feat will find a great deal of useful advice and experience to guide them. Nor is he a devoted slave to a simple list; his campaign, although not this book, is interspersed with expeditions all over the world that are much more exploratory in nature. But the simple, steady goal of completing the list becomes a lodestone in his life, something familiar, even quotidian, with which to measure out his life. He chooses Robin Collomb's list of 52, and offers a persuasive argument for doing so, reminding us that Karl Blodig's tally of 76 on the newer list of 82 would cause the great man agonies. 'His achievement should not be hostage to the vested interest of alpine committees,' Wynne-Jones adds. Such a long career offers a grand perspective from which to judge the scene. He has warmly embraced innovations along the way, and from deep experience has useful perspectives on a range of topics, from navigation to training, from weather to the inevitable decline of the passing years and how to stave it off for as long as possible. He has certainly drunk deep of the Pierian Spring. He is modest and plain speaking – 'we cannot all be poets', he writes in the introduction – but as the years and the adventures accrete the book achieves a quiet authority. It is richly illustrated, and his able eye records the changing fashions as the years pass. Wynne-Jones sets great store in friendship and in his partnerships, old-fashioned it may be but truly valuable, in climbing as in life. He notes that the Alps are quieter now than when he started, beyond the honeypots, but this book offers a persuasive case to return.

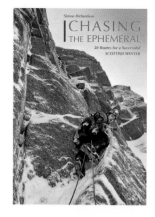

Chasing the Ephemeral
50 Routes for a Successful Scottish Winter
Simon Richardson
Mica Publishing, 2016, pp256, £25

For climbers of a certain age, the compendium *Cold Climbs*, co-authored by Ken Wilson, Dave Alcock and John Barry, is the ultimate British winter climbing book, even though it was first published in 1983 and some of its photography could now usefully illustrate a museum display. This book, written and often illustrated by one of the most prolific and dedicated leading lights of Scottish climbing, must be considered as equally indispensible. Its great strengths are an attractive and useful design coupled with superb and superbly reproduced photography. Richardson doesn't just title the book for the fickle nature of Scottish winter climbing, he offers all his years of experience on how best to manage that problem, offering advice on where best to go taking account of weather and conditions; the book's organising principle is splitting the 50 selected climbs into when they are best attempted or most useful as objectives: early in the winter, or late, during lean conditions, or those increasingly rare golden periods when everything is in. There are lots of well-known routes here; several are common to *Cold Climbs* but there are lesser-known gems too. It's aimed more at the broad mass than the elite, with not much that's very hard. But, as Richardson himself explains, that's not really the point. 'The routes described in this book are all excellent climbs, but they are not meant to represent the very best winter routes in Scotland.' Neither is the book meant to compete with *Cold Climbs* in terms of literary richness: the writing here is succinct and practical. But it's a fascinating and absorbing read nonetheless and a profoundly useful one. It requires us to be more in tune with the mountains and less a slave to the preconceptions that form between our ears and then boss us around.

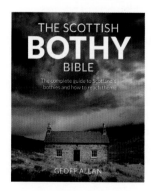

The Scottish Bothy Bible
Geoff Allan
Wild Things Publishing, 2017, pp304, £17

If there's a more enchanting place on earth than Kearvaig bothy in the northern Highlands then I should like to see it. A broad sweeping bay of white sand looks out on the north Atlantic that in the evening light of May has a beauty that catches your breath. Even better, you can stay here for free. The former hunting lodge, built in 1877, is one of the best and best-positioned refuges featured in this excellent guidebook to those bothies under the management of the Mountain Bothy Association (MBA), which renovated the property in 2009. Yet while Kearvaig is among the most appealing this book is stuffed full of remote and wondrous places. The culture and meaning of bothies, the complex history, mixed as it is with the abusive Highland Clearances, which tinges this idiosyncratic and useful tradition with a tinge of melancholy. For those concerned that the publication of this book will see a rush of undesirables that will overwhelm and perhaps destroy something special, this list has been available online for some time, and 10% of the profits will go to its work. One assumes the MBA thought long and hard about the impact of this book, which has already proved immensely popular. Geoff Allan has certainly done justice to the principles and history of bothies, as well as richly describing them and their approaches. The only criticism is the limited quality of the guidebook's one and only map, though perhaps that is deliberate.

Obituaries

Tryfan, Carnarvonshire
George Fennell Robson (1788–1833)
c1827. Watercolour, gouache and scraping out on thick,
moderately textured, cream wove paper. 18¼ x 29⅞ inches.
Yale Center for British Art, Paul Mellon Collection.

In Memoriam

The Alpine Club Obituary	Year of Election (including to ACG)
George Blades	1990
Nick Clinch	1959, Honorary 1999
Katharine Gebbie	LAC 1959
Ron Giddy	1981
George Lee	1960
Alan Lyall	1991
Peter Mallalieu	1992
Des Rubens	2012
Fleur Rutherford	1998
Harry Sales	1968
Mike Teague	Asp 1991, 1997
Hans Trüb	1948
Joe Walmsley	1960
Ken Wilson	1973

As usual, the editor will be pleased to receive obituaries for any of those above not included in the following pages.

George N Blades
1922 - 2016

George attended a number of schools, ending up at Felsted when war broke out. The school was evacuated to Ross-on-Wye where, on Home Guard duty as part of the Air Training Corp (ATC), he was knocked off his bicycle, badly damaging his shoulder. He was unable to join up.

He was accepted on a sandwich degree course in mining engineering at Nottingham, where he joined the ATC. In 1942, he was released from this reserved occupation and joined the RAF. As his large build prevented him from becoming a pilot, owing to getting his knees stuck under the control column, he became a navigator and bomb-aimer in Coastal Command. He sur-

George Blades

vived the war and was demobbed in September 1946.

George never went back to finish his degree as by then he had married Bridget, who died in February 2016. He joined British Insulated Callender's Cables (BICC) and worked with that company until his retirement at 60, by which time he had reached the top level of management.

He was a keen rugby player; when the war ended, he took it up again. He played for Edinburgh Wanderers, London Scottish and was captain of the Notts, Lincs and Derby combined counties. He was also selected for three international trials for Scotland. He never forgave himself for giving away an easy penalty when playing for the 'Probables'.

Inspired by a trip to northern India in 1982 at the age of 60, George went on an Alpine course in Chamonix, where he met Roger Payne. Every year until his eventual retirement from the sport he went to the Alps with Roger, sometimes accompanied by Roger's wife Julie-Ann Clyma and his son Peter.

Peter Blades

James C Smith writes: As a young RAF Coastal Command navigator during the Second World War, George's duty was to search the north-western approaches to Britain and to report the sighted position of German U-boats.

George had studied mining engineering at Nottingham. Owing to improvements in safety in the mining industry, power cables to electrical machinery were required to be robust and well insulated. This development attracted George sufficiently to join BICC and he progressed to become the company's commercial director.

His main sports were rugby and golf. His build made him a natural No8. When his rugby days came to an end, George's life lacked something: he filled the gap with a winter weekend in Scotland, climbing the *Central Gully* of Ben Lui, followed by nearby Ben More. George's climbing continued in Scotland, to include a winter ascent of *Tower Ridge* on Ben Nevis but his natural habitat was the Alps. The genes of the hunter-gatherer showed themselves in the way he felt at home there. He followed the classic routes in his Alpine progress, from the Chamonix Aiguilles to the lower peaks of the Eastern Alps, like the traverse of the Fletschhorn and Lagginhorn to the Weissmiess hut and then to the Weissmiess itself. From the Albert Premier hut, he completed the traverse of the Aiguille du Chardonnet, while from the Britannia hut he went to the Allalinhorn and enjoyed a marvellous day's climbing on the Rimpfischhorn.

For George, there was much more to mountaineering than mountains. To quote Eric Shipton: 'The ascent of a mountain, like any other human endeavour, is only to be judged by the spirit in which it is attempted.' The bustle of Chamonix, a quiet pension in Saas Almagell, or a thirst-quenching drink with friends at a village inn were all an important part of living among the mountains. Companionship and friendship were vital to him; his gift as a raconteur brought enjoyment to many a table.

Roger Payne and George became close companions, and it was Roger who led us to the summit of Mont Blanc from the Grands Mulets hut. My memory of a great day spent with them started with a night inn at the Torino hut, then an ascent of the Aiguille de Rochefort. Roger's death in an avalanche on Mont Blanc brought shock and grief to all who knew him, especially to George.

For George, there was more to life than mountaineering. His 'A' Team was his family. They are all, his three children, seven grandchildren and twelve great-grandchildren, the keepers of the spirit and memory of a fulfilled man who knew how to live and enjoy life to the full.

Nicholas Clinch
1930 - 2016

Betsy and Nick Clinch *(Courtesy of Mountaineers Books)*

Nicholas Bayard Clinch III was born in Evanston, Illinois, and grew up mainly in Dallas, with high school years at the New Mexico Military Institute in Roswell, influenced by his father's and grandfather's careers in the military. A number of Nick's preteen summers were spent at Cheley Camps near Estes Park, Colorado. There, as junior counsellors, our lives intersected and our lifelong friendship began.

Nick received a BA in political science from Stanford University in 1952, followed by a law degree three years later. His education superseded classrooms, as his muse became the mountains that he shared with other members of the Stanford Mountaineering Club and the Sierra Club. Their playground took them from the Sierra and Yosemite to the Coast Range of British Columbia in 1954 and the Cordillera Blanca of Peru in 1955. After graduating from law school, Nick put in a stint with the US Air Force, based in Iceland; he retired to the reserves as a major in 1957, setting the stage for a future life of mountain exploration.

In 1958, Nick collected some friends and acquaintances to pull off the first ascent of Gasherbrum I (8080m), also known as Hidden Peak, in the Karakoram, the only one of the 8,000m peaks first ascended by Americans. With his appetite for expedition organising whetted, Nick was back in the Karakoram in 1960, now, 'having done the high one, to attempt the hard one.' This was Masherbrum (7821m). I was invited along as climber and doc, my first big expedition experience. With no lack of thrills and spills, Willi Unsoeld and George Bell pulled off Masherbrum's first ascent, followed a couple of days later by Nick and Pakistani teammate Jawed Akhter Khan in a 24-hour saga that tapped the depths of Nick's reserves. They topped out as the sun set on K2, then descended through a moonlit night. Nick was never a physically strong climber, but this climb is testimonial to uncommon tenacity and skill.

In 1966, the American Alpine Club asked Nick to fuse competing teams from the Pacific Northwest and the Northeast into a unified effort to attempt the first ascent of Antarctica's highest peak. The expedition not only made the first ascent of Mt Vinson (4892m), it then proceeded to top off about everything else in sight, including the committing ascent of Mt Tyree (4852) by Barry Corbet and John Evans.

Nick's expedition to Ulugh Muztagh, in 1985, was perhaps the most exotic of all his creations. He and Bob Bates consulted with Eric Shipton on the biggest unexplored blank left on Earth's maps. With Nixon's opening of communication with China, this expedition became the first joint Chinese-American mountaineering effort. Ulugh Muztagh (6973m) is a mountain in the Kunlun range, first spotted by Saint George and Teresa Littledale in 1895 during their attempt to reach Lhasa. Five young Chinese, supported from the highest camp by Schoening and me, attained the summit. They opted for a night descent, and two of the climbers fell, sustaining moderate injuries and immoderate frostbite. The Americans then gave up their own summit aspirations to rescue the two injured climbers.

With Ulugh Muztagh, Nick and team had so endeared themselves to their Chinese hosts that they were pretty much given carte blanche to return, freed from the bureaucratic hassle faced by most expeditions. Nick had found a photo in a 1926 *National Geographic* depicting an alluring peak named Kangkarpo (6740m), rising above the Mekong where it descends from the Tibetan Plateau, and in the late 1980s and early 1990s he led four trips to the range. These were the final chapters of Nick's expedition-creating life.

Nick became a member of the American Alpine Club in 1954 and served as its president from 1968 to 1970. He was a visionary who saw the need for the AAC to transition from an exclusive club to a national organisation and voice for American mountaineering. It took a decade of patient planning to finally open membership to all comers, during the term of his partner-in-change, Jim McCarthy, as president. Nick brought not only vision but also patient backroom plotting to this evolution; he was always working on ways to effect change in a way the old guard could accept. This was a role he loved to play, not only within the AAC but also during his terms as a board member at REI, and, I suspect, during his time as executive director of the Sierra Club Foundation.

Another outcome of Nick's vision and priceless negotiating skills was the creation of the Grand Teton Climbers' Ranch in 1970. It is fitting that the club opted at its annual meeting in 2017 to name the ranch's main building the Nicholas B Clinch Historic Lodge.

Along with many expedition accounts and other writings, Nick was the author of two books, *A Walk in the Sky*, published 24 years after the ascent of Hidden Peak, and with his wife Betsy, *Through a Land of Extremes: The Littledales of Central Asia*, published in 2008, restoring the memory of two great British explorers largely forgotten in their native country. He became an honorary member of the Club in 1999.

Nick had a gift for storytelling and inexhaustible (and at times exhausting) humour, which served to shield his inner dreams and doubts. The only one I knew who could outdo Nick as a talker was Betsy. Once I was visiting their Palo Alto home when their planned book on the Littledale explorers was still gestating. Late one evening I asked a question. About an hour later, after midnight, as I snuck away to bed unnoticed, they were still totally absorbed in intense exchange with each other.

Nick died from an untreatable sarcoma of a leg. On 30 November, in full dress uniform, he was buried at Arlington National Cemetery near his father and grandfather. Nick, among many other things, was a quiet patriot who believed in his country as well as its and the world's wild places.

Tom Hornbein

Warwick Deacock OAM
1926 - 2017

Warwick Deacock died in Australia on 3 April. He was 90. A mountaineer, an adventurer, a soldier, a visionary and a successful entrepreneur, he would probably prefer to be remembered as a conservationist: a friend of the wild places. Indeed, in 1997 he was awarded the Order of Australia for his services to conservation and the environment.

British mountaineers of a certain vintage will recall his name as a lead-

ing member of Mike Banks' joint-
services expedition of 1958, which
made the first ascent of Rakaposhi
(7788m) in Pakistan but he had
earlier bagged two virgin peaks in
Alaska with Jimmy Mills' four-
man Parachute Regiment team, had
climbed in Japan and Indochina and
was an alpinist of wide experience.
He was elected to the Alpine Club
in 1959, proposed by Jimmy Mills
and seconded by John Hunt, but
resigned nearly 40 years later for
'geographical reasons'.

Deacock emigrated in 1959 to
Australia with the twin briefs of
starting the first Outward Bound
School in Australia and introducing the Duke of Edinburgh's Award
Scheme, tasks which he accomplished
with great success. But mountain
adventure still beckoned, so true to
his personal maxim 'give it a go or
you'll never know', travelling officially as assistant scientist on an

Warwick Deacock *(John Cleare)*

Australian Antarctic Division expedition, in 1963 he attempted with two
companions to climb Big Ben (2745m), the unclimbed active volcano that
tops remote and glacier-shrouded Heard Island in the Southern Ocean.
The attempt was unsuccessful, and having lost all their gear and food and
balking at eating raw penguin breasts, they were lucky to survive.

Nevertheless the mountain was still there, so in 1965 he organised his
own expedition to climb it, persuading Ed Hillary to be patron and Bill
Tilman to join as sailing master of *Patanela*, the 63ft schooner he'd chartered
for the eight-week, 5,000 mile voyage. There is no landing place or anchorage on Heard Island and the weather is appalling. While the five climbers
attempted to land on the open lava beach, their inflatable capsized three
times in the surf, prompting the claim that this was the first mountaineering
expedition to start below sea level. Tilman and the five crewmembers who
remained on board then had to run 300 miles to Kerguelen for shelter.

It says much for Warwick's organisation and leadership that the summit was reached and the climbers were eventually re-embarked safely,
as planned. Incidentally, Mawson Peak, the highest point on the caldera
rim of Big Ben, is the highest summit on Australian Territory outside the
Antarctic continent.[1]

1. W Deacock, 'Spirit of the Storm', *Alpine Journal*, vol 70, 1965, pp273-80.

Although a modest man, the resultant publicity enabled Warwick to foster mountaineering in Australia. He will be remembered by many as the father of Australian mountaineering and adventure travel. There are only small mountains and no glaciers in continental Australia, and unlike in New Zealand, there was no tradition of alpinism and expeditionary mountaineering. But with a family to support, his wife as business partner and in conjunction with Mountain Travel, the firm his old friend and ex-Gurkha colonel Jimmy Roberts was creating in Nepal, he started Ausventure, the world's first specialised adventure travel agency. They had realised that the expeditionary trek to the foot of a Himalayan mountain would make a superb holiday, and Ausventure organised the first ever trek to Everest Base Camp in 1967.

The concept caught on and was widely emulated, thousands of Australians were introduced to the Himalaya and to wild places worldwide, the business prospered, and thereafter Warwick made frequent trips to Nepal, India, South America and elsewhere pioneering fresh itineraries and scouting new trekking areas, in 1988-9 spending eight months trekking the length of the Nepali and Indian Himalaya with his wife: a then ground-breaking journey yet completely unpublicised. For 10 years he served as the honorary Nepali consul-general in Australia.

In 1975, Warwick announced the time was ripe 'to expose climbers from Down Under to the needs of Up Yonder' and he organised and led the first home-grown Australian expedition to attempt a Himalayan peak: Mulkila (6517m) in Lahaul and a few years later an Australian attempt on the rather more serious Annapurna III (7555m). Australian mountaineering came of age in due course with the pioneering of a new route on the north face of Everest in 1984.

Although Ausventure itself was a commercial enterprise, Warwick always shunned extensive sponsorship for actual mountaineering, claiming it was essentially a self-indulgent holiday. 'An expedition,' he wrote, 'is when you get together with a group of chums, sell the car and go off into the unknown for a good time. No letterhead, no publicity, no free milk powder.'

Warwick Deacock was born in London in 1926 and educated at Stamford, the Lincolnshire public school. He discovered an affinity for the wilder places when the school was evacuated to Wales after the outbreak of war, but not before he had served briefly in the school holidays as a bicycle messenger boy during the Blitz. Perhaps this adventure prompted him to abscond from school in 1943 to join the Royal Marines where he gained his green beret and in due course a commission. The war was virtually over by the time he arrived in the Far East where he soon found himself OIC at Stanley Prison in Hong Kong, the interrogation centre for suspected Japanese war criminals. Then followed a more appropriate assignment hunting opium smugglers in a fast motor launch, before being demobilised in 1947: yet another young officer looking for a job.

He had learnt to climb in the Commandos and for three unsettled years he financed frequent Alpine climbing forays and sailing trips with a variety of jobs, memorably as a long-distance truck driver in France, before he reenlisted, this time as a regular officer in the Middlesex Regiment. As a subaltern he represented the army at rugby and boxing and carried the Queen's Colour at the 1953 coronation parade. He enjoyed attachments to both the Parachute Regiment, and as a fluent French speaker, to the Foreign Legion in Indochina. He served a tour as CO of the British Forces Ski and Mountain School at Schmeltz in the Austrian Alps and was instrumental in introducing adventure training as part of the military curriculum of all three services. Then in 1956 he volunteered for the SAS.

Apart from the Rakaposhi interlude, Warwick's SAS activities are veiled, but suffice to say he undertook several deep penetration patrols in the Malayan jungle during the communist insurgency, before being sent to Oman to join the little-publicised war against Arab revolutionaries. By now promoted to major, Deacock was disgusted to discover the enemy he was fighting was being trained by the CIA and in 1959 he resigned his commission. With his South African wife Antonia, herself a pioneering Himalayan climber and author of *No Purdah in Padam*, the story of the 1958 women's expedition to Zanskar, and infant daughter Kate, he emigrated to Australia.

Having completed the Outward Bound assignment, the family, now also with baby son Nick, spent a year circumnavigating Australia in a VW van, with the purpose, Warwick said, of 'de-pommie-fying myself,' working between times as a gravedigger in Queensland, a biscuit-creamer in Melbourne and a pub bouncer. In 1963 the Deacocks purchased Chakola, an 80-acre wilderness property in scenic Kangaroo Valley some hundred miles south of Sydney, to create an experimental adventure centre for children, which they later gazetted as a wildlife refuge. Appointed secretary of the Australian Conservation Foundation and among the founders of the Australian Wilderness Society, Warwick was known to be interested and interesting besides being given to quirky aphorisms, and he soon found himself hosting a regular outdoor slot on the ABC TV show *On the Inside*, while writing frequent commissions for magazines and newspapers.

Warwick had worked briefly with camels in Oman and was fascinated by the potential of camel travel in the Australian Outback where Afghan camels had been commonly used for transport before the advent of the motor truck in the 1920s. Today thousands of feral camels roam the Outback, and in conjunction with Rex Ellis, who was re-domesticating camels, Ausventure engaged in long-distance camel treks in the deserts of the interior. In the early 1980s Warwick himself made a 31-day camel crossing of the formidable 500-mile Gibson Desert, the first since 1876, during which he conducted the initial botanical transect, earning an RGS Thompson Medal. In similar fashion he later traversed the Simpson Desert and in 1997, now in retirement, he led his old Rakaposhi comrade Mike Banks' British party on the first camel crossing of the Great Victoria Desert.

With his architect wife Antonia, Warwick moved from the Sydney area in 1989 to the innovative, environmentally friendly home she had designed at Maleny, overlooking the spectacular Glass House Mountains of southern

Queensland. Officially retiring in 1992 he was kept busy as patron of Youth Challenge Australia, council member of the Queensland RGS and charity work with Sherpas in Nepal, only returning south with Antonia in 2011 to be nearer his family. After Antonia's death in 2012 he spent time living in a yurt in the bush at Chakola then returned to Sydney. He died peacefully here after a stroke. He leaves Kate, Nick and three grandchildren.

John Cleare

Katharine Blodgett Gebbie
1932 - 2017

Katharine Gebbie, a visionary astrophysicist and senior US government research administrator who supervised and mentored four Nobel laureates in physics, died on 17 August 2016, in Bethesda, Maryland. She was 84.

Dr Gebbie worked at the National Institute for Standards and Technology (NIST) for more than 45 years, served as director of NIST's Physics Laboratory from 1990 to 2011, then of its successor, the Physical Measurement Laboratory, from 2011 to 2012. Under her leadership, NIST staff won four Nobel Prizes in Physics: William Phillips in 1997; Eric Cornell in 2001; John Hall in 2005 and David Wineland in 2012, as well as two MacArthur Fellowships (also known as 'genius grants'). The most advanced laboratory building at the NIST campus in Boulder, Colorado, the Katharine Blodgett Gebbie Laboratory, is named in her honour. At the dedication ceremony for that building, she was praised for her supportive management approach to leading a staff of creative PhD scientists. Dr Gebbie described that style as, 'plant, water and watch them grow.' At the time of her death, she was serving as a senior advisor to the current director of the PML, which includes more than 1,000 scientists, technicians, guest researchers and administrative staff.

An astrophysicist by training, she began her career at JILA (Joint Institute for Laboratory Astrophysics) in Boulder, Colorado, in 1968. JILA is a joint institute managed by NIST with the University of Colorado at Boulder.

D Anderson writes: Katharine Gebbie received many honours, including the Presidential Rank Award in 2006, the Government Women's Visionary Leadership Award in 2006, the Service to America Medal (Career Achievement Award in 2002), the US Department of Commerce Gold Medal, and election to the American Academy of Arts and Sciences, among others.

She was well known worldwide in the scientific community for her leadership of NIST's many advanced physics research efforts in fields as diverse as nuclear non-proliferation, quantitative medical imaging, atomic timekeeping and quantum computing.

In addition, Dr Gebbie was a strong advocate for supporting and increasing the number of women and minorities in science, technology, engineering, and mathematics careers. For example, two world-renowned physicists at JILA who worked for and were mentored by Dr Gebbie won MacArthur

Fellowships: Deborah Jin in 2003 and Ana Maria Rey in 2013. She is also credited with helping to found NIST's Summer Undergraduate Research Fellowship programme, which employs more than 200 college students in NIST laboratories every summer.

Inspired by her famous aunt, Katharine Burr Blodgett (a distinguished American scientific researcher and the first woman to receive a PhD from Cambridge), after whom she was named, Dr Gebbie's fascination with science began at an early age. She graduated from Bryn Mawr College with a BA in Physics in 1957, and went on to earn a BSc in Astronomy and a PhD in Physics from University College London in 1964.

Katharine Gebbie was married to Hugh Alastair Gebbie, a Scottish physicist who died in 2005. She is survived by her sister Margaret B Alkema of Meredith, and her long-time friend and housemate, Sara Heap, of Bethesda, Maryland. Since 1990, Dr Gebbie had lived in both Bethesda, Maryland, and Boulder, Colorado, and worked at the NIST headquarters in Gaithersburg, Maryland.

Reproduced with kind permission of National Institute for Standards and Technology.

Pamela Holt, Catherine Moorehead and Paul R T Newby write: Katharine Gebbie joined the LAC in 1959. She became a committee member of the LAC in 1963 and treasurer in 1964. She is also mentioned in *Pinnacle Club: A History of Women Climbing* by Shirley Angell, published by the Pinnacle Club in 1988.

She became a Pinnacle Club member after climbing in Turkey with several Pinnacle Club members, and making guideless ascents in the early 1960s. She and Alastair climbed in the Atlas, Morocco, in 1966. As a member of the LAC, she and Alastair also climbed in Kashmir in 1979. She was known by that time to be 'thoroughly experienced on snow and ice'. On this trip, she and Alastair climbed two routes on Mahadev (3966m), with further peaks climbed in the Thajwas area, near Sonamarg, and between Gulmarg and Aru.

Dr Gebbie's early experience of climbing in the USA extended to the White Mountains in Washington State, a traverse of Mount Katadhin, the highest peak in Maine, and the Grand Tetons in Wyoming. Outside the USA, she made an unsuccessful attempt on Popocatepetl in 1956. In 1965, Dr Gebbie was climbing in 'Dorset, Scotland and Wales', as well as completing an extensive set of guideless climbs in the Pyrenees. In the LACJ, 1960, p46, there is an engaging account of an extended research period – *Climbing for Science* – at the Jungfraujoch Research Station.

Omer B Tüzel's guidebook, *The Ala Dag: Climbs and Treks in Turkey's Crimson Mountains* (Cicerone, 1993), mentions the 'English Ladies Expedition, August 1963' in Appendix C on p277. Margaret Darvall is listed as leader, and Alastaire [sic] and Katharine Gebbie are there as members. For a full account, see *LACJ*, 1964, pp10-23.

Sara Heap writes: Katharine and her husband Alastair were enthusiastic climbers and trekkers from the mid 1950s to at least the mid 1960s, when they lived in London. She told me about hiking or climbing in Switzerland, the Atlas and Cappadocia. I know she had a healthy respect for mountains in Switzerland with their dangers of avalanches. (Editor's note: Dr Gebbie made at least three guided ascents of the Mönch by the *South-East Ridge*, followed by ascents of the Jungfrau, the Finsteraarhorn and the Aletschhorn, as well as unguided ascents in the Oisans and Valais mountains. In 1959, she also ascended Kebnekaise (2097m), Sweden's highest mountain.) On one occasion in Kashmir, Alastair and Katharine persuaded me to go on what they called an alpine-style 'hike', by which they meant getting up at 2.30am and doing the bulk of the hike before sunrise to avoid possible avalanches. I still remember Katharine getting excited as the sun came up so that she could get warm.

In the Boulder area, Katharine and Alastair would go on hikes in the local mountains. One time, around 1970, we hiked up Long's Peak, which had received a lot of snow the week before. It was a long slog with the ice crust hitting me in the shins at each step, and the metal safety-lines snowed over, so we had to rope up. But it was glorious at the top and a fast ride back down.

When I was living in England in the autumn of 1976, Alastair and Katharine introduced me to the Fell and Rock Club. (I took a hike with the club somewhere in the Lake District. Everyone said, 'Isn't it lovely the rain is so warm!') On earlier visits to England, a number of technical climbs had been made, including *Slingsby's Chimney*, Deep Ghyll, in 1958.

In 1979, Katharine, Alastair, and I visited Kashmir. The leader of the trip was Alwine Walford, who grew up there and did all the negotiations with porters. The home base was a houseboat in Srinagar; we would take two to three-day hikes in the mountains within a hundred miles of town. The food on the houseboat was terrible. I remember Katharine returning from lunch to my cabin, where I was lying down feeling not well enough to eat, and she said, 'Just because you didn't come to lunch, you didn't get any less chicken than the rest of us!' The chickens in Kashmir were very scrawny.

In the early 1980s, Katharine, Alastair, and I went trekking in Nepal with Ruth Gelber and Elizabeth Hall. The first trip was a trek up the Marshyangdi river, around Annapurna, over the Thorung La, and down the Kali Gandaki to Pokhara. We all agreed this was the best trip ever. I think that we went the first year that the Annapurna Circuit was open to foreigners. There was no rubbish or toilet paper from previous thoughtless hikers to be seen; the Nepalis were incredibly friendly, and the Sherpas who guided us were jovial, hard-working and caring people. Katharine, Alastair and I returned the following year, this time hiking the up-and-down route to Namche Bazaar. The following year, Katharine and Alastair hiked to Everest Base Camp.

While Katharine and Alastair were physically separated, Katharine in Bethesda, Maryland, Alastair in London, Katharine would join Alastair in June of most years for climbs in Skye. Katharine loved these trips and offered to let me join them, but Alastair was not up to strenuous hikes for the last ten or so years of his life.

Ron Giddy
1930 - 2017

Ron Giddy was born in South Africa, of British-Afrikaans parentage, and remained scathing about apartheid. He was an accountant by training, graduating from a clerkship in the Supreme Court in Cape Town to a position in the East Africa High Commission (British Colonial Service) before becoming commissioner of Inland Revenue for Hong Kong, which he thoroughly reorganised and modernised. He took early retirement from the HKIR in 1979, when for his services he was awarded the CBE in the Birthday Honours. He was one of the prime movers in the formation of the Hong Kong Mountaineering Club, which he sustained through his persistent enthusiasm.

In his teens, Ron completed numerous solo rock climbs on Table Mountain. His African mountaineering began in 1958 with an unsuccessful attempt on Mt Speke, in the Rwenzori, which he climbed successfully the following year. Three ascents of Kilimanjaro and an ascent of Mount Elgon (4321m) on the Kenya-Uganda border quickly followed. His next climbs appear to have been in the late 1960s in Hong Kong, where he led at Mild Severe and seconded to Very Severe.

In the 1970s, his principal climbing decade, Ron appears to have undertaken at least three solo treks in Nepal, assisted by a sirdar and porters. The first, in 1971, followed the Gandaki gorge to Jomsom area, returning to Pokhara via the Tilicho Pass. The second, in 1974, followed a high level route to the Barun valley and thence to Makalu before returning to Lukla. Finally, in 1979, he spent eight weeks trekking from Bahrabise to the Rolwaling via the Tashi Lapsa La. Following an unsuccessful attempt on Mera Peak, abandoned at about 21,000ft, he returned to Dharan via the Hongu river then through the Arun valley to Chainpur. In 1973, Ron again travelled alone this time to the Gulmarg area of the Pir Panjal for an ascent of Apharwat Peak (4390m).

His Alpine experience was necessarily limited, being largely confined to a solo ascent of the Breithorn in 1971 and ascents of the Wetterhorn, Wildspitze, Similaun and Kreuzspitze with John Swift in 1974. He did not join the Alpine Club until 1981.

Perhaps Ron's most remarkable mountaineering occurred in 1976 on the Hong Kong Kanjiroba (6883m) expedition, with Dick Isherwood, Dave Holdroyd, sirdar Pemba Lama and Pasang. After difficult gorge walking on the way in, an advance base was established at around 17,000ft, this being Ron's highpoint. Isherwood and Pemba made a successful ascent of the peak, following approximately a previous Japanese route. Holdroyd stopped at around 19,000ft, having not acclimatised well.

Ron was a quiet and reserved person. Dick Isherwood, however, observed that Ron had done more trekking in the wild parts of Nepal than anyone else he knew, which coming from Dick was a real endorsement. While a trekker on the Kanjiroba expedition, he was clearly capable of coping with rough going. He was very modest about his achievements, which tended only to be revealed in passing.

He and John Swift semi-joined an AC trip to the Karakoram which Steve Town helped to organise in 1985, by which time he was retired. Apart from being very active, what Steve most remembers about them was their latter-day colonial style, an extra porter or two, chairs and a table in camp, and a cook serving tea and meals: not the norm in the Karakoram.

Ron removed himself to Australia sometime in the 1990s, but for many years returned to Europe annually to walk in the Alps and to lunch with friends in his London club.

Catherine Moorehead, with Steve Town and David Balston

George M Lee
1939 - 2016

George was brought up in Ainsdale, on Merseyside. As a boy, he was known as Martin, to distinguish him from his father, also called George. When he was thirteen, Martin was left in his mother's care following his father's death. It was fortunate that a friend of his father, Harry Spilsbury, took an interest in his welfare: it was arranged that he should henceforth be educated at Merchant Taylors' School, Crosby. At some point after his father's death Martin preferred to be called George, as the earlier distinction was no longer necessary.

While still at school he was taken climbing by Hugh Banner. He also became involved with the Snowdon Scout Group, where he met Phil Gordon. Both George and Phil became good friends and began to go climbing together, hitchhiking to get to the most desirable climbing areas. When George and Phil were about 15 or 16, they did the *Girdle Traverse* of the west buttress of Clogwyn d'ur Arddu in black plimsolls. Harding's 1955 guidebook to Llanberis Pass describes the *Girdle Traverse* as Exceptionally Severe and the most arduous expedition in North Wales.

Nearer to home, George climbed on Helsby, and was part of the 'Helsby All Stars'. He introduced Roger Heywood to Helsby, persuading him to attempt *Hangover*. Hugh Banner later produced a revised version of H A Carsten's guidebook to Helsby. This was superseded by George's new guide, published by the Wayfarers' Club but under the name Martin Lee, no doubt due to Harry Spilsbury, who continued to use George's boyhood name. Harry, as a member of several mountaineering clubs, including the Wayfarers', had also influenced George's climbing so it was no surprise when George, at 18, was elected to membership of the Wayfarers' in 1957, subsequently becoming the hut secretary in place of Harry following his death in 1970.

In 1957 George also entered the faculty of law at Liverpool University. It was of course inevitable that he joined and became a leading member of the Liverpool University Mountaineering Club (LUMC). He and Roger climbed together regularly, often in Llanberis Pass but also on White Ghyll in Langdale, where all the 'Not' routes were climbed in a day.

He continued to climb with Phil; in 1961 they went to Chamonix, where they climbed the Mer de Glace face of the Grépon and the east ridge of the Dent du Crocodile, the latter classed as TD sup with pitches of V and A2, according to the Vallot Guide of the period. When the weather turned bad at Chamonix, they moved to the Dolomites, where they camped under the Tre Cime. They climbed *Spigolo Giallo* (*Yellow Edge*) on the Cima Piccola and the even more demanding *North Face* of the Cima Grande.

The following year, 1962, George again climbed at Chamonix and for a time was joined by Mike Gee, who well remembers an ascent of the *Forbes Arête* of the Aiguille du Chardonnet, on the descent from which George, having dropped his ice-axe, produced a stream of choice words. Nevertheless, they both managed to jump across the bergschrund and arrived safely back in Chamonix. Nearer to home, George led *Gordon and Craig's* route on Dow Crag. Both George and Mike climbed a snow gully in Nethermost Cove followed by a swift descent, as a cornice gave way and hurled the two down. George's ice axe cut his leg open; Mike was uninjured but shaken.

In 1960 George graduated and became articled to a firm of solicitors in Southport. Towards the end of his period of articles he attended law school in Guildford, as did Mike Gee. Although away from the hills, they were both able to climb on sandstone at Harrison's Rocks. Finally, from this period, and most important of all, George returned from a winter ascent of Bowfell and Crinkle Crags with the news that he had met a great girl during an impromptu football match on the ice at Three Tarns. George and Ray were subsequently married, with Mike as best man.

George and Ray soon started a family and had three boys: Robert, Jonathan and William. Roger also had a family and they both often went to the Lee family caravan in Anglesey, from where George and Roger combined rock climbing with family duties. George qualified as a solicitor and became a partner in a solicitor's firm in Wigan. Family life made him eschew the more extreme and dangerous climbs. He spent as much time as he could with Ray and the family, initially using a VW campervan and later a small cottage, rented from the local landowner, by Loch Arkaig.

During the 1970s, a group of Wayfarers', mainly Bintley, Minett, Salisbury, Stroude and Stuart but joined by George and others from time to time, had become hooked on Scottish winter climbing and spent several weekends each winter based at Glen Nevis Youth Hostel. From there they climbed all the classic ridges and gullies on the Ben, including some, such as *Zero* and *Point Five*, which, in those far off days, were considered noteworthy. From this group there emerged the Merseyside Himalayan Expedition 1977, which included George and had designs on the first ascent of a shapely peak, Sattu Da Par, in the Garhwal.

On this expedition, unlike some others, friendships were cemented rather than fragmented. But the team failed to climb the mountain, partly because they had chosen the post-monsoon season of October and winter arrived early, but mainly because the serious illness of one member, Tom Wright, had a morale-sapping effect on the rest of the group. Tom was not fit to fly home with the main party, so George and Fred Smith gallantly volunteered to stay in India, living on very little, for as long as it took – several weeks – until they could safely escort Tom back to the UK and a London hospital, an effort not forgotten by the surviving members of that trip.

Latterly, George took up climbing at a Liverpool climbing wall, as well as sport climbing with Ray and often also with Pete Burrows. In 2012 a severe stroke left him disabled but a gradual recovery allowed him to return to the climbing wall. He gave up driving, explaining that a further stroke was very possible and he could not live with being a danger to others. His fears proved all too accurate: he died on 23 July 2016, following another stroke.

Mike Gee, Ben Stroude and Roger Heywood

Roger Heywood writes: I first knew George when I joined the Liverpool University MC in 1957. I was a beginner, but George already had a reputation. Amongst other things he had done the *West Buttress Girdle* on Cloggy, and of course taken the obligatory leader fall from *Kaisergebirge Wall*. Helsby's Tennis Court Buttress had recently been found and my introduction was top-roping *Hangover*. I was impressed watching George and the others on some of the other routes there.

We became regular partners for the next year or two. During 1959 we psyched ourselves up to try some of the Brown-Whillans routes and were surprised to have some success. We always tried to pick brains to find out if the routes provided any runners, but still had some scary runouts.

We teamed up again in the late 1960s. George had a caravan on Anglesey and we both had young families. We would get up early, do a route and aim to be back at 10am as dutiful parents. I was now teaching and took small groups to the hills to climb. George was an enthusiastic part of this, but it was difficult to persuade the boys that he was a lawyer, as we often dossed in some squalor, with clothing to match.

After a break, I was persuaded to start climbing again around 1995. I went with George, and Pete Burrows, to Carreg Alltrem. They ordered me to lead *Lavaredo*. I began to tie on but they looked on in horror and asked where my harness was: I was ordered to go to Betws to buy one. By now, George was spending most of his leisure time at Loch Arkaig and I enjoyed some great times there, courtesy of Ray and George's wonderful hospitality. He was doing little climbing by then, but I was a regular at the climbing wall. George was mildly scornful about this but when he had a try he became one of its most frequent clients. This led to trips to the Costa Blanca, and we enjoyed routes on the Peñon and Puig Campana, as well as innumerable sports routes. One of the last times we climbed was at Helsby.

George of course wrote one of the early guidebooks. I remembered the fun we had with the usual grading controversies, for instance *Crack of Doom*: 'A great deal of energy gets wasted on this route. The correct method is bridging, which is not strenuous at all.' I believe he wrote this after watching my desperate struggle in the early days.

Paul Davis writes: George also made various trips to the Écrins with the Wayfarers' Club in the 1980s (me among them although I was not then an AC member) when we did such things as the traverse of the Aiguille de Sialouze and rock climbs such as the *Fissure d'Ailefroide*.

By kind permission of the Wayfarers' Club.

Alan Lyall
1932 - 2017

Alan Thomas Lindsay Lyall was educated at Malvern College and Cambridge. He became a solicitor in Liverpool, a job from which he took early retirement when he developed rheumatoid disease, which descended gradually on him from the age of 50.

Alan Lyall

He was a distinguished mountaineering author and bibliophile who also enjoyed marathon running: he thought this was excellent preparation for the sustained effort needed on a long mountain ridge or traverse. He was a strong mountain walker and used to say, 'Why be here when you could be over there?' when his companion felt like slacking.

From 1961 until his accident in 1972, Alan mountaineered alone with a local Swiss guide, mainly in the Bernese Oberland. He climbed the Matterhorn in 1962, and followed this with the *bonne bouche* (Frank Smythe's term) of the ridge linking the Balmhorn to the Altels, or traversing the tremendously steep ridge linking the Zinalrothorn to the Besso. He also managed to cause and get caught in an avalanche on the north face of the Pointe de Zinal. He was sure that he was saved here from burial by his correct use of the ice axe. He had nightmares about this experience until one day he sat down and wrote a detailed account of the event, after which the nightmares ceased. So did his mountaineering, and thereafter he was a keen Swiss Alpine walker from June to September, and a skier in winter. I heard him speak of his mountaineering only when I specifically pointed to a peak or ridge and asked him about it.

Alan met the Naylor family every year in the Hotel Bella Tola at St-Luc, from 1962 to 1973, and thereafter in other valleys. He also climbed and walked with the Toms and Yates families, then with me from 1978 to 2014. The Naylors say he took them on walks which turned out to be too long or too terrifying for their daughter Vivien, who was quite young at that time. After a particularly long and gruelling walk Vivien commented that they

Alan Lyall, left, demonstrating his ability to balance a walking stick on his boot.

should have searched his rucksack that morning for a plastic inflatable cross which would have forewarned them! Alan's favourite mountaineering centres were Zermatt, Kandersteg, Saas-Almagell, the Lötschental and the Gasterntal, although he also stayed in Soglio, Maloja, Mürren, Spiez and Gunten. He tried about 25 hotels in Zermatt before he found one he liked.

In the UK, he furthered his enjoyment of Snowdonia by buying a cottage there, near Beddgelert, which I visited only once, in about 2000. We did one walk only, up and down Cnicht. Alan was already suffering from rheumatoid disease, and on the descent he accepted my loan of a stick, contradicting his strong strictures against walking sticks; he referred to them as 'quarter zimmers', and in an article in the *Alpine Journal*.

Alan's lasting contribution is his *The First Descent of the Matterhorn* (Gomer, 1997), a bibliographical guide to the notorious accident and its aftermath. It was the major source for most subsequent enquiries about this disaster. Being a solicitor, Alan weighed up the evidence concerning the causes of the Matterhorn accident exhaustively and objectively, and corrected errors and simplifications in earlier books.

Alan's memorable final contribution to mountaineering history came in Meiringen in September 2014. I believe he cajoled the locals into organising an event to mark the hundredth anniversary of the death of the guide Melchior Anderegg. The event started with a church service at which there were speeches by local dignitaries and choral singing by guides from the locality and from Chamonix. There was then a procession led by the guides plus members of the Alpine Club (and me), and the sculptress, to her full-sized clay model for a newly commissioned sculpture of Anderegg leading Leslie Stephen to the top of a 'Golden Age' peak. This was followed by a dinner with a top table for guides and another for the Alpine Club, represented by Alan and about five other members, plus me as Alan's guest. This was the last time I saw Alan and it was his last visit to the Alps.

Alan was a superb alpine photographer, taking Kodachromes with his Leica Rangefinder camera. These record his climbs, mountain wildlife and also Swiss customs and costumes that no longer exist. Latterly, he spent about two years digitising the best of these onto memory sticks. The whole collection has been left to the Alpine Club. He was also a lover of German wines and once discovered that a case he had bought for pleasure was now worth so much that he felt obliged to auction it for ten times what he had paid for it. Alan loved everything Swiss. He once found the top model of

Swiss Army knife on one of his walks, and on another a discarded Swiss cowbell, which decorated his home, along with an inflatable Swiss cow suspended from the kitchen ceiling. He amassed a superb collection of books on mountaineering and its history, some very rare and beautifully illustrated with lithographs.

Alan contributed three book reviews to the *Alpine Journal* and a scholarly article on the 1865 Gustave Doré Matterhorn lithographs. Stephen Goodwin favourably reviewed his book in the *AJ* 1998.

Alan was slim, lithe and tough, with striking blue eyes. After walking from St-Luc to the Meiden pass one day, he and the Naylors picnicked beside a group of trumpet gentians; Adrien Naylor was struck by the fact that his eyes were the same deep blue as the gentians. Alan never married and had no children. His only sister predeceased him.

He bore his final illness without self-pity, although for one season it confined him to a chair in a hotel in Mürren. Methotrexate revolutionised his mobility, albeit temporarily. He then continued to walk until Parkinson's disease and old age curtailed all further activity.

Mark Boxer

John Toms writes: Alan bought Brynllinos, Nantmor, near Beddgelert, about 50 years ago, as it was in the heart of the mountains he loved. He was an indispensable guide to the mountains of Snowdonia of which he had an intimate knowledge, seemingly knowing almost every rock. I enjoyed many memorable expeditions with him, in alpine conditions, in deep snow, cutting steps up snow slopes in Welsh mountain cwms and traversing precipitous snow-covered ridges, with an ice-axe in one hand and our little dog under my other arm.

One such trip took us up the Watkin Path in knee-deep snow to the col between Snowdon and Y Lliwedd, then to the Pen y Gwryd Hotel over the rest of the Snowdon Horseshoe, without seeing a single soul. Alan made many ascents of Snowdon, some 500 or more in total. We spent many happy hours in the nearby pubs in Beddgelert. He entertained us splendidly with beautifully cooked dinners accompanied by fine German wine and his very special trifle. He had a passion for the music of Gustav Mahler; we spent many pleasant evenings in his cottage.

Stuart Leggatt writes: Alan's interest in climbing and its literature began in the late 1950s. After school and college, work in Liverpool gave him the opportunity to climb in North Wales, and in 1960 he climbed for the first time on the Continent, in Austria. The following year, he visited the Swiss Alps, and returned regularly to climb there until 1972.

Alan began collecting books in the late 1950s, his first being a copy of Geoffrey Winthrop Young's *Mountain Craft*. In a Liverpool bookshop he discovered for sale the library of William Ernest Corlett, a Liverpool-based solicitor who climbed extensively in North Wales, and was one of the originators of the Climbers' Club: his 1888 climb on Y Lliwedd is described in

George Abraham's *Rock-Climbing in North Wales*. Some of Corlett's books were purchased on publication, and for this reason Alan was only the second owner of such books as the 1902 edition of A W Moore's *The Alps in 1864*. Frederick Jacobs's copy of John Auldjo's seminal work *Narrative of an Ascent to the Summit of Mont Blanc* (Longman, 1828) also came from Corlett's library. Alan's work often took him to London, where the book-sellers, Francis Edwards, proved a rich source of mountaineering books. His visits to the so-called King of Hay, Richard Booth, were equally rewarding, Booth pricing up books that Alan plucked from the unsorted stock. Among the prizes found at Booth's shop were two copies of Charles Hudson, and the superb subscriber's copy of Marc-Théodore Bourrit's *A Relation of a Journey to the Glaciers*.

Early on, Alan began to collect books that reflected not only his interest in the topography of the Swiss Alps, but also the history of its peoples, and the exploration of its peaks and valleys. Among his collection are some important historical accounts, the earliest of which is his magnificent copy of Johann Stumpf's chronicle in its 1586 edition. Illustrators of the Alps feature prominently, with such artists as Lory *père et fils*, Brockedon, Bartlett, and Elijah Walton. The collection offers several view-books of the Bernese Oberland, and a particularly rare panorama of the Alps by Dill that once belonged to the alpinist Thomas Hinchliff. Depictions of the peoples of the Swiss cantons can be found in several volumes of costumes.

Alan's book collection also embraces the scientific endeavour of studying and describing the Alps, and his library extends to valuable contributions on their geology and glaciology by such savants as Simler, Scheuchzer, de Saussure, Charpentier, Agassiz, Forbes, and others.

Vivien Bradley, née Naylor, writes: Most of my memories of Alan are of his taking us on walks which turned out to be too long or too terrifying to people like me with no head for heights. He never learned, and probably didn't want to: he was not overly blessed with that kind of imagination. My husband and I would go for supper with him at his Welsh home. He was most hospitable. And the most notable feature was the wine: absolutely fabulous white wine, like liquid gold, with which we were plied in endless quantities. My other abiding memory of him in these latter stages of his life, and when I was adult enough to appreciate it, was his indomitable and uncomplaining courage. He had made the adaptations to his clothing and his home and his lifestyle with apparent matter-of-factness. The prognosis was never good for the conditions he had but we never heard any word of worry or of the deprivations and hardships he was enduring. He seemed to concentrate on what he *could* do: manageable trips to Switzerland, music, photos, Alpine artwork, wine, friends, memories. And he was very warmly welcoming. We enjoyed our time with him very much.

Peter Mallalieu
1937 - 2017

Peter Mallalieu, who was the honorary keeper emeritus of the Club's paintings and was known to many Alpine Club members, very sadly passed away in the Sir Michael Sobell House Hospice, Oxford, on 6 March 2017. It was much appreciated by Peter's family that several members of the Club were able to be present at Peter's funeral, in Banbury, on 17 March.

Peter Mallalieu

Peter was born in Stockport, then part of Cheshire, in 1937. After leaving school, he graduated with a physics degree from Durham University; he then took an MSc degree at what was then Sunderland Polytechnic. Peter went on teach physics at Sunderland High School for Girls. His enduring knowledge and love of art demonstrated itself early in his career where he also managed an art gallery in Sunderland.

In 1967, Peter and his family moved south when he took up a post as a physics master at St Edward's School, a co-educational boarding and day school in north Oxford. And in 1980, Peter married Jenny, a union of 37 years, although they were, in fact, together for 43 years. He remained at 'Teddies' for the next 25 years, until taking early retirement. Peter was a popular master: he was well known for always being willing to help struggling boys, as letters received after his death attested. An extremely keen and very competitive sportsman, Peter played rugby, cricket and golf to a high standard and coached many St Edward's sports teams. Peter was a *bon viveur*: he had a great wealth of knowledge about wines, particularly French wines. At St Edward's, as well as becoming a resident boarding housemaster, Peter took an active role in the Duke of Edinburgh's Award Scheme and also the school's Combined Cadet Force. He led expeditions to Morocco's Atlas mountains in 1967, to the Canadian Rockies in 1974 and to the Pyrenees in 1980.

I first met Peter in 1986 when we were selected as members of the Royal Navy and Royal Marines Mountaineering Clubs' 1987 expedition to East Africa (*AJ* 1989-90, pp154-161). At the pre-expedition meeting in the Peak District, and in East Africa, we found we had similar professions and interests, particularly skiing and mountaineering. We had a wonderful time together on Mount Kenya and on Kilimanjaro and we quickly became firm friends. Together with our wives, we started spending our holidays together, skiing in the winter season and mountaineering in the summer months. Our first Alpine mountaineering routes together were in the Dauphiné Alps in 1987 and 1988: these included routes on Mont Pelvoux and the Barre des Écrins.

In 1989, having had enough of renting expensive apartments in the Alps in both summer and winter, four of us, Peter and Jenny, my wife Stephanie and I purchased a rather ramshackle Savoyard barn in the hamlet of Le Villard de Montagny, on the hillside directly opposite Courchevel's La Tania. We spent the following few years turning the barn into two semi-detached houses and, with a complete lack of imagination, named the building 'La Grange'. We have both always been delighted to welcome Alpine Club members to stay at La Grange. Although building work took up much of our time, we nevertheless took time off from construction to climb a number of routes, in the summers, over the next few years: the Aiguille de la Vanoise, Pigne d'Arolla, Signalkuppe, Castor, Breithorn, Allalinhorn, Weissmies and the Lagginhorn.

I was very happy to propose Peter as a full member of the Alpine Club in autumn 1992, seconded by his colleague Richard Anderson, and he was delighted when, after due process, he was elected. Peter quickly made many very good friends in the Alpine Club, such as Bob Lawford, Glyn Hughes and Jerry Lovatt. The Club recognised Peter's outstanding knowledge of art: he was appointed to the position of honorary keeper of the Club's paintings, of which he was extremely proud. Peter quickly noted that many of the paintings in the Club's unique and valuable collection were being kept in less than ideal conditions. He was instrumental in ensuring this was changed and, where necessary, he also became responsible for arranging much-needed restoration work on paintings. Together with Jenny's help, Peter organised many mountain art exhibitions at Charlotte Road and in 2011 produced the well-researched and richly illustrated 240-page book, *The Artists of the Alpine Club*, the proceeds of which went to the Club's climbing fund.

Neither of us was in the full flush of youth and time had taken its inevitable toll upon our bodies. Nevertheless, over the years, Peter and I had many great times together on the hills, linked by our umbilical rope: we completed a number of respectable routes including the Grande Casse in the Vanoise National Park and Italy's Gran Paradiso. We had also commenced ski mountaineering and, in 1996, were both delighted to ski the Haute Route from Chamonix to Zermatt. Nevertheless, we were both slowing down and, although we greatly admired the young tigers of the Alpine Club and the many incredible routes they were putting up, we were both realistic and, of necessity, had to cut our coats according to our cloth. Our days of climbing 4,000m mountains ended and we became content and very happy to climb lower, much less-frequented mountains, of which there are a considerable number in the Alps.

Following Peter's heart attack, about a decade ago, our Alpine days came to an abrupt end. Although Peter had recovered well, we quickly recognised he was suffering badly when, in the Vanoise National Park, the four of us made the two-hour ascent from Plan Fournier to the CAF Refuge du Grand Bec (2398m). Although low by Alpine hut standards, the altitude clearly had a serious and deleterious effect upon Peter's heart and, consequently, Peter and Jenny sadly decided to sell their half of La Grange, situated at 1,120m, and relocate to the lower altitude of the Auvergne.

We kept in touch by telephone and met occasionally for a get-together. Although Peter had ceased his mountain activities, he continued with his art exhibition work at the Alpine Club until he eventually gave up this dedicated work. However, he was delighted to be given an emeritus position by the Club in recognition of his outstanding contribution.

My wife and I were greatly saddened when, last autumn, Peter rang to inform us that he had bowel cancer and that it had, unfortunately, metastasized and spread to his liver. After discussing his options with Jenny, Peter, who was also suffering from Parkinson's disease, courageously decided to forgo any chemo or radiotherapy treatment or any operation. In early December my wife and I had lunch with Peter and Jenny in their new home in Oxfordshire and, sadly, that was to be our last meeting.

Peter had a full and very happy life: he had much to celebrate. He will be sorely missed by his family and many friends. When my wife and I return to La Grange, I know that I have skied and walked with Peter over everywhere I can see. Peter and I were very close friends for over 30 years. My wife and I have wonderful memories of the many happy times we had together in the mountains. We will never forget him.

Nigel Gates

Tony Robinson writes: I first met Peter at the bar at Charlotte Road in about 1997 and we struck up an immediate friendship. Exhibiting his warmth and generosity, he had invited me to visit his Alpine home in the Vanoise before we had concluded our first conversation.

In the next few years I developed an enormous respect and admiration for him, both as a person and for the variety of talents and achievements he had fulfilled. Because we had met so relatively late in life our friendship was cut short, first by distance between our UK homes and finally by his death.

My first visit to the Mallalieu home in Montagny, overlooking the Bozel valley, and across to Courchevel, was for skiing lessons. I was over 60 and had never skied. Peter took the matter in hand and took me through to red runs. While I was practising, or climbing, he might be getting an early start to drive to Val d'Isère to ski down into Italy with local chums, to have lunch and bring back delicacies to savour at home. This was way beyond my skiing grade.

The home in Montagny, created by Peter and Jenny (and Stephanie and Nigel Gates) out of an ancient barn, was a masterpiece of creativity despite the problems of French property and inheritance laws, and relatively low capital cost. Peter, whose French seemed fluent, had many local friends, and arranged for one to accompany me up the Grande Casse, the big peak dominating the head of the valley. On another occasion he took me to the foot of the Aiguille de la Vanoise, a dramatic local feature, which I had been fascinated by, and wanted to climb. He left me there to solo, and returned to collect me several hours later.

During long chats into the night I learned about his life of teaching at St Edward's and the nearness he got to being an international rugby referee, as well as his enthusiasm for golf and membership of Royal St George's, at Sandwich. Peter was generous, warm-hearted, talented and a great character to be with. I shall be one of the many who will miss him greatly. We shall be thinking of Jenny.

Catherine Moorehead writes: When I was writing *The K2 Man*, my biography of K2's discoverer, H H Godwin-Austen, I realised that Godwin-Austen's vast output of very accomplished watercolours, many of them the first western views of parts of Kashmir and the Karakoram, could not properly be assessed by me. I therefore turned to Peter to help me out. He immediately applied great skill and assiduousness to this task. And with his natural pleasantness of manner it quickly became a real privilege to work with him. Not only were his critical analyses of the paintings themselves much appreciated, but his scholarly research into Godwin-Austen's influences (two paintings of which were unearthed by Peter in the National Archives of Canada and are published in the book) and artistic history combined to bring a completeness and originality to the assessment which makes his chapter in this book such a gainful pleasure to read, as well as a fine piece of art history in its own right.

I am sorry we, and Jenny, have lost a man of such skill, knowledge and goodness.

Jerry Lovatt writes: Nigel Gates's obituary has captured very well the wide range of Peter's skills and interests. However, there is one additional aspect of the man that lends emphasis to all of this. Unlike many people with his breadth of abilities, Peter was self-effacing almost to a fault. However untrue it may have been, the other person in the conversation was always made to appear more knowledgeable, have climbed bigger routes or have a better collection of this, that or the other. While it is right and proper that Peter should be remembered for his achievements, he should also be remembered for the modest way in which he invariably presented them.

Des Rubens
1952 - 2016

Des Rubens was born in Perth and brought up in Carnoustie, the middle of three sons, all powerfully built. His father was a horticultural consultant in the county of Angus, and annual family holidays in Arisaig introduced the boys very early to the delights of the West Highlands. Educated at Dundee

High School, Des excelled at running and competed at county level. In his later years he attributed his sore knees to excessive road running in his youth.

Des was introduced to climbing when he began studying physics at Edinburgh University in 1970, although he had already done much hill walking while at school. Through the university mountaineering club (Edinburgh University Mountaineering Club) he met his wife and lifelong companion, Jane, and made many close, lifelong friends. As a young lecturer, my introduction to him was in the smoky recesses of Rutherford's Bar, where he was holding court as EUMC president. Soon after, however, I began to hear interesting tales. At the start of the new term, Des had taken a novice to climb *Big Top* on the west face of Aonach Dubh in Glen Coe, but the unfortunate second had swung off high up and been unable to complete the route. Undaunted, Des had solo-

Des Rubens about to climb a pinnacle at the summit of an unnamed peak on the perimeter of the Borumbar glacier in the Thui range of Hindu Raj. *(Geoff Cohen)*

ed the top pitch (the exposed crux) and found someone at the top of the crag who was able to assist him to get down to the marooned fresher and deliver him safely. Throughout the 1970s, Des climbed frequently all over Scotland, and acquired a reputation particularly for his boldness in winter and his new routes in out of the way corners of the Highlands.

Having hitchhiked round Syria and Turkey at 18, with only a duffel bag for baggage, Des embarked on his first Asian climbing trip a couple of years later, joining Ian Rowe for a trip up the Bashgal valley in Afghanistan. In 1975 he took part in the first EUMC expedition to the Hindu Raj in Pakistan. We drove overland to Pakistan in a Ford Transit van whose registration AWG was interpreted as either 'Always Willing to Go' or 'Allah Will Guide'. Either way, we broke down in every country en route, finally arriving in Rawalpindi and enjoying the legendary hospitality of Colonel 'Buster' Goodwin, who regaled us with tales of colonial days.

After flying in to Gilgit, we eventually made it to a base camp on the Borum Bar glacier below the Thui range and made first ascents of several 6,000m peaks, one of which featured a steep rock pinnacle that Des led very smoothly. With our great friend George Gibson we attempted a peak later known as Thui III via a long couloir, which had to be climbed at night for safety. By early morning, with several hundred feet still to go, George was tiring; Des bravely carried both his and George's sack to speed up our exit to safer ground. Towards the end of the expedition Des and I made a six-day attempt on Thui II (6660m), a fine peak that had repulsed several previous parties. After a long approach up an unknown glacier we spent a day of bad weather confined to a small tent on an isolated col below the final ridge. Typically, Des remained cheerful and good company the whole time. We decided to retreat next day, fearing the monsoon was approaching, only for the weather to improve again once we had committed to the descent.

After our Pakistan expedition and Des's graduation, he took a teacher-training course. Following a short period teaching physics at Craigroyston Community High School in north Edinburgh he decided on a change of direction and moved to Broxburn Academy as a teacher of outdoor activities and finally found his true vocation: he soon became a competent canoeist and skier and moved back to Craigroyston as principal teacher. The school was in a rather deprived area of Edinburgh and many of the pupils had little opportunity to develop an interest in the great outdoors. I am sure that it was entirely due to his patience, warmth and sense of humour that Des was able to successfully take even the most reluctant of kids into the local hills. Some were really enthused, and after his sudden death comments such as 'he was the best teacher I ever had' were posted on social media.

Lothian schools in the 1970s still benefited from the far-sighted policies that had been developed by Eric Langmuir, who recognised the huge value of outdoor activities for schoolchildren, and had set up a very supportive network. Unfortunately, local authority support waned over the long period in which Des dedicated himself to outdoor education, and eventually he was left as the only such teacher at this level in the whole region. Never losing his commitment and enthusiasm, Des later completed a master's course in education and wrote a dissertation developing a well-thought-out rationale for outdoor education, a thesis much appreciated by colleagues when outdoor activities began to make their way back into the tertiary curriculum.

There were two occasions when Des probably saved my life. One was in Kashmir in 1977. We had climbed an unknown mountain and were returning to a village at the end of a long, rainy day. The Himalayan torrents were quite swollen and at the last one I began to get into difficulty. Des had already crossed but immediately stepped back into the waters and helped me to safety. The other occasion was on the north face of Les Droites in March 1989. We had climbed about a third of the way up, but decided to retreat in the face of poor snow conditions. On the descent I was hit by a large rock from above which broke my shoulder and ribs. Des was able to shepherd me down, half lowering me for pitch after pitch until we reached the glacier, where I was rescued the next day.

In 1980, Des returned to Pakistan to join Dick Isherwood and me in the Karakoram. We had great ambitions in the Charakusa valley, but these were somewhat tempered by our near-minimal equipment. Our first mountain presented some quite difficult ice pitches and at times Des would fall asleep at the belays (due to lack of acclimatisation) only to be woken to lead some really steep bit of ice.

Unfortunately he abandoned his sleeping bag at our second camp and was then forced to endure a cold night on a very exposed bivouac ledge followed by another night on his own, after he had decided to wait while Dick and I tried to complete the ascent without him. Sadly, we were unsuccessful, but when we were all reunited Des was as unflappable as ever, despite having spent the previous 24 hours alone on the tiniest of ledges in an awesomely exposed place, not knowing if or when we would return. Later, we tackled another very fine mountain, Drifika (6447m). It gave us a tremendous climb with some of the most spectacular views we had ever seen. By now Des was fit and fully acclimatised and had the honour of leading the hardest pitch of the climb, but we still reached the summit not long before dark and had to endure an extremely cold night without sleeping bags on the descent.

In 1985 Des and I organised our most ambitious expedition, to Gasherbrum III (7952m), which had only been climbed once. We were joined by Paul Nunn and Clive Rowland, but both had to go home prematurely, leaving the two of us to make a lonely attempt on a ridge which is still unclimbed. In a difficult bivouac at about 7,250m, Des was the one who contrived with great persistence to provide a brew. We turned back in strong winds at about 7,500m and after a few unpleasant nights, Des suffered frostbite, which in due course led to his losing a small portion of his big toe. When his children were young and unwilling to go to bed he might threaten to show them his toe: usually enough of a sight to send them off. His frostbite injury did not deter him from having a crack at Nanga Parbat in 1992. On this expedition Des and Ally Kellas reached 7,500m before altitude sickness and poor weather halted progress.

Des was also a key participant in the 1988 SMC centenary expedition to the Shiwakte range in Xinjiang, which he recorded in a brilliant contribution to the *SMC Journal*. While the mountaineering achievements were relatively meagre his account of our wrestling with the Chinese bureaucratic leviathan and our complex camel-assisted approach via the Karatash Pass was delightful.

Asia was not Des's only climbing destination. With Dave Broadhead he made a successful visit to the Caucasus in 1984, enjoying several fine ascents including Ushba and Elbrus and returning with copious quantities of caviar and champagne, the only commodities, along with titanium ice screws that Russian climbers could trade for much-envied western climbing gear. Also in the 1980s he had some very successful rock trips in the USA, climbing classics in Yosemite, the Californian Sierras and the Wind Rivers. In the new millennium he made new routes in Peru's Cordillera Vilcanota and Canada's Coast Range. Returning to Zanskar in 2012 he recorded his experiences in a memorable article in the *Alpine Journal*, musing on the changes that had transpired over the 35 years since his previous visit. Finally, in 2014 he fulfilled a longstanding wish to visit Kumaon, joining an expedition to the Nama glacier in the remote Adi Kailash range.

Des loved these travels not just for the mountaineering but also for the variety of peoples that he met, as well as the spectacular scenery and the adventure of untrodden ground. As an enthusiastic photographer, he always returned with three times as many pictures as anyone else.

Interspersed with his many expeditions Des enjoyed a steady Alpine career. In the 1970s and 1980s he accomplished many classics such as the *Walker Spur* and the north face of the Dru. More recently, following his retirement and now in his sixties, we joined up in a pattern of regular Alpine holidays, with a vague notion of collecting the 4,000m peaks. Route quality was always more important than just peak bagging, so we spent wonderful days on, for example, the Peuterey Ridge and the Täschhorn-Dom traverse. We made a harmonious team after so many years together, fully aware of each other's strengths and weaknesses and yet still always enjoying the banter. With his powerful chest, Des was usually faster than me going uphill, but suffered badly with his knees on the downhill, so we developed a routine where he carried the heavier sack on the way up and I took the bigger load on the way down.

In recent years Des developed a keen interest in Alpine ski mountaineering, enjoying several tours with his good friends Stan Pearson and Steve Kennedy. With his ineffable good nature he also allowed Steve to persuade him to return to Yosemite to attempt some big wall climbing. His unquenchable enthusiasm compensated for a lack of experience of the required techniques so that they returned high on their enjoyment of the ambience of the Valley and full of hopes for further explorations.

In 2009, Des was very proud to be elected president of the Scottish Mountaineering Club. Thanks to his teaching experience he was able to chair the AGMs with great skill, navigating contentious waters without upsetting too many sensibilities. His greatest contribution was reviving the SMC's Edinburgh winter lecture programme. By finding a suitable venue in Princes Street and involving the AC and JMCS, and most importantly by selecting a wonderful list of speakers including scientists, poets, historians, expeditioners and young tigers with hard new winter routes to relate, he was able to vastly increase the audiences and made this an important event in Edinburgh's climbing calendar.

Des had a certain lack of self-consciousness that had many positive aspects. Friends would rib him for his hideous snakeskin shirt or his amazing bulging rucksack but he would always just laugh and never take offence. I always felt that if he was unaware that a pitch he was about to lead was the crux he was quite likely to float up it quickly, whereas if he were told to expect difficulty he would definitely experience it.

Apart from his total commitment to climbing in its broadest sense, Des was by no means narrow in his interests. He was a keen lover of opera and theatre, so much so that after his death his wife Jane was appalled to discover how much he had spent on advance tickets for the Edinburgh Festival. Their home is full of books and original paintings, and visitors always received a warm welcome at a loaded table. He was a good cook and had an unrestrained love of food, which might on occasion lead to consumption of all the goodies in the house. Despite his absences in the mountains, Des was a devoted family man who loved to climb with his son Andrew and was delighted when his daughter Catriona also began to take an interest in climbing. Before they had children, he and Jane had accomplished many long walks together in Scotland as well as Alpine seasons in the Ortler and the Écrins.

Des' outstanding characteristics were his warmth, his easy-going unflappability and his inimitable sense of humour. He had plenty of ambitions to achieve in the mountains but this was tempered by sound judgment and a proper prudence when necessary. His calmness in difficult situations must have helped many a beginner to overcome their trepidation. He remained always the most loyal and greathearted companion one could wish for.

Geoff Cohen

Fleur Rutherford
1948 - 2016

Fleur Rutherford was brought up in South Africa, in Cape Town, and lived there until she was 16. She was an energetic and enthusiastic child. Because of her husband's work at Faslane, the family moved to Scotland, where her earliest mountain ventures were into the hills above Loch Long. One outing included carrying her son Sam, aged three months, up a hill in a Royal Navy issue grip bag.

She was first married to Vice-Admiral Malcolm Rutherford CBE, who died in 1997, after whom she married Mike Boyce. She had two children, then became a second mother for her grandchildren, Zara, Mack and Freddie – not just during the often adventurous and difficult holidays (of which there were

Fleur Rutherford

many), or the special events, but also through the humdrum of their daily lives in which she immersed herself with total enthusiasm and excitement: she showed how to make the mundane wonderful.

She was a huge enthusiast for the Alpine Club, not just for the climbing but for the opportunities it gave to people from all parts and levels of society. She loved the mingling of 'high' and 'low', different backgrounds joined by a mutually shared passion for climbing. Her only frustration with climbing was having the view from the top obscured by cloud! She read, from cover to cover, every year's *Alpine Journal*.

Fleur took part in a variety of expeditions. A number of family climbing holidays took place in the Alps and Himalaya, the Weissmiess and Island Peak being particularly remembered. Perhaps her most notable climb was with the British Services Everest Expedition of 1990. Her last climb, with mules, was with the family to Hudad (3287m), a plateau within the Ethiopian Highlands, where she spent Christmas 2015.

When not climbing, Fleur enjoyed tennis, and sailing with Mike, especially around Corsica, Greece and Turkey. Their base was on the Solent, where her parents had a boat at Beaulieu, though the family also sailed in the Bahamas. She was, throughout her career, frequently employed as a trouble-shooter, brought in to turn failing companies around. Towards the end of her life she was running Cappa, a company specialising in a new and patented valve caps for trucks and cars, a remarkable statement of her versatility.

Those who have been touched by her memory include many individuals and a myriad of organisations: village, parish, county, the Royal Navy and Royal Marines, the Drapers and other livery companies, the Cinque Ports, the Royal College of Defence Studies at Shrivenham, the Pilgrims, and many others. The hundreds of personal cards and letters received after her death included those from Her Majesty the Queen, with whom she attended many events, and Archbishop Desmond Tutu, whom she had come to know during her early years in South Africa.

Fleur was intrepid, tough, brave, as anyone who has climbed, sailed or skied with her knows well; her courage, evinced through her unflinching response to the illness which led to her premature death, was as much physical as moral, but she was always gentle and generous with all whom she met, whoever they were. That is not to say she was not also something of a disciplinarian, especially at home where Ps and Qs certainly had to be watched. Her enthusiasm for life spilled over into frustration at so many ambitions left incomplete.

Sam Rutherford

Harry B Sales MBE
1918 - 2017

Harry was born in Stockport. He attended Stockport Grammar School and qualified as a solicitor before he was 21, taking his degree at Manchester University while working as an articled clerk to his solicitor father. He eventually became town clerk of Aldershot. Later in the 1970s he became a barrister, specialising in local government law, and planning law in particular. As a barrister he freely gave advice to the British Mountaineering Council and the charity, Friends of the Lake District.

He married his first wife Elsie in 1940 and they brought up four children. After they divorced, he married Patricia, with whom he shared many adventures in the mountains.

Harry started painting in the late 1930s. He became a director of the New Ashgate Gallery in Farnham, Surrey, and the artist-led organisation Free Painters and Sculptors, with whom he exhibited regularly. When his sight began to fail he turned to sculpture, painstakingly sculpting driftwood, sometimes with the help of a chainsaw, to make human and other figures. The gift of daffodil bulbs started another enthusiasm: for years, he grew the flowers wherever he could find space, competing in shows and developing new varieties.

Harry Sales

Harry joined the Alpine Club in 1968. He was a lifelong climber. As well as the Alpine Club he was a member, vice-president and president of the Climbers' Club.

In 1971 he joined a mini expedition to Greenland to climb in the Roscoe Bjerge in Liverpool Land. The team comprised three Englishmen and three Scots: Jack Derry, Peter Mould, Harry Sales, Peter Cromer, Stuart Kermack and Malcolm Slesser. Various peaks were climbed by this party. In 1974, Harry was part of a team that sailed to Sark and recorded a number of new routes there.

Harry and Pat made a number of visits to the Himalaya to trek through the mountains, including Kullu and Ladakh, often in the company of their good friends John and Joy Hunt and Michael and Sally Westmacott. In 1989, at the age of 70 and with one artificial hip replacement, Harry reached the summit of Mera Peak (6476m), with John Atherton, Hamish Nicol, Charlie Rose and a young lady called Beetle. This was one of the treks that Hamish used to organise from time to time for friends who had 'outgrown' serious mountains.

Harry had climbed in Cornwall many times before he and Pat came in 1997 to live in the village of Paul, near Penzance. On his 80th birthday, Ron Chambers took Harry up *Commando Ridge* at Bosigran. I occasionally climbed with him and I well remember in April 2000, with Janet and Pat, we went over to Bosigran and I led him up his last climb, *Alison's Rib*, when he was 81. He kept up his interest in the climbing scene and enjoyed visiting the Count House at Bosigran when there was a meet, so that he could catch up with old friends.

Harry was enthusiastic in all he did: he had a great love of life. He relished his years in Cornwall. He and Pat made many friends among the local artists. Harry was full of fun and was up for anything. He involved himself fully in many village activities including bell ringing, which he kept up until he was 90. He was well known and well liked in the community.

We send our warmest and deepest sympathy to Pat and the family. We will miss our good friend and companion of many adventures.

John Atherton

Bob Allen writes: Harry was president of the Climbers' Club from 1975 to 1978. I had joined in 1970 and that is how I got to know him, as a mountaineer. One day, probably in 1975 or 1976, he phoned me: 'Bob, do you let out your house in the Lake District by any chance? Because a friend really needs to get away for a week and I thought of you.' I said, 'Harry, this friend wouldn't happen to be a lady, would it?' Well, of course it was, and it was Pat. I told Harry that I definitely did not let out my house, but that he was more than welcome to make use of it for a week anyway. When Marj and I returned home on Friday night for the weekend, the fire was blazing: I knew within minutes that that week had been a defining one in Harry and Pat's relationship.

I also recall Harry's highly unusual presidential speech at the Climbers' Club's annual dinner, probably in 1978. He delivered it all in trochaic tetrameter, the style in which Longfellow wrote his epic poem *Hiawatha*. Harry's version went something like this: 'By the Helyg doorway watching;/ Watching weather over Tryfan;/Stood the climber hairy bearded;/Draped in ropes with friendly Moacs;/Chalk in bag and full of hoping;/Waiting for the rain to lessen …'

A few minutes of this was very entertaining, but Harry's speech covered every aspect of the club's activities during the year. The problem was we couldn't get him to stop. Impatient members began to heckle, but Harry ignored them and finished his recitation anyway. He showed us all why he made such a good barrister: he never gave up.

In July 1969, Harry, Pat, Nicola, Lois, a friend Diana, Lin, three months-old Jonathan and I went to the Austrian Lake District. We camped by the lake, the Hallstattersee, on the north side of the Dachstein, which Harry, Diana and I intended to climb. We found ourselves on a long rock rib at the edge of the Dachstein glacier; in places it was a bit awkward. For speed we were climbing unroped. Harry had not become CC president without some climbing ability, and maybe this was just an off day but, on this occasion, his methods seemed very odd. He had a definite tendency to grab a spike, or ledge, with his hands and then waggle both his legs around in the air until one part of either foot touched something; he would then attempt to stand on it. I watched this performance a few times and then got scared because I thought I could see an accident waiting to happen, so we roped up. That slowed us down considerably and we only made it to the lower summit before we had to retreat to the valley. We were too late for the chairlift and had a three-hour walk through dark woods, at night. Large amounts of wine assuaged the disappointment.

Ten years later, in July 1979, we were in Kenya. We had some ambitions for the famous ice climb, the Diamond Couloir, but discovered that it had largely melted and disappeared, which caused a change of plan. Lin took Jonathan down to Mombasa while Pat, Harry and I set off to climb to Point Lenana on the mountain, which is not a technical ascent, but is still very high, only just under 5000m: it would be my own highest altitude. We had our porters carrying far too much food through the infamous 'Vertical Bog' and, apart from Harry getting dehydrated so that we had to pour two litres of water into him immediately, we got there.

Pat and Harry became regular visitors to us in Grasmere, hospitality always generously reciprocated. On the visits north the objectives always included some challenging walks or scrambles and even when his eyesight was failing Harry would insist on a walk over Scafell Pike or something equally demanding.

The Harry I knew was irrepressible, always giggling, highly intelligent, enormously charming, endlessly patient. In some ways he never grew up, which was part of his charisma. He was very artistic and the house and garden, at least in Old Woking, always had large paintings which were too abstract for me, but his sculptures always seemed to incorporate large ladies with enormous breasts, which I appreciated rather more. He adored Pat: with her he seemed complete. He certainly lived a very full and exciting life. I am privileged to have been a friend. Pat will certainly have many memories of a remarkable man.

Dave Atchison writes: It was 1974 and proved to be the last Climbers' Club Annual Dinner to be held in London. Harry was a Vice-President at this time and destined to be club president the following year.

On our table was Colonel Hugh Wright, a friend of Harry who was seeking a crew predominantly of climbers with a view to a sailing trip to Sark while doing some routes along the way. Several of us signed up straightaway. Hugh was in the Royal Electrical and Mechanical Engineers and had access to a cadet training yacht complete with a fin keel and Bermudan rig. It was a 30-footer and could accommodate a crew of six.

We assembled at Gosport, boarded *Seahorse* and set out at dusk. Navigation by night was new to most of us but we made it to Yarmouth. Next day saw us cross Bournemouth Bay to Swanage. Some of us were a bit green at this stage having not yet got our sea legs, so getting ashore was some relief. We sought out a newsagent's, to look for confirmation of Harry's MBE appointment.

The next move led to Poole Harbour and upriver to Wareham. We then headed off round Peveril Point to Boulder Ruckle and Subluminal and dropped anchor just offshore. The dinghy was now used to get us to the foot of the climbs, much to the surprise and delight of others who had abseiled in. Harry climbed with Hugh; several routes were ascended.

The following day we crossed the Channel. Having arrived safely in

Cherbourg, Harry and party set about climbing the huge slab beneath the Citadel. This was probably a first ascent and was completed before dusk and followed by a celebratory meal in town.

Passage through the Race of Alderney to Sark was thankfully smooth. We explored the area and found several climbing possibilities. Near the seaward side of the Gouliot Cave, Harry and his party climbed several corner cracks. For the return trip involving a night crossing, Harry, unperturbed by the boat's motion, kept us going with food and hot drinks. A most enjoyable trip greatly enhanced by Harry's inimitable contribution.

Sally Westmacott writes: I feel as if I've known Harry forever. I think I first met him at the end of the 1950s or beginning of the 1960s when I first started climbing with the Climbers' Club. As I got to know him better, I realised what a remarkable man he was: not only was he a painter and sculptor, but he also bred daffodils.

After he retired as a solicitor he read law and became a barrister and was instrumental in getting a much needed 10mph speed limit on power-boats on Windermere. Very often he did not even charge for his services. He had a love of music, played the piano and was a bellringer at his local church. And of course he was a keen mountaineer: I have happy memories of many walks together in Surrey, the Peak, North Wales and Cornwall. And we trekked in Kullu, Lahaul and Ladakh with John and Joy Hunt, among others.

He had a wonderful sense of humour and a keen sense of mischief which included him pushing me (the smallest member of the party) through a half open window at Ynys Ettws in the middle of one night: I have no idea why! One of my fondest memories is his reaction to his remarkable 70th birthday cake, decorated with a team of ladies, totally naked except for climbing boots. John Hunt's face was a picture and even Harry almost blushed.

He made friends easily and after his move to Cornwall, the Athertons remarked that he had got to know more local people in a short space of time than they did after 30 years. He bore his increasing blindness with fortitude and humour: I never heard him complain. He was a real character; we will all miss him greatly.

Hans Trüb
1922 - 2016

Hans Trüb was born on 23 August 1922 and spent a happy childhood with his three brothers in Aarau, the canton capital of Aargau, Switzerland. His love of the mountains began when he was 15 years old: he joined the Swiss Alpine Club (SAC). Every Saturday after school he would travel to the mountains for climbing and mountaineering trips with friends.

During a stay abroad in England he got to know Hilary Longley-Cook, with whom he climbed extensively in England and Switzerland.

This close friendship remained throughout his life. Hans also climbed with his wife Ciglia and later undertook several extensive hiking tours in the Alps, which included overnight stays at SAC huts, with their three children.

He was also fascinated by the national parks in America. Among other excursions, when he was 75, he made a river-rafting trip through the Grand Canyon with his youngest son, Roland, who lives in the USA. He

Hans Trüb, with Alphorn, in the Grand Canyon.

brought with him his alphorn, a traditional Swiss instrument, and played Swiss Alpine songs in the most beautiful places in the Canyon.

Up to the age of 92 he was in the habit of visiting friends on the Beatenberg, above Interlaken, from where he could marvel at his three favourite mountains, the Eiger, Mönch and Jungfrau. Unfortunately he never had the opportunity to climb the Eiger, but nevertheless he knew all the interesting stories about the mountain. He did make one ascent of that other famous Swiss mountain, the Matterhorn. He used to tell the story of this climb: because of bad weather his group were forced to bivouac on the mountain. Hans wanted to climb back down on the next day, but a fellow climber stayed with him and persuaded him to climb to the top anyway. Hans was overjoyed and to the end of his life remained grateful. His love of mountains, rivers and lakes remained throughout his life, and he continued to read articles and reports in the Swiss Alpine Club magazine with great interest until his death. Hans passed away on 29 March 2016 at the ripe old age of 94, peacefully falling asleep in the close circle of his family.

Franziska Hänni, translated by Alain Trüb and Catherine Moorehead

Michael John Teague
1954 - 2016

I first met Mike Teague (or 'Teagie' as he was known to his friends) in the mid 1980s after I moved to Southampton. I was looking for a climbing partner; the owner of the climbing store in Shirley suggested that I meet him. That introduction started a friendship and climbing partnership that lasted for almost two decades. Our initial forays were spent on the sea cliffs of Swanage. As we became more confident with each other, our excursions gradually took us to pretty much every main climbing area in England and Wales. Soon, we were spending most weekends at one crag or another. Other than Swanage, our favourite destinations were Cornwall and the Lakes. Winter saw us making regular visits to Scotland. Our climbing bond eventually led to us making trips further afield, including Chamonix (winter and summer), the Calanques and Mont Aiguille.

Most of the trips were planned and initiated by Mike, fuelled by his love of reading guidebooks. He was forever compiling his list of the 'Top 10' climbs that he wanted to try and then dragging me off on another adventure. At times, there was talk of a trip to the Greater Ranges, with a potential new route on Hiunchuli being an oft talked-about objective. As with many of us, career and family prevented this trip from ever materialising.

Whatever Teagie turned his hand to, he was always very competitive, whether on a crag, golf course or within the four walls of his beloved squash court. This winning attitude clearly helped to shape his approach to climbing. Mike was loath to ever acknowledge that a climb was too tough for him. This undoubtedly helped us to get up some routes that we had no business getting up!

I recall fondly our wide-ranging chats during the long night-drives back from Chamonix or Fort William. He was intelligent, articulate and had a great sense of humour. When we had driven from Southampton to Scotland and back, for two days of winter climbing, he would frequently compare the adventure that we were returning from with how the rest of his work colleagues had spent their weekend. Mike was a sales person by profession and nature. By day he very successfully sold high-end acoustic technology engineering projects, while during his non-working hours, he used his skills to sell the next route we were going to attempt.

Teagie was a self-acknowledged gear freak. He loved spending time in climbing stores looking for his next new toy. This love of gadgets extended beyond climbing, as his BMW M3 Ducati (red, of course) and high-end road and mountain bikes attest. While Mike loved to be surrounded by the better things in life, by contrast he was willing to endure all sorts of privations while he was on a climbing trip: we once spent five winter nights camped under the Aiguille du Midi with almost no food, waiting to climb the *Chèré Couloir*. He would rather wait it out than give up. He was also something of a traditionalist: he loved trad climbing and was completely underwhelmed by both climbing walls and bolted routes.

Life in Mike's company was always fun and often memorable. He was naturally gregarious, always chatting to someone on his phone, even sometimes while on a route, and getting himself into and out of trouble. Even when he got into trouble, such as when he dislodged a large flake at Swanage, crushing two fingers, he remained calm and composed and was able to climb out of danger and straight off to hospital. If anyone wants to know who pulled off the large flake on *Zig-Zag* at Swanage now you do.

Sadly, our careers then took us to different parts of the world, Mike to Malaysia and me to Canada via India. Mike spent the later part of his life living in Kuala Lumpur, holding senior roles with Petronas, ABB and Shell. His life seemed to be filled with regular travel to far-flung parts of the world, based on hydrocarbons rather than peaks and crags. His final work at Shell was on a revolutionary floating liquefied natural gas project called 'Prelude', the first of its kind. He was very proud of this.

While the years passed, the memories do not. I will treasure the images of Teagie sitting at the top of Coire an t-Sneachda in a howling blizzard, sipping wine at a pavement café in Cassis, cooking a meal at the Count House and most memorably watching his feet disappearing high above me on another three-star classic at Boulder Ruckle.

While he never lost his love for climbing, during his later years, his active time was more likely to be on a squash court, on a bike, running or racing cars round a track. Mike was also a fellow of the Institute of Mechanical Engineers and was proud of his Yachtmaster certification.

In February 2014, Teagie was diagnosed with an aggressive form of prostate cancer. By the time it was discovered, it had already spread to his spine. Actually, that's how he found out: he had had back pain for ages and thought it was just a sprain from playing squash. Typically, Mike remained positive right to the end. Even two weeks before he passed away, he was still planning the next trip he was going to make.

I am so grateful that I was introduced, all those years ago, to Mike: he brought so much energy, joy and life to everyone with whom he came into contact. Teagie has gone far too soon, but his memories live on. Mike is survived by Guen Loh, his partner for the last 14 years, and his ex-wife Debbie and their son Jamie.

Ralph Newbigin

Ken Wilson
1941 - 2016

Ken was not a leading climber but his influence on British climbing and mountaineering for over 40 years was substantial. He was controversial and cantankerous: not for nothing was he known at one time as 'Citizen Ken' or even 'The Mouth', but, love him or loathe him, his heart was in the right place.

Born in Birmingham and educated at Solihull School, he initially studied architecture at Birmingham Art School before turning to photography. He moved to London to work as assistant to Henk Snoek, a leading architectural photographer of the 1960s.

Ken Wilson encounters Cesarino Fava at a conference discussing the controversy around the now widely discounted first ascent of Cerro Torre. Despite his sceptical expression, Wilson was momentarily swayed by Fava's charisma – but not for long. *(Leo Dickinson)*

He had started, aged 13, hillwalking and climbing with the Scouts, and thereafter climbing became his major motivation. He graduated to the Austrian Alps in 1960 from where, after a Mountaineering Association course led by Plas y Brenin instructor Kris Paterson, he moved west and with Dave Cook, later a notable communist organiser, climbed most of the classic Arolla peaks. His Alpine record over the following decade, much of it in the Eastern Alps, included the Badile's north face, climbed in 1967 with Dick Isherwood.

He was still a student in 1961 when I first met him, a fellow guest at a Christmas house party at Paterson's Nant Peris cottage, where he accused me of prostituting my photography by working for a glossy fashion magazine, and surprised us all by refusing to join a jolly Christmas Day expedition to the Pen y Gwryd, preferring to remain at the fireside engrossed in Karl Marx's *Das Kapital*. We thought this perverse: only later did we realise how it fitted. Ken was a political animal, although once he found himself in London working for Snoek, and then as an entrepreneur himself, his thinking rapidly matured to merely that of a benevolent radical.

By the mid 1960s Wilson was, not surprisingly, already known as a talented climbing photographer: one of the best. His images, powerful black and white compositions typically shot on medium format, included both dynamic action and powerful crag studies, owing much to his background in architectural photography and his strong design sense. As a discerning picture editor himself, these qualities soon proved invaluable.

In those days, besides the regular club journals, there were but two semi-commercial magazines devoted to our game: *Mountaineering*, the useful little BMC quarterly, and the more lavish but rather amateurish *Mountain Craft*, the organ of Jerry Wright's Mountaineering Association, but owned by the YHA. The ageing Wright operated from north London, not far from Wilson's flat, and was persuaded by Ken to let him redesign the magazine, and then take it over completely, producing in autumn 1968 a cracking first number, devoted entirely to Patagonia and highly priced at five shillings.

The January 1969 issue was renamed *Mountain* with the objective 'to break away from the commonplace mountain journalism that has been prevalent for so many years ... and of such high standard that it will be a must on every climber's bookshelf.' Nothing like it had been seen before. It was fully professional, avant-garde in style, visually enticing and above all authoritative, for by then Ken knew the game intimately, as well as many of its key players. That first issue became a collector's piece. Thus, Ken became a full-time editor and mountaineering journalist, staunchly supported by his wife Gloria, the London girl whom he had married in 1971. *Mountain* went from strength to strength, to international acclaim; in fact by the early 1970s the circulation figures abroad outstripped those for Britain.

Wilson was in an ideal position to crusade. While characteristically loud and outspoken, he was knowledgeable and unafraid of rocking the boat, believing passionately that the ethics of mountaineering were worth preserving. Elected to the Climbers' Club in 1965, and eventually to honorary membership, he campaigned for women's membership; he fought against the proliferation of chalk and particularly of bolts on British crags; he exposed fantasists who falsely claimed first ascents – notably that of

Cerro Torre in 1959 – and printed in-depth analyses of such things as the controversial international Everest attempt of 1971 and the Cairngorm Tragedy that autumn. Especially he deplored 'record seekers'. Despite vociferous objection from several senior members, he was elected to the AC in 1972, proposed by Mick Burke, seconded by Bonington.

His first stab at publishing was *The Black Cliff*, a definitive biography of Clogwyn du'r Arddu, written together with Pete Crew and Jack Soper, which he designed and coordinated. Published by Kaye & Ward in 1971, it was highly successful. *Hard Rock*, frequently revised since, first appeared in 1974, following an approach from Hart-Davis, MacGibbon. Compiled, designed and edited by Wilson, it is a coffee-table anthology of over 50 prime British rock routes, each described by a notable climber, profusely illustrated and presented as a glossy, large format tome.

Ten years running *Mountain* was enough, and while the magazine continued under a new editor and ownership, in 1978 Wilson started a publishing company, Diadem, together with the late Ken Vickers, the AC member who owned Cordee, the well-known book distributors. Installed in his new base on the western fringe of the Peak District, 'nearer the nerve centre of British climbing', there followed a steady trickle of memorable books. Most conspicuous were the large, full-colour volumes in *Hard Rock* style: *Classic Rock*, *Classic Walks*, *Extreme Rock*, *Cold Climbs* and others. There were anthologies of essays, notably *Games Climbers Play* (1978) and *Mirrors in the Cliffs* (1983) and Irvine Butterfield's excellent *High Mountains of Britain and Ireland* (1986). A fresh departure was publishing compendium editions of Tilman's *Seven Mountain Travel Book* (1983) and Shipton's *Six Mountain Travel Books* (1985). Some of these titles were jointly published with Mountaineers Books of Seattle for the American market. There can be few mountain aficionados who have not owned or read one or more of them.

Not surprisingly for such a small firm, cash flow was crucial, and at first each book financed the next, so it was something of a relief when Diadem was sold to Hodder & Stoughton in 1989, allowing Wilson to continue at Diadem but under the wing of a major publisher with a reputation for successful mountaineering books. Perhaps the most memorable title published under this new regime was *The High Mountains of the Alps* (1994), a lavish coffee-table volume translated, adapted and redesigned from the original German publication. Such books are expensive to produce, but although selling relatively few copies annually, are definitive and will continue to sell for many years. Always passionate about his books, Ken rang me one morning in tears: Hodder had been taken over, the accountants had moved in, the unbound pages of *High Mountains* occupied warehouse space and had therefore been pulped. (Publishers print a long run of pages but bind up volumes only as required.) Not only was the book out of print, never to appear again, Diadem itself was surplus to requirements.

Ken rose from the ashes: Bâton Wicks Publications Ltd was registered, and by 1997 he was prospering afresh, publishing titles such as Frank Smythe's *Six Climbing Books* compendium, while steadily reacquiring the rights to, and republishing many of the titles on the Diadem list. Once again Ken Wilson had become an important creative force in mountain publishing until tragically, early in the new millennium, he developed Alzheimer's; new publishing tailed off and in 2013 the business was sold to Vertebrate Publishing as a going concern. Ken died on 11 June 2016, aged 75, but not before the Boardman Tasker had conferred on him a well-deserved lifetime achievement award. For 40 years Ken Wilson had been an integral part of the British mountain scene.

John Cleare

Ed Douglas writes: Now we email, then we talked and Ken Wilson would call at pretty much any time of day. The telephone was his window on the world and he kept the window open, broadcasting his high-voltage crackle of energy around the world. Joe Tasker told the story in his book *Savage Arena* of how, on returning to London from a new route on Dunagiri, he borrowed Ken's phone for some reason, and how agitated Ken became. 'It wasn't the cost – I was paying for the calls – he just felt out of touch with world mountaineering for as long as his phone was occupied.' At that point, in the mid 1970s, Ken was at the height of his powers, editing *Mountain* magazine, capturing the zeitgeist of world mountaineering like nothing had done before.

I remember being woken by the phone ringing early one morning when I was living in Manchester, editing a small rock-climbing magazine inspired mostly by Ken's example, like so many others following in his footsteps. This was in the late 1980s, when rock climbing was going through a seismic shift, perhaps its greatest, and Ken was arguing with characteristic passion a line that set him at odds with a large proportion of the new elite. I crawled out of bed, and picked up the receiver. It was Ken, sounding me out, trying to get to the bottom of what I believed. He did it with everyone. When he was publishing Ed Drummond's Byzantine collection of essays, *A Dream of White Horses*, Ken wrote to him asking precisely that: who exactly are you?

At first, he was just a wall of noise coming out of the earpiece, a Girolamo Savonarola of the heights, treating climbing as though it were a world religion whose fundamental precepts were under threat. This was Wilson the polemicist, spittle-flecked and somewhat disagreeable. Later, I came to appreciate and value the complexity of his character: his insatiable curiosity, his wisdom and his kindness, his surprising vulnerabilities.

Ken was not your typical binary thinker. Yes, the world could be divided into good and bad, black and white. Part of him revelled in that. He loved hierarchies. The early editions of *Mountain* magazine, the title that defined the first part of his career, were full of definitive lists, lassoing world climbing and wrangling it to the floor. Back then, in the late 1960s, no one behaved with such gleeful directness. He was Prometheus unchained, defining the world he was trying to describe. Very few editors get to do that. The side effect was a mood of competition, of taking climbers from their natural context and setting them against each other.

Yet his instincts were also profoundly libertarian, a paradox that explains how someone so opinionated could welcome such diversity. He adored the rough and tumble, and lacking self-importance took the consequences on the chin. *Mountain* thrived on a broad cross-section of voices and standpoints. He understood the complexities of teamwork, was warmly respectful to talent but would never genuflect. If *Mountain* sometimes drifted towards pomposity, there were writers like Tom Patey and Ian McNaught-Davis, two of climbing's best satirists, or the genius of cartoonist Sheridan Anderson, to dirty the tone a little, to have a laugh and let some light in. The letters pages were vibrant, critical, sometimes outraged and always manicured, like a garden, to provoke debate.

What drove Ken, I think, was his passion for the authentic. He took that very seriously. Publishing essays like Reinhold Messner's 'Murder of the Impossible' was the definition of what Ken was trying to do. What is it that makes climbing so compelling and satisfactory? It is a game with rules, but none of them written in an arena not of our own design, a competition with no clear winners, a place to impose our will and then have it ripped away. He was powerfully influenced by Lito Tejade-Flores' essay 'The Games Climbers Play', anthologising it in his classic essay collection of the same name as the lead article.

He took the more journalistic parts of the job very seriously, mounting determined investigations. He provided excellent and concise coverage of the Cairngorm Tragedy of 1971. Fraudsters were of particular interest. He was quick to expose the fantasist Duncan McCallum who was claiming routes that he clearly hadn't done. His inquiry into the claimed first ascent of Cerro Torre in 1959 was far more significant. Even after he stopped editing *Mountain*, he remained a sounding board and advisor for those like Rolo Garibotti who had the courage to keep pressing.

His books were underpinned by the same principles that *Mountain* had thrived under: scope, ambition and passion. *Hard Rock* serves as the best example, an eclectic smorgasbord of essays about British rock climbing at a particular moment that somehow contrives to give a sweeping overview, like a painting by Bruegel.

He was nervous around more literary writers. Drummond's collection was his only real attempt to bring something of such complexity to press, although he used Jim Perrin to great effect as an editor for *Mirrors in the Cliff*, his second compendium, and for new editions of H W Tilman and Eric Shipton. His great strength was in his organisational ability, his scope, his enthusiasm and his clear visual imagination. He made books to last, books that rewarded close attention, and readers responded warmly. Ken was likeable and so were his books. He was such a presence, such a commanding figure, bristling and industrious, that even though he was largely gone by the time he died, the feeling of loss was profound.

OFFICERS AND COMMITTEE FOR 2017

Area Club Notes

Cader Idris
Samuel Davis (1757-1819)
Undated. Watercolour, with pen, in brown ink and graphite on medium,
slightly textured,cream, wove paper, mounted on, medium,
slightly textured, cream, wove paper, 16 × 20⅛ inches.
Yale Center for British Art, Paul Mellon Collection.

Paul Mellon: Generous Helpings from a Silver Spoon

This year's section frontispieces celebrate the philanthropy of Paul Mellon (1907-99), in particular his enthusiastic collection of British art, with mountain drawings from that collection. Fifty years ago his endowment was in place to build the Yale Center for British Art as a home for his enormous collection of prints, drawings and books, and forty years ago the Yale Center was completed and opened to the public. In 1970 he founded the Paul Mellon Centre for Studies in British Art in Bloomsbury. Mellon was continuing the philanthropic tradition established by his father Andrew, who had endowed the National Gallery of Art in Washington, and furnished it with his collection of European paintings.

Mellon began collecting in 1948 along with his second wife Bunny (born Rachel Lambert) who was a well-known horticulturalist and garden designer, eventually designing the White House gardens.[1] Bunny collected American and European art (which mostly passed to the NGA in Washington) and Paul collected British art. Initially he concentrated on art close to his own interests in country sports and horse-racing – he was the owner of the famous stallion Mill Reef – but around 1959, under the guidance of art historian Basil Taylor, his interest shifted to English watercolours and drawings, and he acquired whole collections from several well-known British collectors. His autobiography made his motive clear: he was trying to give British art the place in the sun that he thought it deserved. He achieved this through exhibitions, by founding the Center at Yale to curate and display the works, and the Study Centre in London to promote scholarship here.

Mountain drawings are not numerous in the Yale Collection. There are perhaps fifty or so that might have been used, from which I made the following selection.

Elijah Walton: 'Sasso di Pelmo'. The Pelmo was first climbed by John Ball in 1857, marking the beginning of our Club, and of climbing in the Dolomites. Ball's route is now a *via ferrata*. Walton's method seems well suited to the highly structured surfaces of Dolomite peaks. This alpenglow drenched Pelmo is drawn from the west, from high ground near Colle Santa Lucia.

Charles Gore: 'Mer de Glace'. Charles Gore was a Lincolnshire landowner, who acquired further wealth by marrying a Yorkshire heiress. He began by drawing the coast and shipping, but seeking warmer climes for the benefit of his wife's health he went on tour by sea in 1773, spending three years in Italy where he met the painter John Cozens. It seems likely that his drawing of the Mer de Glace was made on his overland return journey from Italy. Although clearly amateur work, it shows some influence of Cozens, and the Moine, Jorasses and Requin are well drawn. It is one of the earliest Alpine drawings. Gore became acquainted with Johan Wolfgang von Goethe at this time and in 1791 he moved to the Ducal Court at Weimar where he remained until his death in 1807.

1. See P Mellon, *Reflections in a Silver Spoon*, John Murray, 1992.

John Robert Cozens: 'The Pays de Valais'. This view, looking down from the Forclaz to Martigny with the fertile plain of the Valais beyond, was a favourite of Cozens, who produced several versions of it, e.g. in the Fitzwilliam Museum and at Stourhead (National Trust). Cozens was a master of light, cloud and distance effects, and his methods imparted an aura of mystery to his landscapes. Constable famously described Cozens as 'all poetry, the greatest genius that ever touched landscape.' He became mentally ill in 1794, and died aged only 45 at the end of 1797. Yale has some other works by Cozens with Alpine subjects, and other fine examples can be viewed online at the British Museum and the Victoria & Albert.

John Ruskin: 'Macugnaga'. Ruskin spent the summer of 1845 in Macugnaga, mountaineering and sketching from a rented chalet: 'little more than a hut. It was next to a torrent, approached by a stony path and a pine bridge, rocks and waterfalls to one side, pines and stunted acacias on the other',[2] so this may well be the hut drawn here. Presumably his guide Joseph Couttet of Chamonix, the son of Saussure's guide, and his servant George Hobbs, had to make do with the former animal accommodation below. The drawing depicts the Valle Anzasca spreading to the east in the late evening light with Pizzo dei Vittini, Pizzo della Moriana and Pizzo della Caccia rising to the south. Despite Ruskin's over-praise and adulation of Turner, his style was very much his own, and his Alpine drawings have seldom been bettered.

Samuel Davis: 'Punakha Dzong'. Davis is a romantic figure who was born in the West Indies to English parents. After soldiering there, he returned to England and made a career with the East India Company in India where he married Henrietta Boileau from a refugee French noble family. He eventually became a director of the EIC after returning to England in 1806. While in India he was sent with a mission to Bhutan and Tibet in 1783, but was left behind in Bhutan where he spent his time sketching the country and its astonishing buildings. Yale has around 140 drawings by him, all of excellent quality. Punakha Dzong, standing at the confluence of the Pho Chu and Mo Chu, is once again the winter capital of Bhutan. The *dzong* and its environs look today much as they did in 1783, a testament to the conservative nature of Bhutan.

William Daniell: 'Loch Scavaig'. Daniell sailed around the entire coast of Britain in the early 19th century, although very often he 'sailed on horseback'. In the course of his voyaging he made the earliest drawings of many Scottish mountains. While he was an able watercolour artist, he is better known as a printmaker. From the sketches made on his circumnavigation he produced a magnificent series of etchings enhanced by the novel technique of aquatint and then hand-coloured.[3] His Loch Scavaig drawing – judging by the position of the Mad Burn – appears to show Gars-bheinn and Sgurr a' Choire Bhig, both greatly exaggerated. Although Daniell was in Loch Scavaig in 1815 in the course of his voyage, the tourists and their vessels

2. T Hilton, *John Ruskin: The Early Years*, New Haven, Yale University Press, 1985, p92.
3. W Daniell & R Ayton, *A Voyage round Great Britain*, London, Longman, 1814-25. Published in eight volumes, Ayton supplied text for the first two volumes only.

imply a later date for this drawing.

John Warwick Smith: 'The Junction of Lyon and Tay'. Smith made around fifty Perthshire drawings for the 4th Duke of Atholl sometime after his return from Italy in 1781. The drawing shown is a version of one of these. By means of a visit to Blair Castle I was able to identify the subject of this drawing correctly, and also a second Yale drawing of the Pass of Killiecrankie.[4] Smith drew the Perthshire mountains, in this case Schiehallion, without exaggeration, and with scrupulous attention to detail.

Francis Towne: 'Ambleside'. Drawn in morning light on 7 August 1786, according to Towne's inscription on the reverse of the mount, therefore looking north.[5] Towne's style seems to fit no artistic context, and to encompass them all: it might be described as an abstract approach to *plein-air* art.

Edward Lear: 'Yewbarrow'. Kirkfell is shown on the right. Most of Lear's 124 graphite drawings from his 1836 tour of the Lake District have survived.[6] He used all forms of graphite – pencil, chalk, stump, charcoal – achieving remarkable effects. He was direly neglected in his day, but is now avidly collected.

Joseph Farington: 'Gordale Scar'. Although the Yale drawing is untitled, it was identified as Gordale Scar by John R Murray, and there seems little reason to doubt this identification, since the resemblance is so close.[7] Farington had at one time the idea of illustrating the poet Thomas Gray's *Journal of his Visit of the Lake District*, which culminated with a visit to the Scar.[8] Farington was a most accurate topographer, of natural features as well as buildings.

Henry Moore: 'High Tor, Matlock'. Henry Moore was brought up in York, and studied there with his artist father until going to the Royal Academy Schools in London. He became established as a maritime artist, but until the late 1850s he drew many attractive landscapes in a Pre-Raphaelite manner. Here, the Tor and the reflecting surface of the Derwent are both very skilfully drawn.

George Fennell Robson: 'Tryfan'. Robson exhibited three drawings of Tryfan at the Old Water-Colour Society in the 1820s. One was bought by G H Pennant, the owner of Penrhyn Castle, and remains there. The Yale drawing is beautifully composed and coloured, with not only Tryfan, but the Bristly Ridge and Y Garn accurately drawn. A very similar version was in the collection of Graham Watson of Bradford (see Bonhams, 4 Feb 2003, Lot 219), where it was titled 'Skye'. The Yale drawing was also originally mistitled, and eventually corrected by Peter Bicknell.

Samuel Davis: 'Cader Idris'. This view of Craig and Llyn y Cau resembles the well-known painting by Richard Wilson from the 1770s. However, Davis,

4. See R N Campbell, 'The Scottish Watercolours of John Warwick Smith', *Scottish Society for Art History Newsletter*, No45, Spring 2014, pp4-6.
5. See T Wilcox, *Francis Towne*, Tate Gallery, 1997, for the full set of Lake District drawings.
6. See C Nugent, *Edward Lear: the Landscape Artist*, The Wordsworth Trust, 2009, for a comprehensive account of the tour.
7. *A Tour of the English Lakes with Thomas Gray & Joseph Farington*, Frances Lincoln, 2011, p145.
8. Gray's journal of his tour was first published in *The poems of Mr Gray. To which are prefixed memoirs of his life and writings by W Mason, M A*, London, H Hughs, 1775.

unlike Wilson, faithfully delineated the form of the crags, and this must be one of the earliest crag drawings. It is unfortunate that the date of his visit to Wales is unknown.

Robin N Campbell

140 Years on: an ascent of Storen
On 21 July 1876, William Cecil Slingsby made the 'most legendary climb of any Norwegian mountain' with his solo first ascent of the much sought after 2,405m Store Skagastølstind, Storen for short, in the Hurrungane's rocky summits of Jotunheimen. It was not only this bold climb by a foreigner which was significant but that it followed on immediately from a multi-day mountaineering traverse unprecedented in Norway. Repercussions, especially from the last day had enduring effects on the mountaineers and on Norwegian mountaineering.

Slingsby and Mohn photographed in Ålesund in 1876 when they climbed Kolåstind (1432m).

Slingsby saw Storen from a road on his first tour of Norway in 1872. Impressed by its rocky tower and forbidding reputation he decided there and then to climb it if at all possible. On the way home from another visit in 1874, he met a 33-year-old schoolmaster, Emanuel Mohn, on the *Bergen* steamship and discovered they shared an enthusiasm for the mountains. With Cecil's sister, Edith, they explored the Jotunheimen the next summer and Slingsby urged Mohn to share their experiences with Norwegian audiences while he himself wrote an account of their climbs. Then through the winter the pair corresponded to plan a grand summer mountaineering tour.

In July 1876, Mohn and Slingsby met again in Oslo to take a cariole to join the leading mountain guide Knut Lykken. The two went on into the mountains but, detained by poor weather, were caught up by Lykken after he had mended his boots. Then came a five-day excursion of first ascents: Torfinnstind, Galdeberget, Urdanostind, Urdanostind North (aka Slingsbytind) and Jervvasstind. After a comfortable evening at a summer farmstead east of Storen, the three set out at 7am on Friday 21 July in unpromising weather. After ascending beside a cataract then traversing round a high spur they dropped into a cloud-filled hanging valley. Cairning their way, they crossed a second spur and a break in the clouds gave them a revitalising glimpse of Storen's 'truly noble aiguille'. By noon they were scrambling steeply down into the rough valley running north-west up towards the peak for an hour's rough going. Slingsby, being better equipped and less tired,

Slingsbybreen above Kjetil Tveranger on the approach to Storen *(Michael Smith)*

was route-finding and turned up the steep glacier heading just east of the summit pyramid. He had identified this potential route the previous summer when with Edith and was confident of it but 45-year-old Lykken had doubts. Footprints on a snow patch had them thinking they had been usurped but, on closer inspection, they were a bear's.

On the glacier and slabs, Slingsby's nailed boots gave better grip while the Norwegians found the going harder and at one point Mohn totters and was held by the rope. Slingsby became impatient, unroped and went ahead and up a ravine to Storen's north col. Arriving there soon afterwards, both Mohn and Lykken came to an exhausted halt and found even Slingsby had doubts. Mohn declared that Storen was patently unclimbable but, after an exchange of words, a fired-up 27-year-old Slingsby continued. Solo he summited the 500ft final rock tower after struggling past an overhanging outward sloping ledge. That overhang required an ice-axe for aid in descent.

Meanwhile, having lost sight of Slingsby, Mohn and Lykken started back down the glacier. Mohn, perhaps regretting that an Englishman and not a Norwegian might first make the summit, said he felt 'strangely indifferent' at the outcome while Lykken was convinced that 'the Englishman will kill himself.' Slingsby caught up with the other two on the glacier, later named Slingsbybreen and, by Mohn's accounts, ashamedly expressed the view that solo climbing like that was indefensibly dangerous. It was an 18-hour day before they were back at the farmstead.

News of the breakthrough ascent spread. So that autumn Mohn lectured on the ascent, opining that Norwegians were not yet ready for such rock climbing. This inevitably brought condemnation for his failure to complete the ascent and for allowing the glory to fall to a foreigner. The criticism, repeated periodically for several years, lay heavily on Mohn's shoulders and may have contributed to his deteriorating health and eventual suicide in 1891.

Lykken revisited Storen in 1878 and again remained at the col while Harald Petersen, solo, made the second ascent by the same route. In Petersen's subsequent correspondence with Slingsby, both were critical of Lykken's mountaineering capability. Lykken though suffered no loss of reputation as a mountain guide.

Slingsby, a strong promoter of Anglo-Norwegian exchange, was convinced that Norwegian mountaineers had the cragsman's skills and knowledge but regrettably lacked interest in summiting their own mountains and lacked snow-craft. However, it has been argued this apparent lack of interest was indifference to the imperialist and aggressively masculine cultural perspective prevalent among English visitors at that time, extolling 'derring-do and toughness in adversity'. The traditional Norwegian ethic is more about preservation of wilderness and being inspired by 'unknown' territory rather than conquering peaks and subjugating nature. Norwegians commonly considered mountain climbing (as opposed to touring) 'extremely hazardous and a meaningless risk to life'.

Repeated assertions of this untapped national capability by Norwegians are found in the early publications of those involved in constructing mountaineering as a national sport, wresting it from the Victorian-era English visitors. Slingsby, still active in Norway, encouraged this development, partly by instructing the first professional mountain guides. By 1910 an all-Norwegian trio's ascent of Stetind had set the seal on home dominance of Norwegian mountaineering. This change was occurring as the country was enjoying successes in polar exploration and asserting its 1905 independence from Sweden. Some commentators note a distinct intensification of mountaineering activity arising from the ascent of Storen, especially through Slingsby's influence.

To mark the 140th anniversary of Slingsby's ascent of Storen, English and Norwegian mountaineers joined forces to make a more modest ascent of the peak. Two members of the Yorkshire Ramblers' Club (Slingsby was the YRC's second president), joined three local mountaineers and a family descendent of the Klingenbergs who ran the Årdal hotel where Slingsby stayed after landing from the Bergen ferry. In the party were two AC members and two board members of the Slingsby Trust (Slingsbystifinga) which encourages youngsters getting out into the local mountains. The AC has recently supported the Slingsby Trust with donations of *Alpine Journals* to maintain the complete set available to the public in the Klingenberg Hotel where it sits beside many items of Slingsby memorabilia.

The YRC pair left the Klingenbergs, walked up the Utladalen valley towards the original approach route and after a night in a mountain hut

Summit photo on the 140th anniversary ascent of Storen: Kjetil Tveranger, Michael Smith, Lars P Bryne, Are John Knudsen, Knut I Tønsberg and Erling Eggum.

dropped into the valley leading to the foot of the Slingsbybreen but kept on to the head and up the Mitmaradalsbreen to spend a night at the bivouac shelter on the Bandet col. They were joined early the next morning by the four who had spent the night at the NKT hut to the north. Poor weather had set in, windy and damp. Rather than Slingsby's route a more sheltered and readily accessible one was called for: Andrew's renne. On his 25th ascent Knut Tønsberg (AC, NKT) was generally in the lead with Michael Smith (AC, YRC, ST) generally bringing up the rear. Several others made an ascent the same day but by other routes.

They descended by abseiling the same flank of the peak then out north to the NKT cabin to dry out while enjoying a meal and celebratory toasts. It was only at this stage that the two AC members realised they had this affiliation in common. Knut immediately disappeared and returned wearing his AC tie. As dusk slowly descended, three continued down to Turtagrø to finish a memorable 19-hour day.

The Times obituary of Cecil Slingsby from 1929 stated: 'For a mountaineer and explorer, he had the ideal equipment – a magnificent physique, exceptional hardihood, grace and agility, an unerring judgement … coolness and courage'. He certainly made his mark on mountaineering in Britain and Norway. Slingsby was named father of Norwegian mountaineering by Knut Tønsberg's grandfather, Henning Tønsberg, first president of the NTK. Cecil encouraged both Anglo-Norse endeavours and mountain exploration, work the AC, YRC and ST continue. If you are passing through

Årdalstangen, do call in and see the library and memorabilia at the Klingenberg and have a chat to Erling Eggum there.

Michael Smith & Knut Ihlen Tønsberg

Acknowledgements: The authors are most grateful to John Snoad and
Johan Kofstad for their assistance in preparing this article. The image of
Slingsby and Mohn probably originated from Jocelin Winthrop-Young,
was provided by Per Gran and enhanced by John Snoad. The other climbers on the 140th anniversary ascent were Lars P Bryne, Erling Eggum,
Are John Knudsen and Kjetil Tveranger (YRC). A bibliography of sources
for this article is available from the editor.

A Mountain Museum for Norway

In June of this year the long-awaited Norsk Tindesenter or Norwegian Mountain Centre was opened by Crown Prince Haakon Magnus in
Åndalsnes in Romsdal, located in its fjord-side building, its architects
having been inspired by the surrounding mountains and snow-capped
peaks. I was invited there a month later for a special event at Romsdal's
Mountain Festival by Fred Husøy, a driving force behind the creation of the
Tindesenter for which he was presented with Norway's 'Mountain Goat of
the Year Award' by a joint committee of the festival and DNT, the Norwegian Trekking Association.

Above the Tindesenter shop and its already popular quayside restaurant
and past a bust of one of Norway's most famous mountaineers, Arne Randers Heen, who lived in Romsdal and whose idea the mountain museum was,
is a stunning 21m climbing wall, the highest in Norway. Adjacent to it is a
library and reading room which has one of Norway's largest collections of
mountaineering literature including English as well as Norwegian books.
Beyond is a multimedia experience depicting 'the motivation, triumphs
and tragedies of Norwegian mountaineering' with 16 diverse interactive
installations about climbing, mountaineering, backcountry skiing and base
jumping. The cinema screen is unique being 3D and simulating a rock wall
whilst the digital archive of over 7,000 photos, videos and summit books
dating back to 1880, as well as newspaper articles and more.

The museum covers Norwegian climbing history from its origins and
includes alpenstocks and boots from Norwegian pioneers in the 1820s
like Carl Hall, Matias Soggemoen and Erik Norahagen, up to equipment
used by Arne Randers Heen: old hawser laid ropes and worn out tennis
shoes and the like that were *de riguer* for climbers before the mid 1950s.
There's more modern equipment and personal stories from lead climbers
of today and examples of early nuts up to today's cams. Also on display
is an early Edelrid chest harnesses used by the 1965 Norwegian Troll Wall
first ascent team. Gear from the simultaneous English first ascent is there
too including my own leather waist belt made in 1963, a precursor of the
Troll Mark 2 and the later Troll Mark 5, the template for almost all modern sit harnesses. Displayed alongside the Mark 5, are the Troll Whillans

and Troll Black Master, the latter billed as 'the first lightweight sit harness'. An eight-metre photo of Trollveggen (the Troll Wall) is almost overpowering in its proximity. A remarkable video of a huge chunk of it falling down is even more scary!

The Tindesenter has been a dream years in the making and is a credit to its designers, so much so it's easy to spend half a day there and still want to go back for more. If you are climbing in Romsdal it's an essential visit even if it doesn't rain. Its website is at *www.tindesenteret.no*.

Tony Howard

Julian Cooper's Marvellous Year

It was something of a shock to Lakeland Arts, the managers of Abbot Hall Art Gallery, that over 400 people turned up for the opening by Lord Melvyn Bragg of Julian Cooper's 70th birthday retrospective exhibition. Among them were members of the Alpine Club, including the president and the *AJ* editor, curious to see the life's work of our member, Julian Cooper, represented by 30 monumental paintings, some of them loaned by AC members. Three things were immediately striking about this work: its continuous search for new subjects, themes, conceptions as perceptions; the sheer hard work of not only organising painting expeditions to the Alps, Peru, Nepal, Tibet, Tasmania, Brazil and the Carrara marble quarries of Italy, but working for months and years in the studio on the studies brought home; and the unifying, shifting, distinctive voice that is more than a style: more a deep understanding that comes from total immersion in the huge and subtle forces of nature. By contrast the new work in 'Upstream' focussed upon familiar fellside becks around Buttermere, the nearest to the artist's Cockermouth home, where that same voice sings lightly, knowingly, of water 'that nourishes and drowns', as Ted Hughes put it. As always in Cooper's work, environmental issues underpinned by human conceptions of natural forces are never far away, as in a Cockermouth artist naming a show 'Upstream'.

The earliest paintings shown here demonstrate both a determination by the Goldsmiths College School of Art graduate to develop a line of work as far away from the family tradition as possible and a fascination with the then fashionable possibilities of abstraction. That Abbot Hall bought the 1970 work 'Ghita' is an early indication of local support for homebred promise and, of its kind, this playful painting stands up well today. 'Sierra' (1973) and 'Matterhorn' (1974) are experimental abstract engagements with water, rock and foliage, and with rock, snow and greenery, respectively. Strangely, both paintings, whilst challenging perception, strongly evoke movement in the present moment and also on a geological scale. There follow narrative paintings based either upon Malcolm Lowry's novel *Under the Volcano* or Edward Hopper-ish bars and buildings in which the figure is marooned in the moment.

But by 1988 Cooper's subjects are less diverse as he seems to have come home to the mountain environment, albeit a challenged one in the pivotal

Julian Cooper's 'Towards the Sea': the only truly allegorical of his works, painted for an environmental exhibition about radioactivity in the Irish Sea.

painting 'Towards the Sea Scafell' (1988), Cooper's contribution to a Greenpeace exhibition called 'Clean Irish Sea' which travelled up both coasts to draw attention to the most irradiated sea in the world. Cooper's father, William Heaton Cooper, had been commissioned to make a painting to celebrate the opening of Windscale nuclear power plant heralding what was to be a new era of 'clean' energy. Julian Cooper's painting foregrounds a strange dark shaft in the colourfully painted summit rocks of Scafell Pike, and takes the eye down Wastwater, past Joss Naylor's little green farmstead and out over yellow fields to a distant sea and a misted Isle of Man on the horizon. The painting's subject, now rebranded as Sellafield, is faintly in the distant right corner. But the eye is drawn back to a feather and two bones on those summit rocks. This appears to be Cooper's only explicitly allegorical painting. But its agenda – human interaction with natural forces – lies behind much of his later work.

In the large-scale studies of light on snow and rock forms in the Eiger series the human history of legendary climbs is an unseen presence. Cooper's major regret concerning this retrospective is Messner's refusal to part with 'The White Spider' (2000), which would have left a huge gap in his famous museum of mountain art. So we have 'Light Patch' (2000) and 'Fluted Ridge' (2001) in which gravity is ever-present in the runs of paint down the canvas. Again movement of the elements of the mountain is suggested by the passing of light over them. In 'Eiger Face' (2005) we are invited to peer deeply into a complex falling face of snow and rock as light is confined to the periphery of the painting. It is work like this that Melvyn Bragg described as almost getting under the surface of its subject. A trip to Brazil produced a cinematic triptych of panels narrating the 'Assassination of Chico Mendes' (1994), in which the union representative of rubber workers appears silhouetted in his shack doorway on a hot night, an easy target for the bullet that crossed the terrain traversed by the panels of his back yard.

It may seem an unlikely parallel, but Cooper's interest in the quarries of the Lake District and Carrara is also concerned with the exploitation of local natural resources and its human legacy. In his 'Honister Crag' paintings of 2003-4 the lines left by quarrying roadways are only slowly discerned in the grain of the fellside, and manmade scree cannot be distinguished from natural scree. Two monumental paintings from a pilgrimage to Mount Kailas (2007) reveal the quite different characters of the north and south faces, each catching the spirit of this holy mountain with quite different palettes. Even the sky is treated differently, contributing to a sense of the aura of the mountain whose summit is almost touching the top of the canvas. Of the square orifices of the Carrara quarries that invite the imagination into the depths of the source of Michelangelo's marble, it is probably best to avoid being too Freudian, but the mystery they evoke is palpable and certainly serious. The most remarkable painting from this series, 'Ravaneto Battaglino' (2009) evokes scale, zigzagging roadways and scarring in a green hillside that persists only in the top corner of this giant canvas. This is high level desecration of pure white rock on behalf of high culture. Tiny industrial vehicles suggest the long history of plunder here, although, as ever, the patterning of the human imprint has its own kind of beauty.

There is only one painting from the brilliantly coloured, fast decaying open mine in Tasmania where Cooper was invited to make artworks that would raise awareness of environmental issues there. And none from the Peruvian trip for which Cooper prepared by carrying camping, climbing and large-scale painting gear in a ski bag balanced on his rucksack into Carnmore to paint the Wisdom Butttress face of Ben Lair. But the local paintings of 'Low Rigg' (2013) and 'Coniston Quarry 2' (2015-2017) return home to trees barely rooted atop complex broken structures of subtley coloured, delicately lit little outcrops.

These works led to the homecoming of the most recent work in 'Upstream', where, after all the monumental displays from long journeys into the world's mountains, a fresh look with a lighter toned palette at the life of local becks amongst working quarries, sheep runs and tree roots appear as a joyous breath of fresh air. Here that voice sings (yes, you can often hear the water in these paintings) with the ease that only a mature insight into the familiar can achieve. The technique seems to be newly liberated from the intensity of those deep searches into vast faces, so that apparently vaguer strokes achieve their cumulative effect only when viewed at a distance. 'Scope Beck' is almost abstract in its sheer joy of colour. The pulsing of water can be seen in 'Rigg Beck' cutting through rock, turf and roots, and heard amidst the miraculous colours and free hand of 'High Rannerdale Beck'. It injects a life force to the side of the workings of 'Force Crag Mine', its falling contrasting with that of the scree on the other side of the surprisingly light scars of the mine spoil tips. Human structures are also there in the single wall that will not contain the full flood force of the deeply cut beck in 'Low Bank' and in the canalised lake channels of 'Outflow 2' and 'Inflow 2' where the quite different colours of moving water is celebrated against stolid mountains on the other side of the lakes. But human presences are humbled and frail in these eroding upstream fells. In 'Outwall (Rannerdale Beck)' it is at first hard to see the wall at all amidst the tonal plays of purple heather, brown bracken and various greens of swelling growth, all ultimately shaped by the falling stream.

In this latest work, after all the bravado of the big mountain pictures, Julian Cooper is delighting in the intimacy of home with all the time to look and feel, smell and hear, with a lighter heart and deeper knowledge, that which has always been giving and taking, joyously and ominously, upstream.

Terry Gifford

• Julian Cooper: Paintings from 1970 to 2017, Abbot Hall Art Gallery, Kendal: 2 April-7 July 2017.
• Julian Cooper: Upstream, Art Space Gallery, London, 28 April-26 May, 2017.

Boardman Tasker Award 2016

The 2016 Boardman Tasker event was a great success. As usual, there was a big demand for tickets and four of the five shortlisted authors were able to attend. Andy Perkins welcomed everyone to KMF with Martin Wragg, the Boardman Tasker chair welcoming everyone and handing over to Stephen Venables, who was to interview the shortlisted authors.

Stephen began by talking with Simon McCartney, the author of *The Bond*. The title is the theme of the book, the bond between mountaineers upon which the author returns to often in his accounts of two epic new routes in Alaska in 1978 and 1980. The effect of the second route on the author was such that he gave up climbing and his story is an extraordinary account of survival in the most extreme conditions.

Next up Stephen talked to Steve Olson, author of *Eruption*. When a smoking Mount St Helens erupted on a spring morning in 1980, 57 people were killed, some over 13 miles away. Steve's book not only tells their personal stories with compassion, but also turns the tension between the science and the cultural assumptions at play on that day into a dramatic narrative that reads like a classic thriller. Steve's total surprise and delight at having his book shortlisted was very evident and there was much admiration for his book.

The third writer on stage was Mark Vallance the author of *Wild Country*. More than the story of 'the man who made Friends', Mark's book reveals how the spirit brought to bear on friendships, climbs, BMC management and tough business dilemmas might be harnessed in dealing with the onset of Parkinson's disease. Mark spoke with great humour of the difficulties he encountered and was warmly received by the audience.

The final writer on stage was Robert Wainwright, author of *The Maverick Mountaineer*, a biography of George Finch. It was the Australian rebel Finch who demonstrated the value of oxygen in reaching almost 27,000ft on Everest in 1922. Robert's biography reveals an eccentric scientist and inventor whose complex personal life extended to his strange relationship with his son the actor Peter Finch. This is a fine contribution to the history of Everest and makes clear the huge contribution Finch made to climbing at high altitude.

The fifth book shortlisted was *Alone on the Wall* by Alex Honnold with David Roberts. Unfortunately Alex was unable to attend. The cover of this book sends a shiver down the spine and the life of an unroped solo climber gives a gripping subject matter. Alex's book delves into this dangerous world with skill, and revealing honesty about the personal costs of his lifestyle and amazing achievements.

The chair for 2016 was Graham Desroy and the other two judges were Helen Mort, chair for 2017, and Terry Gifford. Graham gave a humorous speech, outlining the difficulties of dealing with 35 entries. He explained the difficulties the judges had in dealing with such an outstanding shortlist. After much deliberation, they decided that the winner of the 2016 Boardman Tasker Award for Mountain Literature was *The Bond* by Simon McCartney.

Alpine Club Library 2016
The 'Les Trésors de l'Alpine Club' exhibition with hundreds of items from the AC collections re-opened for the winter season in the Chamonix Musée Alpin (see *AJ* 2016, p424); this followed a break to change the AC watercolour paintings on show, to limit their exposure to light. After over 20,000 visitors, it closed in April 2016. Subsequently, the ACL team has given lectures, celebrating 150 years since the Golden Age to a number of schools, colleges and special interest groups around the UK.

In January, the Library played a part in the book launch at the AC of *The Maverick Mountaineer* by Robert Wainwright. The 'maverick' was George Ingle Finch; his grandson, Francis Russell, spoke fondly of him. Finch was a member of the expedition to Everest in 1922. He took on the task of understanding and maintaining the oxygen kits from the Air Ministry, developed for high altitude pilots, now to be used by mountaineers. It was a useful occasion for us to gain more understanding about the photographs and artefacts held by the Library.

Above: Visitors to 'Les Trésors de l'Alpine Club' exhibition examining Whymper's ice axe, alpenstock and map of his travels.

Above: Edward T Compton's 'Meije Pic Orientale, 1870' capturing the first ascent by Miss Mary Brevoort, her nephew W A B Coolidge, Christian Almer, and his son Ulrich. A large wall hanging of this painting featured in the hugely successful 'Les Trésors de l'Alpine Club' exhibition in Chamonix.

Right: Barbara Grigor-Taylor, new honorary librarian.

We have often wished for 'rolling stacks' (bookshelves on rails) to fit more books into our limited space but the expense was prohibitive. Then the auction house Bonhams decided to rearrange their warehouse in Acton and dispose of a set. On the basis that we dismantled them and took them away, they agreed to donate them to us. Now, was this good or bad news?

ACL teams were mobilised, dismantling the racks, numbering the pieces and transporting them. These components covered the floor of the lecture room. Next, we moved out metres of books from existing shelving and built a false floor in the basement: this involved accurate levelling for the racks to roll freely with no fixings to penetrate the waterproofed floor. Then we re-assembled and aligned all the components. A mammoth task, but it gained us a compact rolling stack providing an extra 130m of shelving.

Glyn Hughes, our honorary archivist was delighted with new material on Everest 1953 arriving from Susan Band and Sally Westmacott, an expedition account from an anonymous donor, and Kangchenjunga material from Norman Hardie who reached the summit in 1955.

Meanwhile, library project work continued: Peter Rowland and Bernie Ingram digitised hundreds more photos and documents; Sue Hare gained good fees for reproduction of our historic photos in books and journals; John Fairley constructed a catalogue, with thumbnail illustrations, of our 700 paintings and prints; John Town made scans – searchable by keywords – of recent *Alpine Journals* and added these to the AC website; Sally Russell added many new entries to the Himalayan Index (including Chinese peaks).

After 26 years as honorary librarian, Jerry Lovatt decided to retire. At the Club AGM Barbara Grigor-Taylor, who has been a trustee for many years, was elected new honorary librarian; Jerry was appointed honorary librarian emeritus in recognition of his immense knowledge of mountaineering literature, and he was presented with an engraved memento at the AC/ACL volunteers' Christmas lunch.

The Library cares for the Alpine Club's collections of mountaineering books, journals, tracts, archives, artefacts, photographs, and paintings. These form one of the most significant assemblies of mountain material in the world. Visit us on Tuesdays, Wednesdays, or Thursdays (except during August and Christmas-New Year week). Do telephone to check if travelling from afar. Catalogues of books, archives, and the Himalayan Index are on the AC website. Also, 2017 will commence with a small version of the Chamonix exhibition at Frenchay Village Museum, Bristol, opening in January.

Once again, congratulations and thanks are due to everyone in the Library team for providing so much willing volunteer work and expertise.

Hywel Lloyd

Contributors

COSMIN ANDRON was in a former life a classically trained philosophy professor but now makes a living as a certified mountain guide based in the mountains of Transylvania. Fond of the seldom travelled and a climber for experience's sake, he shares at least one expedition a year to the far corners of the world with his wife Cristina, also a mountain guide.

JONATHAN BAMBER is a professor of glaciology at the University of Bristol and president of the European Geosciences Union. He completed his PhD at the Scott Polar Research Institute, University of Cambridge, in glaciology and remote sensing before spending eight years in the Department of Space and Climate Physics, University College London. He is a world authority on the ice sheets covering Antarctica and Greenland and how they respond to climate change. He is also an adventurer, long-distance runner and mountaineer.

MALCOLM BASS has always been fascinated by exploration. At first he focused on caving and cave diving, but his head was turned by a winter trip to Ben Nevis and since then he has been absorbed by the process of trying to climbing new routes in Scotland, Alaska, Pakistan, India and China. He and Paul Figg were nominated for a *Piolet d'Or* for their ascent of the west face of Vasuki Parbat in 2010.

ANTONIO GÓMEZ BOHÓRQUEZ is a librarian and information scientist and lives in Murcia, Spain. He has climbed since 1967 and specialises in ascents in the north Peruvian ranges. He has written two books: *La Cordillera Blanca de los Andes, selección de ascensiones, excursiones y escaladas* and Cordrillera Blanca, Escaladas, Parte Norte.

KESTER BROWN is the managing editor and designer of publications for the New Zealand Alpine Club. He produces the club's quarterly magazine The Climber and the annual NZ Alpine Journal. He is a rock climber and mountaineer of many years' standing and lives at Taylors Mistake Beach, New Zealand.

ROBIN CAMPBELL has held every office in the Scottish Mountaineering Club for which administrative competence is not required, including a long stint as Editor in the 1960s and 70s, and as Archivist since 1997. Retired from a desultory career as an academic child psychologist, he now wastes his time and money in collecting and studying old drawings and watercolours, particularly those depicting mountains before they were trampled into familiarity by the boots of mountaineers.

JOHN CLEARE has been a freelance professional photographer for over 50 years but a climber for rather longer. Business and many expeditions have taken him all over the world, while he has several dozen books, several films and live TV broadcasts, more than a few new routes and several virgin summits to his credit. An ex-vice president of the AC and an ex-president of the Alpine Ski Club, he lives in remote Wiltshire.

MICK CONEFREY is a filmmaker and writer, specialising in exploration and mountaineering. He's the author of *Everest 1953* and *The Ghosts of K2*. His film on the first ascent of K2 won several international awards. He is currently at work on a history of the first ascent of Kangchenjunga.

ROB ESTIVILL was brought up on the sunny coast near Barcelona. After the Pyrenees he moved to the Alps with the excuse of getting a PhD in physics. Discovering the potential of ski mountaineering was a turning point and he has never looked back since. He enjoys mountain and travel photography and organizing the next trip, be it Iran, Scandinavia or the neighbouring Alps.

MICK FOWLER works for Her Majesty's Revenue and Customs and, by way of contrast, likes to inject as much memorable adventure and excitement into his climbing ventures. He has climbed extensively in the UK and has regularly led expeditions to the greater ranges for more than 27 years. He has written two books, *Vertical Pleasure* (1995) and *On Thin Ice* (2005). Mick served as president of the Alpine Club from 2010.

TERRY GIFFORD was director of the annual International Festival of Mountaineering Literature for 21 years. Former chair of the Mountain Heritage Trust, he is the author of *The Joy of Climbing* (Whittles, 2004) and *Al Otro Lado del Aguilar* (Oversteps Books, 2011). Visiting professor at Bath Spa University's Centre for Writing and Environment and profesor honorífico at the University of Alicante, he celebrated his 70th birthday appropriately on Wreckers' Slab.

DENNIS GRAY started climbing on Yorkshire gritstone in 1947. Secretary of the ACG, first national officer, then general secretary of the BMC, Dennis has visited over 60 countries, most recently travelling widely in China. He has written two autobiographies, two books of stories, a novel and a volume of poetry, plays the banjo and sings on three CDs of climbing themed songs.

LINDSAY GRIFFIN lives in North Wales, from where he continues to report on developments in world mountaineering. An enthusiastic mind still tries to coax a less than enthusiastic body up pleasant bits of rock and ice, both at home and abroad. He recently completed his term of office as president of the Alpine Club.

GLYN HUGHES is a some-time hon secretary of the Alpine Club, but now carries out the equally important roles of hon archivist and barman: or as the AC quaintly puts it, 'chairman of the Wine Committee'. In 2014 he took on the near-impossible task of following Bill Ruthven as hon secretary of the Mount Everest Foundation.

SUSAN JENSEN grew up in Anchorage, Alaska, and started climbing some time shortly after the millennium while living in Surrey. Now in Scotland, she has a day job doing statistics for NHS Scotland and also works with the Scottish Mountaineering Trust publications on the climbers' guides. These are fit in around summer and winter climbing, expeditions, sleep and cakes.

TOM KEIRLE is a history of medicine graduate and works in laboratory science. Having spent many childhood summers on Skye's Cuillin, he has a love for the mountains and devotes his spare time to rock, ice and anything with an incline. He writes the blog *londonoutdoorsman.com*.

TOM LIVINGSTONE is a 26-year-old climber and writer based in north Wales. He has a penchant for trad, winter and alpine climbing: the bigger and harder the better. Among his recent successes are ascents of *Divine Providence* (ED3), and a winter ascent of the *Walker Spur* (ED3), but he's still hungry for more. He works as an outdoor instructor, holding the Mountain Leader and Single Pitch Award, and as a Rope Access technician.

JIM LOWTHER started his climbing career with 13 trips to east Greenland, completing over 45 first ascents in the Lemon Mountains, Watkins Mountains, Schweizerland, Kronprins Frederik VI Land and a late winter icecap crossing with parachute sails in 1987. He sailed in *Suhaili* to Greenland with Chis Bonington and Robin Knox-Johnston in 1991 and has since been on several expeditions to the Indian Himalaya (Rangrik Rang, Saser Kangri II, etc) and Tibet (Sepu Kangri). He enjoys rock climbing in the Alps and lives in the Lake District with his wife and four children.

ANDY MACNAE is a former national officer at the BMC and leader of numbers expeditions to the likes of Latok, Gasherbrum IV, Cerro Kishtwar and the Ogre. Nowadays he divides his time between politics and a day job as CEO of Venture Xtreme. He remains a member of the BMC International Committee and is the BMC's rep on the Mount Everest Foundation Board. He is still occasionally seen in the hills and in recent years has been drawn to the dark arts of road cycling.

CATHERINE MOOREHEAD recently retired from being Mistress of Scholars at the Royal Grammar School, Guildford. She became a 'Compleat Munroist' in 1996, and has led expeditions to the Mongolian Altai, Kazakhstan, Zanskar, Xinjiang, Tibet and Bhutan. In 2013, she published *The K2 Man*, the biography of Godwin-Austen.

TAMOTSU NAKAMURA has been climbing new routes in the greater ranges since his first successes in the Cordillera Blanca of Peru in 1961. He has lived in Pakistan, Mexico, New Zealand and Hong Kong and has made more than 30 trips exploring the 'Alps of Tibet'. In 2010 he retired as editor of the Japanese Alpine News but continues as contributing editor. He received the RGS Busk Medal in 2008 and more recently the Japanese Sports Prize.

DONALD ORR is a member of the Scottish Mountaineering Club and recently retired from a career in theology and fine art (which does beg questions!) He now spends his time climbing and writing (and being irresponsible with his grandsons). His writings on mountaineering and the mountain environment have contributed over the years to the Scottish Mountaineering Club Journal.

INES PAPERT grew up in the northern Saxon town of Bad Düben. She comes from a musical family and plays piano and saxophone. A qualified physiotherapist, she discovered the mountains when she moved to Bavaria. A former world champion ice climber, in 2015 she made the first female ascent of *The Hurting* (XI,11) in the Cairngorms. In 2013 she made the first ascent of Likhu Chuli (6719m) in Nepal, reaching the summit by herself.

ROB POWELL is an active alpinist, skier and rock climber. Born in South Africa, he now resides in Saint Gervais-Les-Bains, France. He was a commercial Director for a large multi-national company but saw the light and is currently a full-time unemployed climbing bum and a mountain guide in Southern Africa. He can be contacted on *saclimber@gmail.com*.

PAUL RAMSDEN lives the somewhat contradictory lifestyle of a mountaineer funded by his work as a health and safety consultant. Since ascents of the classic alpine north faces in his teens he has continued to climb in most of the world's greater ranges. He is the recipient of four Piolet D'Or. He puts his success down to a very tolerant wife and family.

SIMON RICHARDSON lives in Aberdeen. Experience gained in the Alps, Andes, Patagonia, Canada, the Himalaya, Caucasus, Alaska and the Yukon is put to good use most winter weekends whilst exploring and climbing in the Scottish Highlands.

C A RUSSELL, who formerly worked with a City bank, devotes much of his time to mountaineering and related activities. He has climbed in many regions of the Alps, in the Pyrenees, East Africa, North America and the Himalaya.

BILL RUTHVEN was made an honorary member of the Alpine Club in 2004 for his service as honorary secretary of the Mount Everest Foundation. Before being confined to a wheelchair, he had built up more than half a century of mountaineering experience, invaluable research for his role at the MEF.

VICTOR SAUNDERS was born in Lossiemouth and grew up in Peninsular Malaysia. He began climbing in the Alps in 1978 and has since climbed in the Andes, Antarctica, Papua, Rockies, Caucasus and across the Himalaya and Karakoram. Formerly a London-based architect, he is now an IFMGA guide based in Chamonix. His first book, *Elusive Summits*, won the Boardman Tasker Prize. In 2007 he received an honorary MA from the University of Stirling for services to Scottish mountaineering.

MARCELO SCANU is an Argentine climber who lives in Buenos Aires. He specialises in ascending virgin mountains and volcanoes in the Central Andes. His articles and photographs about alpinism, trekking, and mountain history, archaeology and ecology appear in prominent magazines in Europe and America. When not climbing, he works for a workers' union.

STEPHEN VENABLES was the first Briton to climb Everest without supplementary oxygen, reaching the summit alone, via a new route on the Kangshung face in 1988. Stephen has climbed across the Himalaya, from Afghanistan to Tibet, making first ascents of Kishtwar Shivling (1983), the south-west ridge of Kusum Kanguru (1991) and Panchchuli V (1992). Apart from South Gerogia, his adventures have also taken him to the Rockies, the Andes, Africa and the European Alps, where he has climbed and skied for over 40 years.

ERIC VOLA is a French climber who lives in Chamonix and Marseille. He spent three years at University College, London, and climbed in the early 1960s with Chris Bonington, Nick Estcourt, Don Whillans and other Brits. In recent years he has translated British mountaineering books, including a selection of Chris Bonington's best stories and Andy Cave's *Learning to Breathe*.

IAN WALL worked at Plas-y-Brenin in the 1960s. Since then he has climbed extensively throughout the UK, the Alps and in Norway. He was involved with the first round of the Kendal Mountain Film Festival in 1980. He has led treks in Africa, Ladakh, Tibet and Nepal, where he now lives and acts as an advisor to the Kathmandu International Mountain Film Festival, Kathmandu Environmental Education Project and in developing and training the Nepal Mountain Leader programme working closely with the Nepal Mountaineering Association.

JONATHAN WESTAWAY is a research fellow in history at the University of Central Lancashire, examining the history of mountaineering, exploration and the outdoor movement, part of a wider interest in the intersections of liberalism, modernity, masculinity, physical culture and imperialism in the late 19th and early 20th century. His research on Eric Shipton's mountain travel writing while in the pay of the British Indian imperial security state, 'That undisclosed world: Eric Shipton's *Mountains of Tartary* (1950)', appears in *Studies in Travel Writing*, vol 18, No4, pp357-373.

SEBASTIAN WOLFRUM is originally from Bavaria but now lives in the UK. Having been taken to the Alps by his grandfather as a young child he rediscovered his love for mountaineering during winter trips to the Scottish Highlands and North Wales. He has since explored mountainous areas in Iran, Madagascar and Africa and is drawn to remote and little explored regions.

NOTES FOR CONTRIBUTORS

The *Alpine Journal* records all aspects of mountains and mountaineering, including expeditions, adventure, art, literature, geography, history, geology, medicine, ethics and the mountain environment.

Articles Contributions in English are invited. They should be sent to the Hon Editor *The Alpine Journal*, Alpine Club, 55 Charlotte Road, London EC2A 3QF, UK. (**journal.editor@alpine-club.org.uk**) Articles, including images, should be sent on a disk or memory stick (with accompanying hard copy as appropriate, e.g. sketch maps) or as an email attachment. With files created in Microsoft Word please confine any extra formatting to italics and bold and set the language to English UK. Length should not exceed 3000 words without prior approval of the editor **and may be edited or shortened at their discretion**.

It is regretted that the *Alpine Journal* is unable to offer a fee for articles published, but authors who are not AC members receive a complimentary copy of the issue of the *Journal* in which their article appears.

Preferably, articles and book reviews should not have been published in substantially the same form by any other publication.

Maps and diagrams These should be well researched, accurate, and show the most important place-names mentioned in the text. It is the author's responsibility to get their maps redrawn if necessary. If submitted electronically, maps and route diagrams should be originated as CMYK .eps files in Adobe Illustrator, Freehand or similar ensuring any embedded images are at 300dpi resolution and CMYK. Hard copy should be scanned as a Photoshop compatible 300dpi tiff at A4 finished size. This can be arranged through the production editor if required.

Photographs Colour transparencies should be originals (not copies) in 35mm format or larger. Prints (any size) should be numbered (in pencil) on the back and accompanied by a separate list of captions (see below). Pre-scanned images should be **300dpi** Greyscale or RGB, tiffs or Maximum Quality jpegs at A4 final size or larger. **Images from digital cameras** should be submitted at the largest file size (quality) the camera can produce, e.g. 'Large' jpegs, tiffs or RAW files. Image files should have **short**, unique names/serial numbers **that correspond to the list of captions** appended to your article, as a separate word processing document, or in an email. Captions should be reasonably detailed and include the photographer's name. Captions must be provided for all images, including any slides and prints.

Copyright It is the author's responsibility to obtain copyright clearance for text, photographs, digital images and maps, to pay any fees involved and to ensure that acknowledgements are in the form required by the copyright owner.

Summaries A brief summary, listing dates, team members, objectives attempted and/or achieved, should be included at the end of articles where appropriate.

Biographies Authors are asked to provide a short biography, in about 50 words, listing the most noteworthy items in their climbing career and anything else they wish to mention.

Deadline Copy and photographs should reach the editor by 1 February of the year of publication.

Index 2017

We are the bond stronger than any rope

Everything we make is designed by climbers, for climbers. Each piece is crafted by peak and crag to give you absolute protection, comfort and mobility when you really need it.

THE MOUNTAIN PEOPLE

WWW.RAB.EQUIPMENT